To the members of
the Los Angeles
Sukyo Mahikari Center —

With best wishes
Andris Telbis
3 Nov. 2006

Kotama Okada, or Sukuinushisama, the founder of the
Mahikari organisation

Seishu Okada, or Oshienushisama, the present
spiritual leader of Sukyo Mahikari

The divine emblem (*goshinmon*)
of Sukyo Mahikari

Suza, the Shrine for the Creator God

Hikaru Shinden, the Shrine dedicated to Sukuinushisama

Hikaru Memorial Museum

Sukyo Mahikari Youth Centre

The practice of True Light

Is the future in our hands?

My experiences with Sukyo Mahikari

Andris K. Tebecis, Ph D

Sunrise Press Pty Ltd, Canberra

Wholly designed and compiled in Australia
First edition (English paperback) 2004

Sunrise Press

Published by Sunrise Press Pty Ltd
65 Finniss Crescent, Narrabundah, A.C.T., Australia 2604

Cover design and book layout by
Web & Multimedia Solutions
www.webmultimedia.com.au

National Library of Australia
Cataloguing-in-Publication Entry

Tebecis, A. K, 1943-
Is the future in our hands? My experiences with Sukyo Mahikari

ISBN 0 9593677 4 8

1. Sukyo Mahikari – Australia. 2. Religion – Australia. 3. Science – Australia. 4. Health – Australia. 5. Biography – Australia. 6. Education – Australia. 7. Agriculture – Australia. I. Tebecis, A.K, 1943-

Printed by Sylog Print System Sdn. Bhd.
No. 20, Block C, Lot 757
Jalan Subang 3, Persiaran Subang
47610 Subang Jaya, Selangor, Malaysia.

Distributed by Mr Steven Tan Kheng Seng, on behalf of Sunrise Press Pty Ltd, Canberra, Australia.

Book orders should be made through Mr Steven Tan Kheng Seng,
No. 25-1, Jalan 23/11
Taman SEA
47400 Petaling Jaya, Selangor, Malaysia.
Tel :   60-3-7053803
Fax: 60-3-7053304
Mob: 60-12-2389499

Acknowledgements

I am grateful for the guidance and nurturing that I received from Sukyo Mahikari administrative staff and members in Japan and elsewhere. I hope I can convey something of what I experienced and learned from the profound teachings that Sukuinushisama, the founder, and Oshienushisama, the present spiritual leader, have given the world. If time shows up any errors, I take full responsibility, with apology.

My wife, Yasumi, and other Sukyo Mahikari members – Paul Taylor and Lynden Howells – made excellent suggestions, for which I am very thankful. In the latter stages the manuscript was read by a number of staff members and was also sent to various people in Europe and the United States for comments. I am grateful to all of them.

The manuscript was typed and retyped a number of times by Bev Prince, Katherine Gould, Tuula Ilander and Susan Lim. Thank you all. Katherine Gould's library skills were also invaluable. I am very grateful to Lynden Howells for the proof-reading; to Rob West for the editing; to Greg and Merle Styles for designing and formatting the book as well as obtaining a number of photographs and incorporating revisions.

I sincerely thank all the Sukyo Mahikari members who allowed me to publish accounts of their personal experiences, as well as the non-Mahikari authors whose words I have cited.

Last but not least, I am very grateful to Mr Steven Tan Kheng Seng of Kuala Lumpur for his support to launch and distribute this book.

Contents

Chapter 9 Spiritually oriented business – the new direction for sound economics

Chapter 10 Yoko agriculture – a collaboration between God, humans and nature

Chapter 11 Establishing the yoko civilisation

Preface

This book is an account of my experiences and understanding of Sukyo Mahikari, a journey with the Light of God (*Mahikari*) and universal laws (*Sukyo*). I came across the Mahikari organisation in 1975 while pursuing a career in brain research, and was so impressed with the fact that ordinary people could radiate a profound energy or power from the hand so simply that I could not help but keep on investigating. In due course I left the field of science and became fully involved in a life that is normally considered religious.

This book is a follow-up of my previous book, *Mahikari. Thank God For The Answers At Last* (Tebecis, 1982) and deals with my understanding of the basics of Sukyo Mahikari based on my studies and personal experiences as well as those of many other people. I do not pretend to have mastered the depths since I continue to grasp things more thoroughly with time.

I hope this book will be helpful as an introduction to Sukyo Mahikari for people who know little or nothing about it, as well as a means to deepen the understanding of those who already have experience with it. Since I wrote my first book on Mahikari, there has been much to update, not only in the progress of the organisation, but my own understanding has grown through experience and there is also a greater awareness in society of many of the issues raised in this book. I hope this book will also help to clarify some misconceptions that have arisen as this organisation evolved, particularly in countries outside of Japan.

Ultimately, though, to really grasp the essence of the Light and universal laws, to make it all come alive, I feel that it is valuable to experience the Light of God as a way of life. Otherwise, acquiring information may remain as an intellectual exercise. It is like apples. One can describe many things about apples. However, to really know about apples and gain benefit from them, you at least have to eat them. To eat them once or twice is not enough either. You have to taste many of them over time. It is the same with the Light of God and universal laws. If this book helps people to experience these, it will have fulfilled another one of its purposes.

Finding the Light

Chapter 1

Finding the Light

Throughout history people have tried to understand the origin of life, the invisible dimensions, the functioning of the mind and a whole host of related topics. For some people such matters belong to religion; for others, to science. However, I have come to understand that religion and science use different approaches to discover the same universal laws; religion starts from the top whereas contemporary science starts from the bottom. A balanced study from both viewpoints is necessary to understand fundamental laws. In reality religion and science are one. It is not surprising then that throughout history many seekers of truth have spent different phases of their lives studying both science and religion.

My education was largely scientific. After completing a PhD degree in neurophysiology and neuropharmacology I did research on the animal brain and later on the human mind. Within this conventional framework, however, I was often attracted to study phenomena labelled paranormal or religious. In 1973 I conducted experiments on the physiology of hypnosis at the Psychology Department of the Australian National University in Canberra, Australia. In addition, I used hypnosis to treat people for problems such as smoking, insomnia, stress and so on. Many of these people occasionally related personal experiences of prophetic dreams, clairvoyance, telepathy, precognition, sighting of spirits and the like. Although not all the stories were convincing, they certainly helped to broaden my mind.

One woman felt she could predict the future when in a hypnotic trance, so on a number of occasions when she was hypnotised I asked her various questions about the future. Some of these sessions were recorded on tape. Although most of her predictions proved to be inaccurate, some were surprisingly accurate and detailed. For example, she predicted I would go to Japan, somewhere in the south, and on my return to Australia write a book about some unusual phenomena I had encountered there. At that time I had no intention of going to Japan, I did not even know any Japanese scientists working in my field, and the only scientific centres I had heard anything about were in Tokyo and Osaka, which are not in the south of Japan.

Less than two years later, however, without any efforts on my part, I was invited to Fukuoka City (in southern Japan) as a Visiting Professor in the Medical School of Kyushu University. While in Japan I came across Mahikari, which impressed me so much that on returning to Australia I wrote a book about it – *Mahikari. Thank God for the Answers at Last* (1982).

My formative years with religion and science

I had little religious upbringing in the formal sense, although I am grateful for the human values and the love of nature that my parents gave me. I was born in Latvia in 1943, registered as a Lutheran. As the Second World War was ending, my parents fled Latvia and migrated to Australia as refugees, to a farm in South Australia, where a family of German descent kindly offered us a home and work. My father had been the editor of a newspaper in Riga, and was now a farmhand. We lived miles from any church, and met with people who did not really care for religion. It was not part of our daily life, although we usually went to church on Christmas Eve and a few other times in the year. Despite the minimal religious training I received during my childhood and youth, however, I often read the Bible and wondered about the possible existence of an Almighty Power, thanks to my parents.

My first intensively religious period was in 1961, when I spent one year as a boarder at Immanuel College in Adelaide, just before entering university. Every day there were prayers before breakfast and last thing before going to bed. There was a morning devotional service before studies began and a shorter service again in the evening. Grace was said before every meal. Two obligatory church services were held every Sunday. At that time I did not fully appreciate all this activity, but looking back, I am grateful to the staff for the teachings I received about Christianity and the Bible.

The following year I entered Adelaide University, and for the next few years I lost contact with organised religion. My life became fully focussed on science in 1966, when I started brain research for my PhD degree in the Department of Physiology at Monash University in Melbourne. I seriously believed I would soon make a major breakthrough in understanding consciousness, memory, thinking, sleep, dreaming or some other poorly understood mental activity.

Laboratory research involved the use of multi-barrelled glass micro-pipettes to record the responses of nerve cells at specific sites in the brain of the cat, while applying chemical substances to them with minute electric currents. Project themes were concerned with the identification of chemical transmitter substances in the central nervous system of mammals. It was necessary to become familiar with a number of techniques, including the construction of glass micro-electrodes, the preparation of drug solutions, the operation of electronic equipment for stimulating and recording, animal anaesthesia, surgery, histochemical methods, photography and the processing of data. In addition, the study of relevant neurophysiological, pharmacological and biochemical literature took much time. A lot of effort went into solving problems that meant little to the outside world. I enjoyed publishing, but daily life was too hectic to be deeply satisfying.

I spent 1969 and 1970 as a Post-Doctoral Research Fellow in the Department of Neurophysiology of the Neurological Clinic at Basel University, Switzerland, continuing the brain transmitter work I had begun in Australia.

The emphasis on drug use in Switzerland was striking. Basel is the headquarters of the giant drug firms, Hoffman La Roche, Sandoz and Ciba-Geigy, and the clinicians I met in Basel prescribed drugs for their patients more freely than I saw in Australia. In fact, it seemed to me that prescribing medication (mainly Valium) was the main form of treatment for almost all the patients who came to the Neurological Clinic at that time. I was not deeply aware then that drugs are toxic and contaminate the body, even though they sometimes relieve distressing symptoms and are probably the preferred choice of treatment under some circumstances.

During my frequent trips throughout Europe I did not become involved in any religious activities at all, nor was I sensitive to any religious phenomena that I may have encountered unknowingly. My life at that time was devoted to hard science.

Early in 1971 I returned to Australia to work at the Australian National University in Canberra. I was given an independent laboratory in the Department of Physiology of The John Curtin School of Medical Research to continue studies on transmitter identification, the very place where Sir John Eccles, the celebrated brain researcher, had earned his Nobel Prize.

About two years later I began to feel somewhat disillusioned with hard science. After seven years of full-time research I was beginning to realise that I knew little more about how the brain works, and even less about life. From a career point of view, things were flourishing. I was working in a famous research department. I had more than fifty publications to my name, including a book on transmitters in the mammalian central nervous system. I had established good contacts with many of the big names internationally. Reprint requests for my publications came in at the rate of several a week. Occasionally people wrote from overseas asking me for a job.

Yet, something was missing. I felt a need to find the real purpose of research and other aspects of life. Nevertheless, I learned much about conducting experiments and how scientists think.

I decided to begin exploring something I was becoming very interested in – the human mind. Over the years I practised yoga, self-hypnosis and various types of meditation. I also spent much of my spare time reading esoteric literature. At the beginning of 1973 I moved to the Psychology Department and collaborated with psychologists in investigating the physiology of altered states of consciousness, particularly hypnosis and meditation.

The early 1970s marked the beginning of a rapid awakening for me to the actual existence of mental and spiritual phenomena, phenomena that cannot easily be explained in terms of the physical laws of conventional science. For example, on two occasions I used self-hypnosis to undergo minor surgical operations on my body, which were done without chemical anaesthesia, thus demonstrating to myself something about the power of the mind. The surgeons and nurses were rather surprised that I showed no signs of pain.

Although I learned something about the mind from research on hypnosis and meditation, it became increasingly clear that mental techniques do not solve or explain most problems either. There seemed to be something more, something that goes beyond the mind. I felt the answer would come from a study of spiritual or religious phenomena, so I decided to visit various countries in Asia in the hope of finding holy or enlightened people who could guide me.

Experiences in Asia

I began with India, to attend the XXVI International Congress of Physiological Sciences in New Delhi (1974) and present a paper on the physiology of transcendental meditation at a Satellite Symposium on Yogic Practices, at Jhansi. From New Delhi I went to Rishikesh, a little town on the River Ganges at the foot of the Himalayas, a centre for many ashrams. Maharishi Mahesh Yogi's Transcendental Meditation ashram was almost deserted and as I walked around to find someone in charge, I met two American TM teachers who were arguing vehemently. My guide (also a member of the TM movement) explained that meditation was causing them to become 'de-stressed'. I spent a few days going from ashram to ashram trying to find a peaceful place, but most of the time there was chanting, beating of drums, blowing of horns and other activity that kept me moving on.

My most vivid experience at Rishikesh came when I took a photograph of a *sadhu* (holy man) who became angry because I offered him only one rupee for taking the picture. He said it was worth at least ten rupees. Shortly afterwards, a very handsome young man, who was also dressed in the typical orange robes of a sadhu, approached me to see whether I was selling LSD. When I told him that my purpose for coming to India was to seek out genuine holy people, he became rather interested. He told me much about the daily lives and aspirations of such people, and that he also had wanted to follow a path towards God. He admitted, however, that he had not been very successful.

I visited temples and other places of worship in Khajuraho and Benares, but during the short time there I did not meet anyone who even remotely resembled a sage. My strongest feeling was one of pity for the thousands of starving and suffering individuals everywhere. If ordinary life is such a struggle, how can anyone think about intangible things like enlightenment? Looking back, I am grateful for my experiences in India, but obviously it was not my fate to meet holy people there. Perhaps I was too insensitive or in the wrong places. I have read that there are a number of genuine, high-level yogic practitioners in India, but they usually live off the beaten track. Besides, one cannot necessarily expect to find what one is looking for in such a short time.

I travelled on to Nepal where I visited a Buddhist monastery on the outskirts of Kathmandu, run by two Tibetan lamas who had stayed at my home in Canberra while on a visit to Australia a few months before. Their hospitality was overwhelming in its simplicity and sincerity. Mahayana Buddhism, with its emphasis on rituals and suffering, did not encourage me to stay very long, but I caught a glimpse of just how dedicated some people can be. Some of the young novice monks were less than ten years old. On leaving, I was touched to find these children had decorated my battered bicycle with ribbons.

Visits to other Buddhist temples in Singapore, Hong Kong and Thailand did not provide any opportunities to communicate deeply with people living or working there. For me these countries provided mainly shopping and sightseeing sprees.

The Filipino faith healers have received much publicity over the years, so I wanted to find out for myself whether their powers were as good as publicised. A two-week stay in the Philippines was not sufficient to meet many faith healers and to witness many operations, but it was enough to form some opinions. It seemed that faith on the part of the healer and the patient was essential for any healing to take place. To encourage belief by the patient, the healers sometimes used props such as animal blood and tissues at the site of the operation. The ability of the healers varied considerably, some of them demonstrating little healing ability at all. In general, those who had established reliable reputations as healers had spent years in religious service. Moreover, despite reports of some impressive cures of certain problems, it was clear that a number of problems could not be alleviated by any of the healers.

Contrary to my expectations, Indonesia provided the most profound mystical experiences of any country I visited other than Japan. The most impressive experiences occurred in Solo, thanks to Pak Ananda Suyono, who had much experience in meditation, a wide knowledge of esoteric phenomena and numerous contacts with Indonesian mystics. Pak Suyono was a member of Sumarah ('surrender'), an organisation which began as an offshoot of Subud, and is mainly concerned with meditation. I went to Sumarah meditations every day and on every occasion a *pamong* (guru or teacher) told me more or less what was going on in my mind. In some way the pamongs tuned in and seemed to be able to feel another person's mental condition by non-verbal communication. I had never taken mind-reading seriously before, but those encounters convinced me that it can be a very real phenomenon.

One pamong's specialty was character analysis. Upon request he meditated on the various character traits (kindness, honesty, aggression, ego or anything at all) of a person and gave a percentage rating (0 to 100%) for each trait. Everyone who had such an analysis was amazed at the degree of similarity between the pamong's percentages and the assessment made by others who knew the person concerned.

My experiences in Indonesia also made me seriously wonder about the actual existence of spirits. Bali is well-known for its awareness of spirits. Offerings to them may be seen in restaurants, in shops and on the street, as well as in less accessible places. Certain rituals performed in paying homage to spirits have become tourist attractions. I spent a week in Bali and was able to get to villages rarely visited by westerners. The mysticism practised there left me with an unsettled feeling.

In Jogjakarta I visited Dr Sastroamidjojo (a nephew of a former Prime Minister of Indonesia), a physicist who had completed his PhD degree at the Australian National University when I was there. He took me to his guru, Pak Darsono, whose specialty was spirits. Pak Darsono told me that I had a friendly spirit in the form of an old man with a beard, in my chest area, and another formless, mischievous one in my genitals. He proceeded to drive the spirit out of my genitals by blowing softly and doing something with a piece of paper. I did not feel any different afterwards but other people in the room claimed that the bad spirit was no longer in my genitals.

Years later, I came to learn that involvement with psychic or spirit mediums can be quite dangerous. Even though they can sometimes demonstrate unusual abilities, it is not necessarily a good thing, nor can such phenomena lead one closer to God. At that time, however, I was intrigued to encounter real phenomena that could not readily be explained scientifically.

While in Indonesia I met Romo Budi, one of former President Suharto's spiritual advisers, who also told me much about spirit life. I watched young girls use some mental technique to split huge blocks of ice and piles of roofing tiles with a single blow of the hand. I heard tales about people in West Irian having the ability to fly. I was told by an eyewitness about a Javanese meditation method to make one invulnerable to bullets. And so on. There was no way of knowing how much of all this was true, but it revealed the existence of many unusual phenomena that are widely accepted by people in Indonesia, even though they cannot be explained by conventional science.

Breakthrough in Japan

I arrived in Japan on 2 April 1975 and stayed there for 18 months. My position was Visiting Professor in the Department of Psychosomatic Medicine at Kyushu University Medical School in Fukuoka City, thanks to the head of the Department, Professor Ikemi, and to the efforts of the head of the Physiology Department, Professor Oomura. My research was concerned with altered states of consciousness. We investigated various psychophysiological aspects of autogenic training and yoga, both with and without biofeedback techniques.

I made a point of travelling often and widely and was always on the lookout for paranormal phenomena, but for the first seven months I did not encounter anything as profound as I had experienced in Indonesia, even though the Japanese people impressed me by their humility, care and respect for people, nature and materials. I visited Buddhist temples and Shinto shrines, talked with Zen masters, witnessed and experienced oriental massage, acupuncture and some of the martial arts. However, my impression was that most of these things are not taken very seriously by the majority of Japanese, who are more concerned about getting a good education, more money, a better position at work and other materialistic pursuits. It was only when I encountered Mahikari that I began to discover the spiritual wealth that exists in Japan.

I first heard about Mahikari on 2 November 1975 at the 4th Annual Convention of the International Association for Religion and Parapsychology held in Tokyo, when I listened to a presentation by Mr T. Asami of the Mahikari organisation. The organising chairman, Dr H. Motoyama, had invited medical doctors, psychiatrists, psychologists, neurophysiologists, social workers, dentists and representatives of some spiritual groups, including an abbot of an esoteric sect of Buddhism, a Zen Buddhist monk and Shinto priests. My purpose was to present a paper on the physiology of blank mind hypnosis.

Mr Asami spoke about possession by spirits and how such problems can be solved by radiating a spiritual kind of energy from the hands. At that time I felt sure that such spirits could be explained away in terms of suggestion. In fact, I probably would not have paid much attention to his talk had I not met an Australian woman at the conference who had come to Tokyo to attend a Mahikari course so that she could practise "healing by True Light".

She said that Mahikari means True Light, a special kind of divine energy or power that purifies the spirit, mind and body. Apparently, anyone could begin to radiate True Light after completing a three-day primary course and receiving a sacred locket called *Omitama*. She told me that if I came to Tokyo in a fortnight's time, after completing the course and receiving an Omitama, I would have great healing power. So I attended the course on 22, 23 and 24 November 1975, a significant step in my life.

Early experiences with True Light

Three weeks after I had first heard about Mahikari, I received a sacred locket called Omitama and was able to radiate True Light from my hand. I raised my hand to radiate Light every day as I had been taught, and gradually received various kinds of experiences that strengthened my understanding. However, in the early days I often wondered whether it was working for me because I did not always experience distinct sensations or see clear effects. Deep down I felt excited and grateful that I had been permitted to find something very profound and significant, but I cannot say that all my questions were answered by attending the primary course. In fact, many new ones appeared. For example, I had some doubts about the teachings on attached spirits, as in my field of brain research, something like that was a very strange concept. Just because people displayed body movement, tears, speaking and other reactions when they received Light, why should this be attributed to invisible entities? The teachings on food offerings to ancestors made me wonder whether this was just an oriental custom. Why was a sacred locket important? Why Japan?

Nevertheless, I persevered with Mahikari with the feeling that at least most of the teachings seemed to be true. There was something unique about the organisation. Deep down it felt right. I had never before encountered any organisation in which a real power could be acquired so easily. If it was really true that anyone could radiate the Light of God from the hand so easily, I would be foolish to give up the opportunity to find out more just because some of the teachings sounded unscientific to me at the time. If things did not work out as taught, I could always discard the whole thing in the future, I thought. I had spent a number of years training in scientific method and knew that understanding is obtained by both experience and experiment, so my feeling was that at least I should give Mahikari the test of time.

So I went to the local Mahikari centre regularly to give and receive True Light. I talked to various Mahikari members about their experiences. I radiated Light to people, plants, animals, food and many other things. As the weeks passed, I noticed that I did not have to try to believe any teachings I used to doubt. They *were* true. All kinds of evidence accumulated that verified the teachings in different ways. I realised that to discover truth, an open mind and perseverance are required. Some of my colleagues whom I brought to the Mahikari centre missed out on discovering the depths, because they evaluated the whole thing from just a few sessions of True Light or by clinging to their preconceived notion that "it cannot be true".

I had spent years reading books on esoteric matters, and even though many authors describe *what* has to be achieved, they usually do not give clear guidance on *how* to go about it. Moreover, even though authors seem to be sincere, they often do not agree with what other authors have written on the same topic, so there is no way to discern what is true or not by reading books, talking or thinking. On top of everything else, many authors philosophise or intellectualise their views so much that a simple fact often becomes too vague or complicated to understand or practise. I was therefore pleased to find that the path of Mahikari enabled me to discover the reality of the unseen realm by *doing* things. Rather than just talk about "receiving Light", "communicating with the divine", "using the power of words", and so on, Mahikari people actually practise these things and as a result, the teachings gradually become a living reality.

Whenever I visited a Mahikari centre, the people there seemed particularly warm, kind, sincere and happy, and almost all exuded a quiet confidence in what they were doing. Nobody was trying to convince anyone of their beliefs either; it was just natural, this practice of giving and receiving Light and practising the divine teachings.

Of course, there is no better evidence than the experience that one receives oneself. It was by receiving True Light and giving it to non-Mahikari people as well as to plants and animals, that I eventually became convinced that it was something very real, not a product of imagination or suggestion as some of my colleagues thought.

The first non-Mahikari person to accept True Light from me was the manager of the Foreign Visitors quarters of Kyushu University Medical School where I was living. The man was 63 years old and had been suffering from a stomach ulcer for approximately one year. He told me that he suffered intense pain in the chest/abdominal area every day and that the only way to stop the pain was to take the pain-killing medication his doctor had prescribed.

I invited him to my room one evening and told him a little about Mahikari and how True Light might help. At first I felt very nervous and wondered what he might think of me, a scientist doing such a religious practice. However, deep inside me I felt I could not let God down, so I plucked up courage and offered him True Light.

He said that he did not believe in God and did not have any time for religious activities. However, since nothing else had worked for him, he was willing to try anything, providing he did not have to have faith in the method. I gave him a session of True Light (about 40 minutes altogether to the forehead, back of the head, neck and the back of the kidney area plus about 10 minutes to the abdominal area). At the end of this time his eyes were shining in amazement and he could not stop talking about how well he felt. He revealed that right up to the time he had entered my room and begun receiving the Light, he had been suffering a burning chest/abdominal pain, but that now there was no pain at all, the first time the pain had been relieved without medication. Moreover, he had an excellent feeling of wellbeing, a rare experience for him. He added that while receiving the Light on the back of the head he had felt sleepy and a sensation of warmth had spread from his neck down his back.

On the following day he happily told me that he had had a wonderful night's sleep, having slept until 10 a.m., an unusual event for him because he invariably woke up before 7 a.m. each day.

This experience was very encouraging for me because an obvious result had occurred from True Light in a man who said he did not believe in God or any so-called treatment from the hands. In my mind, the power of suggestion was not a likely cause for his improvement.

After that it became easier and easier for me to offer God's Light to non-Mahikari people. In many cases neither the receiver nor I observed any obvious changes after one session of True Light, but overall, most people experienced something, particularly as they continued to receive Light, and my confidence in giving True Light grew with time.

Nevertheless, having been involved in psychosomatic medicine, including hypnosis, I was reasonably familiar with the scientific literature on how people may improve by feeling positive or enthusiastic about treatment, so I also wanted to try True Light on non-human systems.

My first experiment was to test True Light on the growth rate of string beans. I placed equal numbers of dried beans of the variety *Kentucky Wonder* on cotton wool in each of four sterile petri dishes (A, B, C, D) of the same size and covered them with 50 ml of tap water. The beans were covered with damp cotton gauze, the covers of the petri dishes were replaced and the dishes were kept at room temperature under similar lighting conditions and spaced 10 cm apart. Every 24 hours at the same time of the evening I radiated True Light for 5, 10 and 15 minutes to dishes B, C, and D respectively, holding the palm of the hand horizontally 20-25 cm above the top of the dish. Dish A (control) received no True Light but was moved every 24 hours in the same way as the other dishes.

The experiment was terminated at the end of the 12th day when the results showed that the longer durations of True Light resulted in more bean ruptures. This was encouraging for me, having come from a scientific background. Beans cannot respond to the power of suggestion as humans can, so it was interesting to see that the Light of God seemed to have increased their rate of germination.

After that, I grew different kinds of seeds and estimated the growth rate by measuring the shoot length, particularly in mung beans, corn and lentils. In these cases I conducted the experiments with bigger numbers of seeds, established average rates of germination first, and used statistical tests to compare the mean differences. (The differences between means was significant at the $p < 0.01$ level in most cases, using a one-way analysis of variance statistical test.) Once again, it became clear that True Light promoted the growth of these plants, taking shoot length as an indicator of growth rate.

I also tested the effects of True Light on the putrefaction of food. In general, the various tests showed that the Light inhibited the putrefaction of boiled rice, fresh strawberries, raw eggs, milk, various kinds of fruit, and other common foods. In some cases there was an initial increase in putrefaction, followed by an inhibition. There were also occasions when I could not interpret what had happened. However, in most cases clear changes occurred from the Light of God and that is what impressed me most. Even though I did not really know *what* was happening, it was clear that True Light was actually causing changes in biological systems. Later I learned that the aim of the Light of God is not for healing or testing and so on, but at that time it was valuable for me as a scientist to see clear effects of the Light on non-human systems, in addition to what I experienced personally by receiving the Light and giving it to other people.

Occasionally I had the chance to give True Light to animals and noticed changes in them as well. Once I was walking in the park with my little dachshund when she took off at high speed and collided with a cat, who was travelling in the opposite direction. There was a loud and painful yelp and the dog stopped in her tracks, looking very sorry for herself, holding up her right hind leg and whimpering. I carried her home, but when I tried to examine her leg with my hand, she started growling, so I left her alone. After about half an hour the injured leg had swollen up to about twice the diameter of the other hind leg.

My immediate impulse then was to take the dog to a veterinary doctor. After a little thought, however, I laid her on her back and began to radiate True Light to the swollen leg. Before my very eyes the swelling diminished with every passing minute, and at the end of about 30 minutes the leg was no longer swollen at all. I could touch the dog's leg freely without causing her any anxiety or discomfort. Within minutes after I had stopped radiating the Light, she was racing around the room in the usual way. I wondered whether this was too good to be true and expected that the next morning the dog's leg might once again be swollen. Next morning, however, there was no sign whatsoever that the dog had suffered any injury the night before.

In my experience at medical schools, sports fields, at home and elsewhere, I have never seen a swelling go down so rapidly after an injury, no matter what kind of medical treatment is administered. In fact, the swelling usually continues to increase over many hours, sometimes staying swollen for days, before it starts to decrease, and recovery may take many days or even weeks. This experience was encouraging and helped to confirm for me that the Light of God has effects on many things and these effects do not necessarily depend on whether the receiver accepts or understands what is going on.

Long-term experience with Mahikari

The Mahikari organisation was brought to the world by a Japanese man called Kotama Okada, or Sukuinushisama, as he is usually known. He was given the mission to give the Light of God and to make it possible for others to do so as well. Sukuinushisama received many divine revelations from before 1959 until mid-1974, when he passed away. These revelations make up the basis of the divine teachings of the Sukyo Mahikari organisation. In one of his final revelations before departing, he was told that his adopted daughter, Miss Keishu Okada, was to become the next spiritual leader, or Oshienushisama. As head of Sukyo Mahikari worldwide for many years Oshienushisama has been receiving revelations and bestowing on people the power to radiate True Light. Near the end of 2002, Oshienushisama appointed her adopted son, Mr Koya Okada, to be the Acting Oshienushisama.

Since 1975 I have had countless experiences with the Light of God and the practice of the teachings. I have come to realise that the purpose of True Light is not to heal disease but to purify people spiritually, mentally and physically in order to restore their innate strength as children of God, and eventually enable them to attain divine nature. The practice of True Light enables people to participate more effectively in what is called the divine plan. Through giving and receiving the Light, together with the practice of the teachings, all kinds of improvements can occur for people as they come closer to God and work on fulfilling the divine plan. There have been countless cases of people who have found relief and even complete recovery from various disorders, improvement in family harmony, breakthroughs in the work situation, human relations and so on. More importantly, people can learn to see their adversities of life in perspective, according to divine principles, and learn how to elevate themselves spiritually over their life's journey, initiating valuable changes in themselves.

Even though I joined the Mahikari organisation in 1975 with some doubts and questions, I have hardly missed a day in giving and receiving True Light since then, as well as studying and practising the teachings. Therefore, I have received profound experiences over the years which have furthered my understanding. I have not kept count, but I must have given Light to tens of thousands of people, not to mention animals, nature, equipment and other materials.

In 1977 Oshienushisama appointed me as the director of the first Mahikari centre in Australia, in Canberra. Later I was appointed as the director of a number of other Mahikari centres throughout Australia, Asia, Oceania and South Africa. In 1985 I was appointed as the Regional Director (a kind of bishop or cardinal if one were to compare this with the roles of the clergy of Christianity) of the Australia–Oceania and Asia regions, which included the countries of Australia, New Zealand, Papua New Guinea, New Caledonia, Fiji, Malaysia, Singapore, India, Sri Lanka, Thailand, Taiwan, the Philippines, Hong Kong, South Korea, South Africa, Zimbabwe and Kenya. Later, the Asia region was separated from Australia-Oceania, and in 2001, when I became its Regional Director, even more countries were added. I have also been able to play a role in bringing Mahikari to Sweden and my country of birth, Latvia.

Every year I visit Japan and have been able to meet Oshienushisama on many occasions, in addition to participating in special ceremonies and activities of Sukyo Mahikari in Japan. I have reattended the primary, intermediate and advanced courses many times, and since Oshienushisama appointed me as a primary course lecturer many years ago, I have delivered the primary course teachings and bestowed Omitama on behalf of Oshienushisama in all the countries of the Australia–Oceania and Asia regions that I have been associated with, as well as Sweden and Latvia. Amongst the thousands who received these courses are people from many different religions, including Christian denominations (clergymen included), various sects and denominations of Buddhism, Confucianism, Taoism, Shintoism, Hinduism, Jainism, Sikhism, Judaism, Zoroastrianism, as well as some people who hold animistic beliefs. The races include

Caucasian, Oriental, African, in fact, practically every race. They include medical doctors, politicians, educators, scientists, public servants, sports people, business people, musicians – an endless list of people from all walks of life. Since 2002 I have also delivered the intermediate course on behalf of Oshienushisama.

I mention all this only to point out that what I have written in this book is based on a rich and long-term experience with Mahikari, as a practitioner, a student and a guide for others. However, I am not pretending that I have understood the teachings sufficiently. In fact, the understanding of divine teachings simply continues to grow, just as my comprehension of God grows deeper with time and experience.

My understanding of Sukyo Mahikari

Chapter 2

ansanable. They are the laws governing the...

My understanding of Sukyo Mahikari

This chapter deals with my understanding of the basics of Sukyo Mahikari – the name of the organisation and what it means; the Light of God; the purpose of the organisation; how people get started; the significance of the holy places that have been established; and how all this fits in with the plan of God. In addition, I give my views on some of the misconceptions and problems that have arisen as the organisation evolved, and how these issues are being dealt with.

All Mahikari primary courses begin with an explanation of the rather unique meaning of the term *Sukyo*, but I sometimes wonder whether this concept can really be grasped quickly by most people. Looking back, it took me a while to grasp its essence.

The meaning of Sukyo

The word Sukyo refers to universal laws that are everlasting and unchanging. They are the laws governing the arrangements that God made at the very beginning of time for everything to function properly and prosper, and they operate whether one is aware of them or not. It is like breathing air, which is a fundamental, essential process for life and has nothing to do with one's faith or beliefs. Human beings and animals breathe in oxygen and breathe out carbon dioxide. Plants, on the other hand, absorb carbon dioxide and give out oxygen. This is one of the laws of the universe that applies to every person, irrespective of whether one is a Christian, a Buddhist, an agnostic or whatever. Even if people say that they do not believe in God, they still breathe in oxygen and breathe out carbon dioxide. Conversely, if oxygen intake is prevented, the people will die, even if their faith is strong and they pray to God for help. It has nothing to do with one's religion. There are universal laws, and if people live in harmony with these laws, they will flourish. If they live knowingly or unknowingly in ways that violate these laws, they will suffer, irrespective of their wishes or hopes.

Some familiar phenomena that involve other laws of a largely physical nature are the force of gravity, the conduction of electricity and the transmission of sound. Sukyo also includes universal laws that deal with more intangible, yet essential aspects of life such as the existence of the Creator God; the reality of the spiritual realm; how ancestors interact with their descendants; the processes of life and death; how cleansing mechanisms operate in the body; how materials come into being; and other matters of the invisible realm. The laws underlying these phenomena apply to everybody and everything just as they do in the case of gravity, electricity and sound transmission. For example, everybody has to die some day. The spiritual realm functions whether one believes in life after death or not. If one studies and understands how the spiritual realm operates, one will be in a better position to take appropriate action in this realm when the time comes. Sukuinushisama taught that Sukyo is really "teachings for all humankind".

What is the relationship of religions to Sukyo? My understanding is that Sukyo refers to the laws of the universe that are the very source of the teachings that gradually came to be called religions. In other words, God set up universal laws at the beginning of creation, and throughout history, some of these were revealed by special people sent by God. Today such people are called holy masters or religious leaders. Their teachings have become systematised into dogma and doctrine and are called religions. Depending on the age, the culture, the customs of the nations concerned and other factors, the emphasis has differed in the various groups, but their origin is nevertheless one and the same; their essence is universal. This does not mean that all the doctrine and dogma, all the interpretations made by people over time, are necessarily correct. There are many conflicting views between religions and even within the same religion. However, the source or origin is the same. Religions have come from the same roots, so to speak. One way of referring to Sukyo would be 'universal teachings that transcend the barriers between religions', even though this is not a translation of the word Sukyo.

Let me clarify this in a different way. In the field of science, there are laws of physics, laws of chemistry and laws of biology, to name a few. No-one would question the fact that these laws or principles apply to everyone and everything no matter what one's views about life may be. Within the field of science, however, there are also theories. Although these theories have been formulated as a result of the study of natural laws, people modify them with time. There are conflicting views between scientists over the same theory and sometimes a theory may be refuted when new data are obtained. This does not take away from the fact that there are laws of nature, does it? It is just that scientists have not always interpreted the data correctly – they may not have had sufficient information on certain aspects or there may have been some other limitation at the time.

The field of religion is similar. There are fundamental laws or principles concerning the functioning of the spiritual realm, the phenomena of life and death, the power of God and other aspects. These are universal and unchanging. However, although many of the teachings have a common essence, people within the field of religion have also developed different understandings, doctrine and dogma that not only vary between races and cultures, but also vary over time within the same culture. In this way, religions such as Buddhism, Judaism, Christianity and others came into being and evolved. Within Christianity there are now thousands of sects and denominations. Within Buddhism there are also numerous sects and denominations. In other words, within the field of religion there are also interpretations of teachings that may not necessarily be correct, as occurs in other fields such as science. However, this does not affect the reality of the unchanging laws concerning invisible phenomena, and these are the essence of all religions. These universal laws are called Sukyo and are the very source of the major religions.

We need to discern between what is fundamental, universal and unchanging – the laws of the universe that apply to everyone and everything (Sukyo) – and what has come about through human knowledge and human interpretation.

I have come to realise the truth of the teaching that the origin of the world is one; the origin of all humankind is one; the origin of all religions is one, and therefore it is best for human beings to live accordingly. God created the world and all its creatures as a whole unit in which all forms of life are interrelated and meant to live harmoniously – a state of coexistence and co-prosperity between God, humans and nature. In the physical dimension, for example, even though there are seemingly separate oceans and land masses, everything is connected. The air intermingles all over the world and the molecules are recycled. The oxygen people breathe in one part of the world may have made up the bodies of animals in another area, even that of dinosaurs millions of years ago, as matter breaks down and is built up again, forming different matter.

Similarly, even though God created human beings by subdividing them into different skin colours, there was no intention of making borders between them. Understanding Sukyo means recognising a world without barriers in which all human beings are like brothers and sisters whose parent is the Creator God. Even though people are born in different countries with different backgrounds, cultures and traditional religions, there is no good reason for any barriers to exist.

In the past, quite a number of universal laws were understood either vaguely or not at all, it seems. From my studies I feel that through Sukuinushisama many universal laws have been revealed by

God more clearly and in greater detail, and some for the first time. That is why people who study and practise Sukyo often gain deeper understanding of their own religion.

In my own case, for example, I can understand the Bible better now that I have experience with Sukyo Mahikari. My reverence for Jesus and gratitude for his noble, dedicated efforts is far greater today than when I used to go to church in my youth. At the same time, my respect for the holy masters of Buddhism, Islam, Hinduism, Judaism and other religions has grown as well. I feel that the understanding of Sukyo helps one to see things in perspective without any attitude of competition or conflict. In fact, a major aim of Sukyo Mahikari is to help integrate religious movements by emphasising their common origin. Sukyo Mahikari is not a religion in the traditional sense, but something which points to the universal core of all religions.

From a legal point of view, the Sukyo Mahikari organisation is registered or constituted as a religious organisation in some countries, but this is because there is no legal category that can recognise the broad nature of Sukyo as yet. The fact remains that Sukyo is not a conventional religion in the sense that religions have been understood up till now.

When people have asked me, "Is Sukyo better than such and such a religion?", I feel it is like asking, "Is nature better than trees?" Trees are a part of nature, which also consists of many other things. Similarly, all religions teach different aspects of universal laws, although between the different religions different areas have been emphasised and there have been many gaps in understanding as well.

So far I have explained Sukyo from a religious point of view. However, since Sukyo refers to universal laws, then naturally it applies to the fields of medicine, science, education, business and everything else as well. In the field of health, for instance, Sukuinushisama has given precise details of the laws or principles that clarify what health is, what disease is, how one's daily life can be lived in order to become free of so-called disease. There are teachings on how to practise purification with True Light, including the body areas and organs to purify in order to help achieve health step by step, and these teachings are integrated with the approach used in conventional medicine. More and more medical doctors are now studying and practising these principles in order to become more effective in their fields. In fact, from one point of view, Sukyo could be regarded as a kind of holistic or whole person medicine.

However, Sukyo also applies to science, a field in which knowledge is accumulated by investigating natural laws. I have some experience with this because my early career was concerned with science, particularly brain research. When I was studying at university I was amazed at the large number of theories in the neurosciences that attempted to explain personality, moods, behaviour and related matters. I am grateful for the valuable information, but have to admit that the theories seemed to be naive and often full of contradictions. Now I know why. Experience with Sukyo has taught me that there are spirits who influence the feelings, emotions and behaviour of people in daily life. For me, this understanding is stronger than the conclusions I reached from the electrophysiological data I acquired over ten years of brain research and which resulted in the publication of dozens of scientific papers. Sukyo deals with these invisible aspects and studying them enables one to become a better scientist by understanding all levels – the spirit, the mind and the body.

I feel that no matter how much we research the functioning of the brain using valuable approaches such as electrophysiological techniques, biochemical methods, molecular biology and behavioural studies, to name a few, the whole field will remain one of gross over-simplification and confusion unless we also understand the actual reality of the existence of the soul, the invisible dimensions, ancestors and other spirits.

Up till recent times, when people encountered the words 'God', 'spirits', 'life after death' and so on, the organisation that used them was automatically assumed to be a religion. If God really exists, however, if there really is life after death, if there really are entities called spirits who interfere with the lives of people, then a medical doctor has to be just as aware of these matters as a priest, since such phenomena apply as much to health as they do to everything else. Similarly, a scientist has to understand such spiritual matters in order to interpret many everyday phenomena correctly. In later chapters of this book I describe how certain universal laws apply to various fields – religion, medicine, science, education, economics and agriculture.

Clarification of many of the universal laws can be found in the teachings that were given by Sukuinushisama. They are based on revelations from the Creator God and make up the topics of the primary, intermediate and advanced courses of Sukyo Mahikari. Many teachings are also published in the Yokoshi Prayer Book (*Yokoshi Norigotoshu*), The Holy Words (*Goseigen*), Short Teachings by the Founder (*Sunkyo*), Great and Holy Master (*Daiseishu*) and other books of the Sukyo Mahikari organisation. Moreover, every month

Oshienushisama (and, since late 2002, the Acting Oshienushisama) gives teachings about the will of God, and these are published in Mahikari journals which are available in many countries throughout the world.

This is not the place to explain the numerous universal laws that make up Sukyo, but there is one law that I was particularly impressed to learn about.

The law of 'spirit first, mind next, body follows'

This can be likened to the functioning of river water, which always flows from upstream through midstream to downstream. If the water is clean upstream (the soul and spiritual body), then that clean water will flow through midstream (the mind) to downstream (the body and the material environment). If the water is polluted upstream, then no matter how much effort is made to clean the water anywhere else, the dirty water just keeps on flowing down. As regards the human, this trinity is 'spirit, mind and body'. As regards all existence, this trinity is 'God and divine matters'; 'ancestors and the spiritual realm'; and 'phenomena of the physical world, the material environment'.

The spiritual aspect is the upstream of the river and therefore influences everything else whether we like it or not and whether we believe it or not. At the same time, however, it is important to recognise that everything is interconnected. For instance, if the body is contaminated, this will also have an impure influence on the soul. Emphasising the spiritual aspect does not mean a neglect of the mental and physical aspects. Emphasising and improving the spiritual aspect in life is also referred to as being 'spiritually oriented' or 'God-centred'.

For clarification, the term 'material-centred', as we use it in Sukyo Mahikari, does not mean being materialistic in the sense that the person is focused on acquiring money and material possessions in a greedy way (although it can include that meaning), but means that the person focuses on the physical rather than the spiritual aspects in interpreting things and conducting his life. It means that the person does not sufficiently consider things from God's point of view or the condition of the realm of spirit, but only from that which involves the material aspect. If one compares this with a river, it is putting focus on the downstream rather than the upstream.

Becoming spiritually oriented or God-centred does not simply mean to believe in God or recognise that the spiritual realm exists, but depends on how one goes about life. One can still be rather material-centred and only pray to improve personal health or for one's business to go smoothly, for instance. It is more spiritually oriented or God-centred to strive so that everyone's health improves and that one's business goes well so that it can contribute to fulfilling the plan of God.

Up till now humankind's approach has largely been to develop theories and ideas based on 'mind-centred' or 'body-centred' approaches. Mental training or mental activity has been generally considered as the highest that could be attained by the human. However, in my experience it is not the highest. The highest deals with the soul.

The problem with relying on the mind is that it is linked directly to the physical body, that is, it is intimately connected with the five senses and is easily influenced by them. In this way, no matter how hard people have tried to remain noble and pure in their mind by studying and practising morals, ethics, philosophies, religious ideals or certain mental states, things have not always gone as they wished because it is not the mind alone that is in control. I believe that unless people become elevated at the level of the soul, it will be difficult to achieve a high-quality life. It is the Light of God that makes this elevation possible.

God is Light

Mahikari is the Japanese word for True Light. It is the Light of the Creator God, the 'true light' mentioned in the Bible (John 1:9). In fact, the word 'light' is mentioned in the Bible more than 50 times. It is the 'Infinite Light' or 'Immeasurable Light' known in Buddhism. For many thousands of years, Christians, Buddhists, Jews, Shintoists, Hindus, Sikhs and followers of the majority of other religions have associated God and light in some way or another. Mahikari or True Light enabled me to understand this deeply for the first time.

Who or what is God? God is supreme, vast, present everywhere and in everything, a kind of essence of all existence, too immense to comprehend. God exists everywhere just like the air that is invisible yet is present everywhere. Just as we live and breathe in the air, and it is air that allows us to live and breathe, so our souls are made to live by and 'breathe' God. Oshienushisama said, "Ultimately, the true essence of Great God is the eternal and undying great life of the universe" and "It is due to an invisible Light and the breath of God filling the shells we call our bodies that human beings are able to exist in this world."

Coming from a Christian background and having been taught that there is "only one God", I understand why some people feel that their basic beliefs are threatened by discovering the existence of various deities. However, seeing things in perspective makes the picture clear. The Creator God is the Supreme Lord of all the invisible dimensions and the whole physical universe. There is no-one or nothing greater. In this sense the monotheistic view that there is only one God is true. However, in order to create and maintain the functioning of all the different levels of existence, the Creator God gave rise to lower gods or deities of different responsibilities and power. In this sense polytheism also holds true. In addition, since everything is directly or indirectly created by Almighty God, everything is a reflection of God. In other words, "God is in everything"– so pantheism is also true. Sukuinushisama explained that monotheism, polytheism and pantheism are different ways of looking at the same thing. All three views are true, but each on its own can be regarded as incomplete.

God has arranged things so that people cannot really understand God deeply except through experience, particularly through the experience of the Light of God. I am not implying that one can know God completely or deeply just by receiving some sessions of Light. However, there is a growing, intuitive, 'knowing' of God, a feeling of coming closer to God, becoming more and more God-centred in daily life, being able to communicate with God, rely on God, be aware of God, as a result of giving and receiving True Light. Mysteriously, one can come to commune with God in a very personal way, being aware that Someone is watching over and controlling everything. As with science, though, the more one learns, the more one realises how little one knows. This is also true with regard to understanding God. Despite the intangible nature of all this, however, God becomes a reality more and more.

This is the most valuable aspect of Mahikari, I feel. Through True Light people can come to understand more and more about God, about the will of God, and become motivated to live in a God-centred way. As a result, their mental aspect becomes elevated in that they become better people – more honest, caring, altruistic and righteous. Physically, the body also functions better and the material environment improves. This is due to the law of 'spirit first, mind next, body follows'.

Sukuinushisama received the revelation that the name of the Creator God is Su. This in itself is a very profound and great blessing, I feel, to be permitted to know the name of the Creator God and to enunciate it when praying. I have experienced instances of profound phenomena, including protection from danger, just by enunciating the name of the Creator God, Su. In my early days, I thought that I had been communicating directly with the Creator of heaven and earth by saying "Almighty God" or "Creator God". Now I can see that these terms have been reverent descriptions, but that something more occurs when one addresses the Creator God as "Su God".

The True Light of Sukyo Mahikari is the Light of Su God, the Creator God. Oshienushisama said that the Light of God is a spiritual energy consisting of invisible particles or waves that are more minute than elementary particles. It is usually invisible to human beings.

I have learnt that when radiated through the forehead of a person to the main soul (located approximately 10 centimetres behind the forehead) True Light rejuvenates the soul and removes spiritual impurities that may have accumulated over hundreds or thousands of years. Inherent in the Light is divine wisdom, will and love. The Light also purifies and gives salvation to spirits who are attached. When directed to the body, True Light purifies and rejuvenates the tissues. It melts and removes toxic material. It gives remarkable protection. It is beneficial not only for humans but for animals, plants, insects, nature – everything. It has wonderful effects not only on creatures but on the air, food, even machinery and other inanimate objects. All this can be experienced.

In the Mahikari organisation the practice of radiating True Light from the hand is called *Mahikari no waza*, which literally means something like 'the practice or art of True Light'. One also talks about giving and receiving purification (*okiyome*). Often, however, people use the expression "giving or receiving (True) Light". According to divine teachings, the art of True Light is what Buddha, Jesus and some of their disciples had practised. Unlike the past when only special holy masters or disciples were permitted, practically anyone today who has the heart of wanting to serve God can be given the ability to practise the art of True Light. One can practise the work Buddha or Jesus did, irrespective of religion, race or background. There is no need to renounce existing beliefs in order to begin radiating True Light.

Omitama, the sacred locket
A person may begin to radiate True Light from the hand after completing a three-day primary course and receiving a sacred locket called an Omitama (which literally means something like 'sacred, precious, spirit'). It is Oshienushisama who makes it possible for the Omitama to link people powerfully to the Creator God through spiritual cords. By having an Omitama on the body one is also being continuously purified to different degrees. Through the Omitama, the link with God is considerably strengthened when one prays, in times

of danger – in fact, at all times. Because the Omitama is so precious, we are guided to respect and protect it at all times.

Occasionally people have asked me why it is necessary to have a physical object to channel God's Light. Surely, God is everywhere, for all people! Of course God is everywhere, but the problem is that due to accumulated impurities, people in general do not have strong communion with God as in ultra-ancient times. The soul of the human was extremely pure originally, but it is said that it has become so impure over many lifetimes (see chapter 4) that people nowadays cannot easily tune in to divine will. For comparison, everyone may receive the sunshine, but a person with a lens can concentrate the sun's rays to the point of producing intense heat. The Omitama functions like a lens that focuses the Light of God in great concentration, even though it is true that God is everywhere.

In order to grow to understand the preciousness and significance of the Omitama, experience shows that it is best to give many people Light and to build up spiritual experiences through this practice. This will not explain how the Omitama works, but it is possible to discover that it really does work. Take the example of television. It is not necessary to know how a television set works in order to switch it on and view a program. Looking inside the set and examining the electric components is neither going to reveal how a television set picks up and displays the transmitted signal, nor add to the enjoyment of watching it. On the contrary, it may lead to damage and disappointment. The Omitama is a mysterious blessing that cannot be explained logically at the present time but may be appreciated through experience.

The practice of True Light

A session of True Light is normally carried out by first radiating the Light for about ten minutes through the main soul, an invisible area in the region of the pineal gland, about 10 centimetres behind the forehead. The hand is held about 30 centimetres from the forehead. The receiver may feel nothing or there may be sensations, such as warmth or tingling in some part of the body. The body may move in a gentle rocking or swaying pattern, or there may be pronounced, specific movements, the face displaying joy, anger or some other emotion. Such movement is called 'spirit movement'. Sometimes people perspire, see visions, cry or talk. Often none of these symptoms occur. Physical changes are not indicators of the effectiveness of the Light. Everyone who receives True Light receives purification.

One learns the 27 body points or areas that are important for purifying with True Light, as well as the significance of purifying them, matters that Sukuinushisama received through revelation. One also learns about the importance of purifying other body areas, particularly where there is fever, pain, hardness, injury or something unusual.

After purifying through the forehead (normally preceded by reciting a prayer of purification), the back of the head (the medulla oblongata area) is purified on both sides, followed by the left and right sides of the back of the neck (the cervical vertebral area). After that the left and right kidney areas are purified. In addition, in a single session, which is approximately 40-50 minutes long, other areas of the body are usually purified with True Light, depending on the need of the receiver.

In this way, a person can be purified spiritually, mentally and physically with True Light, ideally every day. The giver of Light also receives Light as he or she channels it to the other person. This can be compared with a well; the more one draws water from a well, the more fresh water flows in. Giving Light to people one after another results in receiving abundant Light oneself.

In April 1998, Oshienushisama said:

We need to be aware of the fact that the art of True Light is of an essentially different dimension from that of other so-called spiritual practices that depend on the individual's own power or that of psychic mediums. The art of True Light is neither a shamanistic-like practice nor a spiritual practice that is based on human power. Mahikari, True Light, is the Light from the highest dimension, given directly by the Creator of heaven and earth, Su God.

31

Mahikari primary course

As I mentioned, in order to become a practitioner, one who is able to give the True Light of Su God, it is necessary to attend what is called a primary course, a course of lectures, at the end of which one receives an Omitama. The teachings are delivered by a lecturer who is spiritually appointed to represent Oshienushisama at that time.

I have come to realise that participating in the course is a spiritual matter that is much more than simply receiving information. It is like soaking in a hot spring or fountain of God's Light. Just to participate in the course means that there has been a close bond with God since ancient times. The course has valuable outcomes for not only oneself, but one's family members and ancestors.

There are three types of Mahikari courses. The primary level course is the first step, which allows a person to begin radiating True Light and to be guided about many basic aspects concerning life. Primary courses are held fairly frequently in many countries throughout the world, sometimes every few weeks in the bigger Mahikari centres. The intermediate level course is a higher step spiritually and considerable experience is generally required before being eligible as a candidate. Intermediate courses are held much less frequently. Regions outside of Japan may hold one only once a year or so and many countries have never held an intermediate course. The advanced level course is an even higher rise spiritually and there are more prerequisites to be fulfilled before being eligible. So far, the advanced course has only been held in Japan, and people travel from all over the world to attend it.

It is not just the level of the course and the act of giving God's Light that are important but *how* one practises. The innermost attitude plays an important role. Training oneself to pay close attention and to give Light with a heart of love towards the receiver results in greater purification and effectiveness.

I have found many aspects of Sukyo Mahikari to be unique. Practitioners of Mahikari are not called by traditional names such as 'followers', 'devotees', 'believers' and suchlike. They are called *kamikumite* (which literally means 'those who join hands with God') or *yokoshi* ('people of Light').

Sukyo Mahikari has nothing to do with faith healing. Of course, one's understanding and belief about God and divine matters become stronger as a result of one's experiences, but belief is not required in order to begin. In fact, I have met some very devoted kamikumite who related how they were atheists when they started with Sukyo Mahikari. They said that they came to the Mahikari course to please their spouse or to try to disprove the whole thing. In the same way as the enthusiastic candidates, these people discovered the significance and power of their Omitama. People are not asked about their beliefs. Also, there are no requirements concerning diet, clothes, lifestyle or related matters.

In the early days it was quite a surprise for me to see the broad range of people who attended the courses. There were elderly people and young people, even children (although there is a lower age limit of 10 years). There were people who were ill and others who were healthy, people who were extremely enthusiastic and others who were receiving the course calmly, even with some doubts. It is no surprise anymore, as I have been seeing this every month for years. In every case, irrespective of health, intelligence, age, gender, race, enthusiasm or anything else – everyone who completes the course and receives an Omitama is able to radiate the True Light of the Creator God.

Hopefully, people who become kamikumite will grow to appreciate being of service to God as a way of life, by helping others and making a better society through steadily purifying others and being purified themselves. How that is actually done depends on the person's interests, commitments and so on. People are encouraged to offer service to God in a sensible way that fits with their lifestyle at home, school, work or wherever, and everyone has the freedom to choose what to do.

Goshintai of Su God, the sacred scroll

Another powerful contact point or link through which the Light of God is received in abundance is the Goshintai, the sacred object or scroll in the Mahikari altar. Goshintai literally means something like 'sacred (holy, divine) object' (article). This Japanese word refers to many objects considered sacred at temples or shrines in Japan. However, in the Sukyo Mahikari organisation the Goshintai refers only to the sacred scroll on which there is a comma-like symbol (Chon) on a golden disk. Through this the Light of Su God, the Creator, gushes out like a fountain, in great concentration. Again, it is a spiritual connection that only Oshienushisama is able to make.

Goshintai, in a divine altar at a Mahikari centre

This Light cannot usually be seen with the physical eyes, although I have occasionally met people who have seen a golden-white kind of aura surrounding a Goshintai or something like sparks emanating. It is an area of intense spiritual power where human vibrations are matched with divine vibrations, a place of strong purification and other divine blessings. Therefore, to offer prayers to the Creator God in front of the Goshintai is more effective than to do so elsewhere. The Goshintai also results in greater protection.

A Goshintai is inaugurated in the altar of all official Mahikari Centres. It is also possible to inaugurate a Goshintai at home when one becomes eligible, after attending the advanced course.

World Shrine

In my understanding, the World Shrine, also called *Suza, Sekai So Honzan* or *Motosu Hikari Okamu no Miya*, is a powerful source of Light and salvation for the world. It is located in the city of Takayama in the central mountains area of Japan. Near the summit of a nearby holy mountain, Mount Kurai, is the Inner Shrine, *Mahikari Motosu Miya*, which is something like the 'holy of holies' of the World Shrine. According to divine teachings, the area of Takayama and surroundings, called Hidama in ancient times, is extremely ancient and holy land, an area of significance long before this country was known as Japan. Suza is in Takayama, Hidama, because Sukuinushisama received a revelation that it was to be established there.

World Shrine

Sukuinushisama received a divine command, a holy covenant, to establish a shrine for the Creator God. Through the immense efforts of Su God, Sukuinushisama, Oshienushisama and countless kamikumite throughout the world, this great mission was finally achieved on 3 November 1984.

The World Shrine is a holy shrine where Su God – the Creator of heaven and earth, the universe – is enshrined and worshipped. It is for all people, irrespective of race, religion or anything else. It can be viewed as something like a 'meeting place' for Su God and humankind. The high point of the heavenly dimension and the high point of earth were connected when this shrine was inaugurated. Now a Goshintai of Su God is inaugurated for the whole world, a kind of gigantic spiritual lighthouse. A major step has been taken to establish the spiritually oriented civilisation. It is taught that it is the base of salvation for the world. People from all over the world visit the World Shrine.

Hikaru Shinden, the Shrine dedicated to Sukuinushisama
Another source of Light is *Hikaru Shinden*, the Shrine dedicated to Sukuinushisama, which was inaugurated on 23 June 1992 at a special site at the foot of the holy mountain, Mount Kurai, about 30 minutes' drive from Takayama. Hikaru Shinden is a place where one can communicate more directly with the divine soul of Sukuinushisama as well as express gratitude and respect to the holy master. It is one of the steps for establishing the foundation for the twenty-first holy century.

Hikaru Shinden

The Hikaru Memorial Museum

This museum, located in Takayama, was completed on the founder's birthday, 27 February 1998, and opened on 8 April 1999. The guideline for establishing this museum was the ideal advocated by Sukuinushisama, "The origin of the earth is one; the origin of the world is one; and the origin of all humankind is one." An aim of the museum is to contribute to the development of a high-level civilisation by facilitating mutual understanding and integration amongst not only local, but also international, communities through academic, artistic and cultural endeavours. Many personal belongings of Sukuinushisama as well as reference materials are exhibited. There are also exhibits related to ancient history highlighting the significance of Japan, including the Hida area. There is also an art gallery that exhibits paintings, calligraphy and ceramics.

Hikaru Memorial Museum

Sukyo Mahikari Youth Centre

The *Sukyo Mahikari Youth Centre*, located near the town of Kuguno, about a 30-minute drive from Takayama, was completed on 5 May 2002. This holy place also serves as a base to help make the twenty-first century a holy one and is particularly significant for the future of young people. The training conducted there focuses mainly on nurturing young people so that they can become leaders of society who have a firm grounding in spiritual values, to enable them to be pioneers for the betterment of society. In addition, the Youth Centre serves other

Sukyo Mahikari members of different Mahikari centres and regions, and is also available for use by the residents of Kuguno.

Sukyo Mahikari Youth Centre

The divine plan

In order to understand why the Mahikari organisation came into being, I feel it is necessary to know something about what is called the divine plan, or plan of God. Very simply, there is order, design and purpose in the universe. Life did not begin by chance. There is a purpose for the existence of humans. Things are not evolving in a random, haphazard way. The Great Designer, God, has created the universe and is making things move in order to achieve certain aims. Before dealing with the divine plan, it is useful to consider the theories of evolution and creation.

Theories of evolution and creation

Many people have given up traditional religion and cling to material-centred science in order to try to explain the origin of the universe, the origin of life and the process of evolution. Summarising the evolution theory, matter was supposed to have come out of nowhere with a Big Bang. Slowly it cooled down and coalesced, organising itself in an amazingly orderly way to form the right stars, moons, planets and so on, all in the right positions. In very ancient times, somehow a single-celled creature spontaneously appeared in the primeval sludge of the planet earth, and from this all other creatures are supposed to have developed. Charles Darwin believed that God initially created just one or a few creatures to get things started, and that new life forms developed from these simple creatures by natural selection.

However, many modern scientists have done away with God altogether in evolution theory, and the new or updated version of Darwin's theory, the Neo-Darwinian view, holds that evolution is simply and totally explained by mutations in the genetic code and by natural selection. Humans are considered highly-developed animals at the tail-end of an evolutionary line of the animal kingdom. These views may sound scientific on the surface, but they have some basic flaws that have never been explained by conventional science and show that the mechanistic theories of evolution cannot hold (Morowitz, 1968; Schroder, 1990; Gottlieb, 1992; Laszlo, 1993; Goodwin, 1994; Stove, 1995; Harman & Sahtouris, 1995).

There are certainly many learned scholars – in various fields of biology, genetics, physics, philosophy, palaeontology and archaeology, to name a few – who do not agree with the mainstream view of a simple mechanistic theory of evolution. Quite apart from such studies, however, I feel that mechanistic explanations for evolution do not take into consideration the existence of life after death of human beings. There is no way that the studies of genetics and natural selection can explain the reality of such existence. I believe that when scholars verify the real existence of life after death of people, the reality of discarnate spirits and the clear evidence for reincarnation, as being scientifically valid (see chapter 4), that alone will show up the inadequacy and oversimplicity of mechanistic models of evolution.

In the field of religion, there are also extremist views about the origin of life and evolution – called creation. The rigid, fundamentalist view of creation is that human beings were created a few thousand years ago starting with Adam. The lineage of Abraham, Isaac and so on mentioned in the Bible supposedly represents some of the early ancestors of humankind. Obviously, such a simplistic view cannot be accepted by scientists or any other open-minded people who are familiar with the archaeological evidence for the existence of human beings who lived tens of thousands, hundreds of thousands, even millions of years ago, in different parts of the world.

I believe that it is possible to combine the viewpoints and see the truth within the fields of religion and science. As a scientist I was inspired to learn that what Sukuinushisama transmitted about the divine plan made sense with what I had learnt in the past – in Christianity, science, medicine or anything else. It was particularly valuable to learn about the direction of change in the divine plan and the reasons why, as well as what we can do as human beings. Knowing about the divine plan answers questions such as: What is the purpose of the life of humans? Why are there humans anyway? Why are there so many different religions? Despite all the faith, why has there been so much suffering? Can we humans influence the fate of the world?

Main aspects of the divine plan

From my studies, saying it simply, the Creator God wants to achieve a paradise on earth, just like the paradise that already exists in the high, heavenly dimensions, but with the use of materials. Su God began creation by giving rise to lower gods and establishing the invisible, heavenly dimensions. He first created the opposite essences of fire and water (yang and yin) and the fundamental laws. Then came the creation of the universe and all the materials therein, including plants and creatures. All this took seven long 'generations' over billions of years. There are teachings about the stages and even the names of various gods who were in charge of the various functions, given particularly in the intermediate and advanced courses. It is only at the end of this long period that human beings were created.

There is no denying that over time extremely diverse forms of life have arisen amongst plants, insects, fish and other creatures. Particular plants or creatures have also changed their form over time. There is no question that evolution has taken place. It is only that it has not taken place by chance but has been directed with a purpose. All creatures have a purpose and when there was a need for a change, the form of the creature was changed. For each form that appeared physically, a spirit pattern, an invisible substance or matrix of the physical, was first created. Then it materialised accordingly.

Getting back to the human being, the big question is, why was the human created? The answer is that human beings are expected to create a heaven on earth using materials, on behalf of God. The soul of the human comes from God. Even though the flesh, the physical body, comes from the physical world, the original, spiritual source is God Himself and that is why human beings are called children of God. In other words, humans have a divine nature. In the Bible are passages referring to this as well: "So God created man in his own image" (Genesis 1:27). Also, "The Spirit of God dwells in you" (Romans 8:9).

According to the divine teachings, even though animals have a spirit, it is not like that of humans. Animals communicate by sounds, not words. There are profound differences between humans and animals, even though humans physically resemble some apes. However, apes do not have a soul that is from God. The ancestors of human beings are not apes.

When human beings were first created, they were spiritually, mentally and physically pure. They lived in harmony with the deities. In fact, they were like deities themselves and God ruled over them directly.

However, although people had strong spiritual power then, they had little motivation to promote material development. Su God therefore arranged for humans to have desires by giving them what is called the sub-soul (an invisible area below the navel). Su God also arranged for emphasis of the water or material-centred aspect rather than the fire or spirit-centred aspect, that is, for yin (dark) rather than yang (light) phenomena to predominate for a while. Desires stimulated people to become motivated, to organise, to develop, compete and therefore improve conditions materially.

As a result of having a certain freedom to fulfil their desires, which was necessary so that material development could reach a sufficiently high standard, God had to temporarily overlook deeds that today would be considered evil or wrong. For example, in competing with each other, families, tribes and races came into conflict and fought each other, often killing people. Nevertheless, this had to be overlooked in the short term, in order to achieve the main aim, to promote material progress. After many reincarnations, people have contaminated their spirit, mind and body, even though material development (which today is called technology, inventions, development in science and so on) has progressed. Excessive desires for material possessions, power, fame, sex and other forms of self-gratification led to various kinds of suffering being inflicted on others. That is what is called spiritual impurity. Although humans have a divine nature, they have become contaminated to the extent that many people no longer even recognise the existence of the Creator God and the invisible dimensions. Many people have simply become obsessed with the pursuit of self-centred materialism.

In my youth I used to wonder why God gave people the freedom to choose how to live if He knew they would eventually transgress divine will. I now know that this was a necessary stage for the promotion of competition, which then leads to the development of material aspects. People striving for power, glory, fame or money have made brilliant inventions, achieved great progress in trade, opened up countries and helped society in many ways. Even wars, terrible though they may be, have resulted in many valuable technological advances, despite the unfortunate destruction and suffering they have caused. European countries have played particularly major roles in material development. They colonised many other countries throughout the world, bringing their trade, inventions and other know-how with them. History shows that material progress has occurred in leaps and bounds over the past several thousands of years.

During this peak of material-centredness – in order to help people maintain some understanding of the existence of God, the spiritual realm, life after death and so on, as well as how to live correctly – God arranged for various holy masters and philosophers to bring guidance to the world. This led to the development of what people understand today as religions, ideologies and philosophies. It was not intended to reveal the divine plan in detail at that time. That is why the teachings of that era deal mainly with morals, ethics and how to live properly.

Despite the valuable contributions of religions and ideologies, there are many people who have lost touch with divinity and have become extremely material-centred, even materially obsessed, to the point that there is danger to the very existence of life on earth. This is why a big step in God's plan was to introduce what is called the major transition or turning-point. Basically, the reversal is from water phenomena to fire phenomena, from material-centredness to a focus on the spiritual. We have recently entered this period. Sukuinushisama received a revelation on its precise beginning. It was on the first day of 1962 that he announced the revelation, "The world has now entered the age of baptism by fire/spirit." Since then, the emphasis is changing more and more from yin phenomena to yang phenomena. Su God is now striving to change the dark, disharmonious, self-centred, material-centred world to a bright, peaceful, selfless, spiritually oriented one by various means – by increasing the spiritual fire energy in the universe as well as the Light of God, by providing divine teachings and in other ways.

The materials, technology and science that have been developed up till now are not to be viewed negatively. It is just that they are not to be pursued selfishly as aims in themselves anymore. It is now particularly important for people to understand the real existence of the Creator God; that God has a plan, that a high-quality civilisation is to be established in which peace and harmony are to reign, a world in which God, humans and nature are to coexist harmoniously, and materials are to be used for the good of humankind according to the will of God. People who make efforts in this way will tend to flourish in their lives, businesses, enterprises and other pursuits, pursuits that used to be considered 'materialistic'. Any approach involving cheating, exploiting, corruption and so on will not succeed anymore. That is why such matters are being exposed more and more.

In order to motivate human beings to become God-centred and work on fulfilling the divine plan, God has given the highest gift of salvation on a grand scale at this time – the practice of True Light. It is possible for people to begin to radiate the True Light of the Creator God after simply attending a three-day primary course and receiving an Omitama. God is permitting this because of the urgency of the times we are now living in. If people cultivate the heart of wanting to be of service to God and go about their lives so that they can be used to fulfil the divine plan, the form the purification takes becomes more and more easy to appreciate.

On the other hand, since the will of God has been reversed from an emphasis on material-centredness to an emphasis on the spiritual, if people are not being of sufficient service to God and not voluntarily removing their impurities, the form of cleansing will be more drastic. This is why in addition to the growth of God-centredness in society at large, there is also increasing cleansing or compensation phenomena in the form of disease, financial problems, human relation problems, disorder in society, natural disasters, war and so on. In other words, opposite trends are growing in society at the same time – increasing goodness, happiness, blessings on one hand and increasing evil, unhappiness and suffering on the other, which are really manifestations of various cleansing mechanisms of the universe. The ultimate aim is to establish a high-quality, holy civilisation.

Predictions and trends

From the late 1950s onwards, Sukuinushisama predicted that as the period of baptism by fire increases to a peak, there will be major problems stemming from the population explosion, the number of big earthquakes will increase, and volcanic eruptions will grow in size across the globe. There will be increasing incidences of inexplicable explosions, unpredictable weather with extremes of heat and cold, and overall the temperature will gradually rise. New diseases will appear, including unusual, incurable ones. There will be food shortages. Crops and other produce will deteriorate from the inside before harvesting, when the soil becomes too toxic from artificial chemicals. Eventually people will even have to eat grasses and the roots of trees. They will discover the toxicity of synthetic chemicals in many aspects of their lives. Ocean currents will change, fishing grounds will change, and the sea level will rise, flooding coastal cities. Global warming will lead to major disasters through floods. The polar ice caps will melt, the differences between summer and winter will lessen and Japan, for instance, will eventually have a tropical climate. There will be various kinds of economic collapse and financial misfortune. The value of currency will decline. There will be serious problems from pollution, acid·rain, 'killer' ultra-violet radiation, desertification, oil shortages, conflict and chaos of all kinds, and many smaller wars will occur throughout the world. Sukuinushisama predicted that the two major nations of opposing power will unite, but that nuclear war and pollution from nuclear disasters will cause considerable destruction.

Sukuinushisama talked about various future problems at a time when these phenomena were not generally known or accepted in society. For instance, he first predicted global warming at a time when some scientists were predicting the coming of an ice age. He predicted these things from the revelations he received from God. Today many of these matters are almost everyday news. A study of the literature, scientific data or even media reports reveals that there has been an increasing incidence of major earthquakes, volcanic eruptions and other disasters, particularly fire phenomena, from the early 1960s onwards. According to divine teachings, it seems that a characteristic of fire energy is to make water move, so great floods and tidal waves are increasing as well.

For example, in mid-1996 Washington's Worldwatch Institute reported that losses from "weather-related disasters" (floods, fires, hurricanes, storms and other climatic catastrophes) in the 1990s were running at six times the level of the 1980s. "Between 1990 and 1995 the world suffered 16 climatic catastrophes that each cost more than $3 billion: up to 1987 there had never been a disaster that cost even as much as $1 billion." By the end of the century, these figures were multiplied. In 1996 the total economic losses due to climate-related disasters amounted to $60 billion. In 1998 the figure was close to $80 billion (Brown, Flavin & French, 1998).

From ancient times, various people who are now known as religious leaders, prophets or ones who could predict the future, have forecast a period of destruction that is to occur, particularly after entering the twenty-first century, and that this is eventually to be followed by an age of peace and happiness for the surviving minority.

About 5,000 years ago the Maya people of Central America prophesied that the period after the turn of the twenty-first century would mark the end of the previous age and the beginning of a new one – a period of catastrophic changes (Gilbert & Cotterell, 1995).

Jesus and a number of Jewish prophets before him made predictions about the so-called "judgement day" at the "end of the age" when fire rather than water will be the major means of purification.

Scientists, economists, politicians and others who are concerned about the welfare of people have also predicted that crises resulting from overpopulation, pollution, food shortages, fuel shortages, global warming, desertification and other human-made problems are expected to reach catastrophic proportions around the turn of the century onwards (Ehrlich & Ehrlich, 1996; Brown, Flavin & French, 2000a,b; Brown, 2001). Increasing violence, family breakdown, divorce, suicide, drug use, crime and so on are trends that go well beyond what could be predicted from the increase in the population in most countries of the world. There are serious economic crises. The rate of traffic accidents is escalating. Political wrangling, terrorism and wars continue.

This may sound like the preaching of doom and gloom. Some media and research reports have referred to Sukyo Mahikari as being a 'doomsday' organisation. This is a narrow view, taking things out of context. The fact is that many organisations – both religious and non-religious – and countless individuals, are concerned about the increasing crises, turbulence, disasters and other major problems in the world. Moreover, it is mainly the scientists, economists, environmentalists, politicians and other professional people who are providing evidence for the increase of such turbulent change.

A point sometimes missed in reports on Sukyo Mahikari is that the teachings emphasise that a high-quality, holy civilisation is to be established, not destroyed, through the turbulence. There would be no sense for God to destroy everything that He had spent eons of time developing. The teachings also indicate that the more God-centred and purified people become in this time of reconstruction, the less will it be necessary to go through compensation with misfortune. This time of reconstructing the world is a time of hope and joy, a time when crises can be turned into good opportunities for change, if one understands the ultimate aim of the divine plan.

Even though many problems are escalating, we can also see many favourable outcomes appearing. Who could have predicted the sudden collapse of the communist regime of the Soviet Union or the end of the Cold War? Who could have predicted the sudden unification of East and West Germany? Who could have predicted the sudden liberation of the Baltic countries? The dismantling of apartheid in South Africa has been an incredible change. There are positive trends such as the greening of the world, the trend towards a global cooperative economy, improved social justice, emphasis on community spirit, teamwork, 'win-win' thinking, noble values, ethics in policy-making in government as well as in the business world.

An aim of Sukyo Mahikari is to raise concern about focusing on excessive materialism as in the past, and to cooperate in a spirit of love and harmony with concerned individuals and organisations in order to help guide humankind in the direction of lasting happiness and prosperity.

How the Mahikari organisation is evolving

Since I wrote my previous book on Mahikari, Mr Garry Greenwood, who was not only a good friend but also contributed significantly to promoting Mahikari activities for about 10 years as a full-time employee (appointed in 1978) of the Canberra Mahikari Centre in Australia in the early years, resigned in 1988. At first he continued to be active as a kamikumite, but after some years he began writing various kinds of grievances about the organisation, beginning with his electronically published book, *All The Emperor's Men* (1995) and other materials on the Internet. These writings included many accounts of events and views that are quite different from what I and many other people in Australia remember. A number of kamikumite left Sukyo Mahikari as a result.

Why is it that some people give up whereas others who have been exposed to similar activities, continue? For instance, Garry's own sister-in-law was the assistant director of the Canberra Mahikari Centre when he was the vice-director (I was the director), and she has enthusiastically continued on the path of Sukyo Mahikari, serving as a staff member at the Canberra Mahikari Centre since 1978. Even though the large majority of members have continued and are growing from strength to strength in Sukyo Mahikari, I am sorry that there are some who have become disappointed and even disillusioned with the organisation. After reflection, I wonder whether I and others in the administration could have done some things differently to ensure a more accurate understanding of the organisation and its teachings in those early days.

From my experience, I can see that the Mahikari organisation has been evolving. Of course, the art of True Light and the teachings do not change, but the availability of more Mahikari literature that is better translated, the consideration of cultural differences, and people's increasing understanding of the teachings, depth of experience and growing flexibility have all helped to clarify various misconceptions and are leading to positive changes.

Better translations and more literature
All the lecturers of primary courses for many years after the beginning of the Mahikari organisation in 1959 were Japanese, and when people from overseas countries attended the courses from the early 1970s onwards, the interpreting and translating were done by Japanese people who had less translating ability than occurs nowadays. All the translators were Mahikari members who were volunteers, and even though their understanding of foreign languages was usually better than that of their fellow members, it was not at a professional level. Another problem with translating teachings is that various nuances or depths of teachings cannot necessarily be understood deeply and therefore translated adequately unless translators have long-term personal experience of the teachings. Their lack of understanding of the diverse cultural differences also led to problems, no doubt.

For instance, the meaning of 'Sukyo' was originally mistranslated from Japanese into English as 'supra-religion', which unfortunately could have given the impression that the Mahikari organisation considered itself superior to other religions. However, this is not the meaning of Sukyo at all, as I explained at the beginning of this chapter.

I say these things without blame, to point out a reality that has to be taken into consideration for any organisation whose teachings are translated, particularly when the language involves technical or rarely used words, as well as entirely new concepts. After all, the Bible is still being translated and retranslated, with all kinds of versions coming out century after century. Improved translations will no doubt continue in the Mahikari organisation.

When I attended my first primary course in 1975, there was practically nothing on Mahikari in English – only a romanised version of the prayer Amatsu Norigoto* and a few pages of experiences in Japanese English. Now there is much more literature available in English – books, journals and pamphlets.

When I was stationed in Asia, to some degree I saw a repeat of the simplistic views that used to exist amongst English-speaking people, particularly amongst people who only knew their own language and where there was little or no literature on Mahikari in that language. For instance, I had thought for years that the Indonesian language is the same as the Malaysian language, but

---

In English, "Heavenly prayer". It is the most important prayer, and has a strong spiritual power of purification. It is usually recited before giving Light and at important activities.

there are many differences in words and expressions, and if Indonesian people receive a translation in the Malaysian language, there are aspects they cannot understand. Language problems will continue to be a challenge wherever Sukyo Mahikari spreads, I feel.

Kamikumite are grateful for the translators and interpreters who offered their service since the beginning of the Mahikari organisation. It is also pleasing to see that in Sukyo Mahikari, particularly in recent years, teams of English-speaking translators from the USA, Australia, Europe and Asia, as well as Japan, have been scrutinising more thoroughly all kinds of Mahikari phrases and concepts. More accurate and understandable translations have been appearing. Similar steps have begun in French, Spanish, Portuguese and Italian, and to a smaller degree, various other European and Asian languages. Hopefully, improved translations will help the divine teachings to be grasped and practised accurately throughout the world.

Taking cultural differences into consideration

I lived in Japan for one-and-a-half years beginning in early 1975, and I have visited Japan at least once every year since then. My wife is Japanese and I also speak the language, so I feel I have been able to pick up some of their culture and compare it with my western background.

The Mahikari organisation began in Japan, and wherever it spread in overseas countries, it inevitably came with a Japanese culture. All the early administrative staff and instructors were Japanese, with limited ability to communicate in foreign languages, so this was a challenge in itself. Non-Japanese people (myself included) who attended the primary courses in the early years had a tendency to use Japanese words, or 'Mahikari jargon', in Mahikari activities. This fact, together with various Japanese customs that were acquired along the way, gave a distinctly Japanese flavour to the Mahikari organisation, even when it was growing overseas. For instance, my first book on Mahikari (published in 1982), is full of Japanese expressions that the organisation now regularly translates into English. It is amusing to recollect that in the early years, a number of enthusiastic Western Mahikari members may have inadvertently promoted a Japanese culture unnecessarily by even putting up non-Mahikari Japanese pictures on the walls in Mahikari centres or replying with "hai" instead of "yes" to a question.

When non-Japanese people first see Mahikari activities – the divine altar, bowing and clapping, chanting in Japanese – some cannot help but feel that they are encountering a Japanese religion, not something universal, as the word 'Sukyo' implies. Nowadays, those aspects that have spiritual significance are naturally still practised at Mahikari Centres, but those that do not are gradually being changed to fit the local culture in different countries.

In addition to customs, cultural differences between Japan and other countries have at times resulted in a different perception of certain teachings, depending on the receiver. For instance, from my experience in Australia where people are mainly from a Christian background, the expression "sins and impurities" has made some people feel guilty or inadequate, particularly if they had had an upbringing in which Christianity was enforced on them in a narrow way or if they had had experiences that led to low self-esteem. Even encouraging such people to offer service to God has sometimes made them feel inadequate or forced to do things, when there was no such intention. In Japan, on the other hand, talking about "sins and impurities" and encouraging people to offer service to God usually does not give feelings of guilt or inadequacy. In Buddhism or Shintoism, the main religions in Japan, even though priests encourage their members to come to the temples and shrines, the members do not feel guilty if they do not do so. They realise it is natural for priests to encourage their flock in this way. They just do what they can. Nowadays, the expression, "sins and impurities" is usually translated into English as "spiritual impurities".

Another aspect that stood out for me is that the Japanese people value harmony more than occurs in the West, even if it means sacrificing some honest openness. Even before encountering Mahikari, when I attended conferences as a scientist, I observed that Western scientists (myself included) were eager to voice their opinions strongly and often found delight in finding mistakes in other people's research. This was viewed as 'scientific honesty'. However, I noticed that Japanese scientists – amongst whom were world-class, respected neurophysiologists – often said nothing because their words would have sounded critical and broken the harmonious atmosphere.

In my observation, this cultural difference has led to some misunderstanding amongst Mahikari members. For instance, in Japan people generally know that there are lots of religions, and anyone interested in something like the Mahikari organisation soon gets to know that the organisation has split into other organisations. However, in Australia and other countries, people in Sukyo Mahikari were sometimes shocked to learn from the Internet that there are 'other' Mahikari organisations. For me and others in the early days, there was no problem because we attended our first primary courses at the time when there was only the one original Mahikari organisation, before any split. When the split came, at times we talked about it, but since it was not part of the routine topics in primary courses and study classes, we usually did not say much publicly. Anyway, years later, when Sukyo Mahikari members learned about this split and asked their staff members why they were "not told", Japanese staff members sometimes responded with either silence or very few words, in order to preserve harmony. However, from a westerner's point of view, this was sometimes interpreted as "hiding things".

It is pleasing that nowadays there are attempts to bridge the gaps between cultural backgrounds. The Japanese are more open and encourage dialogue, even on sensitive issues, and westerners are also trying to be more reflective and cooperative rather than leap to conclusions.

More accurate and deeper understanding of the divine teachings

I feel that some of the teachings of the Mahikari organisation have been viewed in a rather simplistic or narrow way, particularly in the early years when there were few experienced instructors and little literature was available. Many of the people in overseas countries who did the instructing – non-Japanese included – did not always have formal training or long-term experience with the teachings. I, for instance, have not attended any training institute of the Mahikari organisation, nor did I have the opportunity to learn in a master-disciple relationship. I picked up what I could from my visits to Japan, from visiting Japanese staff members, my own experiences and the limited literature that was available. I feel sorry that no doubt I have limited people's understanding with my own limited understanding, particularly in the early days.

People formed their views largely from what they picked up from the primary courses, study classes and from each other. Sometimes Mahikari members may have perceived things incorrectly and then shared their views with others. It is a well-known observation that within a group of people who attend a talk with the same lecturer, there can be striking differences in what the individuals perceive and write in their notebooks. If courses are held frequently, discrepancies can be rectified, but this was not always possible, as the number of well-trained staff members was low. More Mahikari literature and more frequent courses and study classes, together with personal guidance, have helped to rectify various misunderstandings.

One misconception, for instance, was that Mahikari was regarded as an organisation for healing and other self-benefit, much more than occurs nowadays. The founder indicated that the aim of

True Light is not for healing disease but to purify the spirit, mind and body in order to restore the original potential of people as children of God. Ultimately, it is to enable people to become divine in nature and participate in fulfilling the divine plan. Yet, the demonstrable improvements that occur with True Light often make people focus on self-benefit, particularly when they first encounter Mahikari.

I, for one, was motivated by self-benefit at the beginning. I was curious whether an energy radiated from the hand could really cause effects in people and whether it could be researched objectively. I had no concept of becoming divine in nature or that God even has a plan. Somehow God put up with me and used me, gradually allowing me to discover the altruistic aims of this organisation.

I have undoubtedly contributed to giving people a self-benefiting image of the Mahikari organisation, which I regret and hope to put into proper perspective. In my previous book on Mahikari I presented many cases of people receiving miraculous benefits, often rather quickly, from practising the art of True Light and divine teachings. No doubt many people came to Mahikari expecting a life of miracles simply because they received the sacred locket, Omitama, and then became involved in some Mahikari activities. When things did not work out quickly enough according to their expectations, some people may have given up Mahikari thinking, "It doesn't work".

Seeking benefits continues to be a major reason why many people start receiving True Light or enquire about Sukyo Mahikari. There is nothing wrong with this provided people can grow beyond this to become more altruistic. After all, great masters such as Jesus also first helped people to overcome their problems before they came to know about God and grow in their faith.

With time, more experienced instructors and more literature available, the Mahikari organisation has been enabling people to gain a deeper understanding that benefits are not the aim in themselves but a means towards awakening to the power of God and how to change oneself in order to become more altruistic and of service to God and others. The guidance and literature provided nowadays gives a more realistic understanding that even if visible benefits occur, they do not occur all the time or necessarily when expected, and that in any case efforts are usually required. A more balanced understanding of the necessity for responsibility and commitment in one's relationship with God is becoming clearer.

§

Another misconception amongst many Mahikari members was that the Light of God could 'fix' almost everything and that there was little need for medical science. Some members even had the view that the Mahikari organisation was against medical science, despite the fact that the founder had taught that true medicine is a balance of spiritual, mental and physical medicine, with emphasis on the spiritual. These misconceptions were unintentional, no doubt promoted by the observations that many and varied miraculous changes, did, in fact, occur through the Light of God, often in a short time. Also, when something is new and shows potential, it is sometimes ascribed 'cure-all' powers that go beyond reason. The Mahikari organisation was certainly a novelty in western countries in the early days.

Nowadays there is a deeper understanding about the need for a balanced, commonsense combination of spiritual, mental and physical medicine when dealing with health. More detailed guidance is now given about this, and many real-life experiences about this combined approach towards health have been reported in Mahikari literature.

In my own case, I can never forget that my wife and I are parents of five wonderful, healthy sons, all born through caesarean section. If it had not been for the technical skills and the equipment used by the doctors and nurses involved, there would be no wife and no sons. I am very grateful for the wonders of modern medicine. At the same time, I also have the conviction that I would not have my wife or descendants in the first place had I not been able to serve God on the path of Sukyo Mahikari and erase some of the spiritual impurities of my family.

§

Another oversimplistic view that still appears from time to time, particularly when people have limited experience with Sukyo Mahikari, is that positive results can be predictably obtained just by giving Light to certain parts of the body. For instance, there are a number of documented cases of people who lost the symptoms of cancer, previously diagnosed as irreversible and terminal by their doctors, as a result of receiving Light. Many people have therefore been led to think that curing cancer or removing some other ailment is merely a matter of receiving God's Light on the appropriate parts of the body. However, life is more complicated than that, and whether one recovers from cancer or not usually depends on many factors.

One of my early experiences with this occurred when my home was used as the Mahikari centre in Canberra, in the late 1970s. Mr John Teagle, who had a malignant melanoma diagnosed as terminal by his doctor and other specialists, came in desperation with his wife to see what Mahikari had to offer. They were strict, practising Catholics, and appeared very uncomfortable as they observed the chanting of 'strange' prayers and bowing and clapping at the Mahikari Centre. However, John was dying so he agreed to receive Light from me. Spirits attached to his body made him move uncontrollably and vigorously when he received Light on his forehead. Even though he was quite shaken by this experience, he was also moved to discover a power that he could not deny. He and his wife attended the next primary course in Canberra and have been offering service to God ever since. All signs of cancer disappeared. According to the medical reports, he was expected to die in the early 1980s, but he is still very much alive.

A few months later, another couple came to the Mahikari centre because the man also had malignant melanoma, although of a milder and less dangerous stage than that of Mr Teagle. He and his wife also attended a primary course. However, the husband never came to the Mahikari centre to give anyone Light after that, and his wife only came a few times before she also drifted away from Mahikari. A few months later we heard that the man had died of his cancer.

This was one of many early lessons for me, showing me that whether it is cancer or any other disorder, improvement does not usually come about merely from receiving a number of minutes of God's energy on certain parts of the body, but that there are many factors involved, and generalisations cannot be made. The Light of God is usually essential for improvement. In addition, however, what is the innermost attitude or motivation of people when they come to a Mahikari centre? As I mentioned, there is nothing wrong with having an initial attitude of seeking benefits. However, in the longer term, there may be a big difference in the results if people come to serve God out of a genuine desire to do something for God rather than simply a desire to be healed. The degree of negative 'karma' or impurities from previous lives of the person and the family members also plays a role. How many other members of the person's family are involved in serving God is another factor. If one does not even believe that one has impurities from the past and there is no heart of apology for one's mistakes, there may only be limited change from the Light of God, even if one is involved in Mahikari activities. Some people may die from cancer even though they do their best for God. In another words, there are various factors that determine what kind of arrangements are received from God.

§

A related narrow view, particularly amongst people of limited experience with Mahikari, is that the outcome of receiving Light is often superficially assessed through only short-term, visible symptoms, not taking into consideration the person's quality of life or whether the person's outlook on life or the future is changed. An outcome from the Light of God cannot necessarily be judged as a success in the here and now, even if it seems miraculous, nor can it be regarded as a failure if it does not fit society's perception of what is success.

I still vividly remember my first case of giving Light to a cancer patient, in 1976, in Canberra, shortly after returning from Japan and before any Mahikari centre was established in Australia. A Latvian man in his 30s asked me whether I could give Light to his mother, who was dying from cancer. He and I had been little boys on the same ship on which our parents came to Australia in 1948, arriving after the Second World War as 'displaced persons'. Latvian society in Australia was rather closely knit so I was well known, having participated in all kinds of ethnic activities over the years. After I returned from Japan and became involved in Mahikari, however, the kinds of comments from Latvians that reached my ears were: "What a pity for us to lose such a fine academic; Tebecis has gone off and lost his mind by becoming a Japanese priest". I therefore hoped that this lady would recover from cancer as a result of receiving True Light from me, and that the Latvian community would recognise the value of the Mahikari organisation.

I went every day to give her Light with sincerity. However, after some days she died. Some Latvians said, "I knew it; it doesn't work. I told you so." However, what can we call a success? I observed how agitated and how much in pain the lady had been at the beginning, and how peacefully she passed away as a result of receiving Light. Her doctor came to visit her on most days when I was there, and after his patient had died he told me: "This is an area that medical science cannot touch. You have done something for her that I could not do, even though I don't really understand what you did. Thank you." I realised that God had provided great blessings for that lady even though nobody at that time considered the result as a success, viewing it from a distance.

It is not possible to evaluate such an outcome using criteria that apply only to the present existence in the physical world. It is not a matter of whether a person lives or dies, but how the person dies, how purified he is and what degree of understanding he has at the time of death, as death is not the end anyway. I would not consider it so successful, even if a person's cancer was resolved through receiving the Light of God, if that person was unable to develop the heart of offering back gratitude to God through some kind of service. It would be a more favourable outcome if the person died of cancer, but died comfortably and peacefully, spiritually purified and with a new lease of life in the afterlife, enthusiastic to serve God there.

Receiving miraculous improvements from God is valuable if the people concerned are able to awaken more deeply to the reality of God and the existence of the realm of spirit, and therefore can develop an altruistic heart to show gratitude and become better people. To view a miraculous experience as an end in itself is too simplistic. As the founder pointed out, sometimes God gives miraculous improvement for demonstration purposes, to help people awaken to the power of God, even if they have not yet made much effort in serving God. Such an experience may serve more as a beginning. At other times God gives miraculous improvement as a reward due to people's dedication in serving God and erasing some of their impurities.

Human beings tend to take things for granted if they occur frequently and easily, and this is true of miracles as well. Many Mahikari members have told me that they had forgotten the miraculous blessings that God had given to them years ago, and were pleasantly surprised to read their own articles about their experiences later. Many of those who have left the Mahikari organisation had had miraculous experiences from practising the art of True Light and divine teachings, and a number of these have been published in Mahikari journals and in my previous book. Having had a miraculous change does not necessarily mean that the people concerned will continue their involvement with Mahikari. The effects of True Light have at times been evaluated too naively and taken for granted too easily. However, as the years pass, generally members seem to be making greater efforts to understand the deeper significance of changes arising from True Light, and are reflecting on what God's expectations might be. More and more people are discovering that generally the best way to improve one's condition is to help others, with the Light of God and in other ways.

What is a miracle anyway? I still do not cease to be amazed just by the fact that the Light of God can come from my hand when I raise it, through no personal power of my own, but because of the special link with the Creator God through my Omitama. I feel that one of the biggest benefits is not whether one sees obvious changes that impress people but the fact that one can learn how to direct oneself towards God through thick and thin, no matter what happens.

§

Another oversimplification, particularly in the early years, was the view that if one was a Mahikari member, one should not have serious problems but be steadily blessed with a life of health, harmony and prosperity. Some Mahikari members have been surprised and even lost their faith in God when they or other members developed a serious disease, got divorced, their business collapsed or there was a tragedy in the family. It is almost as if having an Omitama should give one immunity from serious misfortune, irrespective of what one has done. The teachings clearly indicate that hardships, difficulties and suchlike are valuable times to strengthen people, and guidance is given on how to grow through such difficulties in a positive way. Despite knowing the teachings on 'ups and downs in life', that cleansing and compensation are necessary if impurities have been made, as well as the existence of God-given trials and training, it seems to be human nature that members still hope that such things will not happen to them. They tend to expect only the gentle aspect of God's love. In fact, there is probably an underlying concept in most if not all religious movements that it is God's job to bless people and fix their problems. There does not usually seem to be much focus on what God's expectations might be of people.

With such a view, it can be particularly shocking when Mahikari members who have been serving God, die inexplicably or tragically. The first major tragedy amongst Mahikari members in Australia occurred in the early years of the organisation and involved a group of youths who were killed in a car accident after they attended a Mahikari ceremony in Canberra and were returning to Melbourne. We were all shocked and full of grief. I was asked by the parents of two of these youths to hold their funerals. The grief-stricken parents did not blame the Mahikari organisation, but some members gave up Mahikari because they felt that as members there should not be such tragedies.

Since then I have encountered a few cases in different countries where Mahikari members have died in tragic circumstances – in traffic accidents, from heart attacks, from cancer and so on. Of course we were deeply saddened to lose friends in such a tragic manner. However, through such misfortune and with time we come to learn that even though we know certain factors can influence our destiny in a positive way – such as serving God, erasing our impurities and resolving spirit disturbance – we cannot judge a situation and make interpretations. I have learnt that there are complex arrangements from God as regards life and death, and that sometimes something that looks tragic on the surface can have a favourable outcome. For instance, through spirit investigations I have had personal experiences in which I found that some Sukyo Mahikari members who died tragically are actually of great service to God in the astral world and have communicated, "Not to worry; we are OK".

This is another area in which I have seen changes for the better over the years, namely, that Sukyo Mahikari people are more careful and less judgemental in trying to interpret phenomena. They tend to reflect on God's teachings by observing things over time. In the early days, members often confidently gave reasons why certain things happened or why they could have happened. All in all, members have been acquiring a more accurate and deeper understanding in their practice of divine teachings, and are becoming more open-minded and flexible.

Better training

One characteristic of the Mahikari organisation is that, unlike companies, government organisations or other professional bodies which offer salaries to trained and skilled people appropriate for their requirements, the Mahikari organisation consists almost entirely of volunteers. Even the small proportion of people who are employed by the organisation offer their service largely for the love of God. It is therefore understandable that in Sukyo Mahikari there are people in the administration with different degrees of skill and ability – in dealing with people, diplomacy, public speaking, writing, teaching, planning, organising, time management, accounting and office procedures – and limitations in these areas can contribute to misconceptions or insufficient nurturing of people. Here too, I think that my arrogance and over-zealous personality, particularly in the early years, may have hurt some people or given a limited understanding of the teachings.

As the years pass, steady progress is being made in the nurturing and training of people in the administration of Sukyo Mahikari. Despite this, we have to recognise that the nurturing of human resources will continue to be a challenge, particularly as the people involved are virtually all volunteers.

Importance of practising the art of True Light

In my opinion the various shortcomings of the Mahikari organisation's human resources and materials in the pioneering years, significant though they may be, are probably not the main reasons for misconceptions, oversimplistic views or people giving up Mahikari. It will always be the case that it takes time to understand the teachings in depth, even with the best literature and the best instructors available, and that continuing to practise the art of True Light is important. It is not a matter of learning things academically.

The founder and spiritual leader often emphasised the importance of practising the art of True Light in order to understand the divine teachings. No doubt many misunderstandings have come about due to a lack of continuing experience with True Light.

I have witnessed many cases of people who had demonstrated a reasonably good understanding of the teachings and practised the art of True Light enthusiastically in the past, yet have sometimes even forgotten their previous enthusiasm, inspiration and miracles, as they lost touch with the art of True Light, and allowed negativity to creep in. If people are negative, they can be manipulated more easily by negative spirits. This is not blaming the attached spirits, as we human beings need to take responsibility for our situation, including the reasons for having attached spirits. Nevertheless, it has been a frequent observation of mine that sometimes well-meaning kamikumite gradually find it more and more difficult to maintain positivity and enthusiasm to practise the divine teachings if they neglect the art of True Light for too long. This is because disturbing spirits are then able to influence them more easily (see chapter 4).

I feel that the Sukyo Mahikari organisation nowadays is striving more and more to help people understand the importance of practising the art of True Light and being motivated to continue.

Media publicity

There is an extreme view on the Internet that Sukyo Mahikari has a hidden agenda – that the Emperor of Japan is going to rule the world and that the organisation is a front to achieve this. Such a distorted view simply could not subsist in Japan. Practically everyone in Japan knows that members of the Imperial family are strictly traditionalistic when it comes to religious matters, following traditional Shintoism and all the rites and practices that come with it. The Emperor of Japan, as any head of state or person in high office, would not show favouritism to any religious organisation in Japan or elsewhere.

Why has this view appeared amongst some previous Sukyo Mahikari members? It could be because the founder gave teachings that things started in the "land of the origin of spirit", and that in extremely ancient times there was a leader from the land of the origin of spirit who was the representative of God for the peoples of the world. These teachings need to be taken in context. In ancient times when humankind appeared on earth, there was no country called Japan, no nationalities or borders, only land. People were all of the same origin and spread out to different parts of the world. Japan today is a part of what in ancient times was called the land of the origin of spirit. Sukuinushisama said that the people of the land of the origin of spirit does not only refer to Japanese people. Various teachings of Sukyo Mahikari point not to 'a chosen people' but to the importance of having harmony amongst people of all backgrounds as brothers and sisters. For example, in the *Yokoshi Prayer Book*, a verse of a divine song (entitled "The Land of the Origin of Spirit") says, *Japanese and Jewish people, you are not the chosen ones*. Another says, *Americans, Russians, Chinese, Japanese and Jewish people are all brothers. It is absurd that you now have discord among yourselves*.

Related to this matter is another allegation made in the media and on the Internet – that Sukyo Mahikari is racist, in particular, that it is anti-Semitic. There is no truth in this allegation. The passage cited above from the *Yokoshi Prayer Book* already makes this clear. Sukyo Mahikari welcomes all people, irrespective of their religion, race or background.

There are a number of Jewish Sukyo Mahikari members in Australia, with whom I communicate. The first Mahikari doctor in Australia is a Jewish woman whom I guided to Mahikari in 1976. In Canberra, I often talk with a good friend of mine, a Jewish man who became a Sukyo Mahikari member in Perth years ago. This man used to be the principal viola player for the London Symphony Orchestra and also had a position with the Carl Pini String Quartet. He told me: "The Light and the Mahikari teachings have not only furthered my progress as a musician and teacher but they have deepened my understanding of Judaism". Another Jewish member in Canberra was the vice-principal of a high school and told me that she found the Mahikari practices invaluable in helping to fulfil her role as an educator. There are many Jewish kamikumite throughout the world. Also, I have attended Sukyo Mahikari ceremonies in the World Shrine where Jewish rabbis and dignitaries made complimentary remarks about the organisation in their public speeches.

I feel that any misconceptions about Sukyo Mahikari controlling or looking down upon other races will gradually be dispelled as the organisation spreads and people find out how altruistic and universal it really is.

§

Another matter worthy of clarification is the allegation on the Internet that Sukyo Mahikari has links with the movement, Aum Supreme Truth, in Japan. The Japanese police have discredited Aum Supreme Truth as a terrorist organisation, so it is understandable that people who know little about Sukyo Mahikari would be shocked by any report that the organisation has a connection with Aum Supreme

Truth. There is no connection with Aum Supreme Truth and never was.

It is true that a Japanese one-time Mahikari member who came to Australia became a member of Aum Supreme Truth, but she did this many years after she had given up Mahikari. I knew her well – Ms Yasuko Shimada, who came to Adelaide in South Australia in 1974 and helped plant the first seeds of Mahikari in Australia, a little over a year before I came across Mahikari in Japan. She married an Australian man and was able to gain Australian citizenship. She was certainly a pioneer for Mahikari in Adelaide. However, for various reasons she got divorced and gave up Mahikari in the early 1980s, years before Aum Supreme Truth was even founded. We heard from acquaintances that she was trying different religions. As far as I know, Mahikari members lost touch with her for years and were surprised by media reports that she had become a member of Aum Supreme Truth years later.

People come and go in all kinds of organisations, and there is no way any organisation can be responsible for what people do elsewhere years after leaving that organisation.

Of course, history has shown that sometimes organisations registered as religions have, in fact, had hidden agendas or have exploited people. It was a good move by governments, not only in Japan but around the world, to investigate religious organisations to assess how genuine they are. Mass suicides in religious movements in Europe and Canada a few years ago, as well as the sarin gas murders by Aum Supreme Truth in Japan, prompted governments to look closely into religious organisations, resulting in some reassurance for the public. The Japanese government enacted religious law reforms in which all religious organisations were scrutinised, and there were a number that were either closed down or are under surveillance. From all this, it became clear that in Japan, Sukyo Mahikari is held in high regard as an organisation that stands for good in society. Media reports in Japan have cited Sukyo Mahikari as one of the fastest growing new religions attracting the public. More and more research reports on new religions in Japan are also indicating their surprise that Sukyo Mahikari is growing rapidly, not only in Japan but overseas.

When shocking allegations appear about religious movements that are not well known, some people are quick to use the words 'brain-washing', 'sect' and 'cult' even though they know little or nothing about the organisation concerned, or even what defines a sect or cult. Sukyo Mahikari is not very well known in society outside of Japan when compared with mainstream organisations that have been in existence for centuries, so it is understandable that the public can become alarmed by negative claims in the media and on the Internet.

I was in Australia in 1997 when media reports criticising Sukyo Mahikari in Australia appeared. At that time, I was the Regional Director of Sukyo Mahikari Australia-Oceania Region. Understandably, a number of Mahikari members became confused, particularly because of some anxiety from their non-Mahikari relatives. In order to help allay people's concerns, I invited the Australian Federal Police to come to our Sukyo Mahikari Headquarters in Canberra and examine our records, files, accounts or anything else they wished. Three Federal Agents came, and during the amicable conversation they raised no concern about the integrity of Sukyo Mahikari. In fact, they offered their support, indicating that they would come quickly to our aid if any problems occurred from people who did not know the facts and wanted to cause trouble.

In 1996 a Parliamentary Commission in Belgium investigated dozens of religious and spiritual organisations, including Sukyo Mahikari. At that time media reports labelled Sukyo Mahikari as a 'dangerous sect'. Sukyo Mahikari staff members contacted the Department of Justice in Brussels about this allegation and the Commissioner General of the Criminal Investigation Department (Department of Justice) in Brussels replied in writing on 26 May 1998 that he had not given any indication that the organisation was dangerous and that he is not responsible for the interpretations by the media. Even the organisation for observing sects, "Information and Advice Centre on Harmful Sectarian Organisations", legally established in 1998 as a consequence of that parliamentary commission, replied in writing on 13 December 2001 that in the documents of the Centre there is no evidence of anything presented before a judge, of illegal practices, harming individuals, families or the society, or disturbing public order, by Sukyo Mahikari.

In England, on 4 March 1999, Scotland Yard wrote to Sukyo Mahikari's lawyers in London confirming that "nothing untoward was found" when officers visited the London Mahikari Centre and that as far as they were aware, Sukyo Mahikari was "not being investigated by the Metropolitan Police for any suspected criminal offence".

Negative publicity can have a good outcome. It usually makes people look more carefully at organisations and how genuine they really are, and as a result many people can be reassured and even discover the value of the organisation. Within Sukyo Mahikari as well, many people's faith has been strengthened through these experiences.

Also, we now feel that we have a responsibility to not be so passive but to help society know more about Sukyo Mahikari so that people can make informed choices.

§

The Mahikari organisation has been spreading mainly by word of mouth. Other than some public talks, public activities and media coverage, there have been no high-pressure campaigns or advertising. Also, not much Mahikari literature has been available for the public.

However, the Mahikari organisation has always been open in that the general public is welcome to visit Mahikari centres, to experience the Light of God, to talk to members, read the literature, attend ceremonies, study classes and so on. There is no obligation to continue, although of course, members are pleased if someone wishes to do so. People may visit once or twice or come dozens of times. They may become members or not. There are people who leave the Mahikari organisation, in which case their views are respected. There are also some people who wish to come back to the Mahikari organisation years later, and do so. Unlike the early years when people could become Mahikari members with little or no prior preparation, nowadays, most Sukyo Mahikari centres have guidelines for preparation in order to help potential members to really know what they are getting into. Such people are encouraged to receive the Light of God many times, to attend some activities, read the literature and talk to members so they can make informed choices. Young children may also become members, but only if at least one of their parents is a member. Teenagers require the permission of their parents if they wish to become members.

Sukyo Mahikari derives no income from any business. It is totally funded by voluntary donations made by members. It is taught that offerings only have significance if they are made willingly and with gratitude.

As Sukyo Mahikari spreads and as more literature on Mahikari becomes available to the public, I envisage that more and more people will be able to see what this organisation stands for and evaluate it appropriately.

The founder
and the present
spiritual leader

Chapter 3

The founder and the present spiritual leader

A brief history of the founder

The Mahikari organisation was founded by Yoshikazu Okada, a Japanese man whose life had been mainly concerned with military and later, business activities, fields in which he had not only achieved considerable success but also undergone great suffering. Later in life, his dedication to God, startling spiritual power and inexhaustible, altruistic efforts for the salvation of humankind earned him the name *Sukuinushisama*, which means 'Master of Salvation' or 'Great Saviour'. I did not meet Sukuinushisama personally, as he had passed away the year before I became a Mahikari practitioner, but I have learnt much about him from other people's reports and experiences.

Yoshikazu Okada was born on 27 February 1901, in Aoyama, a district of Tokyo. He was the only son and he had five sisters. He came from a respected family of scholars. On his father's side, his ancestors were from the Oda family, and on his mother's side, the Tokugawa family, both samurai families that flourished during the age of the feuding warlords and that had a notable influence on the history of Japan. His grandfather was a tutor in the employ of a feudal lord (*daimyo*) of the Kishu clan in Wakayama. His father, Inasaburo Okada, was a military officer with the rank of major general, who had studied military strategy for three years in Germany after the First World War.

Yoshikazu had set his hopes on making a contribution to his country by becoming a diplomat or a politician, but when he was 15 years old, his father's dying wish was that he enter the Military Academy of the Imperial Army. Feeling compelled to do this, after high school the youthful Okada became a student at the Military Academy. He achieved the distinguished rank of Equestrian Flag Bearer of the 1st Regiment of the Imperial Guard.

A classmate in the Military Academy, Mr Kiyoharu Tomomori, spoke affectionately about his friend, Mr Okada, who later became his superior in rank, in this way (Shibata, 1993):

He was obedient, innocent and truly childlike. There was nothing false about him. He said exactly what he thought and believed what he was told. There was nothing cunning in his nature at all. He was extremely considerate, placing great importance on friendship. He did not get angry or blame, accuse, hate or hurt anybody. He did not worry about trifles, was broad-minded, never complained or made a fuss. He solved problems with humour. He had no attachment to money or material things, and he freely spoke his mind. He was enthusiastic in everything he did . . .

Mr Tomomori considered the young Okada as handsome, his noble features suggesting his family heritage, having a lively manner and a speech that was sophisticated and refined. Apparently he was the best student at conversation in their English class.

I still remember the words of another of his classmates (at that time 92 years old and not a Mahikari practitioner) at a Sukyo Mahikari Ceremony in Tokyo in 1991, who related his early experiences with the young Okada. Amongst other things he said, "... there was no doubt that of the 365 members in our class, Okada-san was the best".

Even though many aspects of Mr Okada's life indicated great success, he also went through great hardships, difficulties and trials. He was involved in military service during the wars in China and Indo-China (serving behind the lines with stores, supplies and transport), which he deeply regretted years later, as many people were killed in these wars. In December 1937, the tragic attack on Nanking took place while Mr Okada was hospitalised in Shanghai due to a high fever, according to military records. Then he was sent back to Japan. He came close to death several times. The most hopeless time was during the Second World War, when he had great trouble with a back injury which he had previously received in Japan after falling from a horse, in 1938. This injury flared up again when he was on military duty as a lieutenant-colonel in Indo-China, in 1941. As a result he developed a disease of the thoracic vertebrae called caries, which could not be cured by any doctors using the most modern treatment in Japan. In his early forties, when he should have been in the prime of life, he was told that he only had three years to live. The apparent hopelessness of his condition made him reflect deeply on life and he awakened to many things about the existence of God and the limitations of relying on human power.

Not being able to stay in active military service because of his disease, he retired with the rank of lieutenant-colonel and went into business. Utilising his family's fortune he established several companies, the main one being an aeroplane-manufacturing company. Spending much time in prayer he gradually regained his health. With time he realised that mysteriously, he showed no signs of dying and that his spinal disease had disappeared even though more than three years had passed since he had been told by his doctors that there was no hope.

Soon after, however, he was devastated again, this time in a material way. His aeroplane company was destroyed by United States bombing raids at the end of the Second World War. He lost everything. He crashed from prince to pauper. The only possessions he had left were the clothes he was wearing at the time. Nevertheless, he looked upon his financial struggle as a great compensation and took on humble jobs such as selling rubber boots to farmers, door to door. Later he joined a construction company as an executive in order to begin paying off his enormous debts.

He finished paying off his debts by January 1959. Then, as he woke up from five days of unconsciousness due to high fever, at 5 o'clock in the morning on 27 February 1959 (his birthday), he received his first revelation from the Creator God concerning the mission of spreading the Light of God. This date is now considered as the spiritual beginning of the Mahikari organisation.

As regards his beliefs before that time, Mr Okada had had a keen interest in learning what he could. His mother Tomi, was a devout follower of the God of Izumo Taisha, a Shinto shrine. He sometimes mentioned with gratitude how his parents had given him a good foundation for his faith. His efforts to grasp the realm of God developed through studying spiritual matters and various religions. However, his research went beyond the field of religion and also covered fields such as history and science, including nuclear physics. On occasions he remarked on the value of studying the Bible. Although he was not a full-time religious professional, it is clear from his words and writings that he received communication from God (including revelations) during the war and post-war years, before 1959. Even though he had learnt much in various ways, the revelations he received from God on his birthday in 1959 and thereafter, marked a new phase.

Efforts to spread the Light and divine teachings

On 27 February 1959 God revealed to Mr Okada that all religions so far had exposed only fragments of divine truth and that he would be given depths of truth never revealed before. The Holy Spirit of divine truth entered Mr Okada, who was told to speak what he heard.

Mr Okada had already gone through considerable suffering as regards his health and his material situation and now he had hardships and obstacles in another way – rejection and opposition to his efforts to spread the Light and the divine teachings. Having been well-known in the military service and in the business world, fields that are normally of a rather secular nature, his talking about God and activities to bring the Light were met with a lot of opposition, doubt and suspicion, even from his own relatives.

In 1959 he received the spiritual name *Kotama* ('Sphere of Light') from the Creator God and later, the spiritual name *Seigyoku* ('Holy Jewel'). However, he felt that these names were 'too awesome' and did not make them public. In 1961 some Shinto priests, who at first had doubts about his divine missions, discovered through their own divine oracle that his spiritual name was Seigyoku, Kotama being a temporary name. Furthermore, much to their surprise, they confirmed that he had special missions from God and was indeed the great soul whom they were expecting. As a result, several Shinto priests attended the Mahikari primary course.

In 1965 Mr Okada received the spiritual name of *Seio* ('Holy Phoenix') through a revelation. Being very humble, he did not reveal this name at first, but after receiving some signs from God to make public his new divine name, he eventually did so, in 1968.

He received numerous revelations from the Creator God, many of which are published in the divine books – The Holy Words *(Goseigen)*, the Yokoshi Prayer Book *(Yokoshi Norigotoshu)*, Short Teachings by the Founder *(Sunkyo)* and others. In 1962 Sukuinushisama launched the journal *Mahikari*, which is still being published every month. Sukuinushisama also transmitted divine teachings at grand ceremonies, monthly ceremonies, the primary, intermediate and advanced courses, meetings of staff members, certain training sessions and on other occasions such as lectures to the general public.

One of Sukuinushisama's missions was to "hold up the hand to "purify the world" with the Light of the Creator God and to share this ability with whoever sought it. He performed many miracles and also passed on the power to do similar things to numerous people by holding Mahikari courses, at the end of which the candidates received the sacred locket, Omitama.

From 1959 until 1974, when Sukuinushisama ascended to the realm of divine spirits, he helped many people with the Light of God. I heard from several staff members who had been with him for a long time that he often gave Light more or less continuously from about nine in the morning until midnight or later. Even at around midnight, on many occasions there were 20 to 30 people still waiting for the Light. It was not uncommon for him to end the day at about one or two o'clock in the morning and then return home for other service to God.

God gave Sukuinushisama missions of considerable significance for humankind including: to enable people to channel the power of Su God, the Creator; to help the major religions to return to their common origin; to build the World Shrine in order to enshrine the Creator God; to awaken people to the importance of the invisible but real dimensions of existence of the spiritual realm; to give people understanding of the actual existence and great influence of spirits; and to change the world from following ideas, practices and directions that do not fit with the will of God to one which follows universal laws.

In addition, Sukuinushisama gave prophecies about the future as well as details of the ancient history of the world, the origin of languages and so on. He made trips to shrines, temples, libraries, archives, archaeological sites and other places of significance in order to show that there was already some evidence for many of the revelations he had received concerning history.

A number of people, including friends, school mates, disciples, acquaintances and others, have given insight about Sukuinushisama as a man, a father, a military officer and so on, published in a book edited by Shibata (1993). In this book Sukuinushisama's daughter, his successor as spiritual leader, wrote:

Witnessing my father's rapid physical and spiritual transformation, I gradually became attracted to the practice of Mahikari and the divine principles about which he spoke. Before long I also came to experience the greatness of God's limitless power and became determined to assist my father.

The expansion of Mahikari, initiated by two people from a small, 12-square-metre room, was not easy. Many were the times when we seemed to be treading a thorny path that defied description. Nevertheless, our hearts remained filled with the warm Light of God's love.

Never heeding the rain or cold wind, my father would venture out on his old bicycle, even in stormy weather, to help people who were suffering from pain and anguish. Out of his deep and warm love, he would travel, day or night, as far as Tachikawa or Hachioji to give True Light and offer guidance.

Miracles occurred around him one after another as he held up his hand in sincere obedience to God's instructions. People in ill health recovered, and those living in poverty or conflict were able to end their suffering and have new hope for the future. Here was a new principle of salvation for mankind, a high-dimensional practice for the resolution of spirit disturbance, something impossible to comprehend in an age when material science was thought to be almighty.

When someone recovered from a long-standing illness thanks to the art of True Light, Sukuinushisama was as happy as if it had happened to himself. The strength of his gratitude and determination to serve God grew increasingly stronger; he was a living example of how to put God first in all things.

No matter how busy he was, he always nobly and selflessly sought the eternal glory of the name of God and the happiness of others without worrying about his own affairs. As my spiritual master, my father guided me in divine matters more strictly than he did anyone else . . .

He had a certain serenity; he was not unduly fussy and never became upset over small things. Sometimes he was childlike, and at other times full of wit and humour. On other occasions he would confidently express his thoughts without hesitation, thoughts which went beyond the common knowledge of ordinary people. He lived life in true obedience to God.

In 2001, one of Sukuinushisama's early disciples, Mr Suzuki, later one of the executive directors of Sukyo Mahikari International Headquarters, reminisced about his experiences in a lecture to overseas staff members, a lecture I also attended:

Sukuinushisama was the kind of person you would not forget once you met him, not only men, but women, young and old – everyone was attracted to Sukuinushisama regardless of their social status or economic background . . . even when Sukuinushisama walked down the street, people passed and then looked back, wondering who he was.

I think Sukuinushisama must have understood God's feelings when God created human beings, as Sukuinushisama could give out love to anyone, anyone at all.

He encouraged people, boosted them so much, making them happy. It wasn't a pretend thing. It was a genuinely happy feeling. Just to be with Sukuinushisama made me happy.

Sukuinushisama was like the sun, so warm. People used to say things like, 'Sukuinushisama, may I put my arm around your arm?' Sukuinushisama would say, 'Yes, of course,' and everyone would swarm around him.

International recognition

Sukuinushisama was respected and admired throughout the world. His wisdom, joy, cheerfulness, warmth, charm, love for humankind, humility, broad-heartedness and other attributes attracted people from all walks of life. He also had the gift of putting the teachings of God in a simple yet awe-inspiring way. A number of scientists (including Professor Hideki Yukawa, who received the Nobel Prize for his contributions to nuclear physics), came to see him; various politicians; ambassadors from many countries; well-known figures in the fields of education, music, art, literature, the theatre, sport and so on, have all come to learn, to show respect and support.

In the field of religion, for example, in the early 1960s His Holiness Sri Swami Rama, a great Indian yoga master and spiritual leader, was asked by his guru (who had apparently received a divine message) to go from India to Japan and seek out a special soul. I met Swami Rama when I went to India in 1974 for an international physiology conference, and although he told me about the Mahikari organisation, it did not register for me at that time. It was only at the end of 1975 that I first learned how much Swami Rama respected Sukuinushisama, Oshienushisama and the Mahikari organisation. A few years later I was given a script of Swami Rama's talks about how he met Sukuinushisama. The following excerpts are from one of his talks in Japan.

I have travelled all over the world and have met all kinds of religious people, but there is nobody as great as Sukuinushisama. Eighteen years ago Sukuinushisama invited me to Motomitamaza several times and I was permitted to talk with him about spiritual matters. Sukuinushisama was so wonderful that he dealt with any person ever so freely, whether young or old or even a small child. For each one Sukuinushisama was always smiling, warm and totally free. If I tell you everything that Sukuinushisama showed me, I'm sure you would be very surprised. Sukuinushisama's prayer wasn't restricted to twice a day, in the morning or evening or anything like that. His life itself was prayer.

Going back to the beginning – I was brought up in a cave in the mountains in the Himalayas and in a way to leave everything up to God, not to worry about anything, that is, not to think about anything secular, so I had made no preparations to go anywhere. However, my master gave me two pieces of paper and told me to take these messages to give to a certain person. I told my master again that I did not understand the language, I did not have money, and how would I find such a person?

After I went through Customs in Tokyo I met a man who asked me where I intended to stay so I answered, 'I'm staying at my friend's place'. He asked me again, 'Who is your friend?' So I had an inspiration and said, 'You are'.

Over time the man took me to various leaders of religions but I didn't feel anything special about any of them. My master had told me, 'When you meet him, you will know and he will know as well.' But I did not meet anyone like that. I also gave lectures at Rissho University, Tokyo University and Nippon University. Also, this man took me to a place in Yamaguchi

Prefecture where the people danced as they prayed. They asked me to dance with them and to write a book about them to help them, but I declined.

However, when I went to that place a man called Mr Yoshida approached me and said, 'I will take you to the man you want to meet. He's a wonderful man, a truly sincere person.' Mr Yoshida is a Japanese who had lived in America a long time so he spoke English very well. I felt at ease with Mr Yoshida, so I said, 'I've been looking for a particular person for two months but I haven't met anyone.' Mr Yoshida telephoned Sukuinushisama and said, 'Someone is here from the Himalayas.' Sukuinushisama replied, 'Yes, please bring him.' So I went to Sukuinushisama's house with Mr Yoshida. Sukuinushisama extended both his arms and said 'Welcome'. At that moment precisely I knew that this was the person I'd been looking for. For a while we uttered no words – just embraced. This meeting was not just the kind of meeting between friend and friend. It was different from a meeting between man and woman. It was a truly holy and sacred meeting.

So I asked Sukuinushisama, 'Sukuinushisama, have you been waiting for the message I brought?' and he answered, 'Yes, I have been waiting.' I thought to myself, 'I would never be able to meet a man like this again.'

The Light of God comes from the one source, from God. The relationship between God and man is very solemn. Do you drink good wine from a paper cup? No, you drink the best wine from the best glass, that which is appropriate. Many people call themselves holy or sacred or claim to be messengers from God, but I believe Sukuinushisama is a genuine holy man or sage, a true child of God and a tool of God.

I've never experienced elsewhere the wonderful joy that I had when being with Sukuinushisama. I feel that there are two different kinds of wonderful people in the world. The first kind of people offer wonderful experiences and have wonderful behaviour. People praise such people as wonderful people. The other kind of great person is a genuinely great character who truly knows God and knows people. It is through such people that God gives Light to people . . .

On many occasions Sukuinushisama and I talked through the night about psychology, philosophy, religious teachings and so on, but amazingly, Sukuinushisama knew most of these things thoroughly. Many times Sukuinushisama tried me and I tried him as well. As we approached each other with deep love, I tried and tested Sukuinushisama to see how much he knew and I too was tested by Sukuinushisama.

Once I asked him a question in this way. 'I'm sure you know the divine principles very well but how do you put them into practice? For instance, what can you do to make small children understand the divine principles or divine truth? I want to transmit divine truth to people, and Sukuinushisama, you too are trying to transmit this. For instance, what would you do to teach

small children?' I have asked many holy people about this, but no-one but Sukuinushisama has ever been able to answer this question satisfactorily . . .

Sukuinushisama replied, 'It is very easy. First of all, do not tell any lies, speak only what God has transmitted to you and then pray to God about everything. Ask God to give you the divine truth and divine principles, and be kind.' These things may sound very obvious matters that have been talked about for many centuries, but knowing something is different from practising it. In other words, knowing teachings is different from putting them into practice. It's easy to study but hard to practise. Many great men have talked about truth and wonderful things, but very few practise it . . .

One day in October, Thursday, about five o'clock, I said to Sukuinushisama, 'Let me tell you about a secret teaching from the Himalayas.' We were very close indeed. I said to Sukuinushisama that I could radiate the power of God and Sukuinushisama said that he can as well. So I said to him, 'We believe in the same God; please let me see.' Sukuinushisama raised his hand. So I said, 'Sukuinushisama, I would like to see the Light of God in a material manner.' Well, near us there was a vase of flowers which were still in the form of tightly closed buds. It looked as though it would take three or four days before they would open. They were tightly closed, but as soon as Sukuinushisama raised his hand towards those buds, they opened up immediately and blossomed as flowers! To remember that day, as a souvenir for the miracle performed by my great friend, and in order not to forget my awe, I have made pressed flowers out of them and am still keeping them preciously in a cave in the Himalayas.

I have been trained in ascetic practices ever since I was three years old, but I know Sukuinushisama is a genuine messenger from God. Sukuinushisama told me that even during the war he had heard the voice of God very often. There were messages such as, 'Why are you in the war? You must save people.'

I want to memorialise the matters about Sukuinushisama so that I can transmit things about my greatest friend.

§

Sukuinushisama's visit to western countries (France, Italy, Belgium, Switzerland) took place in 1973, beginning in Paris. A group of people accompanied him on a boat trip on the river Seine in Paris. A staff member later reported that as the boat approached the Cathedral of Notre Dame, there was a sudden clap of thunder and a heavy rainstorm began. Sukuinushisama then gave the following explanation:

In ancient times, beneath the site where the Cathedral of Notre Dame is built, there was an altar dedicated to the gods of fire. This storm is a divine signal to confirm that the mission of bearing witness that Light comes from the East has been accomplished. This storm will stop once the boat goes back past the Cathedral of Notre Dame.

Exactly as predicted, the storm ceased gradually once the boat passed the Cathedral of Notre Dame again. People were astounded.

Two days later Sukuinushisama gave a public lecture at Paris's Salle Gaveau concert hall. An article in *Le Monde* had aroused the interest of the French people, and over 500 people attended the three-hour talk.

§

I met Father Andrew F. Morlion, a Dominican priest of Flemish origin, when he participated as a speaker at the First International Yoko Civilization Conference held at the World Shrine in Takayama in 1986. In his lecture he said:

It is with this criterion of wisdom that we objectively conclude that Okada is one of the great sages sent by God to bring the people of this century back to the essence of faith, the only real source of hope. . .

Thus Mahikari is not a new religion; it is the constant appeal to all to unite in one religion. Okada concentrates on the essentials which give new vigor to the abstract idea that God is omnipresent.

Mahikari members have no ambition to become the only power that changes society. The Mahikari movement is not a hierarchical organization dependent on structures made by man. Mahikari is thus not just one new group competing with others; it is a thoroughgoing universal religious challenge to obey the will of God (Morlion, 1987).

§

In one of the revelations (*The Holy Words*) that Sukuinushisama received in December 1965 (which he was very reluctant to reveal to the public at first, because the revelation is from God to kamikumite about Sukuinushisama himself), the words of God are:

The master of you kumite is not the master just for you. He is now the master of the eternal life of all humankind as the true representative of God for this world . . . Consequently, he has become the master who is not only for you kumite. He is the soul that I shall make the master for all humankind and that I shall use for the work of establishing a heavenly world. He is the one whom I made the master of guidance and the master of salvation . . . the holy messenger to help humans achieve true liberation through true spiritual elevation.

Sukuinushisama's departure

Sukuinushisama departed from the physical world on 23 June 1974. He had gone to bed and fallen into a deep sleep. On the morning of the 23rd he did not answer when people called him. Then his breathing stopped like a quietly receding tide. His heartbeat could no longer be heard through the doctor's stethoscope, but mysteriously his pulse could still be felt – now strong, now weak. Other unusual things occurred. Even after the doctor had pronounced Sukuinushisama dead, his pupils did not dilate. His eyes continued to shine. His body temperature did not go down. His whole body was soft, with no change from the time he went to bed. The colour of his complexion was good. Smiling, he looked as if he might start speaking at any moment. Finally, a quiet spiritual energy permeated the room and Kotama Okada, the holy master and saviour, ascended to the realm of divine spirits.

On 26 June a private funeral was conducted by staff members. Although it was the rainy season, on that day the weather was particularly fine without a cloud in the sky. When the funeral ceremony began, gold flakes, materialisation of the Light of God, rained down out of the sky over the headquarters building. Reflecting the light of the sun, the flakes were dazzlingly, almost blindingly, radiant. This miracle occurred in broad daylight before the eyes of many Mahikari members standing outside the building.

The official funeral was held at the Nihon Budokan (Japan Martial Arts Hall) in Tokyo on 13 July. Approximately 20,000 people had gathered from all over Japan and different parts of the world. Most of them laid flowers before the altar, including Swami Rama.

Viewing the Mahikari organisation in perspective

Over the years, there have been a few occasions when people have suggested to me that Sukuinushisama had formed the Mahikari organisation using teachings from other religions. It is true that Sukuinushisama sometimes referred to Buddha or Buddhist teachings, to Jesus and some things that have appeared in the Bible, as well as to other religions. He had knowledge of the Talmud and other teachings of the ancient Jews. There are people who have said that many of the teachings have already appeared in Shintoism and in some new Japanese religions, particularly Sekai Kyuseikyo (Church of World Messianity). In some academic publications I have read the view that Sukyo Mahikari is a 'syncretistic' religion, that is, made up of bits and pieces of other religions. This view can only be held by people who examine the subject superficially, I feel. It is like saying that rugby is the same as soccer or that one was formed from the other, just because there are some similarities in the games (people chase a ball, try to score goals and so on).

There is no doubt that Sukuinushisama learned many things in his life – in the military service, in business, from his religious background (in Japan most people are both Buddhists and Shintoists) and from everything else – things that enabled him to fulfil his role in the Mahikari organisation more effectively. For instance, by referring to people or texts his listeners were familiar with, Sukuinushisama was able to present the teachings in a way that could be understood more easily. That is a far cry, however, from thinking that the Mahikari organisation is just made up of teachings from other religions.

Whatever experiences and learning Sukuinushisama had had in the past, the fact remains that the Mahikari organisation began with a very important revelation from God on 27 February 1959 and Sukuinushisama continued to receive revelations thereafter. From studying the contents of the revelations, particularly those in the *Holy Words*, for me it is clear that there are countless aspects that have never been revealed before or as deeply before, as a result of the progress of the divine plan. There are also many things that do refer to what had been given already by other holy masters. This is only natural as all religions have the same common origin. For example, Jesus talked about "Judgement Day", "Baptism by Fire" and so on. However, he did not say much more than that. In the teachings revealed through Sukyo Mahikari, very specific details are given with time frames. Sukuinushisama also said that he cannot make public everything that God revealed to him. For instance, he said that at this stage people cannot even begin to comprehend the "whole" divine world.

The second spiritual leader, Oshienushisama – the succession and subsequent divine service

Ten days before leaving for the divine spirits world, on 13 June 1974 Sukuinushisama received a revelation of momentous importance. God revealed that the spiritual leadership of the Mahikari organisation was to pass to his daughter, whom he had adopted. Her spiritual name was *Keiju* ('Blessed Jewel'). The ceremony of succession took place at Hidama Motomitamaza in Atami, the special holy shrine and place of divine service of Sukuinushisama and his daughter, Keijusama. That morning at 11 a.m. Sukuinushisama, wearing his ceremonial robes, bowed respectfully before the altar of God at Motomitamaza, his daughter behind him, and recited the prayer of purification, Amatsu Norigoto. After that he turned to Keijusama, his face very serious, and said, "This morning I received a revelation. Your Omitama is to be replaced by another. Give me your Omitama." He then gave his daughter the special Omitama he had been keeping around his neck. He said that God had given him the revelation, "Give the Omitama of Yo to your daughter." Then, his face full of affection, he gave guidance concerning the succession both strictly and gently. That is how Keijusama became the second Oshienushisama, which means 'Master of Teachings' or 'Great Teacher', and inherited all the divine missions from Sukuinushisama.

§

Oshienushisama has undergone many trials. Shortly after Sukuinushisama left the physical world, Mr Sakae Sekiguchi, who had a high administrative position in Mahikari Headquarters and who had been asked by Miss Keiju Okada to help her by taking the lead in expansion activities, wrongfully told some administrative staff members that before passing away, Sukuinushisama had indicated that he, Mr Sekiguchi, was to be the next spiritual leader of the organisation. In their grief and confusion, a number of the staff, not knowing about the revelation that Sukuinushisama had received concerning his daughter being the next Oshienushi, were directed to arrange other staff at Headquarters as well as Regional Directors, to give their signatures in order to approve Mr Sekiguchi's position as the spiritual leader. (One of the senior staff members who gave his signature without thinking, told me personally how much he regretted his action, when he came to Australia to hold the first primary course in Canberra, in 1976.) Mr Sekiguchi took the matter to court with the aim of becoming the official leader of the Mahikari organisation. Even though the important revelation concerning the succession was later made available, it did not carry legal weight. After years of legal proceedings in which a number of appeals and re-appeals occurred, in July 1982 the Tokyo High Court decided that it did not have the power to determine the rightful successor, and according to the indication by the judge, a compromise or amicable settlement (wakai) was reached – both Keiju Okada and Mr Sekiguchi would head independent organisations.

Most members followed Ms Okada. They knew that she was the only one at that time to be given the highest course of spiritual training, called tokkyu kenshu, 'special level course' by the founder, and that she had always assisted the founder closely in his service to God, even making decisions on his behalf from time to time. In fact, in April 1964 it had been officially announced (in writing) that Ms Keiju Okada was the 'representative of Oshienushi' ('Oshienushi' referring to Sukuinushisama at that time). In other words, while still in the physical world, Sukuinushisama had already let it be known that Keijusama was his representative.

Also, in October 1972 Keijusama had completed the special 10-year training called sento no gyo, the only person ever to do this. Keijusama had to undergo spiritual tests from God. Even while Sukuinushisama was still in the physical world, Keijusama helped him with all kinds of divine work, including preparation of the Goshintai and other sacred objects.

Before the above-mentioned court's mediation, in 1978 Sukyo Mahikari was established as a religious organisation in order to achieve the holy mission given to Sukuinushisama – the construction of Suza, the World Shrine for the Creator God. Mr Sekiguchi's group retained the original name of the organisation, Sekai Mahikari Bunmei Kyodan, which later spawned a number of small organisations as others broke away to form their own groups.

On the Internet is a detailed account of legal proceedings that are supposed to validate that Sekai Mahikari Bunmei Kyodan is the legitimate Mahikari organisation. The fact is that things were not so clear for many people. The spiritual value of a revelation written on a piece of paper has no legal bearing in a court of law, yet, in my mind, this is the most crucial point.

My wife happened to participate in the very ceremony where a senior staff member made a public announcement that Keishu Okada is to be the next spiritual leader. Later in the same ceremony, Mr Sekiguchi's staff made the same staff member who had made the announcement, go back on stage again to indicate that "there was a mistake" in his announcement. In a fluster he then said that the leader is to be Mr Sekiguchi. It was no wonder that a number of people were confused about the leadership in those early days shortly after Sukuinushisama passed away.

I have been impressed by how Oshienushisama has continued to serve God and guide kamikumite about the importance of love and sincerity, without a single judgemental word about Mr Sekiguchi. She has given guidance to kamikumite on various occasions not to criticise or blame anyone but to "be grateful to God for everything," as the teachings indicate. I have also been impressed by the fact that Sukyo Mahikari members have never tried to recruit members from other Mahikari organisations.

Mr Yoshinori Shimada (1996), a journalist who has written about many Japanese religions, has given an account of the "legitimate spiritual lineage" of the Mahikari organisation, arriving at the conclusions outlined above. He is a non-Mahikari person who has examined the facts and has no reason to favour one side or the other.

§

Ten years after Oshienushisama became the second spiritual leader of the Mahikari organisation, on the day of the inauguration of the World Shrine in November 1984, it was publicly announced that on 13 June 1974 Sukuinushisama had received by revelation his daughter's new spiritual name, *Seishusama* ('Holy Jewel'). Because the World Shrine had not been completed, Oshienushisama, being very humble, did not reveal this publicly for ten years, until the day of the inauguration of the World Shrine.

§

At Mahikari ceremonies in Japan, I have witnessed politicians, government officials, ambassadors, scientists, medical professionals, famous artists, mayors and other respected members of society express their gratitude to Oshienushisama for her efforts. In my travels around the world, I have noticed that politicians and diplomats, in particular, are usually rather reluctant to praise any religious organisation publicly, no doubt for diplomatic reasons, fear of reprisals or concern for possibly causing misunderstandings that could affect their reputation. In the case of Sukyo Mahikari, however, it seems that many such leaders have come to realise that this organisation is not a religious order dealing only with its own members, but a movement that benefits people throughout the world.

There are many stories of how people have improved by being in Oshienushisama's presence, from receiving handshakes and in other ways. My wife once attended a ceremony in which a young blind girl offered flowers to Oshienushisama, who shook the girl's hand. A little later, there was great excitement in the auditorium, as the parents of the girl discovered that their daughter could see! I have had the privilege of meeting Oshienushisama on many occasions year after year, and I can say that it has always been inspiring in some way.

§

Oshienushisama visited Latin America – Mexico, Brazil and Peru – in May-June 1986. Then, in May-June 1993 she visited Europe and the Middle East to take the Light of God to nine countries – Luxembourg, Germany, Switzerland, Italy, France, Israel, Egypt, Greece and England. In September 2000 she visited Australia and New Zealand. The details and spiritual significance of these trips are documented in the Mahikari journals and other books.

For me, Oshienushisama's visit to the Australia-Oceania Region at the time of the 2000 Olympic Games in Sydney gave rise to many treasured memories. As Regional Director I was able to accompany Oshienushisama every day on the whole trip, so I could experience first hand many aspects that are not normally known to people in general.

For instance, the changes in weather were surprising. For a few days just before Oshienushisama arrived in Australia on 9 September 2000, the country was battered by turbulent weather. When I was to fly from Canberra to Sydney on the evening before Oshienushisama's arrival, for example, my plane was delayed for one-and-a-half hours because the winds in Sydney were blowing so strongly. However, when Oshienushisama's plane from Tokyo touched down in Sydney the next morning, there was a sunny, clear blue sky with no wind whatsoever.

On 10 September, a Special Gratitude Ceremony for the Sukyo Mahikari Australia–Oceania Region was held at the National Convention Centre in Canberra. The purpose was to offer gratitude for the divine protection of Su God and to promote renewed determination for people to do their best to practise faith directed towards God. Another purpose was to celebrate the Olympic Games in Sydney, the opening ceremony of which was to be held five days later. According to divine teachings, the Olympic Games mark the gathering of the fire lineage gods, in addition to being a festival of sport to foster world peace. The five rings of the Olympic flag represent the five races of different colour, that is, all humankind, and is a symbol of the unity of humankind.

People from all over Australia, New Zealand, Papua New Guinea, Fiji, South Africa and a small group of visitors from South East-Asia and the United States attended the Special Gratitude Ceremony, an event full of joy and gratitude, with tears of emotion visible everywhere. The ceremony was attended by Mr Gary Humphries, the Deputy Chief Minister of the Australian Capital Territory Government, who shortly after became the Chief Minister. His Excellency, the Governor-General of Australia, Sir William Deane, sent an encouraging message.

Some of the distinguished guests told me they were very moved by the teachings concerning peace and harmony, saying that they could feel the love from Oshienushisama through her words, and that they now have a better perspective about their life and the significance of Sukyo Mahikari.

I kept encountering people who related various changes after meeting Oshienushisama. For instance, a Mahikari Youth Group member from Brisbane Mahikari Centre received a handshake from Oshienushisama as he left the Special Gratitude Ceremony. For many years he had suffered from skin dryness and itchiness in both hands, especially the right one, which would often result in uncomfortable and painful skin cracks. The only moderately effective solution to this problem was the application of a strong handcare lotion to his hands immediately after washing them, more than once a day. If he did not do this, the skin would quickly dry up and crack within a few hours. He had resigned himself to having this problem forever as he had tried various ways of solving it over the years. However, after receiving a handshake from Oshienushisama he noticed an instant change in the condition of the skin on the palm of the right hand, the one that he had extended to Oshienushisama. It was no longer dry and cracking. Months later he reported that the skin still had not cracked, despite no application of hand cream, something that had not happened for years.

The day after the Special Gratitude Ceremony, the sky in Canberra was overcast and there were patches of drizzly rain now and then. When Oshienushisama was being photographed in front of the new Parliament House, we were surprised that there was no rain whatsoever over Oshienushisama, yet a few steps towards the cars where the rest of the entourage was standing, there was some rain.

September is the beginning of spring in Australia, and Canberra looked beautiful, green from the rain of recent weeks, with flowers and trees blossoming everywhere. On the day Oshienushisama departed from Canberra for Sydney, 12 September, she agreed to stop at Telopea Park so people could say farewell. Amongst the people gathered were dozens of children, some of whom offered Oshienushisama flowers they had picked from their home gardens. It was moving to see Oshienushisama receiving each gift so attentively. I was next to Oshienushisama and received these flowers from her in turn so that she would be free to shake people's hands. At one stage the petals from a little twig of plum blossoms that one of the children had given to her started to fall off, and Oshienushisama caught the little petals and then passed them to me – she took every part of the gift preciously, not regarding the fallen petals as being insignificant. This made me realise how much Oshienushisama values everything.

On 13 September, the day after she returned to Sydney, Oshienushisama travelled to Uluru, or Ayers Rock. Uluru is a place of considerable spiritual significance to the Aboriginal people, and is also treated with respect and interest by the thousands of tourists who flock there. It is interesting that Uluru was the first Australian destination for the Olympic torch before it was carried all over the country and eventually arrived in Sydney.

After Uluru, Oshienushisama returned to Sydney again, and on 15 September she attended the opening ceremony of the Olympic Games in Sydney. This was an event of great joy and exuberance for everyone in the stadium, it seemed, with its seating capacity of 110,000 people, the biggest stadium in Olympic history. People everywhere were particularly warm and friendly. The Olympic Games were characterised by a focus on love and harmony, peace and goodwill to all humankind, something that was obvious to all participants – athletes, spectators, staff and volunteers. Many of the words of the songs and speeches referred to world peace, love and harmony, goodwill, friendship, integration and sharing. Items of entertainment included fire, positivity and light of all kinds, with fireworks exploding and torches being flashed. All spectators were given hand torches and wristbands that would twinkle like stars in the night sky as they moved their hands. When the athletes paraded in, there was much joy, pride and applause. Of great significance was the unexpected sight of the North and South Korean athletes parading as one country, which brought tears to the eyes of many people.

The highlight of the ceremony was the lighting of the Olympic cauldron. The fact that Cathy Freeman, an Aboriginal woman, was chosen to light the Olympic cauldron symbolised the earnest desire of Australians to improve relations with the Aboriginal people.

At the end of the Olympic Games the President of the International Organising Committee, Mr Juan Antonio Samaranch, declared the Games "the best ever". Sukyo Mahikari members, particularly the youth of Sydney Mahikari Centre, had been purifying the Olympic site with True Light every month for several years before the Olympic Games.

The day after the opening ceremony of the Olympics, Oshienushisama visited Sydney Mahikari Centre and graciously shook hands with all the people there, which again moved everyone considerably, many to tears. A woman who was downstairs waiting to bid Oshienushisama farewell said that as she stood in front of

Oshienushisama's car waving goodbye, she could feel divine Light radiating towards her lung and chest area. She had been smoking cigarettes for over twenty years and had tried to give up on many occasions. When Oshienushisama went past, she had a profound feeling of a force letting go within her, and since that day has largely lost the desire to smoke cigarettes.

On 17 September, Oshienushisama departed from Sydney Airport for New Zealand, and arrived in Wellington, the capital. In Wellington Mahikari Centre, kamikumite and their families and friends were delighted to meet Oshienushisama and receive handshakes.

On 19 September, Oshienushisama was driven from Wellington to Rotorua, a small town in the middle area of the North Island of New Zealand, known for its Maori culture as well as its hot springs, sulphur pools and geysers. On the way, we stopped for refreshments at a little place that caters for travellers. Shortly after we entered, the lady manager – who could not take her eyes off Oshienushisama – came to kamikumite and said, "That lady must be a very special person." None of us had told the restaurant staff who we were or why we had come. This lady was fascinated by Oshienushisama, staring at her all the time. When Oshienushisama was about to leave, the manager asked whether she could give Oshienushisama a present from her souvenir shop. It is not a custom for people in New Zealand to do this with visitors. Oshienushisama graciously received the gift, offered the lady a handshake and was photographed with her.

On 20 September, Oshienushisama left Rotorua by train and paid a courtesy call on the Maori Queen, Te Ariki-nui Dame Te Atai-rangi-kaahu, in her own meeting place (*marae*), near Hamilton. Te Ariki-nui is considered an important person, not only by the Maori themselves, but by the New Zealand Government and many people overseas. Dignitaries such as Queen Elizabeth and other heads of State have visited her. I was able to be present and observed that the Maori Queen was very moved to meet Oshienushisama and asked for a spiritual blessing. Oshienushisama prayed to God and gave her Light, firmly shaking hands. In a teaching later, Oshienushisama indicated that the Maori Queen "is of a very high spiritual level".

Oshienushisama travelled on to Auckland, and on 21 September she visited Auckland Mahikari Centre, much to the delight of about 100 people. Many children gathered there, which was an obvious joy to Oshienushisama. The next day a lady kumite reported to me that her 4-year-old daughter had asked, "Mummy, why is Oshienushisama so pretty?" The surprised mother answered, "Because she is close to God."

After a cruise on Auckland Harbour (with a surprisingly calm sea), Oshienushisama returned to Japan the following day. Practically all the kamikumite and a number of relatives and friends of Auckland Mahikari Centre came to the airport to bid farewell to Oshienushisama on 23 September. Again, there were tears of emotion from many people. Some people reported gold flakes on their hands, a materialisation of divine Light, after shaking hands with Oshienushisama.

About a week after Oshienushisama left New Zealand, I returned to Auckland to hold a Mahikari primary course. A number of the Auckland Sukyo Mahikari members spoke of the experiences·they had received as a result of Oshienushisama's visit. Some people felt a new depth or ability to concentrate and seriously practise the art of True Light.

One very busy mother with four children under the age of eight and a husband who works up to 100 hours a week, had been having difficulties getting to the Mahikari Centre to offer service to God. However, after meeting Oshienushisama, she has been able to offer more service to God with joy than she had been able to for a number of years. At that particular primary course she was only able to reattend for three hours, but said that she understood more in that short time than she had in the past when reattending for the whole three days.

An Auckland kamikumite, who had offered his car to be used for Oshienushisama's travel in New Zealand, said that the right-hand stereo speaker of his car radio had not been working for several months, but that after Oshienushisama had travelled in the car, the speaker worked perfectly, although no-one had touched it.

One lady reported that for some months there had been discord within her family. After meeting Oshienushisama, she was able to give Light to her sisters, as if a new harmony had been established – something that she could not achieve before.

Another mother reported that she had been suffering pain in the ribs for the week prior to Oshienushisama's visit, to the point that she could hardly sleep at night. For instance, the night before Oshienushisama arrived, the pain kept her awake till four o'clock in the morning. She was able to meet Oshienushisama and shake her hand for the first time, and that night she had no pain at all and slept deeply and peacefully all night.

As Oshienushisama indicated later in teachings, "It is truly significant that the Light of God was taken to the countries of the south, Australia and New Zealand, and that the deities of the fire lineage assembled there."

Odairisama

On 5 October 2002, Oshienushisama appointed Mr Koshi Okada, her adopted son, as Acting Oshienushi or Odairisama in order to play a more 'up-front' role to achieve Oshienushisama's responsibilities.

Born as Tairoku Teshima in October 1947, he became a kamikumite in 1964. He played a significant role in the development of the Mahikari Youth Group in the early years when Sukuinushisama established it in Japan.

In March 1970 he graduated from Kokugakuin University with a major in Shinto Archaeology and entered the Doshi (Staff) Training Institute to become a disciple of Sukuinushisama, the first class. He was appointed as a doshi later in that year. After serving as a staff member in three different dojos in Japan, he was appointed as Instructor at the Doshi Training Institute, in 1974. In 1976 he was appointed Section Chief of the Planning Section, and in 1984 he became Assistant Director of that Section as well as Assistant Director of the Ceremony Department, at Sukyo Mahikari International Headquarters.

In 1993 he married Ms Kimiyo Yamazaki and in the same year he was adopted by the Okada family.

Since 1976, he has been offering divine service close to Oshienushisama and has been receiving special training. For instance, he accompanied Oshienushisama on all her overseas visits. In March 1994 he became Director of the Planning Section at International Headquarters. In 2000 he became Director of Motomitamaza.

The year 2002 proved to be a considerable change for Mr Okada. In February of that year he was appointed Assistant to Oshienushisama, and in June he completed the special level course (*tokkyu kenshu*), the only one to do so other than Oshienushisama. Then, in October he was appointed representative of the Second Oshienushi. Shortly afterwards, he received the divine name *Koya* (literally, 'Sun/Light', 'exceedingly').

I was privileged to see much of him when he visited Australia and New Zealand in 2000, and I could not help but notice his strong dedication to God and his deep humility towards everyone.

The reality of the spiritual realm

Chapter 4

The reality of the spiritual realm

As I was growing up, I often wondered whether there is life after death. Religions teach that there is, but how can we be really sure? If life exists after death, what is it like? Is it something vague and intangible or do feelings and consciousness continue in the same way as in the physical world? I read about spirits who haunt places or possess people, but how good is the evidence for this? Are people born into the physical world again? If so, why and how? These kinds of questions came to my mind even more frequently when I was involved in brain research. Questions that neuroscientists continue to ask are: Is human consciousness something that is separate from the brain? What really constitutes the mind? Is it a result of the functioning of brain neurones or is there something more?

Now I feel more confident that I can answer some of these questions to significant degrees. Through experience with the Light of God and the teachings of Sukyo Mahikari I have come to know that the spiritual realm really exists, as well as something about how it functions, including the life and death of human beings. The functioning of the spiritual realm is not merely a matter to do with religion, but involves all aspects of life. At least some understanding about it is essential if we are to explain human consciousness, personality and behaviour. This chapter deals with my understanding of the spiritual realm. Firstly, I would like to clarify the terminology I am using, as some expressions about spiritual phenomena have come to mean different things for different people.

About terminology

There is a lot of confusion in society about the word 'spiritual'. For example, people say things like, "He is very spiritual". This is vague, as everybody has a soul and an invisible form, so everybody is 'spiritual' in a sense.

Sometimes the term 'spiritual' is used to describe people's *physical* activities such as living alternative lifestyles, growing vegetables organically, drinking herbal tea and so on.

Often people use the word 'spiritual' when they are really referring to the *mental* aspect. For instance, people say, "He is very spiritual; he meditates". Even though the usual aim of meditation is to "achieve enlightenment", to elevate oneself spiritually or something like that, the actual process of meditation (repeating a mantra, focusing on breathing, stilling the mind, to name a few) is a mental activity.

Sometimes the opposite happens, that is, a spiritual matter is regarded as something to do with the mind. People ask me what I do, and when I reply that I am involved in radiating the Light of God to purify the soul, sometimes they comment, "Ah, that is an interesting philosophy" or, "It sounds similar to meditation," which puts the activity in a mental framework. In general, people have not distinguished clearly between the spiritual and the mental.

Some practices referred to as 'spiritual' are neither God-centred nor people-friendly. For example, there are people who think that a person who can go into trances, communicate with the dead or practise other psychic medium activities is 'spiritual', implying that the person is of a higher level than ordinary people. Such practices do not necessarily mean that the person is coming closer to God and can help others to do so. On the contrary, many so-called psychic or 'spiritual' activities (in the sense used in the literature) are making people more prone to disturbance by spirits and are taking them away from the path to God (see the section on 'Spirit disturbance' later in this chapter).

§

In this book, the expression 'spiritual realm' or 'spiritual world' refers to the invisible realm in which spirits reside (from the very highest dimensions of deities or highly-evolved souls to the lowest dimensions of the astral world, or hell). In another sense, the term 'spiritual realm' is used for the invisible aspect (the spiritual and astral cells) of all things.

The 'spiritual aspect' or 'spiritual condition' of a person refers to the condition of the soul and spiritual body.

'Spiritual impurities' refer to sins, impurities, wrongdoings, mistakes and the like, caused by oneself or one's ancestors in previous lives or the present one, that contaminate the soul and spiritual body.

When an activity or approach to life is described as 'spiritual', it means that it is spiritually oriented or God-centred, that is, it focuses on the 'upstream of the river' (explained in chapter 2). For example, for brevity, a 'spiritual way of life' is sometimes used for a 'spiritually oriented way of life'. Similarly 'spiritually oriented economics' is also called 'spiritual economics' (chapter 9).

Lastly, in a less common usage the term 'spiritual' refers to something invisible and non-physical, such as 'spiritual cords' and 'spiritual functions of words'.

Matter – three types of cells

In physics, chemistry and biology we learn a lot about physical matter. Everyone knows that tissue consists of physical cells, and that in their depths cells consist of molecules. Molecules in turn are made up of atoms. Quite a lot is also known about the elementary or subatomic particles that make up atoms, although this is a field in which new discoveries are made frequently.

It used to be thought that protons, neutrons and electrons were the smallest subatomic particles possible. Over recent years, many new subatomic particles have been discovered, particles that make up the protons, neutrons and electrons. For example, protons and neutrons consist of quarks, whereas antiprotons and antineutrons consist of antiquarks. The smallest units of matter have been considered to be leptons and quarks (more generally categorised as fermions). The existence of quarks and leptons can explain the behaviour of the larger elementary particles under a variety of normal conditions, but to explain phenomena under more extreme conditions, studies have shown the existence of hundreds of subatomic particles (neutrinos, bosons, gluons, etc.). Interestingly, scientists in the U.S.A., working with Fermilab's Tevatron particle accelerator (the most powerful in the world), have observed an unexpectedly large number of violent collisions between quarks, which is the kind of effect one would see "if quarks were not fundamental particles but had some sort of internal structure" (Glanz, 1996). If true, this would indicate that quarks are not fundamental building blocks of matter (as proposed by the so-called Standard Model) but that even finer particles exist. The possible subdivision of quarks is still a controversial subject in physics, but it is clear that over time, science has been discovering that matter in its depths consists of finer and finer particles.

Sukuinushisama taught that in the depths of the elementary particles there are what are called 'astral particles', particles that have not yet been discovered by science today. Furthermore, in the depths of the astral particles there are ultra-minute particles called 'spiritual particles', even finer than astral particles. The spiritual, astral and physical particles make up the spiritual, astral and physical cells of all matter.

My studies and experiences have led me to believe that astral and spiritual particles are not a figment of the imagination or some vague, nebulous notion, but actually exist, just as physical particles do. In fact, it is the spiritual particles that give rise to the astral particles, and it is the astral particles that give rise to the physical particles. Matter cannot exist in physical form without the inherent spiritual and astral matter. This realm of spiritual and astral particles is called the 'spiritual realm', a realm that is invisible to people normally. Sukuinushisama predicted that one day science will deal with astral particles as freely as it now deals with elementary particles (electricity and nuclear power). There will be 'astral particle science' and later, 'spiritual particle science'.

Make-up of the human

The human body consists of spiritual, astral and physical cells, as does all matter. Just as the physical cells together make up the physical body, the astral cells make up the astral body and the spiritual cells make up the spiritual body. The spiritual and astral tissue continues on, unlike the physical tissue, which breaks down and returns to nature, particularly at the time of death. It is only due to the existence of the spiritual and astral bodies that the physical body is formed, an exact prototype of the spiritual body. The astral and spiritual bodies are the same shape as the physical body except that they are invisible.

It is the invisible aspect that is the basis of life, whether in the physical world or the spiritual realm. The physical body can only live if the spiritual and astral bodies occupy it. These three bodies are intimately intercommunicating and their functioning is extremely complex and precise. In the field of science this is still completely unknown. Oshienushisama predicted, "I expect that these matters will be elucidated to a certain extent as the convergence between science and religion advances."

The astral body, which is related to the mind, is something of a semi-material nature. There are people, so-called psychics, who have demonstrated various degrees of ability to tap into this and move objects by the power of the mind. The spiritual body is closely related to the soul, and to what is in the depths of the mind – the innermost attitudes, notions, outlook or mindset (called *sonen* in Japanese).

The human is a special creation. According to Sukuinushisama, in addition to the spiritual, astral and physical cells there exists what is called the 'main soul' (located behind the forehead), which is a part of the soul of God. It is normally just referred to as 'the soul'. This is what drives the spiritual body and makes the human being unique amongst all creatures. Because of this soul which was divided off from God, deep down human beings want to be united with God. It is because of impurities built up over numerous lifetimes that many humans have lost a conscious awareness of God, but deep down all people are seeking God, as they receive the vibrations of wisdom, love and will of God through the main soul.

This main soul, invisible to the physical eyes, is located in the area of the pineal gland, about 10 centimetres behind the forehead. For thousands of years it has been known that there is something special about this area. In religious literature people refer to it as the third eye, a special chakra, and in other ways, but in the past its definition has been rather vague, I think. Sukuinushisama explained that the soul is situated there and for this reason, a session of True Light normally starts with radiating the Light through the forehead to penetrate that area.

The most important aspect of the human is the main soul together with the spiritual body.

Dimensions of existence

Similarly, all existence can be broadly viewed as consisting of a trinity – the divine world, the astral world and the physical world. These are intimately interconnected, interwoven and intercommunicating while at the same time being at different vibrations of existence. (Things are really much more complicated but this is not the place to go into detail; it is a topic for the Mahikari intermediate and advanced courses.) Broadly speaking, the divine world or realm and other high dimensions, which are extremely pure, beautiful and joyful, are realms for gods or deities and certain holy spirits, ones who have become sufficiently purified and elevated to go there. The divine world cannot be seen or experienced consciously to any great extent by ordinary people.

The astral world is a kind of intermediate dimension which includes the realm where people go after death in the physical world. The astral world is itself subdivided into many dimensions, from the relatively warm, comfortable higher or intermediate dimensions, to the cold, dark, sorrowful, unpleasant lower dimensions, or training places referred to as hell in some religions.

When a person dies in the physical world, the normal procedure is to go to the astral world and do various kinds of appropriate practices or training until permitted to reincarnate in the physical world again. (The subject of reincarnation is dealt with later in this chapter.) This cycle of birth and rebirth between the astral and physical worlds goes on for tens of thousands of years. That is why religions use the expression "everlasting life" for a human. Even though the astral world is normally invisible, sometimes people can have certain experiences of it through practising the art of True Light.

Su God is at the very top of the divine world. Lower than this is the realm of great gods of heaven, but no human souls. Still lower is a dimension where deities and those human souls who have become holy spirits reside. In the middle regions (the astral world) are levels where human spirits can do training that is relatively pleasant such as reading, cultivating the mind and so on, in an atmosphere of warmth and brightness, with music and the like. As one descends through the levels of the astral world, existence becomes darker, colder and more unpleasant.

People are ranked according to their spiritual level, which is a result of their experiences and training in the physical and astral worlds. In other words, although there is eternal life, this can be spent in joy or misfortune, or different degrees of both, depending on one's deeds and attitudes. What is accomplished in one life will determine the spiritual rank or circumstances of the next life. Our present situation is an indication of what we have done in previous lives, even though we normally have no conscious memory of our previous lives.

The physical world is the world of the five senses that people are very familiar with. However, even while living in the physical world, one is constantly influenced from the spiritual realm according to one's spiritual level and spiritual condition, that is, one is subjected to the laws that inter-penetrate all three realms. The law of 'spirit first, mind next, body follows' applies to everything. For example, our situation in the physical world (condition of the family, financial means, health) depends mainly on our relationship with God and our spiritual level; then, the condition of our ancestors and attached spirits; and lastly, our attitudes and activities in the material world.

What is death?

Through practising the art of True Light and studying the divine teachings, I have come to understand that there is no real death, a conviction that is as strong as anything I can experience with the five senses in the physical world. What we call death is really birth in the spiritual realm, more specifically, the astral world. When a person dies, the physical body returns to nature in the physical world and the soul and spiritual body together with the astral body, the inner or invisible entity, goes to the astral world. Such an entity is called a 'spirit'. This spirit is really the same being, the same person, except without a physical body. Only the outer shell or container is discarded. Other than that, everything for the person continues as it was when he or she left the physical world. In other words, the person's (the spirit's) consciousness, all the good and bad points, the understanding about life, the hopes, wishes, doubts, fears, desires and so on are the same;

any pain, injuries or diseases continue – everything continues in the astral world unless the person changes through purification and awakening. Death is just a change of dimension, but life goes on for the person where he or she left off in the physical world.

If a spirit's descendants or other relatives in the physical world offer service to God or do other things that help to erase the family's impurities, the spirit's condition can improve more quickly, but normally, if a person dies in suffering, the spirit of that person continues to suffer in that way for a long time.

Several authors have documented people's experiences shortly after death (peace; a bright light at the end of a tunnel; meeting relatives and so on), but these do not give an accurate picture of the more permanent fate of the individual after physical death. In the past, very few people have been given a glimpse of what happens in the long term in the astral world. Sukuinushisama taught that for 49 days after physical death the person (spirit) is generally free to go anywhere. After that the spirit must go to a specific, more permanent place in the astral world, depending on his or her level of purity and previous deeds. Wherever one goes, it is important to give up all attachments to things in the physical world (such as material desires or longing for a loved one) within 30 years.

The astral world is a realm of training to achieve awakening. The training may be rather pleasant, involving learning that cultivates the soul, or it may involve various kinds of suffering that last until the person has compensated sufficiently and awakened to why he or she is undergoing that practice. If one is suffering, it is important to ask, "Why am I suffering like this? What do I have to awaken to from this?", and to apologise and make appropriate changes. Then one's level will soon rise to a higher and more pleasant place of training. Unlike the physical world where it is possible to avoid certain unpleasant situations for a while, in the astral world one has to go where one is matched, and there is no escape until one achieves awakening.

God wants human beings to learn from their mistakes, compensate for their misdeeds and rise spiritually. If the lessons in the physical world are not learned by accepting advice, devotedly serving others and society, being purified with True Light or some other relatively pleasant way, they must be learned the hard way. For example, if someone destroys property or living creatures by fire in the physical world, he may have to endure fire in the astral world until he understands, apologises and compensates for his error. If someone is wealthy in the physical world and wastes food without sharing, he may go to an astral dimension where food is available but he cannot put it into his mouth. These are examples of the law of cause and effect. Spirits can quickly rise from their environment of suffering to higher, more pleasant levels of the astral world by realising their mistakes and apologising for them (or compensating for them in other ways).

After a period of time (usually some centuries), the spirit returns to the physical world again with a new physical body. This is called reincarnation. The physical body is not the same one as before, of course, but is gradually built up from new physical material, beginning through the mother's body. The cycles of birth and rebirth are repeated until the spirit is sufficiently purified. Eventually the spirit can become a highly-evolved soul or holy spirit and reside in the upper dimensions of the spiritual realm.

Any problems that are unresolved in the physical world have to be solved in the astral world or future lives. In other words, misfortune in the physical world cannot be avoided by dying. Sometimes people think that suicide is an escape from suffering, but the reverse is true. Not only do the problems remain, but more bad karma is made by taking one's life and this normally results in more intense suffering in the astral world. If physical death is painful, this condition can continue for a long time in the astral world. It is good to die a natural death, not tragically. That is why it is valuable to live one's life so that one's destiny can improve and for that life not to end in tragedy. Pain is more difficult to bear in the astral world where there is no physical body to act as a buffer. If one dies of disease, the problem will usually last for many years in the astral world. We cannot ignore or escape our wrongdoings. We must compensate for them sooner or later. It is much better to compensate through voluntary service to God and others while still in the physical world, where living is still relatively comfortable.

The more we learn to follow divine laws in the physical world, the easier it will be to understand the reason for our training in the astral world. With purification and elevation through God's Light and dedicated service to God in the physical world, as well as efforts towards attaining divine nature, it is possible to become purified so rapidly that after physical death the level in the astral world will be relatively pleasant or at least bearable.

Purifying after death

Apparently, at the time of death in the physical world the spirit usually leaves the physical body through the forehead. Because the spirit has occupied the physical body for a long time, there are extremely dense, invisible spiritual cords interconnecting between the physical body and the soul and the invisible spiritual and astral bodies, even though the latter have departed from the corpse. This is why it is valuable to purify the person's 'dead' body with the Light of God for many minutes or even hours if possible, after physical death. The transition from the physical world to the spiritual realm is a period when much can be done to influence the wellbeing of the individual. True Light radiated to the forehead area of the corpse has the remarkable effect of purifying the person's soul. If one radiates Light to, say, a cancerous area on the corpse, that area of the person in the spiritual realm will receive purification through the spiritual cords. Obviously, the more the person awakens and is purified, the higher and more pleasant the level in the spiritual realm. Purification with God's Light after clinical death (before burial or cremation) could mean the difference between a joyful, bright existence and a sorrowful, gloomy one in the astral world.

I have witnessed remarkable changes in people's condition as a result of giving Light after they have died. It is nothing short of amazing to see a dead body with a grim-looking face, for example, become a smiling face; a bluish-green complexion becoming yellow-pink; a rigid limb becoming soft and supple, and things like that. Many Sukyo Mahikari members throughout the world have witnessed marked changes in dead bodies as a result of purifying with the Light of God shortly after death.

One of my most vivid early experiences of purifying a dead body concerned my own father. My father died at the age of 74 on 4 August 1980 in Mount Gambier Hospital (South Australia), where he had been trying to recuperate from a hip operation. Over the few months before that, his health had been deteriorating rapidly. For some years he had been taking several pills daily to lessen the intense pain in his hip.

It was only a matter of time before my father's kidneys gave up the struggle against the continuous intake of artificial chemicals. The doctors said he had died from kidney failure. My mother, who had been at his side, told me later that his death throes had indicated much suffering. Minutes before his death he had vomited blood mixed with faeces and urine. He had been in excruciating pain, and in the last stages had cried out for help like a child (in Latvian) calling for his mother.

Within an hour of my father's death my mother telephoned me in Canberra (about 1,000 kilometres from Mount Gambier). With my wife, Yasumi, I made special prayers to the Creator God that we might help my father to the astral world smoothly, and caught the next available flight to Mount Gambier. The hospital authorities permitted us to see my father's body 30 minutes after we got off the plane. The body had not yet been cleaned up or prepared for burial.

My father's face was not a pleasant sight. It was pale blue with a gaunt expression, showing obvious signs of suffering. The lines showed that he had undergone stress. His mouth was open with smudges of blood in different parts. I tried to close it, but it could not be moved.

Yasumi and I began giving him True Light immediately, chanting the Amatsu Norigoto prayer of purification almost continuously, interspersed with other Mahikari prayers. After 20 to 30 minutes his face was noticeably brighter and more peaceful. My mother came in at that stage and helped in giving Light and chanting the Amatsu Norigoto prayer for another 45 minutes or so until the morgue attendant took my father's body away.

Early next morning we went to the undertaker, who had already taken my father's body from the hospital morgue. He was reluctant for us to see the body because it had not been prepared yet. I told him that this did not matter as we only wanted to give salvation spiritually. He placed father's body in a separate room where we could give True Light for hours, and arranged that we could stay there in the evening if we wanted to.

Over the next two days we gave True Light for hours to him, chanting the Amatsu Norigoto prayer and offering other divine teachings and songs. Every now and then I talked to my father in Latvian about various divine teachings.

The most astounding thing that happened was that father's face kept changing as he was being purified with the Light of God. It was particularly noticeable after we returned from lunch and later, from dinner. His jaw became quite flexible and we were able to close his mouth. His face became much softer, losing some lines of stress. His complexion became a normal colour, with touches of pink around the eyes where it had been bluish before. The wrinkles around his eyes and the corners of his mouth showed a faint smile, whereas before there had been a look of anguish.

This was so startling that my two brothers, my twin sister and their spouses, who arrived from other states a few days after us, were all amazed to see how peaceful my father looked. It was quite a shock to them, especially after hearing about the way he had died. There was no doubt that the Light of God had given profound salvation to my father. Instead of feeling grief, which often occurs at funerals, I felt an inner joy and deep gratitude to the Creator God, and I have had a contented feeling about my father ever since.

§

How can God's Light affect a dead body, people may ask? As I said, the reason is that there are numerous and dense spiritual cords connecting the spirit (soul and the invisible spiritual and astral bodies) who has just departed, and his corpse in the physical world. The three bodies, having been together for a long time, are still inter-connected with dense spiritual cords for a while. That is why the Light of God can have a profound effect on a person who has just died, if people give Light to the person's corpse. There have been numerous cases of such a departed spirit temporarily attaching to a relative and expressing gratitude for the improvement received as a result of the Light of God. A number of cases have been reported in my previous book (Tebecis, 1982) as well as in the monthly Mahikari journals throughout the world.

In my opinion the most frequent and convincing evidence for the existence of life after death and continuing consciousness after death can be obtained by giving True Light to people. I have had countless experiences in which so-called dead people talked to me, that is, the spirits of departed people communicated with me through the body of the person to whom I was giving Light during a spirit investigation (see the section 'Spirit disturbance', later in this chapter).

For example, in October 1995, a male member of the Perth Mahikari Centre was killed in a traffic accident while visiting Zimbabwe, shortly after I saw him in Durban. It was very sad for everybody. A lady kamikumite in Zimbabwe went to give Light to his body and reported clear signs of salvation. This man's wife (who was in Perth) was not a kamikumite at that time and did not understand the kinds of things I have written in this book, but said that she was very grateful that her dead husband had received God's Light. She came to the Perth Mahikari Centre when a memorial service was held for her dead husband. While at the Mahikari Centre, the spirit of her dead husband temporarily attached to a kamikumite who had been a close friend, and communicated with the staff member who was giving Light to that friend on the forehead. What was particularly striking was that the dead man's wife witnessed the manifesting spirit of her husband. She recognised her husband's mannerisms and way of speaking as he was manifesting through this female kamikumite. The wife became very relieved because the spirit of her husband said that he was now all right after receiving the Light of God. His wife attended the Mahikari primary course at the end of 1995 and became active in serving God.

Reviving people from death

When I first attended the Mahikari primary course I learned that Sukuinushisama had revived people who had been pronounced clinically dead. For example, at a wake for a Buddhist family, Sukuinushisama gave Light to the dead body of an old man, who after some time, got up and started eating rice. I was very surprised when I first heard this story and at that time even wondered whether it was true. Over the years, however, I have come across cases where kamikumite have, in fact, revived people from the dead. Of course, this is not a frequent occurrence. It is just very interesting that it happens at all and really goes to show the profundity of the practice of True Light.

At the second Yoko Civilization International Conference held in Takayama, Japan, Dr Doi (1991) reported a case of an 85-year-old lady who "rose from the dead" as a result of receiving True Light from a kamikumite. She had been admitted to hospital and early one morning her condition took a sudden turn for the worse. Her brain waves and heartbeat stopped and her pupils dilated. At 5 o'clock in the morning a medical doctor pronounced her dead due to acute cardiac insufficiency. Her relatives were informed, but could not get to the hospital until several hours later, at 9 o'clock that morning. The body of the old lady was in the morgue by then. One of the relatives, a kamikumite, began giving True Light to the dead body. After a while, the heartbeat and breathing of the old lady returned. A medical doctor quickly moved the old lady to another room to administer medical treatment as well. The relative kept radiating True Light in the direction of the old lady from outside of her room. At 11 a.m. she regained consciousness and her normal condition. Later she was discharged from the hospital. At the time of reporting this case Dr Doi said that the woman was still alive (at that time 92 years old) and living in high spirits.

After her revival the elderly lady said:

I don't know whether you believe it or not, but I left my body. I passed through darkness and came out into brightness. I met many ancestors and friends who had already passed away, but two of them, turning their back on me, didn't welcome me. When I looked at them closely I found that one of them was my close friend from my childhood and the other was my relative. Why didn't they welcome me? What was the reason? While I could not make up my mind whether I should join the ancestors or not, I was called back into my body and found myself lying on the bed.

This is what the lady related about what had happened during the time she was pronounced clinically dead, that is, when her brain showed no electrical activity and her heart and breathing had stopped. I feel this experience confirms that life continues to exist even after the person leaves the physical body. It is clear that consciousness continues normally as well. Even though this woman had physically lost her consciousness for more than six hours, she remembered clearly what she had experienced during that time and could describe it verbally. She identified her ancestors and friends who had welcomed her. The fact that identification took place means that cognition was functioning. Saying that the spirit has consciousness is really saying that there is a mind functioning after leaving the physical body. It is clear that the consciousness does not come from the body, because in the physical world there was no consciousness. The consciousness returned physically only when the spirit of the lady returned to her body.

§

Hosaka (1993) reported a case of a Japanese man, a kamikumite, who died in hospital. "Three hours after his heart stopped, however, he came back to life." In a frenzy, the man (Mr Kawada) cried out that he had returned for his Omitama, the sacred locket enabling him to radiate True Light. His Omitama had been left at home to avoid any problems at the hospital.

§

Another case of 'resurrection from the dead' through the practice of True Light was reported by Alvarez (1995) and occurred in a clinical setting with doctors and other medical staff to confirm it. Mrs Alvarez is a kamikumite of Sukyo Mahikari in Peru and her husband runs a maternity clinic, so she often gives True Light to mothers and their newborn children. On 15 December 1992 a patient had difficulty in giving birth to her child and required a caesarean section, according to the attending obstetrician, surgeon and a nurse. The doctor thought that the baby was probably already dead as its head was caught between the hip bones of its mother, whose pelvis was very small.

The kamikumite prayed and offered Light to the mother's forehead, and five minutes later the mother had a strong contraction, at which time the baby came out quickly without the need for a caesarean section. Even though the mother had a narrow escape from death, the newborn baby was purple all over and did not move at all. When the doctor cut the navel cord, not a single drop of blood came out. The baby was diagnosed as dead. Nevertheless, for about half an hour the medical staff carried out heart massage, administered oxygen, patted the baby's bottom and did all that they could to revive him. However, the baby did not come back to life and was declared dead.

The medical staff took the mother away and left the room. The kamikumite then gave True Light to the back and front of the baby's heart, kidneys and lungs for up to half an hour. Lastly, she gave Light to the baby's soul for ten minutes and then asked the child to open his eyes. To her surprise, the baby's eyes opened. Then he started to cry in a small voice and turned his face towards her. Soon the medical staff returned and the nurse brought in the mother, whose eyes were swollen from crying. Everyone was overjoyed, saying that it was a great miracle. The child recovered completely and is growing in good health.

Reincarnation

The process of reincarnation is not something new for people to understand, as most religions originally taught the existence of reincarnation. However, Sukuinushisama gave details about why this process occurs, its ultimate aim, how long it usually takes, its various stages and what is actually involved.

I learned that ideally, people reincarnate only after losing all conscious memory of their previous life on earth. Normally, a stay in the astral world is about 200 to 300 years, although there are many exceptions. Because of strong attachments, for example, spirits may sometimes force an incarnation well before 200 years. Conversely, those spirits who do not learn their lessons satisfactorily in the astral world or who attach to people in the physical world cannot reincarnate for many hundreds or even thousands of years.

The form of the body may change as well, which is then called transmigration. For example, a man may be reborn as a woman or vice versa. There are also cases when humans may transmigrate into animal form if they lived their life in the physical world with excessive animal-like attitudes. Only humans reincarnate. Animals do not generally reincarnate although they exist in spirit form after death (see the section on various types of spirits, later in this chapter).

Reincarnation is the basis for progress of humankind and the flourishing of civilisations. There is so much for humans to learn that many lifetimes are usually required to achieve significant progress. It takes lifetimes to become accomplished in skills such as musical ability, dexterity with the hands, remembering languages and so on. Along the way, if spiritual impurities accumulate, time is spent not only in learning new lessons but in compensating for misdeeds (negative karma). It is valuable to awaken to and follow divine will as much as possible, otherwise years of precious lifetime can be wasted in confusion and suffering.

When I was younger and more involved in traditional Christianity, I was told by many Christians that reincarnation does not exist, that it is just a belief of Eastern religions. However, when studying Christianity more deeply, I found that people who followed the teachings of Jesus originally looked upon reincarnation as a normal part of life and that this understanding was lost only centuries later. For example, at a meeting of the Second Council of Constantinople in 553 AD, centuries after Jesus Christ's time, the Pope and other leaders of the Christian Church decided that it was not good for people to know about reincarnation and that this concept should not be preached (Head & Cranston, 1967). The teachings survived, however, in the various Gnostic movements that continued underground and broke out occasionally in open defiance of the church.

Studying the Bible with an open mind indicates that early followers of Jesus understood about reincarnation. For example, people thought that John the Baptist was an incarnation of Elijah the Prophet. Thus,"Jesus asked his disciples, 'Who do men say that I am?' And they told him, 'John the Baptist; and others say, Elijah; and others one of the prophets'" (Mark 8:27-28). To me this indicates that people at the time of Jesus believed that people can reappear in another physical body.

The disciples understood that Jesus was talking to them about John the Baptist when he said, "But I tell you that Elijah has already come, and they did not know him, but did to him whatever they pleased . . . Then the disciples understood that he was speaking to them of John the Baptist" (Matthew 17:12-13). In fact, people asked John the Baptist directly whether he was Elijah the Prophet (John 1:21).

Once when Jesus was walking he saw a man who had been born blind. His disciples asked him, "Rabbi, who sinned, this man or his parents, that he was born blind?" (John 9:1-2). How can a newborn baby have sinned unless he has lived before?

Spirit disturbance

When departing from the physical world, ideally a person's spirit (the soul together with the spiritual and astral bodies, that is, the invisible entity) would accept his or her training in the astral world until permitted to reincarnate on earth with another physical body. However, many spirits leave the astral world or do not even go there at the time of death in the physical world, but instead, attach to the physical body of people in the physical world for one reason or another. The spirits of animals may also attach to people. Such invisible entities are called 'possessing spirits' or 'attached spirits'. In the literature one may also encounter the words 'discarnate entities', 'disembodied beings' or (when partly visible) 'apparitions'.

If a spirit attaches to the flesh of a person in the physical world, this is breaking one of the laws of the astral world. It means that the spirit has escaped from the astral world and this is a transgression against God. In my experience such spirits include ones who have strong resentment (a grudge or hatred) towards the person in the physical world due to that person's wrongful deeds in a previous life or those of the person's ancestors. There may be other attachments such as having a strong selfish love for a spouse or a lover from a previous life. There are cases of spirits who do not know where to go after death. There are spirits, including ancestors, who escape from the astral world because their suffering is severe in some dimension of hell or because they feel they can be saved more easily by attaching to a person in the physical world. There are also spirits who have a strong desire for some pleasure in the physical world, crave food and so on. Whatever the reason, attaching to the flesh of a person means committing the sin of escaping from the astral world, and because this results in accumulating impurities, the spirit's condition sinks towards hell even more, resulting in more suffering.

A person in the physical world may have many spirits attached, either for similar or different reasons. Sometimes a spirit may just attach temporarily, but usually it is long-term. There are also cases where a spirit may not be attached to a person's flesh in the physical world, but may be living in the person's house or some place in the environment. Whether they are attached spirits or spirits in the environment, they interfere with, disturb or manipulate the people they are associated with in the physical world. This occurs even if the spirits mean no harm, as in the case of some deceased relatives. Often they do mean harm, however. All such interference is called 'disturbance by spirits' or 'spirit disturbance'. The degree of interference varies, depending on the person's attitudes, mistakes and impurity from previous lives, physical condition, the power of the attached spirit or other reasons. According to Sukuinushisama, more than 80% of the world's problems – ranging from minor problems in individuals up to large-scale, global problems – are due to disturbance by spirits. In other words, almost everybody is affected by spirits to different degrees.

I can now say this with confidence, having had years of personal experience in giving God's Light of salvation to people and spirits. At the beginning of my involvement with Mahikari, however, I often wondered whether spirits can really influence people to the degree that Sukuinushisama taught. Having done brain research for a number of years, I was reluctant at first to ascribe the many unusual phenomena I witnessed through the practice of radiating the Light of God to anything other than changes in brain mechanisms. I did not want to believe that they were due to spirits. I tried to find other explanations, using expressions such as 'motor incoordination' due to mental changes and so on, but none of the explanations accounted for all the facts. The influencing of a person by a spirit is not usually a visible process, so it takes time to understand spirit phenomena, but their reality is something that anybody can experience.

I have found that attached spirits can change people's personality, moods, feelings, thoughts; can make them move their body, have certain desires, become angry, force them to say things and change their behaviour to a considerable extent. In fact, in my opinion it is impossible to understand human behaviour, consciousness, emotions and desires to any great degree without understanding the phenomenon of spirit disturbance. This is not to say that one does not play a role oneself. One should take responsibility for one's life, and strive to improve oneself with all the abilities, talents and education one has acquired. It is just that we cannot be sure that our thoughts, desires or behaviour are totally our own because of the possible influence of attached spirits.

When True Light is radiated through the forehead of a person to the main soul, not only does that person receive the Light, but attached spirits also receive it. Even in cases where spirits may normally have to stay in dimensions of suffering for centuries, the Light of God can enable them to awaken and be saved much more quickly. This is why giving True Light to people steadily results in the salvation of spirits.

At times the attached spirit may manifest by making the person move, cry, speak, write and so on. This is called 'spirit manifestation'. When the face, head or body moves, it is called 'spirit movement', which is one form of spirit manifestation. Spirit movement is only one indicator of a person's spirit disturbance, however. In many cases when people receive True Light they do not experience obvious physical sensations or movement. However, lack of physical manifestation does not necessarily mean lack of spirit disturbance. It is common for resentful spirits to try to 'hide' (not reveal their presence by moving and so on) when the person they are attached to receives Light.

Certain Mahikari staff members are trained to do what is called a "spirit investigation", which involves talking with the attached spirit, in order to help the spirit to be saved. Occasionally such spirits confess what they have done in previous lives and why they are now attached to the person. I have also had experiences in which the attached spirit spoke a language that the person attached to did not understand. In Sukyo Mahikari we do not necessarily believe what spirits tell us, but with experience, spirit investigation can sometimes be valuable to help and guide spirits so that they can be saved by God, which is the purpose of spirit investigation.

If spirit manifestation were a rare phenomenon, perhaps I would not be so sure of its reality. However, it is something one can witness practically every day if one gives the Light of God to people one after the other. By receiving the Light one can sometimes experience this personally. The phenomenon of spirit possession is not new in the literature, but the living reality of it in everyday life is something that most people have not understood or accepted widely before. Throughout history there have been many reports about so-called demons or devils possessing people or about unusual phenomena resulting from practices done by people involved in psychic medium activities. These are just extreme cases. What I am describing here is something that has a close relationship with practically everybody in everyday life. Spirits are attached to people who are highly educated, who lead balanced, sensible lives, who are respectable citizens in society, who may have no interest in spirit phenomena or may not even believe in God. A man's attached spirit, for example, may be that of his own dear mother, who died recently, means no harm but by attaching to him nevertheless unintentionally interferes with her son's life because her condition is naturally reflected in her son.

As I mentioned, disturbance by spirits may be the cause of problems ranging from minor injuries, personal discomfort and negative moods through to serious accidents, diseases, crimes, suicide, murder and other tragedies. When resentful spirits cooperate in groups, large-scale misfortunes such as mass destruction, mass hysteria, riots, revolutions and wars may result. Spirits who bear strong grudges may plot the misfortune of a person over many years and may take their revenge on the person's descendants as well. If a problem due to spirits is not resolved in one generation, the descendants inherit the problem in subsequent generations until it is resolved. In other words, our ancestors' impurities are also our own.

The suffering caused in ignorance by the attached spirit of a relative may be as great as that caused by a resentful spirit seeking revenge. One kind of spirit disturbance can easily lead to another. Whatever the reason for attaching and whatever the disturbance caused, most attached spirits are really crying out for help, as they are suffering. Through the Light of God such spirits can be gradually saved.

Experiences

Every day Sukyo Mahikari members can obtain convincing evidence for the existence of spirits from different levels of the astral world, by observing the manifestation of spirits during the practice of the art of True Light. Even though spirits can, in a sense, escape from the astral world by attaching to the physical body of humans in the physical world, their current situation is a reflection of the dimension of the astral world to which they belong, and this may be ascertained by observing them manifesting as they receive True Light.

For example, I have personally encountered cases in which True Light on the forehead area has caused a person to become extremely hot (showing flushed cheeks, beads of perspiration and so on) within a few minutes, even on a cold winter's day. In some such cases the person has cried out in anguish, "Fire! Fire everywhere!" (or something similar). It was not the person, of course, but the spirit attached to him who reacted in this way. I have also witnessed the reverse, when the Light of God caused spirits in the freezing part of hell to manifest. Even on a hot summer's day such spirits caused shivering, chattering of teeth, goose bumps and so on in the people to whom they were attached. On a number of occasions in my experience attached spirits have verbally described places of fire, intense cold, total darkness, fearful monsters, repetitive and aimless labour, mud and slime, snakes, a pool of blood, worms and different kinds of aggression. The following case is an example.

On 5 December 1978 I gave True Light to a 26-year-old Czechoslovakian woman from Canberra who had cancer in the left breast and had had a long history of throat problems. During Light to the forehead an attached spirit manifested. Unlike most such spirits, this one was very eager to speak, which it could do loudly and clearly. The spirit said that she was the woman's grandmother and that she had died ten years ago. The grandmother spirit confessed that she had hated her husband, and one night during the Second World War she had killed her husband by stabbing him in the heart and throat with a knife. She had then set fire to their house and fled with her son, feeling confident that the Russians, who were then invading

Czechoslovakia, would be blamed for the crime. Her crime was not exposed but later she became so miserable that she eventually hanged herself.

I asked her (the spirit) how she felt now. She exclaimed that her "neck and throat hurt terribly". I asked her whether she knew about the existence of the world after death. She cried out, "Of course I do, you fool, it's terrible! I couldn't stand it! I ran away. I was burning and they were all at me with knives. There was fire everywhere and they kept on stabbing me! I don't know why I didn't die; it just kept on going!"

After I had finished giving the woman Light I asked her whether she remembered her grandmother. She said that her grandmother had hated everybody and everybody had hated her. One day about ten years ago when she (the girl) came home from school, her grandmother was hanging from a cord in front of the entrance to the house. She had hanged herself. Frightened, the girl ran away.

This experience illustrates how the grandmother suffered from stabbing and fire in the astral world, the same things she had inflicted on her husband in the physical world. It strengthened my understanding of the law of cause and effect. There is no way to escape one's karma, not even by dying. Suicide did not put an end to the grandmother's unhappiness; it made things worse. This experience also confirmed something else I had learnt, that people develop the same conditions their attached spirits have. The girl to whom the spirit had attached had throat and breast problems, the same areas of injury and suffering as in her attached grandmother spirit.

§

A vivid experience of an attached spirit who was in freezing hell was reported by Knobel (1995), as in the following excerpt.

When I received Light to my forehead I started to feel extremely cold. My breath was so cold the staff member giving me Light could feel her hand becoming cold. Afterwards she told me the spirit attached to me seemed to be in an extremely cold level of the astral world. As she gave Light, the spirit's condition changed from not being able to move at all to being able to move slightly, and for this improvement the spirit cried with gratitude.

When I got home I went to bed, rugged up in three layers of warm clothes plus two feather quilts, trying to keep warm. Even with the heated waterbed, I was still freezing. As I fell asleep an unusual dim light surrounded me and with it came a horrible silence, loneliness, and worst of all, an unbearable cold. All of this seemed to last an eternity.

When I woke up more than forty hours later I felt my kidneys and bladder quivering and shaking from a tremendously icy cold feeling. I felt as if I were encased in a gigantic block of ice that was trying to crush and suffocate me. There was a very heavy, cold weight lying on top of me, causing an almost inhuman pain and cold within and around me. I had to get out of bed somehow, and after several attempts and offering a prayer, I finally managed to lift the bed covers and sheets off me only to realise with horror they were a solid mass of icy cold material. Looking at it in absolute disbelief I questioned my sanity. 'This is not real – this cannot be!' The frozen feeling and pain when I tried to move was a reality as were the icy sheets and bed cover. I managed to get to the bathroom and prepared myself a very hot bath. All I wanted was to get warm. Unfortunately, the steaming hot water turned cold within ten minutes. I got out of the bath, worried that I might be enclosed in a frozen mass again. It was a shocking awakening to realise what spirit disturbance can cause. I went outside and knelt in the grass and prayed.

'May I ask You, Su God, for Your mercy and salvation for the attached spirit. May I humbly ask You for Your forgiveness for the spirit's sin of escaping from the astral world and attaching to human flesh. I sincerely apologise for whatever I or my ancestors may have done to cause this spirit's suffering. May I be of any assistance to help the attached spirit return to the astral world to a level that is filled with warmth, peace and happiness.'

I went inside again and proceeded to give Light to the house and the surrounding area for about half an hour. As I stepped outside again into the crisp cool morning air, it was as if I had never before felt the warmth of the rising sun. The bitter cold within me was slowly replaced by a cosy warm feeling and the tears of agonising pain from the unbearable cold turned to tears of joy for having been able to experience, feel, see and receive such physical and spiritual cleansing.

§

Many diseases are caused by the spirit of a person who had that disease while alive in the physical world, and who then attached to a relative or a friend after death. As already explained, a person's disease usually does not disappear just by dying in the physical world, but continues in the astral world. The same is true for pain, injury, paralysis or any other condition. The condition is reflected through the person in the physical world some time after the spirit attaches. For example, grandfather may die with asthma, and if the spirit of grandfather then attaches to his grandson, that grandson will become an asthmatic in due course, even if the grandson had no obvious problem with his chest before that time.

I have witnessed such phenomena again and again over the years. One lady in Canberra, for example, a kamikumite, had a close friend who developed cancer in a part of the intestine on the left side. The friend's abdomen swelled up and she was in very great pain on the left side. Even though her kamikumite friend wanted to help her with True Light, she refused to receive it. A few months later she died with her disease. Within two days, the kamikumite came to me very concerned because her belly was now swelling up and she had pain on her left side, precisely where her deceased friend had had the cancer. When I gave True Light to the lady, sure enough, the spirit of her recently departed friend manifested, and very embarrassed, confessed that she had attached to the lady kamikumite because she felt lost. When she was still alive in the physical world, she could not believe in the actual existence of the spiritual realm and had just relied on modern medicine to save her. Now that she had died, she did not know what to do. As I gave Light I guided her about the functioning of the astral world and her role as a human being, and after a few days of Light she left her friend's body and went to the astral world. In a short time the swelling in the kamikumite's abdomen disappeared, as did the pain. I wonder what would have happened if it had not been for the art of True Light and the divine teachings that enabled the spirit to understand what to do. It is possible that her friend could even have died from cancer as well. Through True Light the suffering of spirits in the astral world can be alleviated. Agony can change to relief and even joy.

Many conditions such as cancer, heart disease and so on run in families, and medically are therefore thought to be due to some genetic reason. However, a deeper cause is often an attached spirit who keeps going from one family member to another, as the relatives die one after another, or the deceased relatives themselves become attached spirits. I feel it would be a major breakthrough if people in the field of medicine were able to understand that spirit disturbance has a considerable influence on disease and that this can be solved.

§

Belief in various religious teachings may not necessarily give deep understanding about life after death or provide comfort to people when they die. On a number of occasions during spirit investigations, while radiating God's Light to the forehead of people, I have encountered spirits who had had religious beliefs while living in the physical world, yet were confused and suffered after physical death. The following is one such experience.

In Madang, Papua New Guinea, is a young, single lady kamikumite who lives with her father, also a kamikumite. Her mother died during childbirth a few years before this event. This lady's younger sister developed a lupus condition in about April 1993, when she was in her early 20s. She was married to a devout Christian and they lived in Port Moresby. Her condition gradually deteriorated. According to her elder sister's description, she became very ill. Her legs became cold, she felt cold at night, she had very little appetite (eating a few mouthfuls only now and then), her upper arms were as hard as a rock and in general she was slow and sluggish in her movements. Her elder sister said that her legs felt so cold that it was like touching the legs of a dead person. Over the months her condition deteriorated to the degree that she could not walk anymore. She could not even go to the bathroom or toilet by herself. At first she was assisted to the bathroom with a special chair and her husband washed her. Towards the end of 1994 she could not even leave her bed so it was necessary to use a bedpan for her toilet.

She asked her husband for permission to go to the home of her father and sister in Madang, which was arranged. Over a period of about two months, she received the Light of God from her father or her elder sister every day, and she continued to improve to the point where she was not cold anymore, her legs did not feel cold, her upper arms were soft and supple, and she even proudly demonstrated that she could walk around the garden unaided.

Early in 1995, her husband insisted that she come back to Port Moresby because he considered that Sukyo Mahikari activities were against those of his church. Even though other members of his church had heard about the miracles experienced by many people through the Sukyo Mahikari organisation and suggested that he permit his wife to continue receiving God's Light, he could not be persuaded and brought his wife back to Port Moresby. After that her condition started to deteriorate once again and in mid-February 1995 she died, aged 24.

I visited the kamikumite in Madang in December 1995, and not knowing this story, noticed that the elder sister did not look like the woman I used to know. She had a puffy look about her and also occasionally complained about the cold. Her father talked to me privately and asked whether I could spiritually investigate what was going on, because his eldest daughter often behaved just like the younger daughter used to when she was in the physical world. Her mannerisms, her way of giggling, the way she scratched her legs – these were some of the things that the father noticed his elder daughter was doing that reminded him of his deceased daughter.

When I gave Light to the elder sister, spirit investigation revealed that the spirit of her younger sister was indeed attached and still suffering with her lupus condition. I gave her Light repeatedly day after day for several days. With time, through the Light of God, the spirit was able to improve.

Various types of spirits

Over the years I have found that there are various kinds of spirits. Possessing or attached spirits may be human, animal or even nature spirits. Oshienushisama has taught that much of the spirit disturbance in the world today is caused by animal spirits, which have a common resentment against humankind because of the despicable ways they have been treated by people over the years. Even the mass production and consumption of domestic animals, exploiting them unnaturally as mere material for profit, results in tremendous vibrations of resentment generated by the animal kingdom. This leads to a mass of negative energy directed towards human beings, manifesting as spirit disturbance, including infectious diseases.

Some animal spirits were originally human spirits who have transmigrated. As indicated earlier, during the cycle of birth and rebirth spirits may transmigrate not only from male to female (or vice versa) but from human to animal forms as well. If people live like animals in the physical world, they may acquire such forms in the spiritual realm and may eventually be reborn into the physical world as animals. Sukuinushisama gave detailed teachings (mainly in the intermediate course) on the different kinds of animal forms that can result, depending on the innermost attitudes of the people concerned. For example, people with strong attachments (greed, selfishness) for material possessions may sometimes transmigrate as snakes; those who are cunning and cheat may be born as foxes; and so on. Even though most animals in the physical world are purely from animal spirit, the fact remains that there are animals in the physical world that were originally humans. When transmigration is incomplete, people may be born into this world with animal characteristics, such as fur, multiple breasts, the vestige of a tail or other characteristics.

Again, such phenomena may be difficult to believe without personal experience. Through practising True Light I have witnessed people crawl on the ground and hiss like a snake, walk on all fours and meow like a cat, flap 'wings' like a bird, behave like a fox, and show other animal-like behaviour, as a result of the manifesting of an attached animal spirit. Fortunately, when transmigrated animal spirits continue to receive God's Light, they eventually awaken to the reason they transmigrated into animal form, and often after purification and apology to God they can revert back to the spirit form of a human. Such human spirits then have the possibility of reincarnating again.

There are also cases of attached animal spirits that were always animal, not a transmigration from a human. Again, the best way of helping them is to purify them with the Light of God. The following letter illustrates how one lady experienced this phenomenon.

For 15 years before I came to Mahikari I suffered severe spinal problems from the neck to the base. Other physical disorders included tension headaches almost daily, hay fever, fast heart rate, shortness of breath, upset stomach and severe pain in the hips when discs in my lower back area pressed on nerves.

I went from regular doctors to chiropractors, to naturopaths and then to a neurosurgeon, who advised cutting the nerves at the base of my skull. (I did not take his advice.) I even went to an eye specialist, who put his patients under anaesthetic and then twisted the head almost back-to-front to adjust the spine! My headaches always continued and discs never stayed in place for more than a few hours after adjustment.

Then, early in 1979 I went to the Mahikari Centre in Darwin, not knowing anything of the healing attributes of True Light, and found beautiful people just willing to help others. I soon attended the primary course and as I continued to give and receive True Light my whole life changed spiritually, mentally and physically. On the physical side I now no longer experience headaches daily (only on odd occasions) and I understand what cleansing is. No more hay fever, no more medication.

My back problems have not been solved completely, but the improvement has been considerable and is continuing. I must admit I was rather surprised to learn that my spinal problems had been caused by snake spirits! During True Light on the forehead, spirit investigations made by the staff of the Mahikari Centre revealed that snakes (three have been identified so far) had attached to my back because my family and I had killed them previously. They were very resentful. They were able to understand English and communicate because they had originally been humans, apparently very greedy in acquiring property. Even more amazing was the fact that they gradually reverted to human form as they received God's Light and tried to give up their attachments over the weeks. For me this really opened my eyes to the reality of transmigration from human to animal form.

Gloria Sutherland, mother, aged 30, Canberra, 20 October 1980

§

The spirit of a person who is killed tragically, such as in a traffic accident, suicide or war, may become earth-bound. Such a spirit can usually move no more than up to 100 metres or so in any direction, until he or she has spent long enough there to compensate for bad karma and becomes purified. Such spirits often cause more accidents and kill more people out of the sheer need for more company. By purifying the area with God's Light and offering appropriate prayers, earth-bound spirits may be released. Even if it is not possible to purify such a site directly, dedicated service to God by the earth-bound spirit's relatives will also eventually result in that spirit's salvation.

Various kinds of spirits may live in houses, caves, waterfalls or other places and may interfere with people's lives without being actually attached to them. They can all be helped with the Light of God.

Helping spirits

The aim is to save or help spirits, not try to get rid of them. The person radiating Light to the forehead area of another should do so with love, sincerity, respect and patience, no matter what the response. It is not good to blame the spirits, but to recognise that one has spirits attached in balance with what one is and what one has done previously. If a spirit is trying to kill a person through some disease or accident, it is evidence that that particular person or the person's ancestors in a previous life did similar things to either that spirit or the spirit's family. Instead of feeling victimised and having attitudes of conflict towards spirits, the best approach is for the person to have a sense of apology for having caused suffering and to go about life so that the spirits can be saved by God. In order to help or save spirits attached to a person, it is important to be compassionate to them, to recognise that they are suffering because of that person's wrong deeds from the past.

Sukuinushisama taught that in resolving spirit disturbance the Light of God is extremely important. Ideally, giving and receiving the Light of God would be a way of life. How the Light is given is also important – the innermost outlook or attitudes. If a person continues to give Light to others merely for self-improvement, God may not permit the attached spirits to be saved and the disturbance may continue. But if the person gives Light to others with the heart of wanting to help people (as well as the spirits), as evidence of his apology and gratitude, the same activity may result in greater improvement. That is why service to God with appropriate attitudes is also very important in the resolving of spirit disturbance. So, in order to resolve spirit disturbance, that is, to save or help spirits, it is valuable to practise the three aspects – radiating the Light of God; elevating the innermost attitudes and so becoming a better person at home, at work and in society; and offering service to God.

Spirit disturbance can be resolved when the attached spirit awakens to what is right and wrong, forgives the person and returns to the astral world. In other cases, the spirit may not leave the body but does not disturb the person anymore. In still other cases, the spirit may still maintain a strong grudge and want to disturb the person, but because of the person's sincere, dedicated efforts for God, it is God who prevents the spirit from disturbing the person by limiting the spirit's power. It is impossible to make any predictions about how long it will take to resolve spirit disturbance, as it depends on the degree of the spirit disturbance, the degree of the person's impurity, how much awakening there is by the person and the person's family members, how much effort they make for God, how much the innermost attitudes are improved, what God's will is for that person, and so on. The best course is to make the path to God a way of life. If one is sincere in serving God and helping others, eventually one will be able to see improvements in one's life as a result of the arrangements made by God.

In my experience, the resolving of spirit disturbance for most people is a gradual process that takes years and years and often improvement is barely perceptible as the person makes efforts for God. It is good to be patient and to use the opportunity to grow in a mature way. Even though God may sometimes show interesting phenomena in the short term to help people to awaken to the real existence of the spiritual realm, spirit disturbance will not usually be resolved, no matter how long one gives Light, if one maintains a selfish attitude and focuses on phenomena (sensations, feelings, unusual experiences) without trying to practise the will of God.

In Sukyo Mahikari the aim is to actualise the plan of God by reviving people's divine nature. The reason we are now permitted to radiate the Light of God is to purify people and spirits so that they can awaken to the real existence of God and be motivated to be of service for the divine plan. On top of that, since the Light purifies the spiritual, astral and physical cells, that is, spiritually, mentally and physically, it also helps to revive the pure condition of humankind and nature as it was originally.

In order for us to be more effective in achieving this, it is valuable to know about the existence of the spiritual realm, including activities of different kinds of spirits, but not to focus on spirits as an aim in itself. This chapter deals a lot with spirits and the spiritual realm, only because it is a subject that is not well known in everyday society. However, this does not mean that we focus our attention on spirits. If that happens, it is not being God-centred anymore.

Ancestor spirits

Everybody has parents, grandparents and so on, some of whom may still be living in the physical world. In addition, everybody has many ancestor spirits who have already passed on but who are very much alive in the spiritual realm. Sukuinushisama taught that every person also has a guardian spirit who is usually a representative of one's ancestors, whose task is to protect, guide and help the person in everyday life. The guardian spirit is associated with the person but not attached to the person's physical body. With the guardian spirit are a group of two or three other helper spirits, who are also ancestors.

In my travels I continue to discover that care of ancestors, including the offering of food, has been practised by people of many cultures throughout the ages, not only in Eastern countries, but also in Western countries. For instance, the ancient Jews believed that there was "a mutually beneficial arrangement between the living and the ancestral dead. The living would provide physical sustenance to the dead; in turn, the deceased ancestors would be expected to provide guidance and protection to the living" (Raphael, 1994). Similarly, in my own ancestry, there are many stories about how the ancient Latvians honoured and offered food to their ancestors from time to time. Today, however, with the passage of time, incorrect procedures have been introduced, important aspects have been omitted and for many cultures, particularly in Western countries, the practice of serving ancestors has been forgotten and given up all together.

Sukuinushisama gave detailed guidance on taking care of ancestors, which has helped countless people. In Sukyo Mahikari, by correctly inaugurating name-tablets in an altar, people are able to pay homage to their ancestors in the spiritual realm and help them do their training.

I learned that there are a number of reasons why we take care of our departed ancestors. Firstly, by tracing back our ancestral lineage, we ultimately go back to Su God, the Creator, so any homage paid to our ancestors is indirect worship of the Creator God.

Since it is our duty as descendants to take care of our ancestors, inaugurating and taking care of the altar is an expression of our apology for the neglect of our ancestors, and a demonstration of our resolve to do things correctly.

It is also a way of showing gratitude to our ancestors. We are in the physical world because of our ancestors and we therefore naturally want to express our gratitude. The guardian spirit is also one of our ancestors. Respect and gratitude in deeds to one's parents and other ancestors is a natural part of life.

The inaugural ceremony and care of ancestors through their altar is also a way of helping our ancestors, particularly by offering food, but also by other offerings such as the Light of God and divine teachings from time to time.

Many ancestors need the 'energy of earth', which they can obtain from food offerings made to them. If they cannot receive food and if the descendants do not awaken to their needs, they may attach to a descendant in desperation and cause gastric or other problems. They give a sign or admonition (warning) like this in the hope that the descendants will awaken to the fact that the ancestors cannot eat. Common admonitions can be problems with the stomach or intestines (poor appetite, frequent indigestion, chronic constipation, ulcer, tumour, cancer, for instance). Admonitions from ancestors may also take the form of head or eye problems, particularly on the left side (the spiritual side). They may include mental problems or insomnia. In fact, if ancestors are really desperate, an attached ancestor spirit may even end up causing a descendant to die. Many everyday problems that people have are found to be due to admonitions from their own ancestors. These problems may be solved by inaugurating name-tablets and an altar and taking care of ancestors properly.

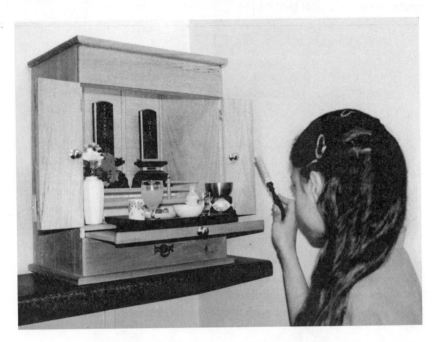

I am not saying that these kinds of problems are always due to admonitions from one's ancestors. There can be other causes, including disturbance by resentful spirits. However, in my experience, a frequent cause is ancestors' admonitions, in which case the problem can be solved rather easily if it is not left too late.

Mysterious as it sounds, after inaugurating suitable name-tablets, through invisible spiritual cords connecting the ancestors and the gold writing on the name-tablets, they can see and hear their descendants, and smell and absorb the earth energy from the food offerings made. I suppose it is a little like television, except in reverse. We can watch television but the television cannot watch us.

Such things can really only be appreciated by personal experience. I remember feeling somewhat reluctant to accept these teachings at first, shortly after I attended the Mahikari primary course in 1975. I was wondering whether the care of ancestors was not some kind of Japanese custom and therefore did not really apply to me. People kept telling me about the importance of taking care of one's ancestors but I did not really want to listen. Then, mysteriously, I became deaf in the left ear. I regained my hearing on the day I bought the name-tablets for my ancestors. Only afterwards did I recognise that the deafness must have been an admonition from my ancestors, who were giving me the message, "You're not listening. Open your ears." After holding the inaugural ceremony and making regular food offerings to my ancestors I noticed that I hardly ever became constipated, something that used to happen often for no apparent reason in the past. In various ways I grew to appreciate the reality and importance of taking care of ancestors.

The following case illustrates how the inauguration of the ancestors altar resulted in improvement of gastrointestinal disorders in a woman from Hong Kong (Lim, 1996).

Twenty-eight years ago, I started to have the most terrible eating habits – which I hated, yet I couldn't stop. Sometimes I would avoid having meals and snacks altogether, and at other times I would eat excessive amounts of food, then make myself vomit, sometimes eating again and voluntarily vomiting again. I didn't want to do this but somehow I couldn't stop myself. Sometimes I would avoid meals and food altogether so that I wouldn't have to eat excessively and voluntarily vomit. I would rather starve myself. However the need to eat would 'win' and I would again eat excessively and vomit.

This went on for 27 years – 27 years of madness! I tried to stop on countless occasions but in vain. I didn't tell anyone about my problem all those 27 years, as I was so ashamed and thinking that I was a bit insane. I was very frightened. At my worst times I might do this three or four times daily and at my best (which was after I joined Mahikari) I did it only once a day. It was impossible for me to stop it altogether – except for one week in Japan, when I was attending the Autumn Grand Ceremony and tour in November 1992.

The medical terms for such disorders are bulimia (eating excessively and then voluntarily vomiting) and anorexia nervosa (avoiding food and starving oneself). They have been termed psychiatric disorders and although many possible explanations are given for these disorders, there is nothing definite. Many people have died of these disorders – Karen Carpenter, the singer, was one of the famous sufferers who died despite all the help given to her. Others go in and out of hospitals living in despair and desperation, believing that there is no hope or real help available. Sometimes they commit suicide. I myself had contemplated suicide on several occasions.

In October 1991, I attended the primary course in Kuala Lumpur. Not long after becoming a kamikumite I attended the ancestors altar inauguration of a fellow kumite and so I started to awaken to the importance of the ancestors altar and looking after ancestors properly.

On 10 January 1993, we inaugurated the Lim family ancestors altar. On that day (without any forethought or intent) I ate normally and I have eaten normally ever since! Twenty-seven years of madness gone – just disappeared upon inaugurating the Lim family ancestors altar. For me this is a miracle – a miracle Almighty Su God has given me to share with all of you.

Interaction of spiritual vibrations

Sukuinushisama taught much about communication between spirits through the vibrations given out – the vibrations of innermost attitudes, thoughts and words. This communication takes place knowingly and unknowingly between God and people; people and their ancestors or other spirits in the astral world; people in the physical world; people and the spirits attached to them; people and their guardian spirits; and between spirits themselves. There really is no barrier, it seems. In fact, the vibrations of our innermost attitudes and our words reach animals, plants and even materials to different degrees.

Spiritual functions of words

I have learnt that words are the materialisation of what is called *kototama*, the spiritual essence, power or functions of syllables and words. This is not the spiritual functions or power of *sound*, which is also a power in its own right (just as there is the spiritual essence or power of *numbers* and the spiritual essence or power of *colour*). Just by enunciating syllables, specific power manifests. This spiritual power or functions of words is a subject studied in the Mahikari advanced course.

In the Sukyo Mahikari organisation, one normally chants the prayer, Amatsu Norigoto, the 'Heavenly prayer' of purification, in a bold, clear voice before giving Light to someone. People who are not familiar with Mahikari have sometimes asked me, "Why chant prayers in Japanese?" It is not a matter of using the Japanese language. The combinations of the syllables and the words have functions of purification, effects of reviving the original power in humans as children of God, functions of opening the positive aspect of the spirit. This applies to anybody anywhere, whether in Australia, in Europe or Latin America. It has nothing to do with understanding Japanese. Naturally, people pray to the Creator God in their own language, but when it comes to purification with God's Light, there is specific power if one chants the Amatsu Norigoto prayer in addition to radiating Light from the hand.

Similarly, after giving Light to the forehead for approximately ten minutes, the practice of calming down the spirit is done by radiating the Light with both hands in a sweeping down motion while enunciating "*Oshizumari*" three times. The spiritual functions of the syllables of Oshizumari calm down spirits. On many occasions I have witnessed an attached spirit showing marked movements, and then being calmed down by the giver's reciting of the word Oshizumari three times. Manifesting spirits will not calm down by saying "Please calm down" in English, for example.

There are researchers who study the meanings of words, but I am talking about the *spirit, essence, functions,* or *power* of words, not their meaning. If translations alone are read, there may be intellectual understanding of the prayers at a certain level, but not necessarily any spiritual purification or understanding given to spirits.

When the Amatsu Norigoto prayer is chanted, possessing spirits of the receiver sometimes manifest in the form of movement, crying or speaking, even before the Light of God is radiated to the forehead from the hand. My first experience with this occurred not long after I attended the primary course, when I was about to give Light to a medical doctor in Australia. I did not have time to explain anything to the lady because she was keen to receive the Light straight away. I just asked her to sit in a comfortable position and close her eyes.

Within seconds after I began reciting the Amatsu Norigoto prayer, she started moving her hands, head and eventually her whole body, in pronounced, jerky movements (that I later recognised to be the manifestation of a possessing spirit). I had not even begun to radiate Light. Her whole body was shaking and moving about in an uncontrolled way, and she made wailing and sighing sounds as her head shook. At one stage tears came from her eyes. This behaviour continued while I gave her Light to the forehead for ten minutes, but after I said Oshizumari three times, she became as calm as she had been before and her eyes were shining in amazement. In fact, she looked elated, explaining that she had been looking for something like that all her life. I did not have the chance to tell her that the spiritual power of words had evoked activity in her attached spirit, but she did not seem to mind. She said that despite her agitated behaviour, deep down she had felt something wonderful happening to her. She said she did not know the language at all, nor had I told her that I would be chanting a prayer before radiating God's Light. Obviously, the Amatsu Norigoto prayer had evoked activity in her by the spiritual essence of the words. I was also impressed by the remarkable calming effect that the Oshizumari had on her.

Oshienushisama has also given guidance about the importance of the spiritual functions of words in general, not only words of prayer. Apparently, words are like seeds; whatever is planted will grow. Words are living. They influence not only the destiny of oneself, but the destiny of others. For instance, offering cheerful greetings to people in the morning – family members at home, others at work, students at school – can lead to all kinds of improvement.

In short, there is very real though invisible communication through the vibrations of one's will or attitudes as well as through one's thoughts and words. In this way, we make spiritual cords with people and those in the spiritual realm. There are also vibrations of resentment, love or attachment that can come from the spiritual realm to people, depending on how much the people tune in to such vibrations. It is valuable not only to be aware of these things but to train oneself to live so that one has pure, elevated attitudes and thoughts; positive, bright words that encourage others; as well as behaviour that is correct. The more positive one can be, the less the negative influence one receives.

Research on death and spirit phenomena

From an academic standpoint there are many views about what happens during and after death, but it is difficult to be sure. Since the first books largely devoted to the near-death experience (Moody, 1975), medical doctors, psychologists, brain specialists and other researchers have studied cases of people before, during and after death in the physical world, and have provided strong evidence that the dying person continues to have conscious awareness of the environment after being pronounced clinically dead (Ring, 1980; Sabom, 1982; 1998; Lorimer, 1990; Owens, Cook & Stevenson, 1990; Almeder, 1992; Becker, 1993; Greyson, 1993; 2000; Irwin, 1994; Morse, 1994; Fenwick & Fenwick, 1995; 1999; Wade, 1996; Bailey & Yates, 1996; Roy, 1996; Tart, 1997; Ring & Cooper, 1999; Parnia, Waller, Yeates & Fenwick, 2001; van Lommel, van Wees, Meyers & Elfferich, 2001; Cornell, 2002). Even though this field is still controversial, a number of academics are confirming what religions have taught for a long time, that life continues after the death of the physical body. One puzzling observation in the early studies was that patients who recalled their experiences after being resuscitated from clinical death had reported only pleasant and neutral experiences.

However, this changed when Dr Maurice Rawlings published his book *Beyond Death's Door*, in 1979.

Dr Rawlings, a specialist in cardiovascular disease, resuscitated many patients who reported experiences they had had after clinical death, and the unpleasant experiences in his studies were at least as frequent as the pleasant ones. He used to regard most after-death experiences as fantasy, conjecture or imagination. Then one evening in 1977 he was resuscitating a terrified patient who told him he was actually in hell. He begged the doctor to get him out of hell and not to let him die. When Rawlings realised how genuinely and extremely frightened the patient was, he resolved to study death more closely. He became convinced that there is life after death and that not all of it is pleasant.

Rawlings concluded that the patients of previous investigators had described only pleasant experiences because they probably had not recalled their experiences completely. He felt that most of the bad experiences are soon suppressed deeply into the patient's subconscious mind, as they seem to be so painful and disturbing that they are removed from conscious recall, leaving only pleasant experiences or no experiences at all. It is possible that after-death experiences, especially unpleasant ones, fade quickly from memory unless recorded immediately, as is often the case with dreams. Few of the previous researchers had ever resuscitated a patient or had the opportunity of recording immediate on-the-scene interviews.

Rawlings related that many of his dying patients who had lost consciousness (according to clinical criteria) had heard themselves being pronounced dead by the doctor and watched themselves being resuscitated. In some cases the patients had looked down upon the scene from a floating position near the ceiling; in others they had stood or floated at the same level as the doctor and nurses. Apparently, all could see, feel, think and talk as before. Some patients reported that after an interval they found themselves moving through a long, dark passage or tunnel at the end of which was a brilliantly lit environment of exquisite beauty where they met and talked with friends and relatives who had died previously. Some were then interviewed by a being of light or a being of darkness. Religious background seemed to influence the identification of the being. For example, no Hindu saw Jesus and no Christian saw a Hindu deity. Then a barrier was usually encountered beyond which they could go but not return. At that stage the patients were resuscitated and regained consciousness.

All of Rawlings's patients who reported a continuance from one life to another, whether good or bad, usually met 'dead' relatives or friends in a type of sorting place that often had a barrier preventing entrance into a more permanent type of existence. In some cases they crossed the barrier temporarily and were given glimpses of where spirits may go after death. Of particular interest are vivid descriptions of unpleasant circumstances. These include:

I was standing near a shoreline of a great ocean of fire . . . burning, turbulent, rolling mass of blue fire . . . lake of fire and brimstone . . . no way to escape, no way out (pp. 103–104);

. . . gloomy room . . . huge giant with a grotesque face . . . little imps or elves . . . Outside was darkness but I could hear people moaning all around me . . . things were getting worse . . . I was crying (p. 106);

. . . the awfullest, eery sounds were going on . . . odor of decay . . . some of the workers were only half human (p. 107);

. . . The further down I went the blacker it became, until it was all blackness. I could not have seen my hand if it had been one inch in front of my eyes . . . Finally, way down below me, I could see lights flickering on the walls of the caverns of the damned. They were caused by the fires of hell . . . (pp. 108–109);

. . . The earth was like slimy mud that sank over my feet, and it was hard to move (p. 113).

A number of Rawlings's patients who had had unpleasant after-death experiences had been active in religious practice, and included clergymen. For example, one such person was surprised to find himself descending through a tunnel lined with fire and opening into a huge, fiery world of horror. Rawlings wrote, *He saw some of his old friends from the 'good old days' who exhibited blank stares of apathy, who were burdened with useless loads, and who were continually going nowhere but never stopping for fear of 'the main drivers' who, he said, were beyond description* (p. 110).

The following excerpt is from an after-death experience of the founder of a Sunday school, a lifelong supporter of the church: *. . . then I saw these red snakes crawling all over me. I couldn't get away from them. I would throw one off and then another would get on me. It was horrible! Finally, I was dragged down to the ground by something and then other crawling things started getting on me. Some looked like red jelly. I screamed and cried out, but no one paid any attention to me* (p. 118).

§

Sir John Eccles has provided neurophysiological evidence to suggest that the mind of the human exists outside of the neuronal interactions within the brain (Popper & Eccles, 1985; Eccles, 1987; Eccles, 1994).

I have great respect for this eminent scientist. His breakthrough research on recording from single central nervous system neurones in mammals earned him the Nobel Prize in Physiology and Medicine in 1963. I inherited some of his research techniques through his student (my professor) when I was conducting brain research at the John Curtin School of Medical Research at the Australian National University. When I first met Eccles in 1970, in Switzerland, I was pleasantly surprised to see how dynamic and insightful he was, seemingly uninfluenced by conventional thinking of that time.

During the 1970s and 1980s, scientific and philosophical discussion of the human brain was dominated by a materialistic and mechanistic view, according to which all processes of the brain and mind, including conscious processes, could be wholly explained in physical terms. It was thought that the brain could be understood as an information-processing machine, operating on much the same principles as a computer. Practically all the modern, great neuroscientists before and during the time of Eccles concluded that the mind or consciousness is merely a product of activities of nerve cells in specific configurations in different areas of the brain. If brain activity stops, there is no consciousness, they postulated.

This was neither the viewpoint of well-known philosopher Sir Karl Popper nor the neuroscientist Sir John Eccles. Eccles strongly asserted that physical investigations of the brain have by no means excluded the role of consciousness and that consciousness did not have a purely physical explanation. He has given clear reasons why the conventional materialist theories cannot be accepted and suggested that there is a so-called 'dualist-interactionist' explanation for the mind. Eccles concluded that immaterial mental events such as thinking can act on material structures such as neurones of the cerebral cortex. In simple language, Eccles had the view that there is a conscious and spiritual self, distinct from the brain, and that it controls the brain.

His view does not deny that interactions with the neuronal machinery of the brain can give a person sensations, feelings and thoughts. It is like comparing a computer with a human being. The computer can do amazing tasks, but it requires a human being to program it and press the right buttons at the right time. The computer does not control the person; it is the other way around. In brief, research by Eccles suggests that the mind or consciousness can exist outside of the brain and have an influence on it.

In his book *Death and Personal Survival,* Professor Robert Almeder (1992) reviews studies largely made by reputable scientists on reincarnation, apparitions of the dead, spirit possession, out-of-body experiences and communications from the dead. He provides the reader with a balanced and informed discussion which includes so-called evidence by sceptics that these phenomena cannot exist. Almeder shows that the views of the sceptics are based on insufficient information and ultimately cannot be accepted. The chapter on apparitions concludes that there is overwhelming evidence that such phenomena do indeed occur.

Dr Harvey Irwin's textbook on parapsychology (1994) has grown out of 15 years of teaching at the University of New England in Australia. In a scientific manner, it covers various topics including reincarnation experiences, apparitions, near-death experiences and out-of-body experiences. Irwin concludes that "if just one of the phenomena should be found to demand a revision or an expansion of contemporary psychological principles, how enriched behavioural science would be".

Dr Peter Fenwick, Emeritus Consultant Neuropsychiatrist of Maudsley Hospital and Honorary Consultant Neurophysiologist of St. Thomas's Hospital in London, has been researching near-death experiences for many years. With his wife, Elizabeth, he has written and reflected on the results of questionnaires returned by about 300 experimenters in the United Kingdom (Fenwick & Fenwick, 1995). This makes it the largest of the major studies undertaken. As a neurophysiologist, Dr Fenwick is interested in brain function and the ways in which it is modified near death. His book is the first full-length account by a neuroscientist who has read the whole range of the literature. Amongst the conclusions made is that out-of-body experiences provide the most concrete evidence of the mind operating non-locally beyond the brain.

Various clinical investigations in recent years have shown that some patients must have obtained information during unconsciousness or clinical death. One startling case was that of a young woman who had had a very deep near-death experience as well as an out-of-body experience at the very time the EEG of her cortex and even her brain stem was totally flat (Sabom, 1998). There are even cases of blind people who reported seeing things clearly and in detail during out-of-body experiences at the time of their near-death condition (Ring & Cooper, 1999).

Up until recently, the near-death and out-of-body experiences researched have been retrospective cases, and it was not usually clear whether the particular experience occurred before, during or after recovery from a period of unconsciousness. Two research groups

– Parnia et al. (2001) and van Lommel et al. (2001) – have made comprehensive long-term, prospective studies of large numbers of cardiac arrest survivors whose subjective experiences were correlated with objective physiological measurements. The results confirmed that memories, though rare, can occur after cardiac arrest and that most of them are near-death experiences. Furthermore, the memories could not have been due to physiological, medical, pharmacological or psychological reasons (possibilities that could not always be ruled out in earlier reports).

The study by van Lommel et al. (2001) of 344 people included a report by a nurse who had attended a 44-year-old comatose man while she was on night shift ambulance duty. A week later, after regaining consciousness, when the staff were trying to find the patient's dentures, he said, "Oh, that nurse knows where my dentures are". He continued, "Yes, you were there when I was brought into hospital and you took my dentures out of my mouth and put them on to that cart, it had all these bottles on it and there was this sliding drawer underneath and there you put my teeth." He had seen all this while in a deep coma and in the process of receiving cardio-pulmonary resuscitation. The man was transferred to a coronary care unit while in a coma and later reported that he had seen himself lying in bed. He had perceived from above how nurses and doctors had been busy with his resuscitation. He was able to describe correctly and in detail the small room in which he had been resuscitated as well as the appearance of those present.

Making conclusions from these studies, in simple terms, people can have memories of experiences they had after they clinically died, that is, when they were medically shown to be unconscious and technically, their brain should not have been functioning. In short, the clinical and scientific evidence is gradually building up to show that consciousness is not generated by brain processes and that life continues after death (Wade, 1996; Russell, 2000; Parnia et al. 2001; van Lommel et al. 2001).

There is also considerable experimental evidence concerning psi phenomena that conclusively demonstrates that living systems can sometimes interact with each other across space without involving normal sensory system contact (Laszlo, 1996; Radin, 1996).

The most comprehensive academic research on reincarnation in modern times has been done by Professor Ian Stevenson, who was Carlson Professor of Psychiatry at the University of Virginia Medical Center. Since the 1960s Stevenson has been engaged in research on people who remember previous lives and he has built up a database of some 2,500 cases (Stevenson, 1977; 1997a,b). He has verified the statements of many subjects throughout the world who claimed to remember previous lives, and has concluded that the idea of reincarnation is valuable in·explaining various aspects of human personality and biology that currently accepted theories do not clarify adequately. According to Stevenson's research, the idea of reincarnation gives greater understanding of unnatural fears and desires in childhood, skills not learned in early life, abnormal relationships between parents and children, grudges, fierce nationalism, certain aspects of childhood sexuality, birthmarks, congenital deformities, internal diseases, differences between identical twins and food cravings during pregnancy. His latest books (Stevenson, 1997a,b) represent the culmination of decades of researching cases in which birthmarks or birth defects are correlated with memories of the people's previous lives.

Almost a third of Almeder's (1992) book is devoted to reincarnation, which mainly refers to the work of Ian Stevenson. Roy Stemman (1997) and Fenwick & Fenwick (1999) have also presented much evidence for reincarnation, based on decades of research.

In chapter 6 (section on solving mental problems) I refer to the evidence for spirit possession, reincarnation and related matters provided by some clinical researchers.

§

I give this information only as interesting confirmation. As I have been indicating, the most powerful evidence for the actual existence of spirits, the real existence of the spiritual realm, life after death and the process of reincarnation, in my opinion, can be obtained by steadily practising the art of True Light.

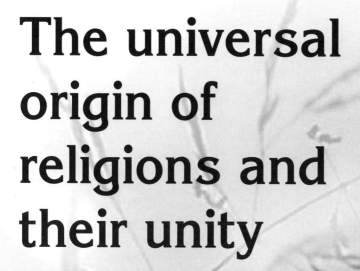

The universal origin of religions and their unity

Chapter 5

The universal origin of religions and their unity

One reason I was originally attracted to the Mahikari organisation, apart from the fact that I could radiate a significant spiritual energy from my hands so easily, was its broadhearted, inclusive approach towards people. Nobody minded what beliefs I or others had. Anyone could become part of the 'Mahikari family', as the teachings were universal; they applied to everyone.

Since then, I have come to learn that one of the major aims of the Sukyo Mahikari movement is to lay the foundation on which all the religions and people of different beliefs can be harmoniously united, that is, to facilitate the return of all religions to their common origin. There is only one Creator God for all people. The origin of all religions is one and the same. The origin of all human beings is one and the same, irrespective of their skin colour, nationality, creed or anything else. There is only one world for humankind. This may sound obvious, but it cannot really be obvious to many people because there is still much conflict throughout the world due to ideological and racial opposition. Unfortunately, religions have been used to justify some wars in the past and some that are still being fought today.

Becoming united does not mean joining a new religion with a new set of dogma and doctrine. Unity can be achieved if people live according to the will of the Creator God through practising the basic universal laws set up by God so that love and harmony can be achieved. In my opinion the Sukyo Mahikari organisation can play a significant role towards achieving this because it enables people to give and receive the Light of the Creator God and helps them to practise universal laws which make up the common foundation of the major religions. The universal teachings transcend the barriers between religions.

I do not think that achieving unity is an easy task or that it can happen quickly. The process of achieving unity requires religions to at least coexist in a spirit of tolerance and to foster an attitude of mutual acceptance and respect for each other. With time, as the common origin of religions and other common ground are recognised and accepted, hopefully religions will be able to unite and work together.

It seems to me that this process has already started. The twentieth century saw the beginnings of a strong movement towards unity amongst Christian churches and amongst different religions. Many important inter-religious agreements took place and there were numerous examples of cooperation centred on the issues of peace and caring for God's creation. It is also a wonderful development that more and more people from different religious and cultural backgrounds are praying together and working together. In this regard, Sukyo Mahikari is grateful to have the opportunity to participate and support many of these joint efforts.

Some viewpoints about religion

During the past few thousand years, people have followed different dogma and doctrine. As a result, division and competition occurred between people. One consequence of this was the promotion of the material civilisation that we have inherited today. According to our teachings, these developments were in accordance with the divine plan. In any case, most religions taught the importance of morals and ethics as the central issue.

From history, we notice that religions were established in places with very different social, cultural and economic backgrounds, and these different backgrounds influenced the way universal principles – revealed through different holy messengers – were passed on from generation to generation. In each case, over time a tradition and a body of doctrine were established. There were often variations or different emphases in these traditions or doctrines, depending on the political or economic situation in each country or place. In most places, until recent times, it was common for individuals to follow the tradition of their families, communities or countries. On the other hand, in some Western countries, since the time of the Renaissance and Reformation, it became gradually more common for people to choose their own particular form of dogma or doctrine. People would commonly say that they were Catholic, Anglican, Buddhist or Hindu as if they were talking about studying science and saying things like "I'm studying mathematics"; "I'm doing physics research"; or "I prefer chemistry". In the field of science people do not normally believe that one discipline is necessarily better than another. They recognise that the different disciplines within science study the same laws of nature, but at different levels, using different approaches. However, when people choose one form of religious dogma and doctrine rather than another, they often seem to believe that in doing so they have reached the real truth, the correct path, a path that is better than other paths and that the other paths must be wrong or incomplete in at least some aspects. Why have people become so divided when it comes to issues of faith or religion?

There is no doubt that religions have given much to humankind over thousands of years – moral fibre, goodness, righteousness, ethics, decorum and other teachings and practices to enable people to cooperate harmoniously. In recent times, many religious leaders have been strong advocates for peace and reconciliation when there have been conflicts. Religious communities have also helped people suffering from natural disasters, poverty and social unrest. Indeed, the practice of altruistic love has become an important practice in many religions. At the same time, however, in the name of religious beliefs, divisions, conflicts and suffering have been caused by people. Coming from a Christian background I have become familiar with some of the history of Christianity – the Crusaders who went to the Middle East and killed people of the Islamic faith; the torturing that took place in the Inquisition; the burning of witches in mediaeval times – all done in the name of God. It is important to realise that God's plan has progressed despite such difficulties. For example, in recent years a process of repentance and reconciliation has emerged from the Christian community and some Christian leaders have apologised for the suffering caused by their churches in the past. Some conflicts and suffering have also been caused by followers of other religions, and varies degrees of repentance and reconciliation have been taking place.

Regrettably, in recent times in some parts of the world, religion has been used as a kind of a business for the tourist industry. In some places there have been cases of moral misconduct. There are also places where religious practice focuses on spirit mediums. There have even been extreme cases where religion has been used as a front for terrorist activities. Such disorder has probably lead to suspicion, doubt or disrespect in some people's minds as far as religions are concerned.

However, I think that the essence of religion should not be damaged just because unfortunate things have occurred throughout human history. There are countless cases of business people who have engaged in all kinds of corruption in high and low positions. However, society has not discarded all matters to do with the business world. There have always been, and still are, honest and well-meaning people who follow ethical business practices that are essential for society to prosper.

I believe that the same applies in the field of religion. Despite unfortunate events and practices that have occurred due to human weakness,. misinterpretation of teachings or spirit disturbance, the messages of the original holy masters are still of great value. There are many people in all religions who make great efforts to live according to the will of God, and in their search to deepen their relationship with God, many of them have come across Sukyo Mahikari and feel that they have benefited from this association. The real essence of religion is important and can be revived according to God's will.

Uniting the essence of religions

The original holy masters, whose teachings eventually became religions, did not preach teachings to divide people, but to unite them. For example, Jesus, who was a Jew, emphasised that his teachings were not just for the Jews but also for the Gentiles (non-Jews). His message of "Love thy neighbour as thyself" is a very powerful message from God that is as valuable today as it was 2,000 years ago. He just spoke to people about the correct way of living, with love and forgiveness, in order to fit with the will of God. Unfortunately, within some areas of Christianity there are divisions that create barriers not only amongst Christians but also with people of other faiths. I think that by allowing such things to happen, many Christians are not putting Jesus' teachings into practice.

The year before I entered university I was studying at a Lutheran college. I am grateful for all the knowledge I was able to acquire concerning the Lutheran religion. I must confess, however, that one thing that disturbed me was the fact that there was another Lutheran college in the same city, the result of a different interpretation of some of the founder's (Luther's) words. Amongst the teachings that my pastors gave during religious instruction was the message that "only our Lutheran faith" would enable people to go to heaven. Even then, as a young student, I could not bring myself to believe that God could be so cruel as to prevent many of His children from being saved simply because they had not encountered my religion. Quite apart from Lutheranism, what about the people who have not even heard about Christianity? What does God do with them? What about the Buddhists? Surely there must be universal laws created by God that apply to all human beings?

Obviously, all aspects of religious doctrine, dogma, ideologies and philosophies that have been promoted over thousands of years cannot be true because there are many conflicting views. Is it not obvious that there must be mistakes or misinterpretations in the various religious movements, even though they have also brought good to the world? There are literally thousands of Christian churches under the umbrella of Christianity; thousands of Buddhist sects, many branches and interpretations of Hinduism, Sikhism, Judaism, Shintoism and so on. Clearly, no single religious denomination has the whole truth, even though they all have different parts of the truth.

Sukyo Mahikari and religions

As I mentioned, Sukyo Mahikari's approach is to encourage people of all religions to practise giving the Light of the Creator God, and in this way, help to restore the original essence of religions – "God is Light".

Sukuinushisama invited Christians, including people of the clergy, to join Mahikari and become even more effective clergymen for their church; Buddhist monks and priests to become even more effective for their temples and followers; and Shinto priests to become better priests for their shrines and their people. Some of them did. There were also religious leaders from outside Japan, who thought highly of Sukuinushisama and what he stood for, even though they did not become Mahikari practitioners themselves (chapters 2 and 3).

In my own experience with the Mahikari organisation since the end of 1975, I have observed people from several religions become kamikumite, including people with roles as priests, ministers or other professional positions in their religion. As a primary course lecturer it has been inspiring to see people who have already been serving God with sincerity, give the Light of God to the followers of their religions. In New Zealand a Catholic priest attended a primary course that I conducted. There was also a Maori kamikumite who was a minister of the Ringatu (Christian) religion, before he passed away. In the Philippines two Orthodox Catholic priests attended the primary course. Two Lutheran ministers were amongst the candidates for the first primary course held in Sweden, when I was the lecturer. A Methodist preacher from Zimbabwe attended the course in South Africa when I was there. Two Hindu priests I met have attended the course. In Malaysia and Australia, there are some elders of the Sikh religion who have attended the course. In Australia, a Jewish rabbi received True Light frequently and asked kamikumite to purify his home and synagogue. After some months he attended the course.

The following is an excerpt of a letter that Father Joseph Carbonell, a priest of the Orthodox Catholic Church in Manila, wrote to me in February 1987, shortly after he attended the primary course.

Since the time I graduated from the Mahikari primary course, I have been busy trying my very best to share the ideas and practise the art of True Light. Truly, the results, as far as I am concerned, are amazing. Amazing in the sense that even if I have reservations on my own and those who receive the Light don't know nor believe in what I do, they get some relief from the malady they are in. On one Sunday right after I held mass, I hesitantly gave Light. The people came one after another, and for the whole day I raised my hand like never before. I only stopped for the evening mass at 6:30. What surprises me is that I never get tired . . .

Some months later Father Joseph published a report, 'More experiences of a Catholic priest' (Carbonell, 1987). Here are some excerpts.

It is already four months since I received the primary course and I can recount tremendous blessings therefrom . . .

Then as I raised my hand to give Light to other people, various kinds of miracles became an everyday occurrence. Two of the 13 candidates that God has allowed me to bring for the course in June were almost if not completely healed of their sicknesses. One had had goitre and the other had been suffering from diabetes and high blood pressure.

Two women who have had problems in not being able to have children became pregnant after a session or two of True Light. One is now four months, and the other, two months in the family way . . .

Thrice have I blessed houses that were considered to have spirits present. The residents found peace after the blessing . . .

Twice I have given Light to the remains of people who died unexpectedly. One had committed suicide and the other had died drinking hard liquor. Both seemed to have signs of struggle and difficulties before. Yet after the Light their bodies showed signs of tranquillity and peace. This is normally quite impossible even if a priest would bathe the remains with holy water and recite all the Catholic prayers.

These are a few of the blessings that God has allowed me to experience. These are the amazing things that have happened which I cannot explain from the point of view of human knowledge. Yet from God's viewpoint I do begin to understand that everything that I learned in that 3-day course is true, good and worthy of deep gratitude from morning till night.

Apart from my personal experiences, I have heard about a number of other professional religious people who have attended the primary course – Catholic and Protestant clergymen in different countries throughout Europe, Buddhist monks and priests in Japan (I met a Zen Buddhist priest who became a kamikumite when I visited Japan in 1988) and Shinto priests in Japan. Needless to say, apart from those with clerical roles, there are many more followers of these religions who are active practitioners of Sukyo Mahikari.

I am not implying that the numbers of Mahikari practitioners who have clerical roles in different religions are high, nor that such cases represent mainstream views of their religions. It is just interesting that it happens at all. It shows that there are religious leaders who have found value in the art of True Light and the teachings of the Mahikari organisation.

Some of these people have indicated that they now have a better understanding of the essence of their own religion and that they can be of greater help to their followers, families, friends and acquaintances. Others have said that they cannot easily accept all the teachings of Sukyo Mahikari, but that within their own religion there are also teachings that they cannot accept or understand easily. In such cases they have put the particular teaching in question 'on hold' until they acquire more experience and understanding.

I believe that as people practise giving the Light and living the universal laws, the true and correct aspects of the different religions will become clearer and be reinforced. Errors and misinterpretations will come to be discarded in a natural way.

This is how science progresses as well. Certain hypotheses are revised or even deleted as a result of new data based on more recent research. If an error is encountered, it does not mean that that particular field of science has to be discarded or that the essence of the old approach is bad. It is a sign of our maturity as human beings to recognise that within religions, as in science, education, medicine and every other field, things progress and not everything one believed in the past is necessarily true for the present. If one believes that the world is flat when it is really round, one will not be able to navigate properly, no matter how strong the belief.

As a person of Christian background, I found that Mahikari teachings and practices clarified and gave me a deeper understanding of the basic doctrines of Christianity. For example, the expression "God is Light" (or variations of this) in the Bible became a living reality as I practised the art of True Light. Similarly, the text, "In the beginning was the Word, and the Word was with God, and the Word was God" (John 1:1), was difficult to understand without deep appreciation of the spiritual essence or functions of words *(kototama)*. I believe that "Let Thy Will be done on earth as it is in Heaven" refers to the divine plan, Su God's plan to materialise the condition of the divine world in the physical world.

For me, Mahikari teachings and practices not only clarify many Biblical passages, but give much more detail about certain topics. For example, the concept of reincarnation is not explained clearly in the Bible although there are some passages which indicate that people believed in it in ancient times. In Mahikari there are detailed teachings about reincarnation, and living evidence can be obtained by practising the art of True Light. Similarly, Mahikari enables people to learn about and understand matters such as karma, possessing spirits, sin and impurity, the realm after death, salvation, the plan of God and many other topics that are only briefly mentioned in the Bible. From my studies, Mahikari teachings also give details on important truths that have never been revealed to humans before.

These are some glimpses of how I, with my Christian background, have been able to reconcile Sukyo Mahikari with Christianity, and actually gain a deeper appreciation of both. I have met Buddhist kamikumite, Hindu kamikumite and kamikumite from other religions who say similar things.

I believe that Sukuinushisama is the man whose appearance was prophesied in the scriptures of religions (see chapter 3). In the Bible the words of Jesus are recorded, "I have yet many things to say to you, but you cannot bear them now. When the Spirit of truth comes, he will guide you into all the truth" (John 16:12-13). Buddha also predicted that a man would come from lay people, approximately 3,000 years after his death, to reveal the innermost depths.

As Sukuinushisama said in 1974, the year he departed from the physical world: *Basically, my founding of the organisation was aimed at reviving the spiritual power of salvation in all religions. Also, I have been given the mission to accomplish the teachings of Buddha and Jesus. That is why I never criticise any religion.*

Progress towards unity

To me, uniting religions really means integrating people who follow different dogma, ideologies and philosophies, including people who call themselves humanists, spiritualists or agnostics. It is not restricted to people who are in a clearly defined movement called a religion.

In many of the traditional religions there have been discussions and other moves by open-minded and concerned members regarding unity, as I mentioned earlier. The Bahai faith has always promoted the view that all human beings are to unite under the one Creator God. Within Christianity, steps have already been taken to unite various denominations within the Protestant Church and also within the Catholic Church. For example, I am pleased to see that the original division of Lutheranism into two broad camps does not exist anymore. The World Council of Churches, a church organisation representing Protestant, Orthodox and Anglican denominations from all over the world, has as its main objective the promotion of unity amongst Christian churches and collaboration with other religions in order to help overcome the divisions that exist between people. As part of its activities, the World Council of Churches has organised many important meetings and initiatives related to unity and the search for peace.

On 14 November 1994, Pope John Paul II said in his publication, *Toward the Coming of the Third Millenium,* "*Christianity, Judaism and Islam stem from the same origin. We should offer a prayer at Mount Sinai in the year 2000 for their unification.*" According to the media, the Pope was quoted as saying that all religions should now unite, not just Christian denominations.

Professor Hans Küng, a religious philosopher and former adviser to the Pope, has provided a set of common denominators amongst the world's religions. These were presented to the Parliament of World Religions in 1993 in the hope that a common basis for global peace could be found, a proposal called the Global Ethic. In his more recent book, Küng (1996) developed the concept of integration further with essays from the fields of politics and culture, the humanist perspective, as well as Judaism, Christianity, Islam and some eastern religions.

The Reverend Marcus Braybrooke (1996) has presented a history of the World Congress of Faiths, showing how its work has provided a basis for the growth of inter-religious understanding and cooperation.

In her book, *Many Paths, One Truth,* Carol Addlestone (1997) pointed out the remarkable similarities in a number of ethical values (faith, gratitude, interactions amongst people, to name a few) between eight long-established religions – Hinduism, Buddhism, Taoism, Confucianism, Zoroastrianism, Judaism, Christianity and Islam. Her work has enabled people to see the common ground in religion and promote the view of unity amongst people.

The mission of the United Religions Initiative (URI), a movement that was first set up in San Francisco, is to create a permanent assembly where the world's religions and spiritual communities will gather on a daily basis, in prayer and meditation, dialogue and cooperative action, to make peace amongst religions so they might be a force for peace amongst nations. The URI has groups on every continent planning its strategic development, organising regional conferences and carrying out research and development work to build worldwide commitment.

The role of ethics in all disciplines is increasingly emphasised. His Holiness the Dalai Lama (2000), for instance, has proposed straightforward and practical ways of practising ethics for the new millennium. He considers that any new hope for the millennium rests on the transformation of people's minds and attitudes, resulting in a new outlook and way of thinking. This will mean a new way of relating, as he himself has demonstrated in his inter-faith work. As a great Buddhist leader, he advocates making pilgrimages to the sacred sites of other faiths, for example, and has described his personal experience at Lourdes, a place considered sacred by many Christians.

In 2000, the United Nations took the unprecedented step of holding The Millennium World Peace Summit of Religious and Spiritual Leaders (28–31 August 2000, New York), a gathering of about 2,000 people, the first time that the United Nations has become involved in religious and spiritual issues on such a grand scale. This came about as an inspiration to the organisers that if world peace is to become a reality, it cannot be left in the hands of political leaders and related government bodies only, but must involve religious and spiritual leaders as well. They worked together to discern shared commitments to peace, expressed in a document, *Declaration for World Peace*. The Secretary General of the United Nations, Kofi A. Annan, said: "This gathering of the world's pre-eminent religious and spiritual leaders in a united call for peace will hopefully strengthen the prospect for peace as we enter the new millennium."

An international conference, held in Tokyo in 2000, a dialogue between representatives of Jewish and Shinto culture, also serves as a step towards the integration of religions, I feel, as scholars have reported some common aspects in ancient Judaism and Shintoism. For years I thought that the Jews and people of Japan were of completely different cultures. It is very interesting to see that there are specific similarities. Since religions today seem to be quite different in many ways, the practitioners of those religions would probably be more inclined towards tolerating, respecting and even making moves towards integrating with other religions, if they discovered that they had common threads in their past.

In this regard, I believe that the Hikaru Memorial Museum in Takayama, with its permanent displays and changing exhibitions on various aspects of ancient history that reveal common ground amongst diverse cultures, also plays a significant role in helping to unite people of different backgrounds and ideologies.

As I indicated, the main way Sukyo Mahikari can contribute to the integrating of religions, I feel, is to enable people from different backgrounds to practise the art of True Light and the universal laws. This does not mean that Sukyo Mahikari hopes to replace the various religions or to be the leader of religions. Sukyo Mahikari is not a religion in the traditional sense as it is open to people of all religions and backgrounds and deals with universal laws for all humankind. All the major religions come from the same common origin, the Creator of heaven and earth. The Light and the teachings can help people to recognise that they come from the same Creator God and that it is not necessary or desirable to have conflict. Every religion can contribute valuable aspects towards the actualisation of a more peaceful coexistence and neutral prosperity for everyone. In this way they can work together to achieve a better world. In maintaining such a common purpose, individuality, diversity, freedom and flexibility are to be encouraged. Unity does not mean uniformity.

It is like nature. A garden consists of many different kinds of flowers, shrubs, trees, vegetables and the like, which all coexist and co-prosper if they are taken care of according to the laws of nature. There is no feeling on the part of nature or human beings that a rose, say, is better than a daisy, or an apple is better than a peach, or that one plant is to control the rest of the garden.

Similarly, as regards the realm of human beings, Sukuinushisama and Oshienushisama have taught that it is not appropriate to regard humankind as "of one colour", but to welcome the differences and, in fact, to take preciously the different ethnic, cultural and other aspects in order for God to make a "beautiful tapestry of many colours". On one occasion Sukuinushisama said:

. . . if people try to unify humankind under one ideology, this would be contrary to the plan of God. If a civilisation was constructed under these lines, it would be a monochrome (single-coloured) civilisation.

Our civilisation is not meant to be like that. Although it is necessary to do away with what is wrong, God wants a civilisation that is like a gigantic tapestry of multi-coloured thread in which all kinds of beautiful shades of colours are combined and synthesised, that is, a civilisation where different nations will display their own wonderful characteristics in all aspects.

The same principles apply to individuals. Although each person's characteristics must be correct, with goodness, beauty and truth, this beautiful individuality should be woven together in the form of families, society, and then made to manifest into a great tapestry as a nation. In this way, our civilisation should be one of unity in which the characteristics of individuals live and shine through vividly.

Academic studies of Sukyo Mahikari

Research studies of religions can also help to achieve integration of religions, if conducted in a spirit of open-mindedness and cooperation. There have been several academic studies of the Mahikari organisation, particularly by anthropologists, sociologists and researchers in related fields, who consider it a religion (Koepping, 1967; Davis, 1980; Hurbon, 1991; Cornille, 1991; 1994; 2000; McVeigh, 1992 a, b, c; 1993; 1995; 1997; Young, 1993; Somers, 1994; Melton & Jones, 1994; Knecht, 1995; Bernard-Mirtil, 1998; Bouma, Smith & Vasi, 2000; Matsunaga, 2000; Clarke, 2000). Coming from an academic background myself, I am pleased to see that different researchers are studying the Mahikari organisation. Good research studies by neutral investigators can help humankind to learn about this organisation with less bias than there may be from some Mahikari members, who may report about themselves or their families with much emotional content and who may not see everything in perspective. On the other hand, if researchers make interpretations or draw conclusions from insufficient data, or if they are biased and conduct their research with pre-formed conclusions, the value of the studies becomes questionable.

By and large, where the researchers cited above reported facts and figures, events, case studies and so on, the studies provide valuable information. It is unfortunate, however, that there are areas where some of the researchers have misinterpreted their observations or have drawn hasty conclusions from too little observation. For example, Davis (1980) gave informative data and case studies of Mahikari people's experiences, based on research he did in Japan over a few months. He is the first academic researcher (a sociologist) to publish a detailed book on the Mahikari organisation and is therefore frequently quoted by subsequent researchers as being an authority on the subject. However, he admitted that he could not believe in the reality of the very phenomena he studied. He wrote: . . . *I accidentally came upon an exorcistic group called the True-Light Supra-Religious Organization, known as Sukyo Mahikari in Japanese, this sect turned out to be the most primitive religious community I had ever encountered in Japan.*

I found little in Mahikari that I could empathize with personally. Its belief in spirit possession, its idea that 'medicine is poison', its latent ethnocentrism and manifest occultism, taxed patience and scholarly objectivity alike (p. *vii*).

He also said that he was not enthusiastic to practise the art of True Light, but instead "much preferred to sit quietly in the empty room beneath the church, interviewing members and recording their miracles and encounters with the spirit world one by one" (p. *x*). With all due respect for the valuable contributions, I feel that it would be difficult for anyone with such a strong and biased view to be objective in drawing conclusions from the observations made. Davis could not accept that True Light produces effects and concluded that the "more dramatic possession experiences I observed in the dojo seem best accounted for by the psychological concepts of dissociation and hypnotic suggestion" (p. 143). In addition, he concludes there are ". . . four ways in which okiyome heals: by ritualizing social interaction, by catharsis, by the quiet restoration of confidence, and by creating a new persona" (p. 159).

Subsequent researchers keep citing many of his views as plausible. I have been an active scientist for more than 10 years and a practitioner of Mahikari for more than 28 years, and there is no doubt whatsoever that there is a very real power in the practice of True Light. In fact, this is the central issue of the Sukyo Mahikari organisation. It is the main reason that people join the organisation, I believe. Without this, the teachings, procedures and customs within the organisation would have little attraction for most people at the beginning. What particularly impressed me about Sukyo Mahikari in the early days was that I could demonstrate the existence of the power of True Light on beans, bacterial growth, bread, plants and animals, in other words, non-human systems – which rules out the implication that the results of True Light may be due to suggestion or belief. Even though my first book on Mahikari (Tebecis, 1982) is cited by most researchers, I feel that this important point about the demonstrable power of True Light has not received sufficient attention in academic studies of Sukyo Mahikari.

McVeigh has published prolifically on Sukyo Mahikari. He became more involved with Mahikari, and over a longer period, than the researchers before him, and he described many aspects of Sukyo Mahikari in painstaking detail. This is admirable. However, it is unfortunate that some of his conclusions and opinions weaken otherwise thorough and detailed studies. For example, in one study McVeigh (1992b) correctly pointed out that achieving purity is one of the central issues in Sukyo Mahikari. However, he concluded that "The centrality of the concept of purification in Mahikari should alert us to its political nature . . . Such a system of thought does not just come into existence. It is the product of conscious decisions made by social actors over the course of time" (p. 100–101). In other words, he implies that the Mahikari organisation has a hidden agenda in trying to keep members by not being totally honest.

Such a view surprises me. Why be suspicious and look for obscure reasons to explain why people do what they do in Sukyo Mahikari? The Light of God really does purify. It can be experienced and demonstrated. The power of the Amatsu Norigoto prayer of purification can also be experienced and demonstrated. It seems to me that McVeigh would have come to different conclusions had he had more experience with the practical aspect of giving and receiving True Light. Nevertheless, it is commendable that he attended the primary course and seriously studied Sukyo Mahikari in other ways.

Hurbon (1991), in a report on a study of Mahikari in the Caribbean, stated that "Every illness is deemed to have its source in the action of 'possessing spirits' (p. 246) . . . Medications and surgical interventions are considered to be 'barbaric' and 'superstitious' practices which one must get rid of as quickly as possible in order to become receptive to the benefits of Mahikari" (p. 247). These statements are simply not true. Sukuinushisama pointed out that most, not all, problems stem from spirit disturbance and therefore, in general, the resolving of spirit disturbance is important. However, he also explained that mental and physical aspects have to be taken care of as well. In Sukyo Mahikari it is recognised that medication and surgery have harmful effects (something that is becoming well known by many people in society and is reported by medical doctors), but that sometimes it is necessary to undergo such treatment (see chapter 6). In such cases one is encouraged to be grateful for the medical profession and the treatment received. It has always been the aim of Sukyo Mahikari to achieve a harmonious integration of spiritual medicine and conventional medical science, that is, a holistic approach to care for the spirit, mind and body.

As regards spirits, Young (1993) stated that "The amulet is thus a shield against harmful influences from the outside, but spirits already residing in one's body can only be dislodged by undergoing the exorcism ritual called okiyome (p. 246) . . . possession is an induced or learned behaviour. That is to say, it occurs only inside the practice hall during the exorcism ritual (p. 247) . . . Spirits . . . are malevolent and therefore dangerous, but they are not absolutely evil either" (p. 247). Unfortunately, such statements are inaccurate and give a mistaken view of the approach in Sukyo Mahikari concerning spirits. As pointed out in chapter 4, the whole aim of giving the Light is to purify people spiritually, mentally and physically as well as any spirits attached, with the purpose of achieving spiritual elevation and salvation for both the people and the spirits attached to them. There is no view in Sukyo Mahikari that possessing spirits are necessarily malicious either, any more than people in the physical world. After all, such spirits may even include one's dearly-loved, deceased father or grandmother. Moreover, possession does not occur by moving into a Mahikari Centre, but is something that is more or less a continuous condition in people. It is simply that at a Mahikari Centre such conditions are sometimes uncovered more clearly through the practice of True Light.

McVeigh (1993), in a study on the role of the body in Sukyo Mahikari activities, concluded that "the body becomes an arena in which cosmic powers – that is, possessing spirits – act out a morality play involving key normative principles" (p. 141). It seems to me that McVeigh has not understood the key issue in Sukyo Mahikari, as he stated later: "Though the word okiyome literally means 'purification', members often use it to refer to an exorcism ritual. However, according to members, okiyome is not exorcism . . . Nevertheless, I believe that this activity, if compared to other similar activities in Japan's religious landscape, both current and past, is in fact an exorcism ritual" (p.142).

Cornille (1994) said that: "the worldview of Mahikari is based on a syncretism of Shinto, Buddhist, and Shamanistic elements . . . The Buddhist influence on Mahikari manifests itself in the beliefs in karma and reincarnation . . ." (p. 92). The truth of the matter is that any similarities between Sukyo Mahikari and religions is due to the fact that religions have various degrees of understanding of universal laws in their teachings, so one would expect to find similarities. As regards karma and reincarnation, for instance, mystics and philosophers from amongst the Celts and Druids, the ancient European races before the advent of Catholic Christianity, certain ancient elements of Judaism and Christianity, Pythagoras, Plato and the Greek mystics, the Sufis, Buddha, the third century Mani and his successors, the yogis and the Hindus of India, people of China and other countries of the East – all these and more have spoken of reincarnation and the law of cause and effect. I do not think that belief in karma and reincarnation can be equated with having a "Buddhist influence".

Amongst the conclusions of many of the cited researchers is that the aim of True Light is healing. I can understand that many would gain that impression if they have limited experience with Sukyo Mahikari, as I explained in chapter 2. However, healing is not the aim. All kamikumite are taught the aim of the art of True Light at the primary course, in study classes, through divine books and (in many

Mahikari Centres) by a sign on the wall: *The aim of the art of True Light, purification, is not to heal disease, but to purify the person's spirit, mind and body, in order to revive the original power as a child of God, eventually becoming divine in nature. The art of True Light is thus a great spiritual practice of salvation which stems from God's great love, a practice enabling all humankind to participate in the holy work of accomplishing the divine plan.* The healing and other benefits of the Light of God are a valuable by-product when efforts are made in directing oneself towards God and being of use to fulfil the divine plan; they are not the main focus of attention (see last part of this chapter).

More recent academic researchers have made efforts to obtain information by conducting research based on participant observation and by verifying their intended interpretations through thorough consultation. Bernard-Mirtil (1998) is a researcher who has made rather accurate observations of Sukyo Mahikari through long-term study.

A study of Sukyo Mahikari in Australia was made by Dr Wendy Smith, an anthropologist, and the results were published by Bouma, Smith & Vasi (2000). She pointed out that ". . . Mahikari members emphasise that the aim of giving the True Light is for purification . . . True Light is best accompanied by the individual's grateful attitude . . . ultimate aim – spiritual elevation" (p. 80).

"People within Mahikari emphasise that the experience of receiving the transmission of True Light is the most important aspect in trying to understand Mahikari. Intellectual understanding alone is not sufficient" (p. 79). She also reported that "According to Mahikari teachings, 80 per cent of health and other human problems with emotional and mental states, relationships and even economic matters, are caused by attaching spirits". True Light is "to purify and help these spirits" (p. 80). Dr Smith participated in various Mahikari activities on a number of occasions as an anthropologist. She wrote, "I too experienced the 'experiences' that Mahikari members talk about – a painful toothache was alleviated and I was able to do without the prescription glasses I normally need for reading" (p. 79). Also, "The atmosphere of the centres is very bright and positive, and the attitude of members is very friendly, welcoming and sincere. The humility of senior members and their altruistic concern for individuals and humankind leaves a deep impression" (p. 83).

Similarly, Matsunaga (2000) has made a largely accurate report on Sukyo Mahikari in the United Kingdom, no doubt because she approached her research as a participant (including participation in the primary course, although she did not receive the sacred locket, Omitama), held interviews and analysed questionnaires – all over a reasonable time period. Also, she did not try to overdo the interpretation of her observations. A common approach of some of the previous researchers on Mahikari, I feel, was to draw rather strong conclusions from very limited observations. I can also understand that the early researchers would have had extra challenges to overcome when the Mahikari organisation was small and not so well-known, there was little or no literature on Mahikari in English, and there were differing views about some issues even within the organisation as it developed (see chapter 2).

§

This is not the place to go into a detailed appraisal of all these academic studies. There are accuracies and inaccuracies. I am merely pointing out some of the more glaring anomalies to show how otherwise good studies can be weakened if they include speculation that is unjustified. One glaring, serious mistake in a research report will tend to make already well-informed readers dismiss the rest of the paper as of little use, even if the rest is accurate. A problem in academic circles is that other researchers tend to quote statements previous authors have made, and these views then become propagated from one to another, gradually taking on the appearance of truth, even though the original premise may have been totally unjustified. I am familiar with this because I used to write research reports myself.

I would like to encourage people who research religious movements, and make three suggestions so that their work can be more valuable. Firstly, that they try to experience thoroughly, preferably long-term, and with respect and an open mind, the phenomena they write about. Secondly, that they put effort into accurate description in their report without trying to interpret everything and drawing firm conclusions. Thirdly, that after they have written up their research report, they show it to appropriate experienced practitioners of the religious movement for comments (preferably more than once).

As regards the first, the importance of experience, take the example of cricket. Academic researchers who have never played cricket may spend months watching it, analysing the 'rituals' and the 'magic', speculating about why 'converts' have been 'recruited' for cricket, and so on, but they would probably make a number of mistaken interpretations and conclusions about cricket. Non-cricketers may be misled by their report and cricketers may dismiss the report as so far "off the track" that it could not be regarded seriously. Depending on the mistakes, the report may also infuriate cricketers or make them lose respect for academics. The report would not be of so much value in the long term. If, however, the same academics were to actually learn the basic rules of cricket, how to score, bat, bowl and field, from experienced cricketers by playing cricket themselves, their report would no doubt be more useful to both non-cricketers and cricketers.

I do not think that the various subtleties of cricket can ever be understood just by recording behaviour as an outside observer or by analysing responses to questionnaires filled out by the cricketers. Interviewing the players would provide some valuable information, but if the interviewer does not have any feel for cricket, and does not respect or take seriously the beliefs that cricketers themselves have about cricket, he would not be able to formulate appropriate questions or be sensitive to the different nuances in the answers. Yet that is how religious movements are often studied academically.

Certain things, particularly involving human consciousness, beliefs, behaviour and so on, cannot be understood deeply without personal experience. The usual academic approach using the 'scientific method' has emphasised being objective by studying the subject as an outside observer. This has certain merits, but I believe that a combination of both the subjective, experiential approach and the outside observer approach is necessary when it comes to studying humans. Alone, either extreme is limiting and can lead to incorrect conclusions.

It is possible to study Sukyo Mahikari effectively through a combination of both approaches. Rich, subjective experiences will be provided through being a practitioner of the art of True Light and building up experiences by receiving and giving Light to others. Doing demographic studies, collecting data through questionnaires and case studies will provide information of another kind. When academics combine the two aspects, preferably long-term, in my opinion their contributions will be far more valuable.

As regards points 2 and 3 – putting effort into accurate description and showing the intended publication to experienced members of the particular religion under study to consider their evaluations before making firm conclusions – I am surprised at how confident some researchers are in making interpretations and conclusions without consultation, based on information from limited interviews or questionnaires involving a small number of people and often conducted over a space of only a few months.

Showing the intended publication on a religious organisation to appropriate authorities in that organisation for their comments is a natural safeguard for researchers to learn from the views of people who are far more familiar with the issues under question than the researchers themselves.

Good research on religion is very valuable for people both within and outside the religion. Accurate information, not necessarily always favourable to the religion under study, can nevertheless be valuable, appreciated and respected by the members of that religion. It can help to achieve understanding, cooperation and unity of people with different beliefs.

Directing oneself towards God

I would like to convey my understanding of the essence of Sukyo Mahikari from a practical point of view, so it can be compared with religious practice in other organisations.

In the Sukyo Mahikari organisation, the term used to describe one's spiritual journey is 'going towards God' or 'directing oneself towards God' (called *kamimuki* in Japanese), an active path rather than a passive *faith* or a *belief* in God. It involves ongoing effort and practice. A Mahikari practitioner is called a *kamikumite*, which means 'one who joins hands with God', someone who has a strong link with God and is active in collaborating with God as a way of life, rather than being a passive *believer*, *devotee* or *follower*.

One's life does not necessarily improve automatically just by having a passive faith in God, simply believing in some of the laws of God or respecting the holy masters whom God has sent. It takes sincere efforts to revive the true self, the essence as a child of God, to its original condition. In other words, one strives to become divine in nature step by step. Another way of saying this is to reform the soul.

In my opinion, the most effective practice that facilitates this is the art of True Light. One gives Light to people for their purification and receives it as well, as much as possible. At the same time, one strives to elevate one's innermost attitudes and practise the divine principles in order to fit with the will of God. It is not a matter of simply knowing the teachings or preaching them to others, but a matter of practising them oneself and actually changing for the better. In this way, one can steadily achieve inner peace and harmony.

The ultimate aim is to achieve a heavenly condition on earth, so service to God and others is basic in directing oneself towards God. For the divine plan to be achieved, it is necessary to have families of love and harmony, and for this to be achieved, it is necessary for individuals to progressively attain health, harmony and prosperity on the road to becoming divine in nature. That is why self-improvement is also important, with the altruistic understanding that it is aimed for the higher good of everything – God, all humankind and the environment.

Some people – society in general, members of various religions, academics and others (even some kamikumite when they begin) – often mistakenly consider Sukyo Mahikari to be a kind of religion for healing or self-benefit. This is not so. The miracles and other benefits that occur are not the main aim, but hopefully, they can help people awaken to the power of God and motivate them to make greater efforts in directing themselves towards God.

It is good to become purified with the Light and to change from within, so that one's innermost attitudes are elevated. To give an example, a person may come to a Mahikari centre every day for years and other people there may think that he is very active in serving God. It may be so, but it may not. What is the motivation? If the person is coming only to become healthy for his own sake, his innermost attitude may be rather self-centred at first. However, if he develops his innate altruistic love to serve God (which includes helping other people and contributing to society), his innermost attitude can be said to be elevating.

Elevating one's innermost attitude is not something restricted to changing one's feelings, mood or thoughts. It is something deeper than the mind – the hidden aspect in the depths of the mind. Sukuinushisama taught that the mind's vibrations are related to the physical body whereas the vibrations from the innermost attitude are from the soul. Mental processes may play a role when making efforts to change, but elevating the innermost attitude is really like achieving a new paradigm shift, a new outlook on life, a new mindset, a new approach or belief.

Taking another example, a grocer may be very charming, polite, well-mannered and cheerful with his customers, but deep down he may not care about the harmful effects that many of his products, which are full of toxic artificial additives, may have on his customers. His innermost attitude may be, "As long as I can make a profit, that's all that matters." Another grocer may be equally congenial, but very concerned about providing only pure foods for his customers. He will not sell products that contain toxic artificial additives, even though he may lose some profit. His innermost attitude concerning business can be said to be more altruistic.

Efforts in directing oneself towards God are made not only in areas normally called 'religious activities' such as praying, giving Light and so on, but also in everyday life, in areas that are normally regarded as secular. The aim is to be God-centred (spiritually oriented) in all situations by becoming a good person in worldly matters – a respectable citizen in society, helpful to others and serving the community wherever possible. Going towards God includes becoming a person who is a good family member, who is achieving love and harmony in the family, who is striving to be a good role model at work. For children, it is important to study well at school, to follow their teachers' guidance and later in life to contribute to society in their professions in ways that fit with the will of God.

How do we practise divine principles in daily life? In Sukyo Mahikari there are many practical teachings – altruistic love, positivity, being polite and well-mannered, becoming bright and smiling and greeting others – teachings that are common to various religions. Amongst the common, everyday teachings for practice, the most basic are the three virtues – gratitude, humility and being accepting of the will of God. A basic goal is to try to become totally grateful for absolutely everything from morning till night. Humility is also important. There are various ways of practising humility, such as not attaching importance to oneself; seeing the good points and respecting others instead of judging them; being grateful to serve God despite having shortcomings and deep impurities. We also strive to positively show apology in deeds for mistakes committed (knowingly and unknowingly) in the past. Showing apology has nothing to do with feeling guilty (which is not really pleasing to God). It is an active practice of expressing regret, learning from mistakes, making a new, positive start and being active in compensating for one's errors through good deeds.

I do not think it is always easy to choose and practise certain divine teachings in daily life. Being human, we can forget or take things for granted. I find that participation in ceremonies, study classes and courses, as well as experience with True Light at a Mahikari centre usually provides inspiration and motivation to continue practising.

Another valuable approach to progressing spiritually, I feel, is to develop some good daily habits with divine matters at home – prayers to God in the morning and evening (including the Amatsu Norigoto prayer); care of one's ancestors; giving and receiving True Light with the people at home; reading the divine teachings; and purifying the home and surroundings with True Light. These good habits would be a part of daily life, as much as is possible in the circumstances.

What role does the Mahikari centre play? It is a place where people come to worship God, practise the art of True Light and offer other kinds of service to God, as well as learn the teachings and how to put them into practice so that there can be real elevation, genuine going towards God. That is, people receive education and train themselves, striving to reform their souls. That is why a Mahikari centre of a certain level is called by the unusual name of *dojo*, which means 'training place'. The Mahikari dojo is a place for training the soul. The expression 'Mahikari centre' is often used for dojo so that non-Mahikari people can relate to the Mahikari organisation more easily, but it is a training centre rather than a meeting centre. The word dojo in itself implies that the path of directing oneself towards God is an active process of making efforts, not a passive state of belief and waiting for benefits. If a judo practitioner neither trains himself often nor tries to tune in to the judo dojo instructor's guidance, he cannot expect to progress much. If he tries to grasp and practise his instructor's guidance and continues to train himself, he is likely to make ongoing progress. In the same way, people going to a Mahikari dojo have the potential to grow very much spiritually if they actively strive to tune in to God and grasp and practise the divine teachings as well as the art of True Light.

The practice of the divine teachings becomes significant when it is done willingly, whether other people are watching or not and whether one is at a Mahikari centre or somewhere else. Knowing a teaching in one's mind is a good beginning, but the aim is to practise it to achieve actual improvement. Similarly, the expression, 'service to God', is of significance when there is the heart of offering this service on one's own initiative, willingly, without expecting rewards. Understandably, we all progress at different rates. It cannot be helped if people begin self-centredly, but God is particularly pleased when people willingly offer meritorious deeds for God with the heart of wanting to fulfil God's wishes.

For example, in the case of prayer, it is good to commune sincerely with God by clasping our hands and kneeling before the altar of God. However, it is also important to strive to make daily life a living prayer, that is, to actually practise altruistic love and other teachings to demonstrate sincerity to God, to be living daily life so that it fits with the will of God. That is true prayer.

In my experience I have found that some people pray to God, attend worship ceremonies and similar activities in order to receive blessings from God. It is also common for people to turn to God only when they are desperate or involved in a tragedy. Conversely, many give up their faith in God when tragedy strikes, thinking that God did not help them. There is sometimes an attitude that it is God's job to make things pleasant as a reward for having some kind of faith in a divine being, no matter how weak that faith may be. However, it is best to seek to understand and practise the will of God, no matter what happens. Directing oneself towards God is not about focusing on self-benefits, but about being able to 'ride' the ups and downs of life, harmonising with the will of God.

There are ups and downs in the life of going towards God, just as in every other aspect of life. It is natural to undergo trials and training from time to time, even if one has the best of intentions and does one's utmost. After all, God's love has both a strict aspect and a tender, merciful aspect. Hardships, trials and problems on the path of directing oneself towards God are to be expected, not tolerated or considered abnormal. It is shallow thinking, a total misconception, in fact, to think that dedicated involvement in religion should result in nothing but sweet blessings. Hardships and trials are opportunities for improvement. From my experience, responsibility and commitment are necessary to continue to grow on the path of going towards God.

Once again, as a kamikumite, one is given the means and opportunities to grow rather rapidly, that is, become purified and spiritually elevated, making significant progress in going towards God in a rather short time, because one can practise the art of True Light in order to help others and improve oneself at the same time. On the other hand, one can also be in the Mahikari organisation for many years and yet not be as bright and cheerful, altruistic or spiritually elevated as others who are not kamikumite. It depends on the ongoing efforts. The idea of 'going towards God' or 'directing oneself towards God' involves *practising* the divine teachings with a willing heart, coupled with giving and receiving God's Light. God-centredness is really being practice-centred, and depends on how we actually live our daily lives.

These are some aspects of the essence of directing oneself towards God, which I am also trying to achieve, with different degrees of progress, as I go through the ups and downs of life.

Whole person medicine – spiritual, mental and physical

Whole person medicine – spiritual, mental and physical

This chapter deals with some health concepts that seem to lack commonsense – fever is good; pain can be appreciated; misfortune is a change for the better, to name a few – but experience shows that they are, in fact, true. In my opinion, Sukuinushisama has given teachings that make it possible to understand what disease really is, why it is increasing, why many people have not achieved long-term health and what can be done about it. One can learn about the original, basic condition of the universe, which is health, harmony and prosperity; some misconceptions about disease; the influence of spirit disturbance; how innermost attitudes affect everything; and many more things related to health. Some of these views are not what is believed by people in general. From my observations, however, through practising the art of True Light and the teachings, one can actually experience increasing health and help others to achieve it. The following is my understanding of some key points regarding health.

Principle of cleansing

Understanding the principle of cleansing is essential to achieving long-term health. According to divine teachings, everything in the universe was originally created by God to be in perfect health, harmony and prosperity, and the principle of cleansing was established to maintain that condition. To put it simply, when things become contaminated, processes come into operation to restore the original condition of cleanliness so that things function properly. These processes are natural and unavoidable. The principle or law of cleansing cannot be bypassed any more than the law of gravity or any other fundamental law. One can only help or hinder cleansing, depending on how one lives. Obviously, due to the excessive impurity produced by humankind, much of the world is no longer in an ideal state of health, harmony and prosperity, but it can eventually return to this original condition if people grasp and practise the principle of cleansing.

Cleansing in nature
Cleansing (also called cleaning or purification) processes operate continuously in nature – in plants, animals, the soil – in fact, the whole environment, the whole world and the whole universe. Wind,

rain, sunshine, snowstorms, lightning and other natural weather phenomena are some of the processes that keep the earth, the air and all plants clean in order to sustain life and enable everything to operate properly. If there were no wind or rain, for example, dust and other contaminants would accumulate on plants, preventing them from carrying out photosynthesis and effective respiration. Eventually plants would not be able to provide enough oxygen for humankind. If there were no wind or rain, many people in industrialised cities would die from the smog. Sometimes the cleansing phenomena of nature become very intense – major floods, bushfires, earthquakes, volcanic eruptions, tidal waves and the like. Due to such natural processes of cleansing, the earth, all nature, including the creatures within it, function in ways towards maintaining health, harmony and prosperity.

Cleansing in humans

Just as there are cleansing processes in nature, they also occur in the human being. The end stages of many cleansing processes appear as discharges – a runny nose, pimples, boils, coughing up phlegm, vomiting, perspiring or eliminating waste in the toilet. If the intake of contamination is greater than the output, these mechanisms are not able to cope sufficiently well and eventually more severe cleansing symptoms appear in certain body areas. Buildup of impurity in body tissue can have detrimental effects both because of its toxicity and also because it becomes hard with time. The latter is due to what the divine teachings call the 'principle of hardening', namely, materials become hard with time. The condition is then described by labels such as 'kidney stones', 'stiff joints', 'hardening of the arteries' and so on. These are just descriptive terms to indicate more serious cleansing in certain parts of the body.

In other words, *disease is nothing but cleansing*. In reality, there is no disease, sickness or illness, in that such a condition is not an attack from some mysterious source through no fault of one's own. It is precisely the result of the body's attempts to maintain purity, and therefore health, that symptoms of so-called disease appear, and the symptoms depend on how much one has promoted or hindered the natural mechanisms of cleansing in the past.

This does not mean that serious conditions can be ignored or treated lightly. Appropriate steps need to be taken. However, a sensible approach to cleansing is possible if one understands why it occurs.

The principle of cleansing is not an accepted concept in mainstream medicine today, but over the years, I have come across authors concerned with health who have promoted the idea, particularly in alternative or complementary medicine. I think it is interesting that over 2,000 years ago, Hippocrates, who today is referred to as the father of medicine, wrote "Diseases are crises of purification, of toxic elimination . . . The symptoms of disease are evidence of the body's natural curative reactions."

I have learnt that cleansing or purification enables everything in nature to function properly, and human beings to fulfil their life span. Hindering or preventing purification (knowingly or unknowingly) results in an increase of what is normally called disease and unhappiness, which are usually more unpleasant or severe forms of cleansing. Since the cleansing cannot be stopped, one's choices will largely determine the degree of pleasantness or unpleasantness of the cleansing.

Cleansing or purification in human beings occurs spiritually, mentally and physically, although it is usually not possible to separate the three categories clearly. Physical cleansing is probably the easiest to understand. Modern-day people are polluting their bodies and environment as a way of life, particularly through the use of artificial chemicals. Most of our daily food contains artificial additives such as colouring agents, preservatives, emulsifiers, agricultural chemicals and other substances of varying toxicity. Drinking water in most cities contains chlorine and often fluoride, both of which are poisonous. The air that is breathed in most cities is becoming increasingly polluted with exhaust fumes from vehicles and toxic gases from industrial installations. Many people routinely take medication, have injections, apply ointments and so on, as well as undergo surgery. The seas, lakes, rivers, roads and countryside throughout much of the world have become dumping grounds for all kinds of rubbish and chemical waste, much of which finds its way back to people via running water, circulating air and food chains. Even radioactive waste is becoming a serious problem.

A well-known fact in chemistry is that even though certain substances may not be so toxic individually, they can become very toxic when combined with other, even originally harmless substances. If we take in many different artificial chemicals in the body every day, there must be various chemical reactions which can form toxic substances.

Another well-known phenomenon is the gradual concentration of toxicity through biological food chains (biomagnification), something that was first brought to people's attention through the pioneering research done by Dr Rachel Carson (1962).

Still another alarming problem is the growing evidence that toxic chemicals soak into genes and chromosomes of the body and can lead to deformities and other abnormalities in descendants, even generations after the use of the chemicals.

The functioning of modern society involves much physical contamination, and the natural cleansing processes make up much of the disease and unhappiness that are occurring. I think it is easy to understand the need to clean up such impurities of physical origin.

Less well known is the fact that negative mental states can also generate impurity. Sukuinushisama taught that innermost attitudes, emotions and moods of negativity lead to contamination within the body. Mental states such as anger, jealousy, resentment, hatred, as well as slandering others, complaining and the like, lead to the formation of toxic micro-particles that gradually materialise as pus and other dirty material that contaminate the body.

Some of the impurity generated from negative mental states may be eliminated through physical discharge. Mental cleansing may also occur through unpleasant social interactions. For instance, if a person is blamed or criticised by someone, he is being cleansed mentally. Whether the criticism or blame is justified or not, he is receiving cleansing. Abuse, reprimands, criticism and conflict are all examples of mental cleansing. Ideally, it is best to avoid reacting to them with anger, fear, frustration or anxiety, as such internal negativity generates impurity. If one returns negativity with negativity, the cleansing does not occur so effectively, and in the future there will have to be extra cleansing. That is why even though unpleasant situations may not be enjoyable, they can still be appreciated if it is understood that one is being cleansed as a result. It is not only the cleansing but also the lessons learned that are valuable. Such situations are often trials to make one stronger for the future, or they may even indicate that there is something to change in order to avoid mistakes in the future.

Even less known by people in general is the matter of spiritual contamination and the need for spiritual cleansing. Spiritual impurities are produced by rebelling against the Creator God, transgressing divine will, killing or causing other kinds of suffering to human beings and animals, destroying nature, to name a few. If such impurity has not been compensated for in previous lives, it has to be compensated for in the present or future life, or it is transmitted to one's descendants. Depending on one's activities, impurities are either built up or erased over lifetimes as one goes through reincarnations. Compensation phenomena, usually associated with misfortune, are forms of cleansing in order to restore the original condition of health, harmony and prosperity, or happiness. This is a reflection of God's love, which is a balance of strictness and tenderness.

Spiritual cleansing of a more pleasant nature can occur through receiving the Light of God directly and thereby purifying the soul and the spiritual, astral and physical cells; purifying others with the Light of God and serving God in other ways; being involved in altruistic activities that lead to salvation, benefitting society and others. These are active, willing forms of spiritual cleansing.

Spiritual cleansing also refers to problems caused by spirits involving the physical body, the mind or something quite external such as materials. For example, cancer is often due to a resentful spirit who is trying to kill the person to whom he is attached in order to be avenged. The spirit often attaches to a body area or organ and gradually makes the cells become cancerous. The 'paying of the debt' through suffering by the cancer patient is his spiritual cleansing. Cleansing of that person may also occur through mental anxiety, depression, anger and all kinds of problems with human relations as a result of the cancer. On top of that, cleansing occurs because the physical body may be in pain and there may be a loss of body functions or organs, the need for an operation, the loss of money and so on. Undergoing various kinds of suffering, including clearly physical phenomena, results in cleansing, the removal of impurity, much of which may have been accumulated in previous lives. I do not think we can clearly separate and categorise cleansing into spiritual, mental and physical aspects, even though one aspect may seem to predominate.

A physical discharge of foul-smelling pus from say, the ear, does not necessarily represent only physical cleansing of medication or artificial food additives, but it may also reflect removal of impurity concerned with injuring the head of the attached spirit in a previous lifetime. In my experience, it is common for people to have disorders in certain areas of the body because they have caused suffering to others in those same areas in previous lifetimes. A tumour or cancer in a woman's uterus or cervix, for example, may indicate something to do with those organs in the past such as a previous abortion, rape or killing somebody with a sword in the uterus.

Any contamination of the physical tissue results in contamination of the astral and spiritual cells as well. Conversely, any cleansing of the physical tissue also reflects cleansing in the other two realms. Spirit, mind and body are interconnecting just like the different parts of a river, although broadly speaking, it is clear that there is an upstream, midstream and downstream.

Applying the principle of cleansing

In order to achieve cleansing effectively, I believe it is valuable to:
(1) Understand that cleansing is natural and essential.
(2) Appreciate the cleansing and show gratitude for it.
(3) Avoid further contamination as much as possible.
(4) Promote purification through the Light of God.

Understanding and appreciating the processes of cleansing
The first step is to recognise that processes of cleansing are natural and essential for survival, in fact, they are vital for the proper functioning of everything, for happiness and much more. Consider a car engine. It is only able to continue functioning well if the oil is changed, if it is lubricated, if the spark plugs, filters and so on are cleaned or changed regularly. The human body works in the same way except that things are considerably more complicated. Waste products are generated through metabolism and various other processes essential for life and the proper functioning of tissues throughout the whole body. These waste products, as well as the impurities generated inside and taken in from outside, have to be expelled somehow. This is what appears as mucus from the eyes and nose, wax from the ears, phlegm from the throat and so on. This does not mean that one is sick. Cleansing of the body may sometimes be uncomfortable, but if it is occurring, it is essential under the circumstances.

It is valuable to accept positively and appreciate the processes of cleansing, even if some things cannot be recognised as blessings at the time. For example, perspiration is a valuable, painless way of cleansing the body through the skin. Much of the toxin that is discharged through the skin is so poisonous that it would cause serious problems if it accumulated within internal organs of the body, so one can be particularly grateful for cleansing through the skin. On top of that, since vitality and the ability to perspire normally decrease with age, if one is able to perspire profusely, this indicates high vitality, something for which one can be very grateful.

Fever is another indicator of vitality. When a person's vitality increases, the power of cleansing increases, often accompanied by fever. Fever tends to increase in areas of the body where cleansing is occurring. It is not a sickness or something bad, something to be feared and stopped, but something to rejoice about, as it indicates that the heart is working well and valuable cleansing is going on. Dirty, hardened toxic material melts from the heat and is discharged from the body, a step towards better health. That is why normally one would not try to stop fever.

Sukuinushisama taught that if a person has a high fever, it is important to be grateful; not to chill the person (with ice packs, ice water, refrigerated air – these are dangerous); to make sure that the person drinks and eats (or that nutrition is provided artificially if the person cannot eat); and to receive God's Light, which melts toxins directly so that the body does not have to consume excessive energy to melt the toxins. With such a sensible approach, there is no need to be fearful of even very high fever. In general, the higher the fever, the more the really old, dangerous, highly toxic impurities melt and become discharged. If a situation appears serious, of course it is important to seek medical advice, but in general, if the guidelines are followed, fever is no cause for alarm, but simply something to appreciate.

Some people have mistakenly said to me that fever may cause convulsions and brain damage in children. However, medical surveys have shown that a high temperature does not automatically lead to febrile convulsions. Some children are simply more disposed to fits than others, and such fits may be brought on by a number of different causes. Besides, there is no medical evidence that febrile convulsions do long-term damage. It is the sudden chilling or lack of nutrition that sometimes leads to problems, not the fever itself.

Nowadays, more and more doctors and medical researchers are reporting that high fever is not necessarily bad for people and need not routinely be lowered using medication. For reference, the *Annual Report For The Year 1996* on Obstetric and Paediatric Mortality and Morbidity of Victoria, Australia, included the following:

. . . *it is rarely sensible to use paracetamol to treat fever. Fever is part of the normal host immune response to infection. . . . Paracetamol does not provide effective prophylaxis against febrile convulsions (Journal of Pediatrics 1995;126:991-995).*

Pain can also be an indicator of cleansing, and therefore one can be grateful for it. Pain often occurs when once-hardened toxins melt and move through body tissues as they are discharged. Pain can occur due to the toxicity of the melted material as it stimulates nerves; the swelling of the toxins; the peeling off of toxins from tissues; a reflex reaction induced to accelerate the discharge; the expulsion of toxins through constricted channels causing irritation; or other reasons. People may also experience pain in an area where there is an attached spirit causing or experiencing the pain. Whatever the reason, pain usually reflects a step towards health, and gratitude for it will promote the cleansing, making it more effective (and therefore less painful). Of course, one does not inflict pain purposely. When it occurs, however, one tries to be grateful for it, as much as possible. Naturally, a commonsense approach to pain is also important, as there may be times when pain indicates a problem requiring medical attention, such as a bone fracture.

I have learnt that recently absorbed toxic substances are usually liquefied and eliminated easily. In general, the older they are, the darker the colour, ranging from colourless to yellow, orange, brown, green and black or combinations of these colours. The darker ones are usually more dangerous to the body, therefore one can be even more grateful when they are discharged. For example, in the early stages of a cold or influenza the main discharge is colourless (runny nose) with little or no pain. At this stage the most recently accumulated and most easily mobilised toxic substances are discharged. As cleansing progresses, fever rises and the greater melting of toxins results in more unpleasant symptoms such as aches and pains throughout the body and darker discharges from the nose and throat. Though less pleasant, these indicate the removal of older toxic substances that have been difficult to move, and one can be even more appreciative.

The common cold is actually of great benefit, not something to be anxious about. It is a natural cleansing that appears in the form of fever, perhaps some pain, runny nose, sore throat and so on. With the Light of God such cleansing processes can be promoted so that it is not necessary to become fatigued and have long-term suffering from more severe cleansing. Normally a cold may last for many days, even up to a week or two. With the Light of God, however, because the Light in itself has the power to melt toxins and also gives vitality to the person, the cleansing may last for only a few days. More effective elimination of toxins is achieved more quickly and afterwards the person generally feels clear and refreshed.

If one understands the value of cleansing, one would not normally stop fever, diarrhoea, coughing or other cleansing processes with medication. Sometimes, however (particularly when a condition is serious or in an emergency), medication may be the best option as a temporary measure (see *Dealing sensibly with the 'downstream'*, later in this chapter), but normally, it is best to use it only when it is essential.

It is best to combine wisely and sensibly the existing medical science with the principles of spiritual medicine so that long-term, overall improvement can be achieved through cleansing. At times people have formed the misconception that Sukyo Mahikari forbids the use of medication or other medical treatment, but the truth is that the organisation promotes the addition of a new dimension – the spiritual aspect – and advises a sensible approach when dealing with the physical and mental aspects, in order to achieve the ultimate goal of medicine, to free people from disease and improve health (see *Yoko Clinic*, near the end of this chapter).

With this understanding, one would avoid the use of synthetic chemicals unless they were necessary. Not only do they hinder the discharge of toxic material already accumulated within the body, but they are additional contaminants in themselves that remain in the body and eventually harden, I believe. If symptoms are suppressed by medication without solving the cause of the problem, the same or different symptoms will appear later and eventually the body's cleansing mechanisms will not be able to cope with the poisons and there will be inescapable cleansing in the form of more severe suffering. That is, the accumulation of toxic substances in body tissues may eventually lead to malignant growths and terminal diseases. Such suffering goes on in the spiritual realm after death in the physical world (see chapter 4).

As in everything, ups and downs also occur in cleansing. Even though not all aspects of cleansing will be pleasant, the cleansing can nevertheless be appreciated. People in general view a disorder in the body, say, as a bit of bad luck, usually having been innocent of receiving it, and therefore expect sympathy from others and want the condition to be stopped as quickly as possible. This is understandable, but we all have to take responsibility for our condition. If we transgress God's principle of cleansing, we receive appropriate outcomes. Whether we have done so in ignorance or wilfully in the past, we still have to reap what we have sown. The best choice is to appreciate the processes of cleansing.

Sometimes severe phenomena of cleansing occur in nature such as major floods, bushfires, earthquakes, volcanic eruptions or tidal waves, which are processes of cleansing not only for nature but also for humankind. The damage or loss of property, injury and even death are cleansing phenomena that people have to go through sometimes. I do not think it is easy to go through such cleansing (also called compensation), but it is helpful to understand that if one receives suffering in some way, it means that one must have caused suffering to others in the past or one's ancestors did so, according to the law of cause and effect (see chapter 4). Another way of saying this is that things are arranged according to the principle of balance. If people have caused others to drown in previous lifetimes, they may compensate by dying in a flood in this lifetime. If they have robbed or exploited others in the past, they may lose their belongings in various

165

ways, such as in an earthquake or bushfire. Everything is arranged so that we reap our rewards, whether it be compensating for our misdeeds or receiving blessings as a result of altruistic deeds.

Sukuinushisama explained that when one leads a life of voluntary compensation, offering meritorious deeds, God makes arrangements in which a potentially major misfortune becomes minor and a potentially minor one disappears altogether. Of course, God's arrangements are very complex so one can never judge a situation, but in general, I have found this pattern to be very apparent.

It is unreasonable to expect God not to give cleansing, because God has made this law or principle, that things have to be cleansed in order for everything to function properly. The freedom we have is to choose *how* we approach the cleansing. If one has killed a person in a previous life and does nothing about it in the present lifetime, there may be no other way for the person to compensate than by being killed. This is passive compensation. On the other hand, if that same person awakens and conducts his life in a way so that he can erase impurity by helping others, with the Light of God, for instance, and working for the plan of God in various ways (active, voluntary compensation), he may not lose his life in a tragedy, but escape with minor injuries.

Using another example, say a person in a previous life had exploited the citizens of a village and through this became very wealthy. If he has not compensated for such ill-gained wealth up till now, he may lose his house and belongings as a result of a natural disaster or he may go bankrupt in his business (passive compensation). However, if the same person awakens in time and uses his materials with the desire to serve God and society, doing altruistic things (active compensation), he may only lose some of his property in the same disaster or have financial difficulties, but avoid the collapse of his business. Whatever the cleansing, it is still out of God's love to clean up the person materially so that he can improve. It is therefore good to express gratitude for all kinds of cleansing, whether pleasant or unpleasant, as it would not happen if it were not essential for improvement. On top of that, since suffering indicates that one has caused suffering, it is good to show apology in deeds.

Even if people are sincerely trying to follow divine will with their own understanding, they will receive cleansing through misfortune if they transgress divine laws unknowingly. For example, a person may pray to God sincerely, but will still receive the consequences of contaminating himself by artificial chemical substances or, say, misusing materials. Conversely, even if people are not aware of divine laws but live in harmony with them, they have a better chance of receiving more pleasant or fortunate arrangements in their life.

The teaching about showing gratitude for cleansing in no way implies that the cleansing is to be viewed light-heartedly. It is natural to have sympathy and a caring heart for people who are undergoing great physical or emotional suffering, for instance. It is just that if one realises why one is going through misfortune, and that it is a step for the better in one's life, one can try to be positive about the cleansing as much as possible, thus leading to a better result.

Avoiding further contamination

As one becomes purified, it is best to avoid contaminating the spirit, mind and body or nature again. As one progresses in purifying the soul and spiritual body, which includes resolving spirit disturbance, one avoids making further spiritual impurities that would arise from living a life contrary to divine principles and hurting others.

I have learnt that one's innermost attitudes and mental state influence one's physical condition and surroundings. Since hate, resentment, anger, jealousy and other negativity lead to the formation of impurities, it is good to change towards being cheerful, positive, smiling, joyful and laughing – all these have a good effect, not only on one's spirit, mind and body but also on others as well. One practice that Sukuinushisama recommended was to look into the mirror and put on a smile before going to bed, then sleep with a cheerful, positive attitude, as this would help to make everyday life more positive.

From a physical point of view, there are many ways of providing food, drinking water, running businesses, operating transport systems or whatever that need not contaminate anywhere near as much as they do at present. Avoiding contamination of the body with harmful, unnatural substances such as artificial food additives, agricultural chemicals, medication and other synthetic chemicals, unless required as a temporary or an emergency measure, is also a big step towards maintaining physical purity.

The practice of True Light

As indicated earlier, receiving the Light of God to the soul results in the removing of impurities from the soul, including impurities that have accumulated from previous lifetimes. In addition, the Light purifies the spiritual, astral and physical cells, as well as spirits attached to the person.

If the soul and spiritual body become impure, it becomes easier for spirits to attach to the person. As spirits receive the Light of God, they may awaken to their own wrongdoings and cease disturbing the person. Usually, however, this does not happen easily unless the person recognises that his own past deeds have caused the spirits to suffer and demonstrates apology through service to God and improving his innermost attitudes (see chapter 4). If the person has not awakened in this way, the cleansing process may involve greater suffering, caused by the spirit. This may take the form of greater marital conflict, a disease, an accident or the like.

As explained, we can never be sure to what degree a problem is of spiritual, mental or physical origin. The cause is usually a mixture of the three. Even a very obviously physical incident such as falling over and gashing one's knee may have a spiritual cause. The accident may have been caused by a resentful spirit. That spirit may be attached to the area of the knee and may well have sustained some leg injury in a previous life from the person to whom he is attached. In any case, the Light of God radiated to the wound will help to purify the spiritual, astral and physical cells and promote healing. It also has the power to melt toxins and give vitality to the person, thus promoting the cleansing. Irrespective of the cause of the condition, True Light has a good effect.

If a person lives a God-centred life and practises purification with the Light of God earnestly, it is possible to gradually become free of illness, free of undue tiredness and other symptoms of poor health or reduced vitality. Such a way of life will eventually enable people to die comfortably in old age. Only a few hours' sleep a night is normally sufficient if one is purified enough. Efficiency can be increased through living like this. I believe that progressively better health is really attainable through the path of Sukyo Mahikari if one perseveres with a sense of commitment and responsibility.

Experiences with True Light concerning health

My experience has revealed time and time again that people's thoughts, emotions and desires are not entirely their own but a combination of those of their real self and those of their attached spirits. Because most people have made others suffer in previous lifetimes, spirits attach to them for revenge or other reasons, causing depression, irritability, anger, loneliness, nervousness and other problems. Such symptoms may also be caused by possessing spirits who bear no grudge but are suffering in similar ways themselves. Problems such as insomnia, neurosis and nervous breakdowns are often (though not always) caused by ancestor spirits who may be desperately trying to indicate something important to their descendants, such as a need for food. Sometimes physical disorders are due to attached spirits. The following accounts of experiences are a few glimpses showing that many disorders can be understood and overcome to different degrees with the art of True Light and changing one's lifestyle to fit with the will of God.

Roman centurion

Amongst my early experiences indicating that a person's disorders were due to an attached spirit involved a man in Canberra, in 1979 (Tebecis, 1982). His son, Chris Flaherty, a 22-year-old clerk, reported the following experience.

My father, Irwin, who is not a kamikumite and knows very little about Mahikari teachings, decided to receive True Light regularly. He started receiving Light every couple of days or so. In the early sessions he displayed no obvious reactions during Light on the forehead. After a few weeks he occasionally shed tears, moved slightly and answered questions in a meek, almost inaudible voice. In every session his face looked humble, and he was bent over in a stooped position.

It was rather surprising for me, therefore, when I was giving him Light on the forehead the other day, his face suddenly changed from a gentle expression to a proud, haughty, very strong and determined expression. Just as suddenly he changed his posture from being bowed forwards, to a straight back, arms smartly placed at his sides, with his chin raised and hands clenched military-fashion as though standing to attention. A little later he lifted up his arms suddenly and went through motions as if ceremoniously taking off a helmet and tucking it under his left arm. In one continuous gesture he moved his right arm as though replacing a sword in its scabbard and brought it smartly up to his chest in a salute. He then began pompously speaking what seemed to be Latin. It felt as if a Roman centurion had walked into our lounge room from a previous age!

When I had finished giving Light my father admitted feeling quite moved by the experience. He said that he does not know any Latin and was quite surprised to hear 'himself' speak in a foreign language.

In this experience, during True Light to the forehead, an attached spirit manifested and behaved like a Roman soldier, speaking what appeared to be Latin. Chris's mother also witnessed the session and confirmed his account. Both were present at all subsequent sessions in July and conversations with the spirit were recorded on tape.

From the behaviour and words spoken it became clear that the attached spirit had been a military leader. As a Roman centurion he had commanded one hundred men. He despised any form of weakness and made no secret of holding the Greeks in contempt. He revealed that during battle he had pushed some of the enemy men down a snow-clad mountain, where they had perished. (While the attached spirit was saying this through Irwin, Irwin was huddled over in a crouching position, shivering and showing other signs of being intensely cold, apparently because of the condition of the attached spirit.) The spirit later revealed that he was attached to Irwin's throat and chest.

On another evening when Irwin was receiving Light the attached spirit made him behave in a way that strongly indicated a reliving of the spirit's agonising death throes. The following description was later written by Irwin's wife, Lorraine, who witnessed the episode.

From the actions and different types of heavy breathing we watched what surely must have been the agony of this spirit's death. No actor could have portrayed the event with more realism. The death must have been caused by a sword or long knife in the left side of the stomach area, just below the rib cage. He clutched this area with both hands, his facial expressions indicating intense pain mixed with disbelief that it was actually happening. He slowly removed his right hand from the wound and looked at it for a little while, then wiped it on his right leg. This leg also seemed to be injured because he grimaced as if in pain when he touched it and used both hands to move it. Then slowly his right hand went back to the belly wound and clutched very tightly at what must have been the handle of the lethal weapon. After much agonised breathing and behaviour that suggested physical exhaustion, both hands pulled the knife or sword from the stomach and Irwin suddenly slumped over on the floor in a crumpled heap. Weakly, he seemed to beckon men (presumably) to continue with the battle.

Lorraine told me afterwards that Irwin had been a soldier from 1948 to 1957 and had been an excellent platoon commander. The troops under his command had invariably excelled in various kinds of military exercises. She said that many times during their marriage Irwin had woken up during the night and asked his wife to rub his back because he felt icy cold. He also often complained of the cold during the day when other people felt comfortable or warm. Sometimes he woke up because of a severe cramp in the right leg (never in the left one). At one stage he had spent three months in bed with his right leg in plaster because of Schlatter's disease. The main problem had been between the knee and the hip, the very area his attached spirit, the 'Roman centurion', had clutched in pain. Moreover, Irwin has a birthmark just above the right knee. Between the age of 30 and 40 Irwin had suffered intense pain from ulcers just below the rib cage on the left. At the age of 28 Irwin had had a non-malignant growth (papilloma) removed from his throat. At the time he began receiving True Light he had a disorder of the thyroid gland which had to be treated by surgery, according to his doctor. As a result of True Light, however, the problem was solved without surgery. All these disorders were precisely in areas where Irwin's attached spirit had presumably been injured.

To me this case suggests that Irwin's career abilities, various experiences and physical disorders were related to, influenced or determined by those of his attached spirit. In my opinion, classical behaviour or personality theories do not take into consideration the very real and significant influence of attached spirits and have therefore never been able to explain behaviour or personality satisfactorily. On top of that, clear physical symptoms may be due to attached spirits, something not considered in conventional medicine.

Soldier

The following is another example of how an attached spirit was responsible for the modification of a person's behaviour (Tebecis, 1982).

Mr K., a 60-year-old war veteran of Canberra, had been suffering from various kinds of unpleasant nocturnal experiences ever since the Second World War. One was a recurring nightmare about the graves of 13 Australian soldiers, one of whom (Eric C.) had been a close friend. This dream was always associated with fear, horror, confusion and nocturnal emission (wet dreams). Since the war Mr K. has been plagued by sexual malfunctions. Even during the day, when in emotional states, he sometimes experienced sexual emission. There had been no such problems before the war. For years he had sought medical advice, but nobody could give him any explanation for his problems, let alone help him. It was just labelled "a war injury".

On 31 December 1979, a staff member of Canberra Mahikari Centre gave True Light to Mr K. and an attached spirit who could speak manifested. The spirit said that his name was Eric C. and that during the Second World War he had attached to his good friend Mr K. because he had not known what to do after being killed by the Germans in a battle in Egypt. He said that he was still suffering from his injuries. He also revealed that he had a strong desire to have sex with women, but could do little about it. In the dialogue during the spirit investigation the following remarks were made.

Eric C.: *Get me a woman, get me a woman!* (Repeated several times). *I want sex; I need a dame.*

Staff member: *But Mr K. is happily married.*

Eric C.: *I don't care. Let's form a foursome.*

Afterwards, the staff member asked Mr K. about his war experiences, and amongst other things he related the following story.

On 23 July 1942 during the Tel El Eisa campaign in Egypt against the Germans, while serving with the 2/48 Battalion Australian Imperial Forces, I had occasion to visit Eric C., a friend of mine in the front line, while my company rested in reserve. On arrival I saw that he and twelve other Australians had been killed by a machine-gun burst from a German tank. Their graves were dug in an area not bigger than an average size room. I have had horrifying nightmares of this scene for over 37 years. Strangely enough, this nightmare has always preceded wet dreams.

To me, the most likely interpretation is that Mr K.'s recurring nightmare and sexual problems were due to the emotions of the spirit of Eric C. who had attached to him. This case showed me once again that attached spirits can have a profound influence on people's mental and physical condition.

Stroke

The physical effects of True Light can be just as startling. I still remember my emotion when I visited my mother in Mount Gambier in South Australia, about a couple of years after I attended the Mahikari primary course. My mother knew that I had come across something valuable while in Japan, and often received Light herself. One day she asked me whether I could go to give Light to a 40-year-old Italian man who used to work in the local sawmill but could not work anymore after he had had a stroke. Apparently there was a blood clot in his brain and he could not move the fingers of his right hand anymore. I felt sorry for this man and went to his home. He could not speak much English so our conversation was very limited, most of it through his daughter, who was the translator. I gave him Light on the forehead and then on the back of the head and neck, after which I directed the Light through the area where he told me he had had the stroke. As the minutes passed, I noticed that he was flexing certain fingers of his right hand. After I finished the session of Light he looked very excited. I came back again the next two nights and gave him Light again. After True Light three days in a row he could move his fingers freely, something he had not been able to do since he had had the stroke about three years ago. It seemed that the Light of God had largely melted the blood clot and whatever else had been preventing his nerves from functioning.

As a one-time neurophysiologist, this amazed me because I know that often the brain cannot be operated on after a stroke as surgery invariably destroys too many central nervous neurones, which do not recover. Many people with brain damage normally have no hope of recovering other than through the body's natural healing mechanisms. The Light of God is particularly valuable in such cases.

Discharge of old medication

In the early days of my involvement with Mahikari, I sometimes wondered about the teaching that I first heard in the primary course in 1975, that artificial chemicals harden and tend to stay in the body. I had used many kinds of drugs in my brain research and had had dealings with several pharmaceutical companies over the years. I had acquired the thinking of the time, that through urine, faeces or perspiration the body is soon able to expel all the medication that it takes in and that synthetic chemicals probably cause little or no harm providing one does not take too much at one time. However, not long after I came to Mahikari, I met several people who reported experiences of discharging medication from their bodies through receiving the Light of God, years after they had taken the medication. The following are two cases that occurred between 1976 and 1978.

Case 1

Judy Small, a 40-year-old nurse of Sydney, had taken headache medication in large quantities for many years, but for four years before she attended the primary course (March 1978) she had not taken any medication at all. In the middle of 1978, she had spent several days exchanging Light and offering other service to God (which also allows us to be purified). At that time, she developed increasing discomfort, which included a sore throat, swollen glands, pains in the joints and so on. The pains became so severe that she was scarcely able to walk or move normally. She consulted a medical practitioner for advice. At that time her urine had been thick with white sediment for several weeks.

The doctor did clinical tests which included sending a specimen of her urine to the Pathology Department of the Royal Prince Alfred Hospital in Sydney. The analysis indicated that her urine contained derivatives of the headache medication she used to take years ago. The report also indicated that she had taken it within the previous 12 hours! She had not taken any medication for the previous four years, so it seemed that the medication analysed had been stored in her body during that time and that the Light of God had melted it.

Case 2

Ananda Auhl, a 35-year-old secretary of Canberra, used to take headache medication daily when she was a younger woman. However, she had not been taking it for some years before she came to Mahikari. Some months after she had begun giving and receiving True Light, weeping sores developed on her scalp. These exuded a secretion that was unpleasant to smell and of great discomfort to her. Her head looked as if it was covered with little volcanic craters slowly emitting liquid. The Light did not seem to alleviate the problem quickly enough for her so she went to a medical practitioner for a second opinion. The doctor was very surprised when he examined her head, remarking that such a symptom used to be common years ago in people who took a certain brand of headache medication (the one Ananda had used). He said that he could not understand why she had that problem because the drug company had removed the particular compound that used to cause such symptoms. Apparently, that compound had been removed from the headache medication several years earlier. Again, the most likely conclusion is that much ingested medication normally stays in the body, and that it can be liquefied and removed by True Light.

Solving mental problems

Mental problems usually pose a big mystery for clinicians and people in general. The teachings of Sukyo Mahikari give insight into mental problems and provide a means of helping to solve them, to a greater degree than anything else I have come across.

In 1975–1976, while collaborating with clinicians in the Department of Psychosomatic Medicine at Kyushu University Medical School in Japan and becoming familiar with the scientific and medical literature on mental problems, I was surprised to learn how widespread mental problems were and how futile were the attempts at solving most of them. New labels were being used to describe abnormal behaviour and all kinds of approaches to treatment methods were being tried, but the fact remained that mental problems continued to increase. Many years have passed since I studied the literature on mental problems and I can see that the problems still continue to increase. In developed countries such as Australia, New Zealand, the United States or Canada, statistics show that every fourth to sixth person has at least one severe mental problem during his or her lifetime. Severe depression is at least ten times more prevalent today than it was 50 years ago, and it now occurs a full decade earlier in life than it did a generation ago. Suicide is increasing at an alarming rate as well, particularly amongst the youth.

Classical psychology has been defined by some as the study of consciousness, by others as the study of behaviour. Neither approach recognises the existence of the soul of a person or the person's attached spirits. I believe that this is why many academic studies of human behaviour and mental activity are so limited. Orthodox theories in psychiatry and psychology often consider human personality to be a product of the person's genetic material inherited through the family line and the modifying influences of the environment, before and after birth. In recent years, however, many open-minded scientists have concluded that behaviour, personality, mental activity and many things about humans cannot be explained satisfactorily in terms of genetics, the environment or a combination of both.

In my opinion, the main reason for mental problems is disturbance by spirits, an aspect that has not yet been recognised in mainstream medical science. This is not denying that sometimes mental disorders occur from physical causes such as a head injury or a biochemical deficiency, or from mental causes such as trauma, fear and the like. However, these are a small proportion of the total. Even when there are physical or mental influences, the original cause is usually deeper – due to a spirit. For example, a person may sustain brain damage from an accident, but the cause of accidents is usually resentful spirits.

The most common form of medical treatment for mental disorders is medication such as tranquillisers, anti-depressants, sleeping pills and the like. In the vast majority of cases the medication does not solve the problem although it sometimes temporarily suppresses symptoms, and can therefore be valuable in helping the person to cope. In many cases, however, it does not help at all. There is also evidence that sometimes medication can be dangerous, not only to oneself but to others (Cornwell, 1996). Since disturbance by spirits is the cause of most mental problems, treatment with medication, electric shock, psychodrama, discussions or other forms of mental and physical intervention usually do little or nothing to solve the basic problem permanently. The cause of the mental problem may be resentment by an attached spirit who had been ill-treated in another lifetime by the person or his ancestors, and such a spirit usually does not lose resentment unless he is appeased or awakened to why the ill treatment happened and how it can be solved.

When a person is manic, severely depressed, suicidal or schizophrenic, the marked changes (sometimes dangerous to oneself or others) occur because there is a spirit attached to the person causing or experiencing those mental states. That is why when people lose control they often say afterwards, "I was not myself" or "I was possessed." There are many cases where sensible, well-educated people suddenly commit suicide. Most of the time one cannot distinguish between one's own will and that of attached spirits.

The understanding and resolving of spirit disturbance are essential not only for resolving most mental disorders, but are also important for explaining and coping with the everyday problems of so-called ordinary or normal people. Outbursts of rage, feelings of anxiety, loneliness, confusion and various other common mental states are often due to attached spirits. It is when attached spirits gain considerable control over a person that symptoms become more pronounced and the person may be labelled a manic depressive or a schizophrenic. In other words, I believe that a psychosis is merely an extreme form of something that goes on in ordinary people much of the time. Sometimes a possessing spirit who has a deep grudge will succeed in killing the person to whom the spirit is attached. This may take the form of suicide, murder, death in a car accident or other tragedy.

To resolve spirit disturbance, that is, to save the attached spirit, is generally a difficult and long-term process, but it can be achieved step by step (see chapter 4). Physical and mental methods may help the person to cope during this time. This is one valuable aspect of conventional medicine. For example, anti-depressant medication may prevent a person from, say, committing suicide long enough for that family to become devoted to serving God, erasing the family's impurities and eventually reach the point where the person is not controlled by the possessing spirit. Similarly, mental approaches such as counselling, caring attitudes, learning to relax and the like all play a valuable, supportive role in helping people to cope. The biggest problem is that they generally do not touch the cause of the problem, the attached spirits, and that is why mental disease is increasing, no matter how well-meaning counsellors are and no matter what kind of medication is used.

Case of schizophrenia

My first experience of solving a mental problem with True Light occurred shortly after my return to Australia from Japan at the end of 1976.

A rather attractive 23-year-old lady came to my house in Canberra because she was desperate for help and had heard that I was involved in "some sort of spiritual healing". She told me that for the past seven years she had been taking tranquillisers every day, and that on three occasions she had been institutionalised in a psychiatric hospital for many months at a time. She said that she had had schizophrenia from about the age of 13. She often became vague, vacant or withdrawn and her moods often swung from euphoria to depression for no apparent reason. She had tried to commit suicide on three occasions. She said that she was also very unhappy in her love affairs; every time she fell in love with a man, the relationship broke up after a few weeks or months.

I gave her a session of True Light, and shortly afterwards she remarked that she felt much better. When she came back two days later, however, she said that she had spent a terrible weekend with even bigger swings from euphoria to depression. I reduced the duration of the sessions of Light for the next two weeks, after which I gave standard sessions of about 50 minutes each about three times a week. She continued receiving Light in this way until she attended the Mahikari primary course five weeks later. After the course she gave and received Light three or four times a week on the average.

About two months after I had first met her, an attached spirit manifested while I radiated True Light to her forehead. The spirit was very uncooperative and showed obvious discomfort from the Light. I tried to investigate why he was there, but he refused to cooperate until about one month later. On this occasion the lady had come to the Mahikari Centre distraught and unsettled. When I gave her True Light to the forehead, the spirit manifested and abused me, saying that I was interfering with him. He confessed he had been the young lady's husband in a previous life of about three hundred years ago. He admitted that he had been ruining all her love affairs because he considered that he owned her, that she was his possession. What surprised me most was that he said he was a Quaker!

From the way the spirit spoke, I gained the impression that he was a cold-hearted, ruthless, strong-willed individual. It was no doubt because of his frustration and strong personality that the girl's moods swung suddenly and paradoxically from euphoria to depression. On the day of his confession, however, after some minutes of God's Light, he suddenly became much more gentle and indicated that he would like to leave the girl's body and return to the spiritual realm. I chanted a special Mahikari divine song while radiating Light to the girl's forehead, and during this time she suddenly rolled to the ground limply. Shortly afterwards she opened her eyes. Her face expressed great joy and there seemed to be a radiance that I had not observed before. When the session was over she told me that she had not seen things so vividly and beautifully since she was a little girl. She felt a new consciousness. It seemed that the possessing spirit had left.

Follow-up sessions revealed that the possessing spirit had certainly left the girl's body. Her new outlook on life and behaviour were stable. She did not need to take medication anymore, nor was she subjected to violent mood swings as before. The last time I heard from her, she had been having a warm, loving relationship with a man for more than a year, and it looked likely to continue.

This was a rather rapid resolving of a spirit disturbance and as a result, of the mental problem. I think that God permitted this experience to demonstrate to me, a one-time neurophysiologist, that the power of God is effective in solving mental problems. In my usual experience over the years since then, I have found that it is usually much more difficult to solve such problems and usually requires serious involvement and support from family members. Nevertheless, it is very encouraging to know the cause of most mental problems and that there is hope to solve them (see also chapter 7 in Tebecis, 1982). Even though the problems are difficult and normally take a long time, one cannot say that mental problems are necessarily incurable.

Mahikari therapists

Throughout the world more and more Sukyo Mahikari mental health workers are incorporating the practice of divine teachings and the Light of God in their professions. When I met Dr Jeffrey Friedman, he was a clinical psychologist in Los Angeles who practised gestalt therapy in order to provide patients with a bigger picture of their current situation and to take responsibility for parts of themselves which they may not like to accept. He is a kamikumite and practises the art of True Light in his daily life, at the Mahikari Centre, in his home and in his workplace. He saw approximately 50 out-patients, most of whom were depressed, and also conducted weekly therapy groups for hospitalised psychiatric patients, most of whom were suicidal. At the Fourth Yoko Civilization Research Conference held in Japan in November 1995, he presented four cases of remarkable improvement in his patients as a result of enabling them to view their lives in positive ways, ways that he had acquired from the divine teachings of Sukyo Mahikari (the importance of elevating innermost attitudes, being humorous, being positive and grateful, offering prayer and so on).

Sydney psychologist Gabrielle Meegan has also integrated a spiritually oriented focus in her clinical work ever since she attended the Mahikari primary course in 1993. At that time she was working in a community home for psychiatric patients with serious mental illnesses who had been hospitalised on a number of occasions. She gave True Light to the work environment and to some of her clients, and assisted them to develop more positive innermost attitudes, particularly through the practice of gratitude. A number of her clients made remarkable progress and these successes were acknowledged by other staff members even though they were not aware of her methods.

Later she began working part-time in private practice and part-time at the University of Sydney, in the counselling service area. She regularly purified her work environment with the Light of God. The most obvious change she noticed from the purification was how much easier it was to support students to manage their difficulties in a spiritually oriented way. She was also able to give True Light to students regularly, usually at least one per day, as well as a few staff members. Amongst the changes she was able to achieve in her students was for them to see their problem situations as a learning opportunity; to identify the behaviours in the lecturer with whom they were having difficulty; to make a commitment not to practise such behaviours themselves as well as to reflect whether they had ever behaved similarly; and to identify and focus on the strengths of the lecturer. As students were able to practise these principles and shift their innermost attitudes from dissatisfaction, complaint and judgement to non-conflict and humility, they noticed amazing improvements in their situations.

Ms Meegan herself regularly gives Light at the Sydney Mahikari Centre and elsewhere and makes a point of studying Sukuinushisama's and Oshienushisama's teachings, particularly those concerned with her work as a health practitioner. As part of the Health Group of Sydney Mahikari Centre, she and the other members make a practice of regularly tuning in to God through prayer; studying divine teachings; giving Light to health-related environments; and making efforts to become God-centred people.

In short, she found that her clients were able to achieve greater harmony within themselves and in their relationships through receiving Light and by working to develop more positive innermost attitudes. Also, as a therapist she noticed that she felt surprisingly positive and energised by the counselling sessions when she was able to use spiritually oriented principles and give Light to her clients. When she gave and received Light regularly, she experienced much less stress and greater joy in her work as a psychologist. Dr Friedman and Ms Meegan are two Mahikari mental health clinicians whom I know personally. I have heard about others throughout the world.

Belief in spirit possession and that it can cause mental and other problems in human beings has been held for many thousands of years by people of probably all cultures. Even though it is not mainstream thinking in modern medicine, in recent decades there have been a number of therapists who have provided convincing evidence for this phenomenon.

In his book *The Psychic Dimensions of Mental Health* (1982), Dr Arthur Guirdham, a British psychiatrist, concluded that every form of severe mental illness can be caused by spirit interference, a view he reached after decades of clinical experience.

Psychologist Dr Edith Fiore has been helping people for decades by performing what she calls "spirit depossessions". In her book *The Unquiet Dead* (1987) she has reviewed the historical observations about spirit possession, clinical evidence for spirit possession, how to do a depossession and related matters. Dr Fiore speculates that nearly everyone at some time in their lives is plagued by some degree of spirit interference.

Dr William Baldwin (1995, 2003), a pioneer in the field of regression therapy and "spirit releasement therapy", has treated thousands of clients who have discovered that attached spirits had been causing their problems.

Professor Dinesh Bhugra's book *Psychiatry and Religion* (1995) also shows that many mental health clinicians are recognising the importance of the spirit, not only the mind and the body, when dealing with mental problems.

There is a *Journal of Regression Therapy*, published by the Association for Past-Life Research and Therapies (California), which consists of articles and book reviews on aspects of past life research and therapy with an emphasis on clinical material and its phenomenological and psychological aspects. In 1995 the International Association of Spiritual Psychiatry was formed. It publishes a regular journal and aims to give psychiatry back its original vocation as a medicine for the soul and spirit.

The old approach – material-centred medicine

We cannot underestimate the value that medicine has provided and continues to provide for mankind. Conventional medicine has contributed greatly towards helping people with ailments, particularly as regards diagnosis, biotechnology and patient care. Valuable as these are, however, we can also see that progress in modern medicine does not seem to result in a reduction in disease. On the contrary, many of the well-known or 'old' diseases continue to increase. New forms of disease are continually arising. The reasons why people 'catch' diseases are often not understood. Moreover, there is growing evidence (from medical professionals in particular) that much of the treatment of disease is in fact making people worse, a phenomenon called iatrogenesis.

Why are there such limitations in conventional medicine? From my understanding, the major reasons are:

(1) The approach is largely material-centred, that is, the topic of health and disease is largely considered in terms of the physical body of a person. Little consideration is given to the mind and even less to the spirit. Even when the importance of the mind and spirit are recognised to some extent, the order of priority is usually back to front, that is, body, mind, spirit, rather than spirit, mind, body.

(2) There is little or no understanding about the major effect of spirit disturbance on disease.

(3) Disease is viewed negatively, as an 'attack' that should not be tolerated but eradicated.

(4) The emphasis is on removing symptoms rather than the cause.

(5) There is an excessive use of medication and surgery. Let me elaborate on these points in turn.

(1) From my studies and experience I have been led to believe that everything in the universe, including the life of human beings, operates according to the principle of spirit first, mind next, body follows. There is, of course, an influence of the body on the mind and spirit, but the greatest influence is from the spirit on the mind and the body. In my opinion, preoccupation with physical symptoms, physical approaches or physical interpretations will never lead to breakthroughs in understanding and maintaining health or alleviating disorders. How many clinicians conduct their medical practice by considering the spiritual condition of their patients? How many even believe in the existence of the soul and spiritual body? At least there is a growing number of clinicians today who are beginning to understand that the mind has an influence on the body, the so-called mind-body approach. Even here, however, the emphasis is still on the body rather than on the mind. In other words, the importance of spirit, mind and body is not deeply understood in medicine, and where it is understood to some degree, the order is usually back to front.

(2) Closely related to this is the fact that most people in the medical profession (and in society in general) have no understanding about spirit disturbance. People in general do not even believe in the existence of spirits, let alone the fact that interference from spirits has a major influence on disease. Sukuinushisama pointed out that at

least 80% of what is called disease, sickness or illness is due to spirits, something that I have been personally able to verify over many years. I feel that if the medical profession does not investigate this seriously, there can be no major breakthrough in achieving long-term health.

(3) Another problem is that disease is viewed as something bad, something that one is attacked by and that has to be removed as quickly as possible. There is little understanding that the symptoms of disease reflect the processes of cleansing, which are as natural and essential as all the other processes that operate in nature. All that one can do is to either assist or hinder these processes. Medicine would do well to recognise this, I feel, and aim to promote the cleansing process in positive ways that can be as efficient, safe and pleasant as possible.

(4) Most of medicine emphasises removing distressing symptoms, something called symptomatic therapy, rather than achieving the health of people. The use of alternative approaches such as massage, acupuncture, herbs and the like is also mainly symptomatic therapy, as the emphasis is on removing pain or giving other relief. Most people think seriously about their health only when they have some obvious unpleasant symptom, rather than being concerned about maintaining or improving health. Clinicians as well often feel obliged to give quick relief to their patients rather than deal with the matter so that their patients are able to improve in health in the long term. It is encouraging to see that in recent years, more and more health professionals are focusing on improving and maintaining the health of their patients, but overall, we cannot deny that most medical treatment today still focuses on ailments.

(5) Another major problem is the excessive use of medication and surgery, both of which often have considerable harmful effects on people, not only physically, but spiritually as well. In fact, the spiritual consequences outweigh the physical ones. According to divine teachings, surgery, injections and ingestion of medication are not only harmful because of the injury and defilement of the physical body but because of the injury and defilement of the spiritual and astral bodies as well. Moreover, if the spirit is damaged or polluted in this lifetime, the problem is carried over to existence in the astral world and may even materialise to different degrees in the next lifetime as well. That is why physical removal of symptoms does not necessarily cure the problem but only temporarily takes it out of sight and may result in worse consequences in the long term.

Of course, such consequences have to be weighed against the benefits that medication and surgery provide. They may be the best option to choose in certain circumstances, particularly if the condition is life-threatening or serious. Every situation has to be assessed on its merits so that the person or family concerned can make informed choices about what to do (see *Dealing sensibly with the 'downstream'*, later in this chapter). Nevertheless, it has become well known, particularly in the medical profession, that much of the time medication is taken unnecessarily when the condition is not life-threatening or serious, or even when the doctors themselves say that it probably will not help. Similarly, surgery, despite its great value in sustaining life or alleviating a disorder at times, is frequently practised 'just in case', when its value is even questioned by many in the medical profession.

Sukuinushisama warned people many years ago about the dangers of excessive medication and surgery. He said that the day would come when medical doctors and the community would realise the limitations of many forms of medical treatment. There would be a limit to human life power or vitality if people continue to use medication excessively, there would be many new and unusual diseases, an increasing incidence of incurable diseases and a growing resistance by old diseases to long-accepted treatment by medication. He indicated that artificial chemicals can even affect the genes and chromosomes.

In recent years more and more clinicians and other professionals have been pointing out some of the limitations and dangers of the old, conventional approach to medicine (Illich, 1976; Taylor, 1979; Mendelsohn, 1979; Weitz, 1980; Scheibner, 1993; Walker, 1993; Fisher, 1994; Australian Vaccination Network, 1998; Lazarou, Pomeranz & Corey, 1998). For instance, Lazarou *et al.* (1998) ranked adverse reactions to medication in hospitals to be the fourth to sixth leading cause of death in the United States – of the order of death from accidents and respiratory disease and greater than that from pneumonia and diabetes. It is obvious that disease is not decreasing but increasing. In some cases it is only the labels that are changing, but there are also many old diseases that are making a comeback, and new ones keep appearing. If the traditional approach of medicine was really successful on a large scale, hospitals would tend to be empty and the number of hospitals and doctors would decrease as modern medicine progresses. However, the very opposite trend is occurring. Many dedicated doctors, nurses and other health professionals sacrifice much of their time and desired life-style for the sake of their patients. It must be frustrating and heart-rending for them to see many of their patients get worse and even die, despite their best efforts. Would it not be beneficial for medicine to examine a possible new approach? Valuable though conventional medicine is, I believe it is important to develop spiritually oriented medicine in order to achieve an even more effective and safe approach to health.

Truly holistic medicine

Incorporating a spiritually oriented approach

Holistic (whole person) or true medicine is a combination of spiritual medicine, mental medicine and physical medicine. The spiritual aspect is the most important and plays the most influential role in a person's health, as it does in every other aspect of life. As Sukuinushisama indicated in a teaching entitled "The trinity of medical science":

> True medicine (great medicine) which can save the world is the trinity formed of spiritual, mental and material (physical) medicine. Materially oriented, so-called cellular sciences, medical sciences of the mind and the body (psychosomatics, psychology, psychiatry and others) and spiritual medicine or the resolving of spirit disturbance, must work together to form an inseparably interconnected, three-dimensional cross. However, spiritual medicine should account for at least 80% of all medicine (particularly internal healing) and mental and material medicine together should account for only 20%. Since at the present time it is just the opposite, the number of sick people just increases, and diseases become more and more malignant. Our movement is dedicated to reversing this trend and initiating in Japan a great science for the benefit of humankind.
>
> Accordingly, we are in a time when it is extremely important for doctors to quickly realise that basing medicine as they have up till now on materialism is medicine's greatest fault and to speedily awaken to the importance of spiritual medicine, and to cooperate in this movement, not for the sake of medicine, but for the sake of all humankind.

The spiritually oriented approach in medicine requires understanding that the most important aspect of the human is the soul, which continues to exist after death in the physical world, and that the condition of the person at the present time is really the net result of many lifetimes of activities, which also includes the activities of the person's ancestors and the ongoing influences of the person's attached spirits. Even though we do not remember what we did in our previous lives, if we understand the law of cause and effect, we have to take responsibility for any disorder we have. Even if a spirit is trying to kill a person, that person must have killed people in the past, so without a heart of apology, shown by appropriate action, there may be no improvement. This is why innermost attitudes are important.

If a person receives medical treatment in a passive way with the attitude that it is the doctor's job to 'fix the problem', then no matter how skilled or well-meaning the doctor is, there may not be much improvement. Similarly, even though the Light of God is valuable in order to solve most problems, if it is looked upon as 'treatment', 'curing' or 'healing', even an initially encouraging result may not be permanent.

In many cases help given to people using the material-centred approach may be only temporary, totally ineffective or even harmful. Certainly, if the cause is not treated, there can be no long-term solution. For example, if a person breaks a leg, it may appear to be entirely a physical problem. The bones may be set by the doctor and the leg will eventually heal. This is very valuable without doubt and is one area where conventional medicine is of great value. It is good to recognise, however, that a deeper cause of the accident may be spiritual. It may have been caused by a spirit who was seeking revenge for something the person had done to him in a previous lifetime. It may be that the spirit had tried to actually kill the person but only managed to break the leg because of the special protection the person received. Whatever the reason, if the attached spirit is not saved, he will continue to disturb the person and there may be other injuries or even death in the future. In other words, the removal of symptoms without treating the cause of the problem can only give temporary relief at best.

Experience shows that it is good if all members of a family (or as many as possible) are active in erasing their impurities, particularly if a person's condition is very serious, as this usually indicates much impurity on a personal and ancestral level. For instance, most kinds of cancer are due to resentful spirits and this usually reflects deep family impurities. If there is only one member, say the one with the cancer, who is interested in serving God, that person may still not be saved from death. If other family members are involved, it may make the difference between life and death. However, since life in the physical world and birth in the astral world is only a transition anyway, ideally one is not attached to the outcome but leaves everything up to God. Even if a person dies from cancer because the body has degenerated too much to continue supporting life in the physical world, it is still valuable if the person is able to be purified thoroughly with the Light of God and the other family members are serving God. This means that the person can be saved quickly in the astral world. Otherwise, suffering from the cancer may go on for centuries in the astral world, until the person becomes purified enough. In any case, what is called spirit disturbance is actually an opportunity for compensation or cleansing of negative karma so that the person's eternal self, the soul, will become purified. This phenomenon is not punishment, but something given as a result of God's love for the person in the long term. Therefore, such 'adversities' are best viewed as opportunities to reform one's soul.

I feel it is particularly important for humanity to adopt spiritually oriented medicine as soon as possible, because we have entered the age of baptism by fire (began on 1 January 1962), and according to divine teachings, the spiritual energy of fire and the Light of God have been increasing throughout the universe since that time. One reason for the increase in many so-called diseases is that the power of melting of toxins is increasing with increasing fire energy, resulting in all kinds of symptoms that people call disease. In the past era when the spiritual essence of water was predominant (up till 1962), the symptoms of disease could be controlled to various degrees by chilling the body and using medication. Today, however, since medication is contaminating material and the spiritual energy of fire is increasing, these toxins are discharged from the body through the power of melting, resulting in the increase of disease.

Also, with the increasing spiritual fire energy there is an increase in the struggle of resentful attached spirits, resulting in more intense disturbance and on a wider scale. Helping or saving such spirits is becoming increasingly important to achieve health.

Dealing sensibly with the 'downstream'
The 'downstream' – the physical and mental aspects – is also important when dealing with disorders. These aspects are not to be treated lightly just because the spiritual aspect is the most important. Many people, including Mahikari practitioners, have been grateful to health professionals – for their diagnosing, skills, knowledge, teamwork and medical technology – that have helped to save lives as well as overcome difficult cleansing periods, restore vitality and generally make cleansing more comfortable. Conventional medicine has been particularly valuable in dealing with acute emergencies and trauma management.

Surgery may be the best or only procedure to choose in certain circumstances, even though it affects the body (the spiritual, astral and physical cells). If a person is injured in a traffic accident, for instance, or requires intensive care treatment for some life-threatening disorder, obviously it is sensible to rely on surgery or other conventional treatment.

Similarly, even though medication is basically toxic to the body, it is nevertheless sometimes the best choice to make under the circumstances, particularly in an emergency, during severe cleansing, when one's vitality may be jeopardised to the point of possible death, and other situations. For instance, people with dangerously high blood pressure would be foolish to stop using their anti-hypertension tablets. Using commonsense, if the blood pressure decreases steadily with daily True Light on certain body areas or other approaches, the dose of medication can be reduced accordingly and terminated altogether when it is safe to do so (and as guided by a medical practitioner).

In Sukyo Mahikari people are taught not to diagnose or try to talk a person out of following the doctor's advice if the person wants to have conventional medical treatment. There is no teaching not to take medication, not to consult doctors and not to have surgery. In fact, in the primary course textbook it is pointed out that there are many situations where traditional medical treatment is essential (when arteries are cut or bones are broken, when blood transfusions are necessary, when accidents occur, dental treatment, during certain breathing difficulties, lack of urination, when certain advanced technology is necessary such as x-rays, endoscopy examination, CT scans, ultrasound tests and so on). If vaccination is compulsory by law, then naturally there is compliance. People are encouraged to have regular medical and dental checkups. The sensible view is that if it cannot be helped and medication or surgery is necessary, it is good to have deep gratitude to God and all the people and materials involved in providing the treatment, including the medication and surgery.

There is a very real need for doctors, nurses and other clinicians. Humankind is still in a transition process of becoming purified, and in this stage of transition, if a condition appears to be serious, unusual or prolonged, it is usually valuable to consult medical professionals in order to be able to make the best decision about how to deal with the cleansing – spiritually, mentally and physically. Hopefully, in the future, as human beings become more and more purified, there will be less and less need for invasive and traumatic medical procedures to deal with their processes of cleansing.

The role of microorganisms
One of the accepted views in mainstream medicine is that when certain pathogenic bacteria ("bad germs") invade and multiply in the body, they cause disease, and should therefore be killed off or prevented from multiplying in the first place. I think there is an

excessive fear of so-called germs or bacteria. The presence of various kinds of bacteria in the body is a normal phenomenon. Bacteria work with their host organism by assisting in the breakdown and removal of toxic materials, and many of them also produce nutriments that are vital to our welfare. In nature, when organic matter within plants and animals decomposes, bacteria and moulds break down the highly complex organic molecules into simple inorganic wastes, which are eventually taken up once again by plants and reorganised. That is, bacteria are minute forms of life which subsist by scavenging dead organic material. In the human body, microorganisms also break up and decompose waste material just as they do within the plant and animal kingdom.

Bacteria need nourishment to grow and reproduce. When there is a dangerous accumulation of waste materials which threatens the body parts, bacteria go into action and perform their scavenging function of clearing the body of filth. This leads to symptoms of cleansing that have been labelled as 'disease'. As soon as the role of the bacteria is complete, their numbers decline. In other words, contrary to what is commonly thought, bacteria are associated with disease processes but are not their cause. Bacteria do not cause disease any more than flies cause garbage. Bacteria proliferate because there is dead organic matter for them to feed on, when there is too much impurity in the host, not because they have suddenly become malevolent. It is the environment and the host which determines disease symptoms and the type of bacteria that proliferate.

I have found that this view, though not common to mainstream medicine, has been accepted by some medical researchers over the years. It is interesting that the French chemist, Louis Pasteur, who is said to have fathered the germ theory of disease causation (even though there were other such researchers before him) himself admitted his mistake around 1880 when he discovered that microbial speries can undergo many transformations. He changed his theory, admitting that a healthy body is resistant and not susceptible to disease. Despite this, his original theory has remained as mainstream in medicine.

In my understanding of the divine teachings, it is not the germs that cause the disease but the impurity in the host that attracts them. Killing off microorganisms may temporarily suppress a condition, but in the long term it is worse because the cleansing is stopped and more toxicity is introduced. Of course, it may be advisable to suppress bacterial multiplication in extreme situations – if the condition is life-threatening or dangerous (as a result of excessive toxins) – but the best approach is to become purified spiritually, mentally and physically so that there is no need for so-called pathogenic microorganisms to multiply excessively.

I have often observed that True Light alone may produce symptoms similar to those associated with microorganisms, as occurs with a cold or influenza (runny nose, sore throat, fever and so on) without the intervention of bacteria or viruses at all. Every now and then when I give Light to the forehead or back of the head and neck of a person, I notice that the person's nose begins running, the eyes begin streaming or the brow begins perspiring. After receiving Light, the discharges subside. In the same way, because one receives abundant Light when one participates in a Mahikari course, offers service such as attending a Mahikari ceremony or cleaning the Mahikari centre, one may experience valuable cleansing reactions that resemble symptoms traditionally labelled as 'illness', even without directly receiving Light from anybody.

Whether cleansing occurs due to the body's natural mechanisms involving microorganisms, whether it is due to the Light of God, or a combination of both, it occurs only because there is something to cleanse, that is, the host has become contaminated. Whatever the reason, one can be grateful for the cleansing.

Experiences with True Light in clinical situations

Many Sukyo Mahikari members have found that the practice of spiritually oriented medicine can result in recovery from problems that are often considered medically impossible cases. Some examples are given below of cases in which the results were verified by non-Mahikari medical professionals who monitored the clinical condition of the patients.

Methicillin-resistant staphylococcus aureus infection

Tanikado (1996) found that through True Light and service to God, his father, who was bedridden in hospital with methicillin-resistant staphylococcus aureus (MRSA) infection, was able to recover miraculously and become very healthy. Before that he had been in a critical condition with anaemia, having had three operations (including blood transfusions) for a hole in the intestine, and ended up in the intensive care unit with tubes in his nostrils, an intravenous drip in his shoulder and many tubes inserted into his abdomen for drainage. Apparently, his father now has joined Mahikari and leads a healthy life every day. He has a better appetite than before his operation as well. Laboratory tests showed that the MRSA had completely disappeared from his body. Such results cannot be explained in terms of the physical views of conventional medicine.

Miraculous recovery from a coma

A lady from Kuala Lumpur reported a remarkable recovery in her father, who had a ruptured blood vessel in the brain, through giving True Light. This happened in the presence of medical staff who were monitoring his condition in the intensive care unit in the hospital, and gave him only a 1% chance of survival. The following is part of her report (Kaur, 1995).

On 20 January 1994 at 7.00 am, I received an urgent call from my sister saying that something was wrong with my father. (He is not a kamikumite.) He was perspiring profusely and had developed muscle spasms on the right side of his neck. He had lost bowel control and could not walk due to dizzy spells.

My husband rushed him to the hospital emergency ward. There we were informed that my father had just had a stroke due to extremely high blood pressure. (His blood pressure was recorded as 256/136.)

At 10.00 pm a brain scan confirmed the existence of a ruptured blood vessel in the brain. My father lapsed into a coma with paralysis on the left side of his body. The doctors gave him a 1% chance of survival because the blood clot was lodged dangerously at the back of his brain. Both the cardiac specialist and the neurosurgeon suggested we transfer him immediately to the neuro-ward in Kuala Lumpur.

A second brain scan revealed that the blood clot had lodged itself in one of the veins and that pressure was building up in the brain. As surgery was too risky, a procedure called "shunting" was done. A two-inch L-shaped cut was made on the right side of the head just above the forehead and a hole was drilled so that a tube could be inserted into the head to drain the excess fluid when pressure built up in the brain.

I was shocked to see the pitiful state of my father. He was breathing heavily and a lot of tubes were attached to his body. Both his arms were swollen due to the drips. He was tied to his bed and had to use adult diapers. When suction was done, his whole body trembled. Fever and pneumonia developed. We were all in tears, hoping against hope that my happy-go-lucky father would become well again.

My elder brother, who is not a kamikumite, kept vigil at my father's bedside, but eventually gave up hope and wept. I then plucked up courage and asked him if I could give Light to my father. After a short silence, he told me to go ahead since everyone had given up hope of my father's recovery.

My husband and I started to give Light as guided. We gave Light with the innermost attitude of love, apology and gratitude, concentrating mostly on the head points. To everyone's surprise my father started to show signs of recovery. Initially, clear fluid flowed through the tubes attached to the brain. With the Light, blood clots both large and small started to drain out before our very eyes. My brother encouraged me and told me that the melting and discharge of these blood clots was helping my father to recover. We continued with the Light and at times my brother would turn my father over so that we could give Light to the points at the back of the head.

On the fourth day of giving Light, clear fluid appeared in the tubes and my father regained consciousness. He could look around and grip our hands. A scan showed that the clot had shrunk. All the tubes were removed and healing was fast. Surprisingly, there was no infection. What a miracle God had shown us!

Now, three months have passed. My father is able to walk unaided, attend to his personal needs, entertain his guests and even play with his grandchildren.

Remarkable recovery from multi-organ failure

A young, non-Mahikari married couple of Perth had a remarkable experience with their new-born son who recovered from acute multi-organ failure, considered medically impossible (Bennett & Bennett, 1994). Several medical professionals were constantly monitoring the baby's condition, doing tests, taking readings and so on, and there was clear medical evidence for recovery. Excerpts of their report are given below.

On 31 August 1993, we were blessed with the birth of Aryn, a beautiful, healthy 8-pound boy, but our joy was short-lived, as after several days his temperature began to rise and his stomach swelled. After many tests Aryn was rushed to the Intensive Care Unit of Princess Margaret Hospital for Children.

On his 9th day (8-9-93) Aryn seemed to reach a critical point in his deteriorating condition and we were told by his doctors that he would not survive the night. His liver had become so badly inflamed that it had enlarged to the point where his stomach was as tight as a drum and had stretch marks over it; his lungs had collapsed so he was placed on a ventilator with 100% oxygen; his kidneys had failed; his heart had enlarged and he had suffered small haemorrhages in the brain. The doctors described his condition as acute multi-organ failure.

The next day, two kamikumite friends, Kingsley and Fran, came to visit and asked whether we would permit Aryn to receive True Light. Knowing how much Kingsley and Fran believed in the giving of Light, we happily accepted, but could not imagine that our son could recover at this late stage. Aryn received two sessions of Light on the first day and Kingsley and Fran asked us whether they would be able to come every day. We were constantly being told by the medical staff that our son would not survive. Apparently no other child with this condition had ever survived. We were later to find out that the virus which Aryn had was called Echo 11, which has not been encountered for seven years. Aryn had caught the worst strain possible. In fact, the specialists pointed out that he is the only child in Australia to have survived for more than two days!

Aryn continued receiving Light from Fran and Kingsley twice a day and continued to be stable. However, with his platelet (clotting) level being extremely low, he began haemorrhaging, with blood flowing from his nose, mouth and umbilical area. Altogether, Aryn required 6 blood, 5 platelet and 6 plasma transfusions during the bleeding!

The doctors informed us that they would bring in a liver specialist to make an assessment. He examined Aryn and said that from a medical point of view and from his experience, there was no possibility of our son surviving, as his blood clotting could not possibly improve and his liver cells were 'dead'. We were informed that his complexion would get greener and greener from the increasing bilirubin levels and that the fluid and toxins (for example, ammonia and so on) in his body would continue to rise to such levels that he would go into a coma and pass away, possibly within days.

However, with the continuation of God's precious Light, Aryn did stop bleeding, his liver cells did start to rejuvenate, the toxin levels did come down and the one litre of toxic fluid around his body passed out through his kidneys (via urine) and stools.

After a few more days and the receiving of Light Aryn started to improve even more. By the 4th week he no longer needed the ventilator; he was breathing on his own! He was slowly tube-fed small amounts of milk, which he tolerated straight away, much to the surprise of the doctors. However, they were still dissatisfied with Aryn's mental responses, and his kidneys, lungs and particularly his liver, were still badly disfunctional (e.g. low blood clotting, critically high level of toxins). They still believed that he could not possibly survive. They therefore suggested that we should take Aryn home to spend his last days away from the hospital.

We went straight to the Perth Mahikari Centre where we were welcomed very lovingly and Aryn received Light. We took him to the Mahikari Centre on both days he was home. When we took him back to the hospital (after two days) for him to be officially discharged, the doctors were amazed at the change in his appearance and how alert and aware of his surroundings he had become. They then decided to do further blood and liver function tests and to once again ask the opinion of the liver specialist.

The results of the tests showed that his toxin levels (ammonia etc.) had dropped to safe levels and his clotting and various other factors had dramatically risen to almost normal levels! The liver specialist was amazed to see the improvement and said that he would like to see Aryn regularly.

We took Aryn to the Mahikari Centre every day for True Light. When we took him to see the liver specialist one week later, his jaundice had decreased dramatically, he was taking full feeds without the help of a tube, and his liver function tests once again showed further improvement. Aryn's improvement amazed the doctor, so much so that he could not stop smiling.

We visit the Perth Mahikari Centre every day to receive True Light and to offer our sincere gratitude to God for the wonderful arrangements that have been made for our son. At present Aryn's blood clotting and jaundice (bilirubin) levels are normal and his other liver function levels are continuing to improve. His liver is still slightly enlarged but is getting smaller and softer. Interestingly, when Aryn first started receiving Light, we asked the nursing staff where the liver was located to make sure he was receiving Light in the correct place. We were informed that it was on the right side. However, after about a week Aryn had an ultrasound test taken of his liver and we were surprised to find out that the human liver actually extends across to the left side as well, and that the part of the liver which had been receiving Light had become dramatically smaller whereas the part that had not received Light had not changed.

Aryn's doctor now believes our son is showing every sign of being a mentally and physically healthy baby. He is progressing normally and doing everything a four-and-a-half-month-old baby is supposed to do.

We were permitted to have copies of all the appropriate medical records, test analyses, diagnostic and therapeutic procedures done, which may be of interest to other medical doctors.

Rapid disappearance of a gallstone

On 19 June 1997, Dr A., a social scientist teaching in a university in Melbourne and a friend of mine, sent me a report with clinical data showing the surprising disappearance of a gallstone in her bile duct. She is not a Mahikari member but receives True Light from time to time. She let me have copies of the reports made by radiologists. Below are excerpts of her report to me.

I had been experiencing bad pains in the upper abdomen from time to time after eating, but after a few attacks they had gone away and I had been too busy to consult the doctor. Then I experienced a very bad attack at work one day. The pains continued every time I ate over the next few days and became worse. One day after having some toast for breakfast, I was so ill in my office that the staff called the doctor to come and help me. I vomited all over the floor and was given Pethidine to alleviate the pain. For the first time I was diagnosed as having gallstones. I continued to experience the attacks, really painful, just like one has at childbirth, and only managed to alleviate them by eating rice porridge and umeboshi (Japanese-style salted plums).

Even then, however, the pain persisted. I went for an ultrasound scan on 10 June, which clearly showed a large gallstone of about one centimetre lodged in the bile duct, which was distended. After reporting this to my general practitioner, I was referred to a surgeon.

The report by the radiologist, dated 10 June 1997, entitled "Abdominal Ultrasound", included the following: "The gall bladder contains two calculi each approximately 7mm in diameter . . . The common bile duct is dilated with a maximum diameter of 8mm. A calculus 10mm in diameter is present at the lower end. There is mild dilatation of the intrahepatic ducts, but the liver otherwise appears normal."

On 12 June, Dr A. went to the Melbourne Mahikari Centre to receive Light (a full session, including on her liver and gall bladder area) from a lady kamikumite. On 16 June she also received Light on these areas from the local staff member of the Mahikari Centre. Later that day she went to the hospital to consult a surgeon who specialises in gall bladder operations. Dr A. wrote:

After reading the report of my ultrasound, my local doctor told me that I would need to have an operation to remove my gall bladder. The surgeon at the hospital confirmed this after looking at the same ultrasound report. He said that the operation would involve a technique in which the stone in the bile duct is removed by a 'scopy' procedure, something to do with lassooing the tube through the very narrow entrance to the bile duct. Apparently this is so narrow that it is almost impossible for the stone to be passed out of its own accord. The surgeon told me that if the stone is not removed, it can lead to a dangerous situation, as infections and other complications may result. He also said that the gall bladder itself would have to be removed at some stage as there were many stones still there and this could lead to cancer. I told him that I was reluctant to undergo any surgery, and as I had been feeling much better and was eating normally without any pain in the past few days, I requested that they perform another ultrasound to see whether the stone was still in the bile duct. The surgeon at first was hesitant but kindly agreed to my request.

I had another ultrasound test done on 17 June and it showed that there was no stone in the duct. After the second radiology report, the surgeon said that it was not necessary for me to have an operation anymore.

The report by the radiologist, dated 17 June 1997, entitled "Upper Abdominal Ultrasound", included the following:

"Biliary ducts are of normal calibre with common hepatic duct measuring 3mm in diameter. No calculi are seen within the extra hepatic bile ducts . . ."

Dr A. has the ultrasound photographs, and is very grateful that through the Light of God the gall stone in her bile duct was removed without the need to undergo surgery.

The practice of spiritually oriented medicine by Mahikari clinicians

Throughout the world, a number of medical doctors, dentists, nurses, psychologists and other clinicians, as well as scientists who are researching clinical sciences, have attended the primary course and are practising the art of True Light and the divine teachings in their profession. (Examples of mental health workers were given earlier in this chapter.) They did not give up their professions just because they discovered that some of their previous thinking and practices were limited or could be improved, but have incorporated a spiritually oriented approach, a balanced combination of spiritual, mental and physical medicine into their practices. They give and receive Light and study and practise the divine teachings at their Mahikari centres, at home and elsewhere in their daily life. Some have formed medical associations and related groups in which they have meetings, workshops, conferences and other activities to strengthen their understanding and incorporate the universal laws into their clinical setting.

Sukyo Mahikari health professionals have presented clinical and scientific data to the public as well. Sponsored by Sukyo Mahikari, the First Yoko Civilization International Conference was held in

Takayama, Japan, in November 1986, involving both Mahikari and non-Mahikari health professionals, scientists, educators and people of religion, dealing with the theme, 'Creating the Future of Mankind'. The Second Yoko Civilization International Conference, again held in Takayama (October–November, 1989) dealt with the theme, 'What Does It Mean To Be Human?' The Third Yoko Civilization International Conference, held in Takayama (August 1999) dealt with the theme, 'Life and the Environment'. The First Yoko Institute International Conference for Europe was held in Luxembourg in May 1993 with the theme, 'Human Responsibilities – Approaching the Twenty-first Century.' In Australia (1988) the Mahikari organisation held a symposium, 'Health and Medicine of the Future,' at the Australian Academy of Science in Canberra, and again at the University of Sydney. A similar symposium was held in Singapore.

Articles by Sukyo Mahikari health professionals have been published in various editions of the journal *Sukyo Mahikari* (Japanese), *Mahikari Australia–Oceania and Asia Journal*, the journal *Sukyo Mahikari* of North America and *Sukyo Mahikari: International Journal*. Below are some examples.

Cancer research scientist recovers from chronic fatigue

Dr Sidney Chang of London, a molecular and cell biologist who had been suffering from chronic fatigue for several years, was able to make a complete recovery through the Light of God and the practice of divine principles after he attended the Mahikari primary course. Excerpts from his report (Chang, 1994) are given below.

For the past twenty years I have worked as a molecular and cell biologist in the field of cancer research. In July 1988, I suffered a severe viral infection from which I did not make a full recovery. Following several relapses it became obvious that a chronic condition had developed whereby I was fatigued all the time, mentally and physically. I ached all over and frequently felt disoriented and depressed.

Two medical consultants diagnosed my condition as post-viral chronic fatigue syndrome. The prognosis for this condition is unpredictable and there is no simple medical remedy or therapy for it. On the recommendation of my consultants I began a meditation practice and had massage. I also underwent counselling, reflexology and shiatsu and took many vitamin, mineral and food supplements. Later I adopted a macrobiotic diet.

Although the various medications and therapies seemed to help me, by October 1990 it was evident that there was still no prospect of a full recovery from my chronic fatigue condition. I was advised to take leave from my research work. It was at that stage that one of my therapists, who was a kamikumite, told me that in his opinion the block to my recovery was spiritual. He introduced me to Mahikari. This was in November 1990.

At that time I had many doubts about Mahikari and its teachings, but I agreed to receive Light because I was desperate to try anything that might help me. On receiving Light I frequently felt the sensation of heat or tingling at some points on my body, and after most sessions of True Light I felt more centred and energetic. On several occasions when I received Light on my forehead, I had visions of brilliant, shimmering Light.

Sometimes after receiving Light I experienced physical cleansings in the form of fever, a runny nose, phlegm, skin eruptions and so on. On one occasion, for about twenty-four hours I had the distinct taste of a medication that I had used for several years and which I had stopped using a year previously.

After a few months of receiving Light I noticed that it had become easier to accept my condition and that I complained less. My improving condition made me more grateful and I was able to offer gratitude to the Creator God.

Through Mahikari I learned that it was important not only for me to receive Light but also for me to change my innermost attitudes. I learned that in addition to offering gratitude to the Creator God, I should also offer sincere apology for sins and for spiritual, mental and physical impurities that had been gathered over many lifetimes by myself, my family and my ancestors.

I found that when I offered both gratitude and apology to the Creator God, I coped much more easily with my chronic fatigue condition. Through my experience I discovered that the classic Mahikari dictum 'spirit first, mind next, body follows' is indeed correct and true.

Step by step, as my condition improved, I was able to stop all medication and therapies, including my meditation practice and special diet. Complete recovery from my chronic condition surprised everyone, including medical consultants, family and me.

In November 1991, one year after I started receiving Light, I was able to attend the Mahikari primary course. At the Omitama-receiving ceremony, the moment I received my Omitama I felt that my body was surrounded by the Creator God's divine Light, and this was a wonderful and reassuring experience. In December I returned to full-time work and I have been well ever since.

Since the course I have had many interesting experiences through giving Light and sharing my experiences with others. In June 1992, I gave Light to a lady who had had excruciating pains on the right side of her back for fourteen years, following an operation for breast cancer. The pain ebbed away during the session of True Light and has not returned.

In February of this year, a friend in New York was diagnosed as having cutaneous T-cell lymphoma, a potentially lethal cancer. After I shared my experience with this friend and recommended that she receive True Light, she received Light four to five times a week. After four weeks she returned to see her medical consultant who was surprised to observe that without any medication or treatment, at least 70% of the lymphoma had regressed.

Through these and other experiences, any doubts I had had about Mahikari teachings disappeared, and I was able to accept the teachings and give Light with more sincerity.

Mahikari in dentistry

Dr Chelvaraj (1994), a dentist of Taiping, Malaysia, reported three cases of significant effects of True Light in his dental practice. One patient, a 45-year-old Chinese lady, had trigeminal neuralgia (a cranial nerve pain) that had been treated with multi-vitamins, placebos and pain killers, all to no avail. This condition is neither understood very well medically, nor is treatment generally effective. This patient received True Light on her gums and teeth every three days, and after very few weeks of Light, the patient had a bout of pain only once every few months, unlike before when she would have very severe, sharp pain whenever a certain area of the face was touched, below the right corner of her lip.

Another patient, a 23-year-old Chinese girl, was diagnosed as having an infected radicular cyst, as she had pus discharge from the upper left lateral incisor after root canal treatment was done by a general practitioner. The pathologist reported that the infective organism was Klebsielle. After some days of receiving True Light to the infected tooth and its surrounding areas, the pus discharge first increased tremendously and after that decreased and disappeared completely. The patient did not have pain or discomfort anymore at all. Dr Chelvaraj published x-ray photographs showing the progress of recovery with True Light.

Another patient, a 20-year-old Indian girl, had an abscess leading to cellulitis on the right side of her face. Her nose was pushed to the left and the swelling had hooded the right eye. An abscess was located on the right side, lateral to and just below the bridge of the nose. The area was warm and tender to touch. Intra-oral pus was seen draining from the socket of the upper lateral incisor. She received True Light for five days and the swelling gradually disappeared. The socket of the upper right lateral incisor healed completely. She said that she had felt a warmth come over her and felt the pain subsiding when she received Light on the first occasion, and even though she was given an analgesic (Paracetamol) with instructions that she was only to take it if she could not stand the pain, she did not use it.

Mahikari doctors in India

The proportion of Mahikari doctors in India is rather high. They are enthusiastic in practising the art of True Light and the divine teachings in their clinical practice. Below are some experiences reported by Dr Jaya Lalmohan Thiruvikkal (1995), the Assistant Civil Surgeon in Mumbai at that time, who herself was helped by the Light of God after a haemorrhage in her brain, just before she attended the Mahikari primary course. She has had a number of experiences with True Light in gynaecology, including resuscitating new-born babies who had been given up as hopeless medically.

The art of True Light was being practised at a place very near our home and from July, my husband and I were regular visitors there. One day in October 1991, I had an unbearable headache. Being a doctor by profession, the nature of the pain made me suspect some serious problem inside my head, so I rushed to the District Hospital. The doctors there examined me and suspected a haemorrhage in my brain. A lumbar puncture test was done, which confirmed their suspicion. Thus the doctors decided that the chances of my survival were very remote.

In the hospital bed I was able to receive True Light from Dr Jagadeesh and Dr Kedarnath, two Mahikari doctors. Dr Kedarnath was kind enough to stay overnight to give me Light. I received a lot of relief from the pain and had a good sleep that night. Next morning I felt better. A repeat lumbar puncture test was done to assess my condition. To the surprise of the doctors who had done the previous test, all traces of red blood cells indicating a haemorrhage had vanished! My recovery was fast and miraculous. I was discharged from hospital within a week without any problems.

Both my husband and I received precious Omitama in January 1992. Barely four days after I received my Omitama, God showed me yet another miracle. I was working in a small Government Hospital in Cochin at that time. On 27 January 1992, I was called to the hospital in the early morning to attend a labour case. On reaching the hospital I found a woman with strong labour pains who was going to have a complicated labour, as the baby was presenting by buttocks first position (breech). For such a case it is advisable to do a Caesarean section without which there would be risk to the baby's life. Since the hospital did not have the necessary facilities for surgery, and furthermore, the labour was progressing quickly, I had no other choice than to pull the baby out. Once the baby was born we found that it had neither any heartbeat nor respiration. We tried to resuscitate the baby by all methods but without any success. Finally abandoning the baby, I went to attend the mother. As procedures were being completed a thought suddenly came to my mind. 'Why not give some Light to the body of the baby?' So I washed my hands and started giving Light to the forehead of the baby. To my surprise, I noticed that the baby's face, which had been blue, was now slowly turning pink, and the colour began to spread all over the body. My staff then gave the baby oxygen and artificial respiration, and then the baby began to cry. The next day the baby developed bleeding from the mouth and nostrils and breathed its last. I am very grateful to God for permitting the baby to pass to the astral world in such a purified, comfortable condition, compared with the suffering it would be in now without the Light of God.

Six months later, in July 1992, when I was working in the major hospital at Cochin, I had to assist another doctor doing a Caesarean section on a lady with high blood pressure and premature labour. When the baby was lifted out of the uterus, it was found that it had neither heartbeat nor respiration. The anaesthetist and the other doctor declared the baby to be dead. Anyhow, I started giving it Light along with the usual methods of resuscitation. After a few minutes the baby started breathing! The mother and child are still living happily. I was also permitted to experience a similar miracle in September 1992. In this case too the child had been asphyxiated and was bluish in colour. I gave Light with one hand and with the other started cardiac massage; the baby came alive.

In September 1993 I was doing a hysterectomy on an elderly lady. Everything was going fine when suddenly she went into cardiac arrest and hypotension. The anaesthetist became panicky as her blood pressure was not rising in spite of the measures being taken. By that time I had finished the surgical procedure, so I removed my gloves, prayed and started giving Light to the chest and feet of the patient. Within ten minutes her condition improved.

Thank You very much Su God, Sukuinushisama, Oshienushisama, for all the guidance, protection and experiences given to me.

Doctor treats doctor

Professor Breminand Maharaj is Principal Physician and Professor at the Nelson R. Mandela School of Medicine and King Edward VIII Hospital in Durban, South Africa. Ever since he became a Mahikari practitioner early in 1994, he has been having inspiring experiences with the Light of God. The following are excerpts of his report concerning the effects of Light on one of his doctor colleagues, who suffered from a serious brain haemorrhage (Maharaj, 1996).

Late last year, when I arrived at work on Monday morning, I was informed that a colleague had sustained an injury to the back of his head over the weekend, which resulted in a brain haemorrhage and a large accumulation of blood called haematoma in both the left and right frontal lobes. These haematomas had expanded and caused pressure within the brain to increase to such an extent that his mental state had deteriorated. He was disorientated and confused and in danger of losing his life. At this stage the neurosurgeon decided to do an operation to drain the blood in order to reduce the pressure in the brain. It lasted more than four hours because the surgeon had great difficulty in controlling the bleeding. Only one side was operated upon because it was considered too risky to operate on both. His life was thought to be in grave danger, and even if he lived, it was questionable whether he would be able to function normally again. Movement of his limbs, speech, memory, intellect and emotion were all likely to be severely affected. In short, he could become what is termed a 'vegetable'. At best it would be at least six months or a year before he could return to work.

I visited my friend in the intensive care unit that afternoon. He looked grotesque. One eye was like an inflated balloon, his head was bandaged, and there were tubes connected to various devices. He bore little resemblance to his usual self. He appeared to be in a coma. I held his hand, greeted him and offered him words of love and encouragement from all. He was unable to speak. I gave him a full session of Light, radiating it through the front of his body.

When I visited him the next day (Tuesday) I was amazed to find that the swelling around his eyes had disappeared, his face was symmetrical and his condition was stable. He was still semi-comatose but responded to commands from the nurses to move his limbs. The pressure in his brain had not increased and the brain scan showed that the haematomas had not increased in size either. I gave him True Light again.

On Wednesday he was in deeper coma and less responsive to commands from the nurse. He was coughing poorly, which meant that he would retain secretions in his chest; this would predispose him to chest infections, which is a serious problem in intensive care units. Also, his blood pressure was high for the first time. I gave him Light. I left the hospital more concerned about his condition than before. I continued to pray for him daily.

On Thursday, although his condition remained unchanged, I was very pleased to learn that the pressure in his brain had not increased and that the brain scan had shown for the first time that the haematoma had decreased in size. I was able to give him Light once again. I then had to leave Durban for the rest of the week.

When I returned on Monday I was delighted to learn that he had suddenly woken up on Saturday afternoon and all the tubes which connected him to the different mechanical devices had been removed. On Sunday he was moved out of the intensive care unit to the general ward. When I visited him, he was sitting in bed conversing with a friend. He recognised me and greeted me by name. His speech was fine but his memory was impaired and his vision was distorted. He moved all his limbs, although there was some weakness and imbalance on the left side. The pupils of his eyes were unequal and one eyelid was drooping. I was very grateful for the dramatic change in his condition from the last time I had seen him in the intensive care unit.

I gave him True Light for three more days in hospital. He made incredible progress. He was able to sit up and receive Light on his back points. His memory was improving in leaps and bounds. His sense of humour and wit were returning. The drooping eyelid improved. He was walking unassisted, reading magazines and feeding himself. The brain scan showed a further reduction in the size of the haematoma. It was decided that he could be discharged home on Friday. The neurosurgeon felt that it would still be at least six months to a year before he could return to work.

I continued to give him God's Light after his discharge, although not as frequently. He continued to make excellent progress. He had lost 18 kg in weight and was slowly gaining weight. The weaker side of his body gained strength. He was able to resume working on his computer and helped us to retrieve all the student data we needed prior to the final examination. He resumed physical training at the gymnasium. He came into the office for a few hours every two to three weeks.

In early December, less than four months after his injury, the neurosurgeon declared him fit to resume work and drive his motor car.

Mahikari clinicians in Japan

The biggest number of Sukyo Mahikari health professionals is in Japan, the country of origin of Sukyo Mahikari. As an example, below is an account of various experiences that Ms Onodera, the Chief Nurse of the Neurosurgery Division of a hospital in Iwate, has had with practising the art of True Light and divine teachings. The full report is published elsewhere (Onodera, 1995).

I heard about Mahikari from my younger sister in May 1978. At the time I thought that it must be a strange religion so I was determined to expose how peculiar it was. On completing the course, however, I realised that the contents of the lectures were what I had been searching for, for a long time. I was really moved, and so received an Omitama.

One day in 1985, I was suddenly struck with cataplexy, a kind of paralysis, on the right side of my body. I was hospitalised immediately and was administered a steroid. My disease was diagnosed as Guillain-Barre syndrome (inflammation of nerves following acute infection). Strangely, I was able to remain quite cheerful and free from any anxiety. Rather, I found myself thinking that I would like to offer gratitude to God for being able to compensate through this illness.

Even though I was not able to move my right arm or leg, I still felt cheered to think that there were many people who are less privileged than

I was. I still had movement in my left arm and leg, and my eyes, mouth and ears were still functioning. I therefore decided that I would take full advantage of the body functions left to me, rather than making efforts to regain the ones I had lost. I dressed myself in a white uniform and went throughout the hospital radiating Light as long as time allowed.

Four days later I was able to go to dojo by myself. Whilst receiving Light from a staff member, an attached spirit manifested who said he was an underground Christian. I used to have a recurring dream in those days. In the dream, a person who looked like a Christian missionary was standing on a grey rock, and a crowd of suffering people were far below him. I would notice that the missionary was communicating his gloomy and sad feeling to me.

The spirit said that I had been a missionary in my previous life. The spirit also said that I was the only person who was able to survive an allegiance test, which involved treading on a copper tablet bearing a crucifix. The spirit said that the spirits of more than three hundred underground Christians had been executed for refusing to step on the tablet. These spirits had been feeling strong resentment towards me, and were attached to the right side of my body.

I was shouting in my mind while receiving Light, 'An image of the crucifix isn't God!!' However, I felt deeply sorry and remorseful that I was somehow responsible for the suffering of these people. I sincerely apologised to God and offered sincere prayers from the bottom of my heart that those suffering spirits might be saved.

Mysteriously, my body gradually regained movement soon after this. The course of the steroids was completed in just one week, and my health returned to normal. A patient, who depended on a wheelchair, and his family members, four people in total, attended the primary course because of having witnessed my return to good health within a period of ten days or so. This marvellous miracle, which stemmed from the great love of God, made me determined that I be further dedicated to helping others through medicine.

Whole person medicine for the public

I believe it is particularly valuable for health professionals to become both active practitioners of the Light of God and the divine teachings, and if possible, to help validate the reality of such practice through medical research. As Sukuinushisama said in a teaching entitled "Revolution in medical science":

No matter how hard I work by myself, I would only be able to save a few tens of thousands of people. It would not come to a significant number, even after twenty or thirty years.

However, when the field of medicine is spiritually awakened and starts studying such things as miracles scientifically, the foundation of medical theories will be overturned. A revolution will occur in medicine and this will influence the salvation of all humankind.

What will happen when medicine acknowledges that the spirit is the main thing, and is based on the principles of health of Mahikari? Doctors will begin to say things like, 'Have you caught a cold? That's good. And you have pain? That's even better'. Doctors will preach about God and the principles of health based on divine principles. That is, medicine based on divine principles will develop and be taught.

If medical doctors are awakened to the divine principles and the world becomes filled with such doctors and hospitals, then the whole world will become free from disease.

That is what I call salvation of all humankind.

Yoko Clinic

Sukuinushisama had the vision of establishing a Yoko Health Centre as an important pillar towards the development of true or whole person medicine.

Under Oshienushisama's guidance, the Yoko Clinic, a part of the Yoko Health Centre, was opened in Takayama at the end of 1989. The Yoko Clinic is for all people, irrespective of whether they are Mahikari members or not. The staff consists of medical doctors (internal medicine, paediatrics, gynaecology and so on), nurses and others who are qualified and trained as is the medical profession anywhere. Most of the staff, including those in the kitchen, supply department and garden, are Sukyo Mahikari members. The clinic has modern, sophisticated equipment (whole body CT scanner, X-ray machine, ultra-sound machine, endoscopy equipment and the like), modern up-to-date diagnostic procedures, first class facilities, in fact, like modern hospitals anywhere. For staff members the day usually begins and ends with prayers to God in front of the divine altar on the top floor. Patients are given True Light if they wish and the rooms are purified with True Light every day.

I have been told that the reputation of the doctors is excellent. They examine each patient carefully and give guidance and treatment after assessing the spiritual, mental and physical condition. They take plenty of time to examine each patient and treat them kindly and politely. (Often when going to a general hospital in Japan, one may wait for hours to see the doctor, even if one has an appointment, and the consultation usually lasts very few minutes.) Depending on the case, much of the guidance to patients deals with changing their innermost attitudes. Where necessary, medication is prescribed and operations are recommended. Apparently, the patients cannot help but feel that they are in very good hands.

One of the nurses who works there wrote:

Here at the clinic we talk with patients regarding matters that are deeper than the mind, more than at general hospitals. Consequently, there are even patients who feel relieved and become cheerful just by speaking about their worries . . . I associate with patients as if they were members of my own family. When we have gatherings where we read divine books, there are even some patients who change their innermost attitudes and burst into tears. When there is no apparent change in patients, we nurses have a meeting in which we reflect on our care of the patients and talk about future measures. This is practised at other hospitals, but at the Yoko Clinic I find it is much more tender and detailed.

The food that is offered to the patients is purified with True Light and much of it includes yoko agriculture produce when possible. Naturally, the staff are all striving to practise the divine teachings themselves, so the atmosphere is generally bright and warm, with smiling, helpful people everywhere. It is really an example of the practice of true medicine, I believe.

Research on rheumatoid arthritis involving Mahikari

Professor Takahiro Ochi, whom I met in Japan in 2000, is an example of a clinician whose research is contributing to the progress of whole person medicine.

Professor Ochi and his colleagues of Osaka University have been doing research on rheumatoid arthritis, a very painful chronic inflammatory condition that is accompanied by progressive destruction of the joints. The cause is unknown. They found that the course of the disease could not be changed by medication or the removal of the lesions through surgery. In trying to suppress the disease with various kinds of medication, they and other researchers have found that the medication produced unexpected adverse reactions, including a significant shortening of the life span.

Since 1991, Ochi and his colleagues have been studying rheumatoid arthritis patients who are members of Sukyo Mahikari and who give and receive True Light every day, while trying to elevate their innermost attitudes and offer service to God at their Mahikari centre. Ochi (2002) reported that most of the Mahikari patients were able to overcome the severe pain from rheumatoid arthritis without medication, and exhibited a high-quality mood (above average on the Face Scale Index), although the progressive joint destruction did not seem to be inhibited. Ochi was very impressed with the data and concluded: "I believe that there is a deeply significant issue for humanity in the behaviors of patients going through spiritual healing that cannot be understood from modern medicine."

§

It is interesting that over the past decade before the twenty-first century, the number of articles presenting original research on the relationship between spirituality and health increased sixfold, exceeding 1,200, according to a report by Associate Professor of Medicine, and Associate Professor of Psychiatry of Duke University Medical Centre in USA, Dr Harold Koenig (2001). Most original research articles on the topic found that there were positive associations between increased spirituality and better health outcomes, and that a significant proportion of patients would welcome doctors enquiring about spirituality. Several leading medical journals in the United States have published commentaries on this topic and many US medical schools and some residency training programs include spiritual issues in their curricula. Beginning in the 1980s, Dr Jeff Levin, an epidemiologist and former medical school professor, has been providing evidence for the connection between religion, spirituality and health. He has summarised findings and implications of scientific research that show how religious and spiritual practice can improve people's health (Levin, 2001). I think these are signs of the progress of whole person medicine, a point I illustrate again in chapter 11 with references to more researchers.

The science of the future

Chapter 7

The science of the future

I have always had a love for science and that is why in my early adulthood I chose to research the functioning of the nervous system. Now, looking back over almost three decades of practising certain universal laws and the art of True Light as a kind of a religious professional, I feel that my horizon of what science is and how it can progress, has expanded. Despite my involvement in religious activities, I do not feel that I have lost my essence as a scientist. In fact, I have come to see that various aspects of Sukyo Mahikari can be studied scientifically, and that conventional science and conventional religion can be integrated in certain aspects. This chapter deals with my understanding of the progress and limitations of contemporary science and how science can progress more if research of the spiritual realm is included to a greater extent.

Progress and limitations of contemporary science

Science has made enormous contributions to the wellbeing of humankind. One of the great benefits that science has provided is the understanding of many phenomena in everyday life. Experimental research has helped to dispel various myths and superstitions of the past. Looking at the progress of science and technology in the past few centuries, we can certainly see amazing advances compared with those in many other fields. Particularly in the developed countries, it would be hard to imagine living without motorised transport, telephones, computers, household appliances and countless other convenient and effective products that we often take for granted. Understandably, science began and has developed in a material-centred way. Despite the valuable contributions from contemporary science, scientists are finding that there are also limitations, and under certain circumstances, even hazards, from the material-centred approach.

Traditionally, science has been regarded as the systematic acquiring of knowledge in which the so-called 'scientific method' is applied in observation and experiment. I used to apply the scientific method for a number of years during my research experiments concerned with the mammalian brain, and to a lesser extent, with the heart of the Port Jackson shark, the spinal cord of the toad and the behaviour of rats. Briefly, in using the scientific method, the experiment must have a precise aim. A hypothesis is formulated and the experiment is designed so that the results attained may either refute or support the hypothesis. The description of the procedure and materials used must be sufficiently clear and detailed so that other people are able to repeat the experiment. The experiment must be designed so that any information gained about the variable under study is not confused by other variables. Variables should be kept to a minimum (ideally, only one) or at least accounted for by controls. Ideally, the variable under study should be quantified in some way. Lastly, the results should be repeatable.

Scientific method assumes that the experimenter is not biased and cannot influence the experiment or observations by his thoughts, feelings, moods, emotions or attitudes. However, in certain circumstances these influences do seem to occur. For many years it has been widely known that the mind alone can mediate changes within the body; this is the 'placebo effect' (Benson, 1996). In the United States, trials have shown that 50% of people get better if given a chalk pill which they think will cure them. In European countries it is more in the order of 30-40%. These are very high proportions and raise the question of how much actual chemical effect do the different kinds of medication have (Davidson, 1992)?

Even more significant, however, is the ever-increasing research data showing that mental states of the experimenter can influence the results of the experiment outside of the body. Dr Robert Rosenthal, a psychologist of Harvard University, has been a pioneer and one of the greatest contributors in this field, having accumulated data over several decades. Many years ago, when conducting research involving mice going through a maze, he told his assistant that he felt that a particular mouse would be able to get through the maze easily, but that another mouse would not be able to do so. The results showed that the mouse he had predicted did, in fact, get through the maze the fastest.

In a larger experiment involving primary school students in San Francisco, children from first grade to fifth grade were separated into three groups and their IQ was measured. The person conducting the experiment had no contact with the students, but told their teachers that he expected a particular group to obtain better results. The IQ test was given again after eight months and it was found that the particular group that he had predicted did obtain better scores than the other groups.

It is becoming more recognised that the way teachers treat pupils and the way children learn is strongly influenced by expectations. The textbook example referred to here is called the 'Pygmalion experiment' and was carried out by Rosenthal. Since then, similar results have been obtained by Rosenthal and various colleagues, in other places as well (Rosenthal, 1976; 1991). Moreover, it has been shown that the expectations of experimenters also influence the performance of animals, such as rats and flatworms (Rosenthal, 1976; 1991; Sheldrake, 1994).

Studies have also revealed that when people practise certain mental states, gradually other people in the area exhibit similar brain wave (EEG) patterns (Benson, 1996).

A method that is gaining acceptance by a number of researchers to assess repeatability in experiments is called meta-analysis. This quantitative technique is widely used in the social, behavioural and medical sciences to integrate the research results of numerous independent experiments. The cumulative database on various kinds of experiments on direct mental interactions with living systems has provided strong evidence that one person's attention directed towards a remote, isolated person, can significantly activate or calm that person's nervous system, according to the instructions given to the first person.

There is also increasing evidence that plants respond to people's thoughts, attitudes and feelings (see chapter 10).

Mental processes can also affect inanimate equipment. Electronic and computer technology has enabled researchers to develop highly automated experiments to study the interaction between mind and matter. Much parapsychological research has been done in recent years using a random number generator based on electronic or radioactive noise which produces a data stream that is recorded and analysed by computer software. In the typical random number generator experiment, a subject attempts to affect mentally the distribution of the random numbers. Great flexibility is combined with careful scientific control and a high rate of data acquisition. Starting around 1985, meta-analyses have been conducted on numerous types of parapsychology experiments. Dr Dean Radin, Laboratory Director at the Institute of Noetic Sciences in Petaluma, California, is a respected researcher who has spent years in electrical engineering and psychology, and then experimental parapsychology, a field in which he has made considerable contributions. According to Radin (1996, 1997), meta-analysis of the database published in 1989 examined 800 experiments by more than 60 researchers over the preceding 30 years. The probability that the observed effect was zero (that is, no mental effect on the equipment) was less than one part in a trillion, verifying that human consciousness can indeed affect the behaviour of a random physical system. Radin's presentation of the scientific evidence for psi phenomena is probably the most comprehensive and forceful ever made.

The influence of the attitudes of the experimenter on the results of the experiment presents a difficulty in promoting the scientific method as an infallible criterion from which to make conclusions with certainty, particularly as blind methodology is rarely applied in scientific research. According to Dr Rupert Sheldrake (1998), the use of blind methodologies is low in the various sciences. In the biological sciences, there were 7 out of 914 papers reviewed. There was a higher proportion in the medical sciences (6 out of 102) and in psychology and animal behaviour (7 out of 143). By far the highest proportion (23 out of 27) was found in parapsychology.

I believe that experimenter bias may therefore be a major reason why many sceptical researchers cannot replicate the data of unconventional researchers who have views that often do not fit with mainstream thinking – in studies of spirit phenomena, the mind, plant communication and so on. If a researcher maintains a strong belief that a certain view is nonsense, it may be no surprise that he cannot find evidence to support the view, despite 'objective' studies.

Experimenter bias is not the only problem in the use of the scientific method. Sometimes an observation can be made only rarely, although it is valid and reliably recorded. Also, many phenomena, although clearly demonstrable, cannot be quantified because they either cannot be repeated or there are no measuring instruments sensitive to the variable studied. On top of everything else, although an experiment is repeated under identical conditions (as far as is humanly possible), it may give conflicting results.

Pointing out various challenges in the use of the scientific method does not mean that the method is to be discarded. I think it is still the main way of obtaining the most reliable data possible in scientific research. At the same time, it is good to recognise that it has limitations and uncertainties, depending on the matter studied and the level of the study.

Even in fields traditionally regarded as hard science such as physics and mathematics, conventional methods sometimes show up anomalies, depending on the level of study. For example, Newton's laws (concerned with gravity, motion, mass and vision) apply very well at a gross level in the everyday lives of human beings. Under extreme conditions, such as at extremely high velocities or within atoms, however, Newton's laws do not apply, hence the reason for quantum theory, a field in which Einstein made great contributions (and for which he received the Nobel Prize).

Quantum theory has called into question the traditional understanding of matter, the basic stuff of which the universe is made. For example, subatomic particles have the capacity to behave as either particles or waves. What is even more unexpected is that what they become depends on the observational situation, that is, which aspect is measured. Moreover, at the subatomic level, no little bit of matter exists with certainty at any one place. It only shows a tendency to exist. In other words, atomic events cannot always be predicted with a high degree of certainty. They only show a tendency to occur. These tendencies are expressed as probabilities, and mathematically as probability waves. This phenomenon is now known as Heisenberg's Uncertainty Principle. In other words, at the subatomic level, there are no stable, permanent building blocks out of which the universe is composed. An atom is a dynamic pattern of particles of energy. Subatomic entities have no independent existence as isolated entities, with discernible positions and velocities. They can only be understood in relation to each other, that is, in their interconnectedness. Even the act of measurement affects them. If observers attempt to predict them by some form of measurement, they find that they are no longer just observers but participants, helping to determine the result.

Quantum theory shows that not only the atom, but also, no part of the universe can be wholly or adequately understood except in its relation to the whole. Moreover, from the atom right up to the living organism and beyond, the universe – the whole – is always more than the sum of its parts; and it is the significance of that whole which scientists often lose sight of in analysis. Quantum physics has opened people's eyes to this, and as Davies & Gribben (1992) have proposed, it forces us to see the universe as "crisscrossed by a network of interactions that weave the cosmos into a unity". Professor Davies summarised this as: *To the naive realist the universe is a collection of objects. To the quantum physicist, it is an inseparable web of vibration energy patterns in which no one component has reality independent of the entirety; and included in that entirety is the observer.*

In recent years, a number of scientists have realised that even quantum theory is inadequate or limited in explaining many phenomena of life – consciousness, psychic or spiritual phenomena, the interaction between mind and matter, to name a few.

Getting back to everyday human life, another limited view in traditional, material-centred science is the belief that by using logical empiricism (objectivism, positism and reductionism, that is, 'sequential processing') and the scientific method, science will eventually answer all questions and solve practically all problems. In my previous field of brain research, for example, many investigators believed that ultra-fine techniques capable of exploring the functioning of individual neurones and even molecules will lead to an explanation of memory, consciousness and so on. The use of molecular genetic techniques, microelectrodes and other sophisticated gadgetry has certainly helped to unravel the *mechanics* of brain processes, but is not bringing us much closer to understanding the underlying processes, including life itself. This micro approach can be likened to the study of the individual components of a computer (transistors, resistors, capacitors and the like) in the hope of tapping into the wisdom of the one who designed and put the computer together.

Besides, despite the value in researching isolated parts of a system, it has become increasingly clear in recent years that different parts interact synergistically when placed together. As Nobel laureate Roger Sperry pointed out, new properties that arise from complexes cannot be predicted from the known properties of their individual parts. These 'emergent properties' only exist within the whole. So we can never learn how whole systems work simply by analysing each of their components in isolation.

Generally, people consider that we live in the age of the most advanced science, because of progress in space research, computers, the information super-highway, robotics, genetic engineering, nano-technology and so on. However, according to divine teachings, most of the science practised up till now is really a kind of provisional science involving manufacturing, processing and chemical transformation.

Albert Einstein was asked one day by a friend, "Do you believe that absolutely everything can be expressed scientifically?" "Yes, it would be possible," he replied, "but it would make no sense. It would be a description without meaning – as if you described a Beethoven symphony as a variation in air pressure" (Clark, 1971).

The pursuit of knowledge using only a materialistic approach has resulted in a limited science that is largely based on analysis rather than on synthesis. In biology, for example, animals, plants, organs and cells are generally studied by dissecting, subdividing, compartmentalising and classifying, often causing damage to the material studied. Similarly, in physics, chemistry, geology and other disciplines, research is mainly done by analysis rather than by synthesis. Material-centred human science has not led to the synthesis of even the simplest living cell. In fact, there is no satisfactory scientific explanation of how a cell lives. The phenomenon of life, what makes something live, cannot be explained at all in terms of present-day human science.

Another problem is that the pursuit of science in a material-centred way is not only limited, but can have destructive aspects, as science has not addressed the matter of values. As Dr David Suzuki (1990), well-known geneticist and internationally renowned broadcaster, said: *The huge increase in material wealth and consumption since the end of the Second World War and the accumulation of powerful methods of extraction of natural resources have generated a sense that science and technology supply the knowledge required to control and manage the entire planet. It is a terrible delusion that is not supported by an understanding of what science provides and the nature of technological power.* The advancement of so-called modern science and technology based on scientific method is so recent that more than 90 per cent of all the world's scientists that ever lived are still alive today. However, although the world's store of knowledge multiplies every year, so do the problems.

For example, emphasis on the material approach has led to a science and technology that, despite its valuable contributions to people's comfort and convenience, has also contributed to pollution, destruction of the environment, extinction of plant and animal species, global warming, destruction of the ozone layer, deforestation, an increase in desert areas, rising sea levels, overcrowding, food and water shortages, energy crises, an increase in disease and greater conflict, to name a few.

After the Earth Summit Conference in Rio De Janeiro in 1991, more than half the world's Nobel Prizewinners signed a petition asking for world leaders to take concrete steps to save the planet, but materialistic preoccupations, particularly in the field of the economy, have resulted in limited positive action, considering the urgency of the problems.

The bio-technology revolution in which genetic engineering and gene splicing are promoted for the sake of profit, with little regard for ethics and hazards, seems to be going out of control (Rifkin, 1991; Ho, 1998). Corporations have won legal battles to patent lifeforms. The whole planet's genetic heritage, including DNA itself, which humans share with other species, can now be turned into private property. Human genetic material can also be manipulated and combined with that of pigs, sheep, mice and other animals, and this is actually happening. The research on cloning is another field of science that gives little consideration to ethics and moral values.

Another uncomfortable fact is that *the vast majority of scientists and engineers in the world carry out work for the military. Such work may be called 'defense research' but ultimately it translates into weapons for killing. After all, the horribly imaginative weapons – neutron, particle beam, chemical, biological – don't come from the minds of politicians or military strategists, but are the products of the fertile imagination of scientists and engineers.*

The majority of the remainder of the scientific and engineering professions works for private industry – for profit. If the primary motivations underlying the application of scientific knowledge today are destruction and profit, it's hardly surprising that the best interests of the general public or long-term environmental effects seldom weigh heavily in determining whether a new discovery will be used (Suzuki, 1990).

Another unfortunate aspect of science – upheld as a field in which scholars are committed and devoted to seeking the truth, enjoying academic freedom in this pursuit, which involves critical inquiry, analysis and evaluation – is the fact that in reality there are many cases where scientists are silenced unfairly if their views threaten the power of the establishment (Moran, 1998). This, of course, is not only an issue of contemporary science, but of any science of the future.

Jonathon Porritt (2000), Co-Founder and Programme Director of Forum for the Future, has reviewed a number of these alarming issues and concludes that modern science can be a destructive model of progress unless it becomes more precautionary, more participative, less arrogant, less compromised by its paymasters, more compassionate and more holistic.

Even if science and technology were promoted with high ethics and noble values, and did not lead to any destruction, I do not think that the present approach in conventional science would lead to deep understanding of the essence of the human, consciousness, the key elements underlying life and death, certain crucial aspects that determine behaviour and the processes enabling growth in living organisms. The main reason for this is that science has been mainly preoccupied with the material aspect, only a little with the mental aspect and almost not at all with the spiritual aspect.

In short, contemporary science has made, and continues to make, valuable contributions for humankind. At the same time, however, the limitations and dangers of material-centred science are making people reassess the basic approach to science.

Towards holistic science

I think it is understandable that science has had a material emphasis until recently, because according to divine teachings, the plan of God over the past many thousands of years has been to develop the material aspects of civilisations. All fields – business, medicine, religion or anything else – have been largely material-centred, something that was in keeping with the will of God, that is, until 1962.

Major breakthroughs have occurred in the fields of science and technology, rather than in religion, because the various people concerned received special guidance and inspiration from holy spirits, according to a revelation that Sukuinushisama received in 1963, entitled 'The happiness of new and true ones with a divine soul within': "During these past several thousands of years, it is difficult to find those who have holy spirits within, except in the fields of science and technology".

Startling breakthroughs have been achieved by various scientific geniuses, many of whom were very conscious of the existence of God. For instance, it is well known that Newton, considered to be one of the greatest contributors to science, and Einstein, considered one of the greatest thinkers up till now, maintained faith in a higher power while devoting themselves to scientific research. Einstein's famous words – "Religion without science is blind. Science without religion is lame," and "God does not play at dice" are frequently quoted to this day (Calaprice, 1996). Rather than denigrate science as being materialistic, one can be full of respect for the contributions made by scientists.

Nevertheless, even though material-centred science has contributed much to the world up till now, particularly in a technological sense, in my opinion, the greatest progress in science is yet to occur. I believe that major advances will mainly occur through scientists who match with the will of God, regardless of religion. Since 1962, the beginning of the age of baptism by fire, the will of God has changed from an emphasis on materials to an emphasis on the spiritual. That is why science is expanding its horizons to explore the spiritual realm more than ever before, I feel.

Mahikari and research

I believe that studying the art of True Light, both through one's own experience and also in an experimental setting according to traditional scientific method, is likely to help achieve significant progress towards an all-encompassing science that involves the divine, astral and physical realms, that is, holistic science. For a start, personal experience with the Light of God will progressively lead to understanding that God really exists and that different dimensions of existence are a reality, as has happened for me.

As I pointed out, various effects of True Light can be both experienced and demonstrated. True Light is a purifying energy, a creative power, a revitalising force and much more, that cannot be fully grasped by the human intellect at the present time. It has a kind of intelligence, it seems to me. For example, experience suggests that when True Light is radiated to damaged tissue, it helps repair those cells that are not irreversibly damaged and makes new ones grow to replace those that have been destroyed. Continuing to radiate the Light does not result in continuing proliferation of cells once the condition has reached normal levels. If True Light were nothing but a mindless creative energy, the cells would continue to proliferate indefinitely. In other words, the True Light of God is not something like heat energy or ultraviolet radiation, which will continue having certain cumulative effects that can even be destructive if radiated continuously. It is a great over-simplification to regard God's Light merely as a purifying energy or healing Light. Saying it simply, it is the manifestation of God, although this does not sound like traditional scientific terminology.

Even if we know that True Light is the manifestation of the Creator God, it may nevertheless be useful for research purposes to use limiting labels such as 'spiritual power' or 'special energy'. In my opinion, providing the ultimate purpose of True Light is appreciated and providing the information about the Light is used for the salvation of souls, the betterment of humankind and fulfilling the plan of God, nothing but good can result from researching this Light at all possible levels.

I am not implying that the study of True Light in a laboratory setting will give deep understanding about God. Rigidly controlled experiments in a laboratory setting are not only unnatural but their experimental design is such that deeper aspects of the energy cannot be measured or even comprehended in the slightest. Nevertheless, such experiments may be valuable because they at least give clear information about certain aspects of this Light.

At this stage we cannot be precise about what True Light *is*, but we can nevertheless study what it *does*. Thus, even though the main purpose of radiating the Light is to achieve purification, some of the data from experiments may reveal something about what it can do, or the importance of maintaining appropriate attitudes during the process. Some kamikumite have implied by their words that every time they hold their hand over plants, food, animals and so on, things are influenced in a predictable manner. Experiments, however, have sometimes revealed different results or no visible change. It is best not to use our human judgement and try to predict what will happen, or what is good or bad, but conduct studies using controlled experiments and just report what happens. The scientific study of the effects of the Light of God may open people's eyes to the existence of divine phenomena that could never be studied before in this way and therefore may lead to a great elevation of the field of science.

There is no doubt that visible effects of True Light demonstrated in a laboratory, hospital or other experimental setting have helped to awaken many initially sceptical scientists and doctors to the reality of God. This certainly had a significant influence on me. In 1975 I was shown specimens indicating that the Light of God had prevented eggs from going rotten, whereas other eggs that had not received the Light of God had decayed. Jars of months-old, cooked rice which had been given True Light, showed fresh-looking, fluffy and white rice, whereas the same sample of rice that had not received the Light of God had deteriorated and become a kind of brown soup. These simple experiments were not done quantitatively with controls and had not been repeated many times. However, the crude data soon showed me, a practising scientist at that time, that there is something real and effective about the Light of God that can be researched.

In my previous book on Mahikari (Tebecis, 1982, chapter 8) I presented some data from simple experiments on the effects of True Light. The results suggested that God's Light facilitated the growth of *Kentucky Wonder* beans, mung beans, soya beans, lentils and corn; inactivated the toxicity of a pesticide or allowed dwarf beans (*Hawkesbury Wonder*) to survive in the pesticide solution; inhibited the putrefaction of boiled rice; changed the growth pattern of a mould cultured on an agar base; stimulated the production of molecular products of inflammation involved in reactions to protect tissue; as well as facilitated the elimination of these products after their protective action was finished. The main reason for presenting the simple experiments (as well as medical case reports) was to show that some of the effects of True Light can be studied using the accepted approach of scientific method. Naturally, such experiments can be improved by including double-blind controls and doing repeated tests, but the main point was to demonstrate that True Light has effects on non-human, living systems, effects that are observable. The fact that the effects of True Light are startling in any cases at all would be enough to make researchers keen to study this energy, I feel.

A new dimension of science?

What if the scientists who hold mechanistic views discover that God really exists, that there really is a spiritual realm, which is dynamic, operates according to verifiable laws and that there is an intimate relationship between the spiritual realm and all that happens in the physical world? Would not a plausible view then be that God created the laws and the processes and that we are merely permitted to study or catch glimpses of some of these at a certain level? If traditional evolutionists, for instance, were able to discover that the soul of a human being exists, that there are entities called spirits who can attach to the physical body of people and influence their thoughts, behaviour and many other things, would not a mechanical explanation of evolution require revision?

It is possible to discover the real existence of God and the spiritual realm. If one receives the Light of God from a Sukyo Mahikari member and becomes even a little familiar with some of the teachings and practices, it is only a matter of course that one will discover the reality of the spiritual realm, I believe. In this way, it will be possible to view many of the conventional theories of science in a new light, differently from the interpretations using the material-centred approach.

The underlying attitude in science would then be that scientists are merely studying something that has already been set up or created with a very sophisticated, high-level divine science. We humans are merely given some stewardship of this earth and permitted to uncover some of its marvels. If such a humble approach were adopted, I feel that science would progress in leaps and bounds.

Broadly speaking, there are three intercommunicating dimensions of existence, the divine, astral and physical, but science up till now has been preoccupied mainly with the physical aspect, and to some degree, the mental aspect, but not the aspect to do with God and the spiritual realm (including the human spirit). There are countless observations by Sukyo Mahikari practitioners verifying that invisible entities or spirits are in communication with people and influence their consciousness, personality, behaviour and other aspects (see chapter 4). Even if new inventions eventually made it physically possible to record from single DNA molecules within neurones or the like, in my opinion, mental processes will not be understood deeply without understanding the phenomenon of spirits and the spiritual realm.

In the Mahikari primary course one learns about the principle of the two-dimensional cross, a fundamental principle of the universe. Briefly, when the two basic opposites (for example, fire and water; vertical and horizontal; yang and yin; male and female) are harmoniously combined, power is generated in a wondrous, mysterious way, a creative power greater than either and going beyond either, a mysterious transformation of something to a deeper or more profound level. Similarly, true science is the study of crossing such opposites, the spiritual and the material aspects of natural laws.

I feel it is important to study spirit phenomena as seriously as material phenomena. As mentioned, personal experience – the subjective intuitive aspect as well as the objective physical aspect used up till now – need to be integrated. The material-centred approach involves a logical, sequential analysis, whereas the spiritually oriented approach involves an intuitive, holistic synthesis. Either approach is limited on its own. Combined, however, such science has the potential of transcending many limitations. It may well be that a new approach to scientific research has to be developed, something that goes beyond either.

For instance, how can a strictly physical approach in science explain the influence of the mind on inanimate materials, not to mention its influence on plants and animals? Oshienushisama indicated that even materials will operate better when there is gratitude, something I have experienced personally time and time again with my car, tools, office equipment, lawnmower and so on. I do not pretend to know how this communication occurs, but that it works is something that I can experience. Sukuinushisama taught that all matter has the wisdom, love and will of God to different degrees. These are not teachings that can be grasped easily through rigid laboratory experiments and physical measuring. Understanding grows with the experience of the existence of God and the spiritual realm, and this experience influences one's interpretation of even physical phenomena.

In a revelation that Sukuinushisama received in 1960 (entitled 'The ambiguous delusion called truth by humans') God revealed that the direction of science from then onwards should be towards "returning to the divine science of the great original spirit". In other words, divine science will be eventually achieved when scientists try to fit with the will of God and combine the materialistic science of the past with spirit-mind science, and later, science of divine spirits.

The future direction of science clearly points towards research on what is beyond the material, that is, the spiritual realm.

By being attuned to the will of God, scientists will have a better chance of receiving inspiration from God, which will no doubt lead to breakthroughs in the progress of science. In 1967 (the journal *Mahikari*, in Japanese, vol. 53, p. 76) Sukuinushisama said:

As regards science, when human beings revive their communication with the fundamental realm and achieve an innermost attitude equivalent to that of the divine spirits realm, that is, when they begin working for the welfare of humankind, tremendous progress will be permitted in science. It is so arranged that this progress will be many times greater than what has been achieved so far. This is because God gives unlimited wisdom to people who acquire innermost attitudes like that of God. It is a matter of course when you think about it. God cannot bestow genuine wisdom on those who oppose God; who doubt God; who may destroy not only the earth but the universe, because it is just too dangerous to do so . . . . According to the degree that people tune in to the 'dial' of God, the doors to high-dimension mysteries will be opened up to scientists and humankind of the future. This will occur in the same way as in the past – most of the great, new discoveries of past science came through inspiration.

From a revelation given by God in 1961 (entitled 'God-given intuition'), Sukuinushisama explained that God-given intuition or inspiration can be received by people when they attune themselves to be in direct communication with the divine soul. The mind must become pure, righteous and good. If a person strives to have a crystal-pure mind and soul and makes devoted efforts in serving God, the Light of wondrous wisdom of God can easily pour into him.

Clearly, it is valuable for researchers to make steady efforts to become purified and elevate their innermost attitudes so that they can tune in to God and receive "good, God-given inspiration" in order to contribute to the development of a high-level science. The practice of purifying with God's Light is an effective way to help achieve this aim.

Comparing views of other scholars

Sukuinushisama taught that the stars, planets and other heavenly bodies in the universe have been divinely arranged so that humans can flourish on earth. Years ago, many scientists concluded that because the universe is so large, the earth and its life forms are merely a speck that came about by chance, and that there is no need to postulate any Divine Being responsible for its creation. It was reasoned that since we humans appeared only some 15 billion years after the Big Bang, we must be some kind of after-thought, an improbable accident that occurred late. In recent years, however, many cosmologists have calculated that all that has been discovered about the universe shows that it could not have occurred in any other way. Life as we know it would have been completely impossible for quite some time after the Big Bang, because life is dependent upon carbon, nitrogen, oxygen and phosphorus as its building blocks. After the Big Bang, the universe was an inferno so hot that these elements could not be formed. Only after considerable time had elapsed to allow for the necessary cooling could the building blocks of life emerge. During this time the stars were formed, particularly the supernovas. These subsequently exploded, scattering matter to become planets and containing, in approximately the right proportions, the very elements which are necessary for life.

All this required a period of no less than 10 billion years, by which time the universe had expanded to be some 10 billion light years in size. Only then were the necessary conditions present for life to begin anywhere. People should not be surprised that the universe is so enormous or so old. It is necessary to have one so big and old in order to produce the first building blocks of life – single carbon-based living cells. Human beings are carbon-based, intelligent life forms and this planet earth is a cosmic object which draws its energy from an average-sized star. According to calculations, the only universe we know of is one which is big enough and old enough to have produced us. To put it more clearly, humans arrived right on schedule in cosmic time, within the parameters set by the physics of the universe.

Even though we can understand why it took the long time it did for the building blocks of life to appear, it is still not possible to comprehend how they came together to produce life, without postulating a special power. As biophysicist Professor Harold Morowitz (1968) pointed out, even 15 billion years is insufficient for unguided, random reactions to produce life. Professor Davies (1994) also estimated that from random chance, it is incredibly improbable that any universe should have the parameters necessary for the support of intelligent life. Everything points to a guiding power, I believe.

Science tells us that the cosmic vacuum, the empty space between stars and galaxies, far from being empty, is a reservoir of unimaginably enormous energies, with each cubic centimetre containing more locked-in 'zero point' energy than the mass energy of the whole of the vast universe. Little is understood about this.

Einstein is said to have likened energy to thought waves of the Central Mind, which is the nucleus of all energies.

In his book, *Disturbing the Universe*, the theoretical physicist Professor Freeman Dyson (1979) considered that "mind is already inherent in every electron". Another well-known scientist who thought along similar lines is Professor David Bohm. In his book, *Wholeness and the Implicate Order*, Bohm (1980) showed that in this implicate order, the universe cannot be described as fragmented into individual parts but behaves in a fundamentally connected, non-localised and intertwined way.

A surprising fact for which evidence has been assembled by a number of scientists over the past few decades is that a mysterious collection of numbers, that may be called the constants of nature, appear to exist. In their book, *The Anthropic Cosmological Principle*, Barrow and Tipler (1986) distinguish between two types of factors upon which planetary life depends. If the ratio of the earth's radius to the distance of the earth from the sun were slightly different, life could not have evolved on earth. The mass of a human being is the geometric mean between the mass of an atom and the mass of the planet. Similarly, the mass of the planet is the geometric mean of the mass of an atom and the mass of the observable universe. These are not pure coincidences but are the necessary consequences of the fundamental constants associated with the interaction between gravitational and electromagnetic forces. Barrow and Tipler go into great detail to demonstrate these cosmic facts, and conclude that the sizes of atoms, planets and people are the inevitable consequences of fundamental forces and values.

For example, if the ratio of the nuclear and electromagnetic forces to each other were even slightly different, then carbon atoms could not exist; that in turn means that human beings could not exist. Similarly, the ratio of the number of photons to protons must lie within a very narrow range if the conditions of the universe are going to allow carbon-based life to emerge. If one or other of various fundamental constants of physics were altered by a tiny percentage, not only would it not suit the conditions for the human species, but it would have been impossible for this universe to bring forth life anywhere at all.

Barrow and Tipler have even ascertained which combinations of the constants have played a role in making possible the existence of human intelligence. This leads to the point that the universe which exists was specifically designed for the purpose of generating life in general and conscious human observers in particular. I feel that all this postulates the existence of God as the Great Scientist.

§

Logical reasoning is ultimately unverifiable in terms of its own methodology (Davies, 1992). The book *Blindness of Modern Science* by the Estonian researcher Dr Undo Uus (1994) is an analysis of the one-sidedness of modern science, ignoring as it does the whole subjective side of human experience and thus failing to ask certain crucial research questions in the mind-brain field. Science in general considers only the formal-structural aspects of reality and ignores the qualitative-content aspect experienced in subjective awareness. It is invalid to explain the latter in terms of the former. Professor John Dupré (2001) shows that human nature cannot be explained in terms of the viewpoints of evolutionary psychology and rational choice theory based on economics.

Many scientific breakthroughs which were later validated and accepted were initially persecuted or ridiculed due to so-called scientific scepticism (Milton, 1994). Humanity now needs to go beyond the analytical, fragmented mind – always dissecting, comparing, evaluating – to add another kind of perception, a direct understanding of life, involving insight and intuitive awareness of the true nature of life. Many eminent scientists – Einstein, Heisenberg, Schrödinger, Eddington and others – have found another mode of knowing, called intimate, direct, intuitive, non-dual knowledge or insight.

Although a new approach is necessary, good science has to play an important role in helping to establish a high-quality civilisation. As well-known population biologist Professor Paul Ehrlich (1986) said: *I am convinced that a quasi-religious movement, one concerned with the need to change the values that now govern much of human activity, is essential to the persistence of our civilization. But agreeing that science, even the science of ecology, cannot answer all questions – that there are 'other ways of knowing' – does not diminish the absolutely critical role that good science must play if our over-extended civilization is to save itself.*

It is scientific to be open-minded and to recognise that there may be many realms of existence, experience or phenomena that have not been touched, understood or interpreted properly using traditional science. Many phenomena of the universe – electricity, the motion of planets, nuclear reactions and so on – were once considered mysterious and not amenable to study for fear of 'treading on holy ground'. As Arthur C. Clarke said, "When a scientist states that something is possible, he is almost certainly right. When he states that something is impossible, he is probably wrong."

On top of being open-minded, it is important to be responsible and ethical in science. For a number of years Professor Håkan Snellman (1995), Head of the Physics Department, Royal Institute of Technology in Stockholm, has been advocating that acquiring knowledge should come with responsibility, and not as a means of gaining manipulative power.

In recent years a great revolution has been occurring in the physical sciences through what has come to be called 'chaos theory' (Gleick, 1987). Simple systems give rise to complex behaviour and complex systems give rise to simple behaviour. Moreover, the laws of complexity hold universally, irrespective of the details of the system's elements.

Another scientific revolution, according to Dr Michio Kaku (1994) . . . *is created by the theory of hyperspace, which states that dimensions exist beyond the commonly accepted form of space and time. There is a growing acknowledgment among physicists worldwide, including several Nobel laureates, that the universe may actually exist in higher dimensional space . . . Light, in fact, can be explained as vibrations in the fifth dimension . . . Higher dimensional space, instead of being an empty, passive backdrop against which quarks play out their eternal roles, actually becomes the central actor in the drama of nature.*

The search for a more spiritual kind of science of the future has been discussed over a number of years by the Islamic scholar Dr Seyyed Hossein Nasr, particularly in his best-known work, *The Spiritual Crisis of Modern Man* (1968), and more recently, *Religion and the Order of Nature* (1996). Nasr considers that the crisis in·man's relation to the environment and nature is a spiritual crisis, stemming from the kind of materialistic science we have been cultivating since the Renaissance. In *The Need for a Sacred Science*, Nasr (1993) pleads for a spiritual science that includes both experience and results from material-centred science, but with a focus on the spiritual or sacred as a means of bridging the gap between God, humans and nature.

Professor E. Laszlo's theory of an underlying universal 'fifth field' which he calls the psi-field, has captured widespread interest amongst scientists. In his book *The Creative Cosmos*, Laszlo (1993), who is an interdisciplinarian in his research, writings and daily life, proposes a working description of how this universal field operates in the world as a connecting medium at the sub-quantum level. He considers that the universe is like an organism that operates by information, sometimes very subtle information. In this new conception we have information arising in one part of the system, subtly sympathising and cohering with another part. The whole system evolves together or co-evolves. All parts evolve as the whole system evolves. His view is that what seems to be missing in current scientific theories is a full scientific understanding of what it is in nature that creates interconnections. We know that individual phenomena are interconnected in very surprising ways, even at the fundamental level of the quantum. On the biological level, we know that there is something that informs genetic mutations, so they cohere better with the environment into which the mutants are entering. We know that the human mind is informed and can interact beyond the range of sensory information, certainly with other minds and even with a broader environment. But we do not understand all this scientifically as yet. His view is that some time in the course of the twenty-first century we will be moving towards a highly unified natural science, a science of a dynamic evolution from cosmos to consciousness. This means looking at the cosmos as an entity, that – at the same time as being a physical reality – is a sacred reality, a spiritual reality. In his book *The Connectivity Hypothesis*, Laszlo (2003) brings his views together in a more formal way by postulating the connectivity hypothesis as the foundation of a new integral science.

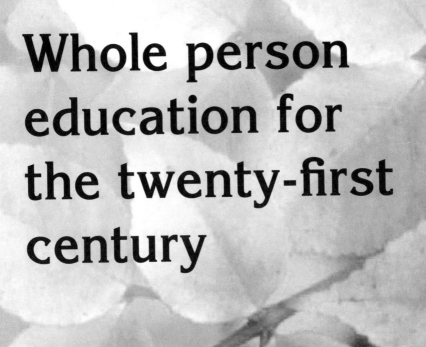

Whole person education for the twenty-first century

Chapter 8

Whole person education for the twenty-first century

When I went to school, and later, to university, where I also did some lecturing after graduation, I did not imagine that education is anything else but learning – the acquiring of knowledge and skills. Now, after years of studying and practising certain teachings of Sukyo Mahikari as well as the art of True Light, I have come to realise that the most important thing to achieve a good education is to elevate the spiritual condition, in addition to acquiring knowledge and skills. I believe that a sound education should emphasise the spiritual aspect and that eventually this needs to be incorporated into education programs, if education is really to progress in a wholesome way. I call this spiritually oriented approach to education 'whole person education'.

Progress and limitations of material-centred education

In modern society in recent years, the main emphasis in education has been on acquiring knowledge and training the body, that is, the mental and physical aspects. This has led to considerable progress for humankind, and continues to be of great value today. It is important for students to study diligently and strive to improve their mind and body. A significant limitation, however, is that nutrition for the soul is not considered much in most schools and society in general. People are taught mainly how to achieve success in a materialistic sense. As a consequence, many people have acquired factual knowledge and skills, but not necessarily virtue and wisdom. I believe it is due to the lack of nutrition for the soul that various kinds of problems have been increasing in educational institutions and society throughout the world – bullying, violence, apathy, absenteeism from school, crime, drug abuse, sexual problems and the like.

In attempting to solve these problems, many educational institutions are trying to restore trust between teachers and pupils; reduce aggressive competition in academic achievement; prohibit extreme physical punishment; increase the number of teachers and provide more diverse curricula. But the problems continue to increase, just as much in modern, developed countries as they do in developing countries, where people live more simply and have limited funding. Youth suicide, for instance, is increasing particularly steeply in well-to-do countries such as Australia, New Zealand, the U.S.A. and Japan, to name a few. Many countries have reported alarming increases in juvenile crime, including violence and homicide, particularly from the early 1990s onwards. Violent crime is no longer only the domain of gangsters but can even involve children anywhere and anytime, it seems.

From my experience, I feel that such problems are a manifestation of the contamination and disorder arising from spiritual aspects or the spiritual realm. Many of these problems can be overcome, or at least greatly reduced, by developing whole person or spiritually oriented education, education in which young people receive God's creative energy, purification and spiritual nutrition. This is the essence of true education, I believe. In Sukyo Mahikari the term 'education' refers mainly to nurturing people so that they can live a good-quality life that is valuable to God, others and themselves. It does not refer to a system of acquiring knowledge by following a curriculum.

Towards whole person education

Sukuinushisama and Oshienushisama have given valuable guidance concerning the essence of education. According to the spiritual functions of the syllables that make up the word 'education' in Japanese (*ki-yo-u-i-ku*), the meaning of education is 'giving the energy of God; of life; filling with divine will'. Saying it more specifically, "The foundation of spiritually oriented education . . . is to purify the soul and spiritual body with the Light of God and to change people's innermost attitudes from material-centredness to spirit-centredness," according to Oshienushisama. Knowledge and skills of a mental and physical nature are important to support the spiritual aspect. However, by themselves, they will usually not result in effective education in the long term.

From my understanding and experience, the key issues to achieve a whole person education are the Light of God; resolving spirit disturbance; elevated innermost attitudes and words of parents; elevated innermost attitudes and words of educators; conveying high values; and creating a home of love and harmony – all in addition to the conventional approach of acquiring knowledge and skills. Each of these aspects is related to some or all of the others. I do not wish to imply that the nurturing of people can be broken down into six issues like following a manual, as many other things can help. However, I feel that understanding the issues discussed in the following pages should be helpful to promote nurturing of the young.

The Light of God

The Light of God is invaluable to achieve a whole person education because it purifies the soul and spiritual body, and helps to resolve spirit disturbance, enabling one's full potential to open up, including the mental and physical aspects. Sukyo Mahikari centres are places where people can be purified and purify others with the Light of God. Those people who are kamikumite can also do this as a way of life at home, at work, sometimes at school and wherever it is possible and practical.

It is valuable to give the Light of God to one's children if one is a parent, to one's students if one is an educator and it is permitted, and to society in general. Many Sukyo Mahikari educators and students have reported improvements as a result of purifying their classrooms, their schools or other educational institutions, not to mention the people with whom they associate. Some people have found that children who did not like studying or who could not concentrate for very long, who tired of things easily, overcame these problems after receiving Light on the back of the head and neck and the shoulder areas. There have been cases of children whose scores in class improved just from receiving Light alone. Teachers have been able to solve various problems by giving Light to students who were unmanageable or distressed in some way.

Resolving spirit disturbance

Many youth turn to juvenile delinquency because they have been hurt inside as a result of discord between their parents. However, in my opinion the inner cause of such discord and juvenile delinquency is manipulation by spirits. Youth are manipulated by spirits, as are people of all ages, a product of society's emphasis on materialism, not understanding the importance of purification and elevation of the soul. The main reason that many youth do not go to school, acquire strange personalities, become involved in bullying, violence, or even commit suicide, is due to their spiritual impurities and those of their families, which manifest as disturbances by attached spirits, usually spirits with resentment. The present age is an age of spirit disturbance in which more than 80% of humankind is influenced by various spirits.

Therefore, it will usually not be possible to solve the fundamental cause of most problems of children and students, no matter how well-meaning their parents and educators may be, and no matter what kind of approaches are used mentally and physically, unless the person's attached spirits who are suffering are saved step by step. This is called resolving spirit disturbance. The disturbance occurs because the person and/or the person's family have hurt the spirits in past lives. Problems occur according to the law of cause and effect, so it is good to take responsibility and go about solving problems in a positive way (see chapter 4).

Even kamikumite who are familiar with the phenomenon of spirit disturbance are sometimes surprised that the education of their own children is influenced by the impurities of themselves (the parents) and their ancestors. One such case is illustrated by the experience of Mrs Nanaumi (1993), given below.

When my son was in the fourth grade of primary school, he was the boy who forgot things the most in his class and his grades were the worst, all Es. I felt uneasy about this and was in considerable turmoil. I scolded my son many times with words such as, 'What do you listen to during class? Look at the blackboard properly and listen well to what your teachers say!' I made him attend additional after-school classes outside his school. Despite all that, his grades did not improve.

Every time I scolded my son, he cried, saying, 'Mum, as you told me, I was listening to my teachers earnestly . . . I looked at the board and took notes . . . but no matter what I do, I can't remember anything!' All I could do was cry with him in anxiety about his future.

One such day, while I was receiving True Light on the forehead, an attached spirit manifested and confessed that he had resentment against the Nanaumi family. In a very resentful manner the spirit said, 'The ancestors of the Nanaumi family used to be my retainers. However, they betrayed me, their lord, and as a result our family was made to perish. Despite this, the Nanaumis are allowed to have two male descendants. I have been trying to kill your sons but I could not do it at all because of this thing called Mahikari! So instead, I am making them suffer by disturbing your son's studies. Your son follows your instructions and stares at the blackboard during classes. But I cover both his ears tightly with my hands during the class so that he cannot understand anything! You deserve it!'

I was utterly shocked to hear this and thought, 'Oh, no! The reason why my son had such bad marks was due to the spirit attached to me! It was all because of my neglect in offering devoted service to God that this spirit has not been saved . . . Despite this, I have just been blaming my son . . .'

I offered deep apology to God for my insufficiencies in my attitude towards serving God and coming closer to God, and changed my life so that I was able to devote myself to serving God.

It was after that when my son's grades began to improve remarkably.

Through this experience, I have realised the divine teaching that the cause of all misfortune lies in oneself and in no-one else, and that if I want things to change, it is I who must change first of all.

§

Beginning in the early 1990s, Sukyo Mahikari in Japan has been holding International and National Educators Conferences. In 1995 I was able to attend such a conference, together with more than 800 Mahikari educators. Several people reported cases of problems resulting from spirit disturbance, for example, of children suddenly refusing to go to school (called 'social withdrawal syndrome'). One school teacher, a kamikumite, reported that a teenage girl in his class refused to go to school for no obvious reason. Her parents just could not persuade her to go to school. This teacher visited the teenage girl's house, but she ran away and hid while he was there so he could not talk to her. The mother of the girl explained that she had taken her daughter to a counsellor, who said it would take about three years to get over the problem, so the mother was very depressed as it meant that her daughter would miss out on classes for a long time. After some discussion the teacher gave Light to the father, the mother and the grandmother of the girl. He made appointments and continued to give Light to the parents. After about two months, the girl began going to school again just as suddenly as she had stopped, and she has not refused to attend school ever since that time.

The Chairman of the Sukyo Mahikari Educators Committee in Japan (a university educator who has a PhD degree) has held private counselling sessions with families that had children who refused to go to school. His main approach was to give True Light to the parents, which in itself resulted in many of these children returning to school. Of more than 100 cases, the success rate was over 50%.

Another problem that was raised at the Educators Conference was so-called 'nocturnal children', youth who tend to stay up at night, listening to rock music and indulging in their hobbies until late and then not getting up in the morning to go to school, but instead, sleeping for much of the day. Attempting to solve this problem through conventional approaches has been rather unsuccessful, but in the cases where the Light of God was given, there was considerable success.

There were also case reports to indicate that the reason some children did not like studying was due to influence by spirits from low dimensions of the astral world attached to them. As they became purified with the Light of God and the service to God offered by their family members, particularly the parents, the children grew to like studying.

Elevated innermost attitudes and words of parents

It is particularly important for the upstream, the parents, to be purified and elevated spiritually, as that is what flows downstream to their children. It is the innermost attitude (outlook, mindset) that communicates most effectively. Sukuinushisama taught that parents and children are connected by inseparable spiritual cords, and according to the principle, 'spirit first, mind next, body follows', it is all the more important for the innermost attitudes and spiritual quality of parents to be elevated in order for their children to become elevated. In Sukuinushisama's words:

Basically, the point is to purify the spiritual realm of father and mother. Let the Light given by God through the purified spiritual realm of the parents penetrate the children.

I consider this the most important point in the education of children. In other words, it is important for parents to become good examples of 'changing others just by being'. Otherwise, no matter how much academic education and discipline are given as has happened up till now, crime will continue to increase amongst children.

If parents pretend in front of their children, behave respectably, give seemingly good advice and so on, but deep down are selfish, materialistic, exploit others, or the like, such low attitudes and low spiritual qualities are transmitted to their children, irrespective of where they are. Conversely, even if the parents cannot be together with their children as frequently as they would like, but make efforts to become elevated, are righteous in the eyes of God, care about others and practise the divine teachings, these high-quality, high-level attitudes are transmitted to their children.

Parents play a major role in the education of their children, whether they realise it or not, because they are upstream. The spirit disturbance of the children is really a manifestation of the spirit disturbance of their parents. Children are mirrors of their parents. They do not acquire what their parents tell them as much as what their parents are and what they do (which depends on the parents' innermost attitudes).

Research has revealed that the biggest influence on people's lives stems from what happened to them while they were children, in fact, while they were still babies. There is evidence that the innermost attitudes of parents while the baby is still in the mother's womb have an influence on the child's future. Psychologists have shown that demonstrating love to a baby can even be assessed physically to various degrees – an unloved infant will have retarded bone growth and may even die early. A stroked infant, on the other hand, grows faster. Basically, the later one leaves things, the harder it is to reverse any problems or to substitute good patterns for bad ones. The value of efforts made by parents to elevate their innermost attitudes and give good nutrition – spiritually, mentally and physically – to their children, cannot be over-emphasised, I feel.

At the 1995 International Educators Conference, I was impressed to learn how great the influence of parents and educators is on their children and students.

For example, a lady school teacher reported that she was able to awaken to the influence of the innermost attitudes of the parents on their children, through her experience with the cleansing of her own son. Her small son had bouts of pneumonia, measles and suchlike, and because the child was small and still unable to speak, she felt very uneasy. Even though she gave Light to her son regularly, she was full of anxiety. Over time she noticed that whenever she gave Light to her son while worrying, his condition did not change much but lingered on for up to ten days or so. When she was grateful for the purification her son was receiving and gave Light with confidence, he was able to recover easily, in a few days.

Another lady talked about how her innermost attitudes influenced her nine-year-old son who often had chest cleansing. The boy would often wake up at night and the mother used to give him Light, but with reluctance, not wanting to be bothered in the middle of the night. She gave Light simply in order to fix the problem. More often than not, this did not lead to obvious improvement in her son. Eventually, through spirit investigations performed by staff members of her Mahikari centre, she came to realise that the chest problem of her son was due to a spirit suffering, someone whom she had killed in a previous life. She was then able to change her outlook and give Light to her son with a heart of apology instead of irritation. The Light of God became much more effective when she gave Light with this attitude.

The words people use are a materialisation of their innermost attitudes. I have been inspired by the guidance given by Sukuinushisama and Oshienushisama concerning the importance of the spiritual functions of words. Words are like seeds that are planted. They germinate and grow. They are living. Filthy, dirty, impure, impolite words cause spiritual contamination, which materialises as unpleasant phenomena. If parents or teachers use such words, the spiritual realm in that environment becomes contaminated and the children will become negative. Conversely, pure, kind, polite words purify the spiritual realm of the environment, including the people there and oneself, resulting in a positive influence.

I was quite impressed at the 1995 International Educators Conference when a school teacher from France got up from the audience and related how they had demonstrated the power of words by calling a certain goat 'Beautiful' (*Belle*) and another goat 'Ugly'. Over the weeks 'Beautiful', did, in fact, become beautiful, with nice, pleasant to touch, silky hair, whereas the goat named 'Ugly' apparently looked scruffy and was not pleasant to touch. Then the names were reversed. The beautiful goat began to look scruffy. The goat that used to be scruffy but was now called 'Beautiful' began to change into a beautiful goat from the very first day it was called 'Beautiful'.

Elevated innermost attitudes and words of educators
Since educators are upstream to the ones they are educating, it is important for them to become good role models in every aspect – spiritually, mentally and physically. Students tend to pick up characteristics of their teachers, their good and bad points. Education involves transferring one's spiritual quality and human qualities to others. That is why it is important for educators to elevate themselves.

The higher the position or role in society, the family or wherever, the more important it is to become a good role model.

It is not the behaviour, but the innermost attitude that has the biggest influence. For example, a teacher may be very skilled in speaking and imparting knowledge, but may lead a despicable life behind the scenes, treating the role of teacher merely as a job to make money. He may not care about his students at all, but treat them with disdain, apathy and irritation. The students will feel uncared for and may become rebellious, with little respect for their teacher. They may not even be consciously aware of why they have these negative feelings despite their teacher's skill in the physical aspect of teaching. Conversely, a teacher may not be highly skilled in imparting knowledge, but if he really cares for his students and their future, this attitude will communicate and draw out the best in the students.

As mentioned in the previous chapter, research has shown that the attitudes of teachers actually manifest in the scores their students receive in tests, quite apart from anything else they do (Rosenthal, 1991). Teachers who have high expectations of their students find that their students achieve higher scores than in cases where teachers do not have such expectations.

In 1983, Oshienushisama pointed out:

Teachers should be role models for children and the youth. Basically, they are responsible for giving children the essence or energy of God and divine truth, but they have not understood what it means to be educators, and have neglected the development of their own character, 'selling' only academic knowledge in bits and pieces. The end result is the desolation that prevails in the realm of education today . . .

If those in society who are called 'clergy' and 'educators' understand that giving education really means transmitting spiritual and human characteristics from oneself; and if they can confidently teach the youth and the children that all so-called difficulties are golden opportunities to train the soul; and can also teach them the need for daily gratitude for the blessings from God, their teachers and their parents; as well as the need for daily reflection; then both juvenile delinquency and violence will decrease dramatically.

Conveying high values

Another important aspect of achieving whole person or spiritually oriented education is the conveying of virtuous principles and moral values, particularly by parents and educators. This involves both the invisible aspect – spiritual quality, innermost attitudes, values, thoughts – that emanate naturally from the parents and educators, and the principles, morals and values that are conveyed in words, writing and behaviour.

In the home, for instance, even though the Light of God given directly and the elevation of the spiritual condition of the parents are the most crucial aspects for the nurturing of children, it is also important to enable children to understand *why* they do things, rather than having views imposed on them just because they are one's children. Naturally, with young children it is important to convey matters to do with God in a simple way that they can understand. Sukuinushisama said:

I think that there are two ways to approach the subject of going towards God with children. One is where the parents make sure that their children follow the path of directing themselves towards God with a good understanding. The other is where the children are made to worship God just because their parents worship God, and because children have to do as they are told, even though they don't understand what they are doing. There will be a major difference in the results between these two approaches in the future.

It will be a big advantage to parents if their children enter the path of directing themselves towards God while still young, gradually resolving their spirit disturbance, and attend the primary course. While feeling joyful for the great blessing of being parents, it is very important to teach children what directing themselves towards God is all about and engrave this in their souls, starting to nurture this when they are very young.

Oshienushisama has taught that before anything else it is important to nurture children so that they are able to offer gratitude for being able to experience the real existence of God. So, to achieve this, the parents should be models of gratitude to God, praying in the morning and evening, expressing gratitude before and after meals and other situations. Essentially, what is important is how the adults practise God-centredness in their everyday life. Do they regularly purify their house with True Light; do they purify their food; do they purify their bodies? If children do not take purification seriously, it may be because their parents do not take it seriously. Are the parents trying to be grateful for everything? Do they greet everybody? In general, children may not always listen to their parents but they will often copy what their parents do.

If parents realise that they do not really own their children, and teachers realise that they do not own their students, the quality of their guidance will improve, I believe. In essence, the children or students entrusted to one are children of God. Just as gardeners are merely stewards or custodians caring for some aspects of great nature and are limited in what they can do as regards the growth of the plants, parents and educators are also merely stewards or custodians who are entrusted with certain people in order to help nurture them so that they can grow more as God's children. In normal circumstances one cannot control or force plants to grow. One can only develop good stewardship so that the plants can grow more effectively. Parents and teachers usually mean well, but sometimes scold or judge their children and students or use words that force them to do things, without gratitude, treating them as if they were possessions. I think this makes children wither just as it makes plants wither. Learning from nature by interacting with it in a humble, grateful, loving way can help one become a better parent or educator, I feel (see chapter 10 on yoko agriculture).

In November 1997 Oshienushisama said:

The ultimate goal of spiritually oriented education is the perfection of human character (personality development). Without personality development, people cannot be truly useful to society. Children will not grow up to be well-rounded adults if they only receive intellectual training. By adding moral training, we can instil manners and a strong sense of responsibility in the young. Furthermore, when we add spiritual training on top of this, young people will be able to return to being true children of God. True education is made up of the trinity of intellectual, moral and spiritual training.

For teachers, I feel that giving moral and spiritual nutrition should not be a matter of holding talks on religion or preaching dogma and doctrine (as this can even sound exclusive or can be divisive) but enabling people to understand and practise the universal laws. Fundamental aspects about existence and how to live can be conveyed without using religious words. For example, the importance of gratitude, humility, cleanliness, dealing with materials preciously and the spiritual influence of spoken words can be conveyed by any teacher anywhere without going against any local regulations or offending anyone. If educators tune in to God and have the sincere prayer of wanting to be of service to God as well as to give spiritual nutrition to their students, it is more likely that inspiration will be given by God as to how to transmit the normal curriculum contents in a God-centred way.

Many good values can be conveyed without much talking anyway. Consider cleanliness and tidiness, for instance. When I went to primary and high school in Australia, students cleaned their own classrooms and the school grounds. This made students feel that it was normal to keep one's environment clean and tidy. By and large, if animals are left free in nature, they do not make their homes and environment filthy. Today, however, in many societies, professional cleaners are brought in to clean up materials around the school. The children are not always taught about responsibility for cleanliness and tidiness, but they are taught in great detail about differential calculus, computer technology and all kinds of things of an intellectual, academic nature. They may graduate without ever understanding that all creatures basically contribute to keeping their environment clean. Schools and the surrounding environment are often littered with rubbish. If people cannot learn the importance of cleanliness while they are young, then it is no surprise that when they grow up, their environment becomes polluted by the misuse of technology or in other ways.

§

There are schools that have an excellent reputation for imparting academic knowledge and this gives status to their graduating students. I have observed, however, that success in life usually has little to do with which school or university people attend. It is much more important for the whole person to be developed properly, something that starts in the home and can be fostered in any school. Sukuinushisama said:

Some people worry too much about which school they should enter. In reality, however, the school that you go to does not have that much influence on your life. Looking at various people, I think that I can safely say that their lives were not determined by the school they graduated from. There is no relationship between people's happiness and the school they attended. A person's happiness is determined solely by how he goes about erasing his impurities . . .

It is important that both parents and children happily do their best with the school they have, bearing in mind that God arranged it and therefore that school is the best for the person's future.

Looking back on my own life and reminiscing about how the lives of my friends are turning out, as well as from reading biographies of various people, it is clear that the ones who were successful in their careers and achieved happiness in their home lives, marriages, careers and so on, did not necessarily go to prestigious educational institutions, nor was the reverse true. There are countless cases of people with good values, morals and integrity, who struggled through hardships, living poverty-stricken lives in their childhood, and who later became great, making very significant contributions to society. There are also countless cases of people who came from rich families, ones who could afford to go to the most prestigious educational institutions, but who later ended up in disgrace, involved in crime, suicide, broken marriages or other unhappy phenomena. To me it is clear that the most important aspect in anything, including education, is elevation of the spiritual condition.

Naturally, it is also important for students to study the subjects of their curriculum. Acquiring knowledge and skills is not treated lightly. It is just a matter of putting things in perspective, the most fundamental being spiritual development.

One of the problems with emphasis on scoring highly, which is part of many traditional education systems, is that there must always be failures. If one is in the top 20%, naturally the remaining 80% are made to feel that they have failed to various degrees. However, children can be boosted by comments such as, "Everyone is good at something. You (John) scored highly in maths, and you (Mary) scored highly in music. You (Jim) are very good at sport. Everybody is good at some things, aren't they?" This approach encourages people to do well without having a sense of failure. In other words, competition need not be fostered between people so much as within oneself. Competition can be useful when it is fostered with the understanding that it is good to improve as children of God and to use abilities for the betterment of the world.

Educators implementing Mahikari principles guide their students that even if people obtain high scores in their studies, their lives will not necessarily improve unless they cultivate a good heart. Even if their students do not score highly, the educators boost them with encouraging statements such as, "You know, your marks may not be the highest, but you are a wonderful person. You have such a lovely, generous heart and you never miss coming to lessons." These are simple things to do, but they are very powerful, lasting influences that may well outstrip academic achievements.

Creating a home of love and harmony
Another important aspect of whole person education is love and harmony in the home. Creating families of love and harmony is the basis of a stable, harmonious society, an essential ingredient in order to achieve world peace. Love and harmony can be gradually achieved where the spiritual level is being elevated and the suffering spirits attached to the family members are steadily being saved. The following teachings by Sukuinushisama summarise the important aspects in order to achieve spiritually oriented education.

It is necessary for parents to purify their spiritual aspect and give the Light of God to their children. This is the most important point in

243

the education of children. Parents must first become purified and be good models, then the behaviour of their children will improve naturally.

It is due to the cloudiness of the family's spiritual aspect that delinquency and accidental deaths are rising amongst our children. To prevent these, cleansing is ultimately essential. It is necessary that the spiritual aspect of both parents and ancestors be purified. Then, the Light of God will enter their children freely and they will improve naturally.

It is also necessary for parents to show love to their children by providing them with emotional sustenance. One way to do this would be to talk about the need for a family to live in love and harmony. Such an approach will result in children having respect for their parents. When children see their father teaching them good things, their love for him will grow. However, if a father lets his children be and does nothing to guide them, they will not look upon him as a parent. Parents need to strengthen the bonds of love with their children and to purify their children's souls by giving them the Light of God.

These points are an essential part of education that parents must provide at home.

In addition, our attitudes and way of life are very important in fostering harmony. Something as elementary as positive, bright greetings ("Good morning!" for example) between parents, parents and children, brothers and sisters and other relatives can elevate the household and family members. If parents use bad words, their children will tend to quarrel and become negative.

At the 1995 International Educators Conference a primary school music teacher related how she was able to achieve love and harmony in her home after she decided to be humble to her husband. She confessed that in the past she had been unable to feel humility towards him, but rather, felt negative and blamed him for refusing to become a kamikumite whereas she had been an active kamikumite for years and often offered service to God. Even though she would greet him every morning and evening, she did it merely as a formality, and apparently, they did not have a harmonious relationship. One day when she had to do something near the school where her husband was working, somehow she realised that her husband was very important for the safety and wellbeing of many children of God. She was then able to have a feeling of humble respect towards him. From that night onwards, she began greeting her husband with sincerity.

Four days later her husband suggested that they inaugurate an altar for their ancestors. Then, some weeks later, her husband wanted to attend the Mahikari primary course, even though he had shown no interest in this during the previous nine years that his wife had been a kamikumite.

This same school teacher also wanted to demonstrate to her pupils how powerful words were, so she grew hyacinths and asked the children to use good words to one and bad words to the other. After a week, the hyacinth that had received good words had many fine roots, whereas the one that had received bad words had only a few thin roots. The pupils were very surprised at the obvious difference and so discovered the power there is in the words we use. They then realised that words act powerfully on human beings as well and soon acquired the habit of addressing their musical instruments verbally, thanking them before and after they played them. This resulted in improved performances, particularly when playing in unity. The teacher said that the music sounded more pleasant and happy, and the tones that they produced on the recorders were clearer and more beautiful.

§

There have been various approaches as regards discipline in education. Over the past few centuries, parents and teachers in many societies were authoritarian figures who gave very strict discipline, including corporal punishment, when they felt it necessary. Many today have adopted the opposite approach where children at home or students at school are given almost unlimited freedom. Unacceptable behaviour is usually not dealt with in a strict way. There have been many viewpoints about the advantages and disadvantages of strictness.

Love and harmony does not necessarily mean a lack of strictness. Love has both a strict and a gentle side. Many young people in affluent societies have grown up being spoilt and leading indulgent lives. There are also children who have been reared with practically nothing but strictness. I believe that a correct balance is necessary in order to enable young people to endure hardships and overcome difficulties in a God-centred way, yet feel unconditional love from the people with whom they live.

Naturally, in the home, if there is love and a trusting relationship between the parents and their children, the children will accept and benefit from some strictness. Similarly, in the classroom, where there is mutual love and respect, the students will learn from any reprimands or consequences, even if they are sometimes strict. It is when an approach is one-sided or extreme that problems can arise.

Lastly, as regards the home, it goes without saying that the points I have made concerning families apply equally well to other people who are living in the home, even if they are not part of the same nuclear family. Some people are not married but are living in the same premises. Some children may spend more time with their grandparents than their parents. Single parents generally have a more challenging task of rearing their children, as they have to try to fulfil the role of both father and mother. Whatever the situation, it is important to strive to achieve a home of love and harmony.

§

In conclusion, in order to achieve whole person education, I believe it is valuable to work on: purifying with the Light of God; resolving spirit disturbance; elevating the innermost attitudes and words of parents; elevating the innermost attitudes and words of educators; conveying high values; and creating homes of love and harmony – all this while giving due regard to acquiring knowledge and skills. This may seem a tall order in the busy world of today, but then again, it is a fact of life that where possible, people generally make considerable efforts anyway to be successful in education, that is, to gain skills and scholastic achievements.

Efforts to achieve a spiritually oriented or whole person education will result in much more than educational success. Such education is the basis for a wholesome, meaningful, stable and fulfilling life, the basis for happiness for the individuals concerned, and in turn, for stable, fulfilled societies and civilisations of high quality.

Youth education

The children and youth of today will have the biggest influence on the progress of the twenty-first century. If they cannot be nurtured to acquire high-quality, God-centred values and live accordingly, any progress made towards a high-level civilisation now can still collapse in the future. One of the missions of the Sukyo Mahikari organisation is to work on the nurturing of young people to develop excellent human resources for the future.

The nurturing of young people of Sukyo Mahikari is conducted mainly at Mahikari centres and in the home, as outlined in the preceding section. Below are some details of how people actually go about it.

More on nurturing young people

Where possible, nurturing of Sukyo Mahikari children and youth at the Mahikari centre is conducted under the guidance of the centre director in collaboration with other staff members, educators, parents, older Mahikari Youth Group (see later) members and support staff members concerned with youth education – five different elements.

Others without such roles also join in if they are willing and able. If the staff members alone provide training for the children, it is not so effective, particularly if the children's parents do not understand the aims and are not supportive. Conversely, if the parents make efforts with their children but this is not followed up by others at the Mahikari centre, it is also not as effective. That is why nurturing involves the different groups of people, if possible.

Some Mahikari centres have a parents group, through which the parents strive to become good parents in parallel with the training and nurturing they offer to the younger people.

For children up to the age of about ten, most of the nurturing is left up to their parents, although many centres do have some organised activities as well (usually conducted by Mahikari centre staff members and parents).

The most important way to nurture young people is to give them the Light of God. Children who have reached the age of 10 years and have the wish to become kamikumite, and who are supported by their parents in this regard, can do so by attending the primary course. From that age onwards, naturally, a major practice for the youth is the art of True Light. The young people are encouraged to practise the art of True Light as a way of life.

What kind of nurturing is given to the young people? Basically, guidance and encouragement are given so that young people can practise the art of True Light and the divine teachings at home, at school or wherever they are. Much of this nurturing is done at home,

but there is also instruction on divine teachings and other programs conducted at most Mahikari centres.

Taking various opportunities, parents who take seriously the nurturing of their children talk to their children about God, why we worship God and how to live in a God-centred way. Emphasis is placed on showing appreciation and respect to God and parents. As much as possible, parents strive to give Light to their children every day and guide them about the importance of the Light in a way that they can appreciate; it is not something that is imposed upon them as a meaningless ritual. Ideally, matters to do with gratitude permeate every aspect of life such as expressing gratitude before and after meals, showing gratitude for materials (including food), not being wasteful and appreciating the blessings of God in everyday life.

Children are nurtured to learn about and appreciate the blessings of nature where possible by cultivating a home vegetable patch or even a potted plant, growing vegetables or flowers in a natural way without using agricultural chemicals, but instead giving them Light and showing gratitude, encouragement, using compost and so on. Manners in the home, at school and elsewhere are also promoted. Children are encouraged to offer greetings not only amongst their family members, but also to their teachers and others in society. They are taught how precious and important words are in themselves – that good, polite and positive words help and encourage things to grow and function well in one's environment, and that it is best to avoid negative words.

Children are taught about the harmful consequences of food that contains toxic agricultural and other artificial additives, and are encouraged to purify the food with the Light of God where possible.

Young people are also taught that hardships, difficulties and problems are training and trials that God gives to people in order for them to have a chance to improve. Hardships are not something to be avoided in order to seek comfort. It is good to appreciate and overcome difficulties in a positive way, to foster endurance, persistence and a strong will to achieve one's responsibilities.

As children become older they are encouraged to avoid any impure lifestyles, spiritually, mentally and physically (such as involvement with narcotic drugs, sexual immorality and so on), and guided to take responsibility for their lives and decisions, to enable them to make correct choices towards pure living. They are taught that sexual activities are permitted by God for people who are married so that descendants will be permitted for the happiness of the family and for the divine plan. Parenthood enables people to understand better how God, the Great Parent, feels about His children. The youth are nurtured to understand that degeneration and disorder in morals leads to the collapse of society and are guided so that they can have pure and wholesome relationships.

§

Where centres have sufficient numbers of people and where there is an interest, education committees are formed to help with the training provided by the educators, parents, Mahikari Youth Group members and so on. In Australia the Sukyo Mahikari organisation is recognised by the Government as an educational institution, in addition to being a religious organisation. The Sukyo Mahikari Educators Association in Japan studies the guidance of Oshienushisama for educators, as well as various approaches to education that have been found to be effective, and where possible, this is conveyed through the regional headquarters to Sukyo Mahikari centres throughout the world.

In Japan, international and/or national educators conferences as well as local education conferences are held regularly. In addition, in various countries of the world, Mahikari regions organise educators conferences, workshops, training sessions and so on.

Many youth and parents have also received inspiration, awakening and improvement in lifestyle as a result of attending youth training camps, Mahikari Youth Group jamborees and other group activities. Reports by some participants have been published in the

Mahikari Australia–Oceania and Asia Journal (August 1994, September 1995, February 1996, December 2000, to name a few).

§

I do not wish to imply that members of Sukyo Mahikari centres are consistently achieving effective nurturing of young people. There are kamikumite who have not yet awakened to the significance of youth education or who do not wish to become involved in organised activities, and that is also respected. There are centres where the numbers of members or the appropriate human resources for guiding are so small that they cannot do much about youth education at present. There are also many kamikumite who have made valuable progress in nurturing the youth at different times, but have not been able to sustain their efforts. There are also kamikumite who have achieved and continue to achieve progress in nurturing young people, despite many challenges. As a staff member, an educator in another sense, and a parent (my wife and I have five sons), I know it is not always easy to continue providing appropriate nurturing of young people. Even if one cannot achieve the ideal situation, however, I feel that if parents, educators and young people grasp the importance and practise what they can, youth education should at least progress.

Mahikari Youth Group

In September 1964, Sukuinushisama approved the formation of a national Youth Group in the Mahikari organisation in Japan. In December, it was renamed the Mahikari Youth Group, and it began its activities as a voluntary service youth group, which is the spirit of the current Mahikari Youth Group. In Mahikari centres all over Japan, the group actively participated in offering service, through giving Light and various expansion activities, such as distributing Mahikari leaflets and holding Mahikari panel displays.

The Mahikari Youth Group uniform was established in 1973. From 1973 onwards Mahikari Youth Group activities began in countries outside of Japan, wherever there was a strong desire to do so. Kamikumite children from ten up to 15 years old can belong to the Junior Mahikari Youth Group. This is a preparatory period towards the Mahikari Youth Group training, which begins from about 15 years old. The Mahikari Youth Group is voluntary and there are Mahikari youth who are content to offer service without joining it.

Today, the Mahikari Youth Group is established in many countries. Some aspects of its original activities have been modified to be appropriate for the culture and lifestyle of the particular country.

The ages of the Mahikari Youth Group members range from about 15 up to the thirties (and sometimes higher), depending on the country. In short, the Mahikari Youth Group is a body of young people from the youth of Sukyo Mahikari and is led directly by Oshienushisama in order to nurture responsible people for the civilisation of the twenty-first holy century. Even though they have various other roles and duties in their families, studies and jobs, being a member means wanting to offer even greater service to God.

Part of the training for Mahikari Youth Group members is to learn teamwork, and one effective way of training is marching exercises and drill. Just as team sport or playing in an orchestra results in training people to cooperate effectively in groups, drill exercise is a way of helping to achieve unity on a large scale and in general is greatly appreciated by the young people. Marching as unity training is not only for uniting as a group, but also for uniting in prayer and purpose. It is also a training to develop spiritual, mental and physical strength as well as willpower and flexibility. Marching exercise gives expression to the energy of youth.

§

From time to time, the Mahikari Youth Group and other youth of Mahikari centres offer community service and other activities for the betterment of society. In Japan, in Takayama, for example, as a result of this organisation's gift of land, a retirement home for the elderly was built near Takayama, and the Mahikari Youth Group as well as trainees from the Doshi Training Institute go and help wash the elderly people, cleaning their apartments and so on, from time to time. Cleaning up litter in the streets is a common practice.

In the Australia–Oceania Region, Mahikari centres are regularly involved in cleaning up the environment, both on special occasions such as Clean up the World Day activities and at various other times throughout the year. They recycle materials and promote awareness of the need to conserve resources. There are tree-planting activities. Sometimes the youth approach local councils, hospitals and invalid homes in order to offer service to the community. In the Canberra area, for instance, young people cleaned and tidied the cemetery of a country town near Canberra, after approaching the local council. Youth from the Canberra Mahikari Centre are offering voluntary service in tree-planting programs (conducted by the Australia Trust for Conservation Volunteers), cleaning the environment, helping out on a telephone advice service called Lifeline, community radio, St John's Ambulance, childcare, 'environment shops' and elsewhere. The more musical ones sometimes get together and go to hospitals or old peoples homes to give joy through music recitals to the people there.

After I moved to Singapore, I learned that members of the Mahikari Youth Group of Singapore Mahikari Centre offered community service for more than three years at a residence for elderly people. Once a month, they visited the elderly folk to chat with them, tell them stories and jokes, and attend to their basic needs, such as eating and going to the toilet (for those in wheelchairs). They also repainted the buildings and repaired and maintained the wheelchairs during this time.

One example of community service is that of the young people of Senegal in Africa, who restored the home of threatened birds and also cleaned the premises of Government House. The following excerpts are from an account published in the *Mahikari Australia–Oceania and Asia Journal*, August 1996.

Faune Nature Reserve is well known internationally as a swamp area where the tern, an aquatic bird, breeds. The terns come from distant Scandinavian countries to Senegal in order to spend the winter and to breed there. Recently, however, increasing numbers of the areas where the birds breed are being devastated. The administrator of the park asked an international institute and the relevant government departments for assistance to construct an island for the birds. He managed to obtain promises of thirteen million CFA francs in grants. However, he has not received any grant yet, and so there has been no progress in his plan.

Mahikari Youth Group members of Senegal established a 'Team United by God' in 1994. This year we decided to train our souls through some activity useful to society, and taking the strong wishes of the nature reserve's administrator into consideration, we decided to construct an island for the terns in the swampland of the nature reserve.

We were to construct three small mounds with a height of about one metre each and with a surface area of 40 square metres, by digging the heaps of sea shells on the bank with mattocks and shovels, and carrying the additional soil for two or three hundred metres in wheelbarrows. By the time the terns would be due to arrive, the dry lake would have been filled by rainwater, and so the mounds would then become safe artificial islands where predators such as jackals would not be able to go. There the terns would be able to breed safely.

Fifty-two Mahikari Youth Group members and trainees participated in offering the service. In six days we made three mounds, where about two thousand pairs of terns would be able to make their nests. Although it was hard work, we did it cheerfully and the atmosphere was lively and friendly.

The administrator of the reserve, the manager of the Department for Mountains and Forests, and the person in charge of the National Parks office came frequently during the six days to see how we were doing. They were very impressed, saying, 'Even though it was such hard work, everyone was truly happy to do it, and you did the work so neatly, even though you are not receiving any payment . . . I honestly can't believe it. I feel as if I am dreaming. What you have achieved is a great contribution to not only Senegal, but for the whole of Africa.'

On April 1, the day after we completed the artificial islands, we went to Government House in Saint-Louis in order to offer service by cleaning it. We did this because when we visited the building in order to go through the correct procedure for constructing the artificial islands, we noticed that the courtyard was very dirty, and therefore asked if we could clean it after we finished the artificial islands.

The officer we asked did not seem to believe that we were offering to do this, so when we arrived at the building at ten in the morning, there were no cleaning tools, nor were there any staff members at all in the courtyard.

It took us two hours to obtain the equipment we needed. We cleaned the whole yard completely. The Governor was unable to hide his surprise that young people had not only constructed the islands but also volunteered to clean Government House.

The next day, April 2, was the day that we had the closing ceremony for the training session. We invited many people to attend the ceremony, including the Minister for the Environment, the Minister for Home, Women's and Children's Affairs, the Minister for Science and Technology (who became a kamikumite recently), the Governor of Saint-Louis, the Belgian consul, and an Assistant Director of Senegal National Park. Before the ceremony, these guests were taken to see the work done by the Mahikari Youth Group. They gave continual words of praise for what the youth had achieved. The following are excerpts from the congratulatory speeches given by the guests at the ceremony.

The Assistant Director of the Senegal National Park:
'Your spiritual group offered service reforesting the animal sanctuary in this nature reserve in 1993 and 1994, planting 4,229 young plants in total. Considering the importance and precious value of the service offered by the Mahikari Youth Group in this park, we are privileged to recognise you as the best partner of the national park.

The Governor of Saint-Louis City:
'I had no previous knowledge of your group, and so was really surprised to receive your offer to clean Government House without receiving any pay. The offer sounded very strange to me, and to tell you the truth, I even felt that you all might be a little insane.

I was quite certain that it was only talk, and that you would not come to do the cleaning. However, when I saw that you had really turned up, I was surprised, and ordered our staff to prepare the tools to complete the work.

After you left the courtyard, I went out to see that the yard was extraordinarily clean. I could not believe my eyes. It is not possible to find young people anywhere nowadays who are enthusiastic in offering service.'

During a news program a reporter introduced Mahikari as follows:

'Sukyo Mahikari is an extremely good organisation. The young people in this organisation are actively working for the protection of the natural environment. Young people of Senegal, let us follow the young people of Mahikari, and create a better society together.'

§

Since this kind of event can only be organised from time to time, individual Mahikari Youth Group members try to be useful to their community, school and family in daily life. The following are excerpts of experiences reported by Jeffrey Lim, a 16-year-old Mahikari Youth Group member of Melbourne (Lim, 1996).

A few months ago I chose to purify my school for approximately 15 minutes every day. I am a 16-year-old pupil of St Albans Secondary College. Like most other schools, it is influenced by drugs, smoking and violence. Our school has a mixed population consisting of Vietnamese, Maltese, Serbian, Chinese and many other nationalities and ethnic groups. It is because of this that I chose to radiate True Light to my school during lunchbreaks for approximately 15 minutes, as my spiritual training.

I could see that the Melbourne Mahikari centre and my school are of two very different dimensions. The youth in school are violent and use very bad language, whereas in the Mahikari centre, youth use positive, encouraging words and have caring attitudes. As I know it is God's will to create heaven on earth and that this can only be done by practising divine teachings in our daily lives, I felt I wanted to make school like the Mahikari centre. I also want to be used as a child of God in service. During the past two months I have observed a slow but steady change in both pupils and teachers, in their actions and their use of the spoken word. Violent clashes between students have decreased. Teachers who usually reprimand students using rough language, instead began using words like, 'Please be quiet'. I became really excited when I saw the effectiveness of God's Light.

Both my parents are kamikumite and it is only recently that we were blessed with being permitted to inaugurate the sacred scroll (Goshintai) in our home. We are privileged to hold purification meetings at my home on Tuesdays and Thursdays. Being able to give and receive True Light is very energising. Whilst my parents take care of the older people, I am able to take care of the younger ones.

My best friend came to my home to sleep overnight. We happened to be holding a purification meeting on that particular evening. I offered him Light and he reluctantly accepted. A few days later when we were having a day out in the city, I asked him if he would like to go to the Mahikari centre. He agreed. I was thus able to take my best friend to the Mahikari centre.

I also take care of one young person who attends our purification meetings with his mother. He was not very enthusiastic about receiving True Light at first. However, after 'breaking the ice' by playing a few video games together and sharing some magic tricks, we became friends and he agreed to receive True Light. He even participated in our June youth overnight stay held at the Melbourne Mahikari Centre and thoroughly enjoyed himself.

Through our purification sessions, I am continuously able to experience the power of True Light, such as observing people's expressions changing after receiving Light, improvements in people's health, people who previously found it difficult to kneel down now being able to do so for longer periods and people who got tired easily after walking only a little while are now able to walk much further. Through these experiences, I have been able to strengthen my faith in God and to trust in God even more.

My parents are both chefs and they work very hard to support the family. Consequently, I am often left alone at home. Occasionally, after I have finished my homework I still have a lot of time so I often help out by cleaning up the house. My usual chores are: taking out the rubbish, sweeping the floor, washing plates and cutlery, fitting up the beds nicely and preparing food so that when my parents return we are able to eat together. When I was asked why I do these things at home, I reflected that it is because they are my parents and I love them. The other reason is that I really feel the need to recompense my parents for all their support, encouragement and their love for me.

§

Mr Taizo Ike of Atsugi Mahikari Centre in Japan, is an example of how a Mahikari Youth Group member can have a passion for serving God, starting at an early age, yet be a responsible family member, student and want to contribute to society in a positive way. Taizo was born with cyanosis, a slightly bluish or dark purple discolouration of the skin due to the presence of abnormally reduced haemoglobin in the blood. He almost died at birth. After being hospitalised for two months, the doctor told his mother that Taizo might lose his eyesight due to his low oxygen intake. The doctor did not think Taizo would live beyond the age of three. I met his mother at that time, a very few years after I became a Mahikari member myself. I could not imagine then that the infant who was about to die would one day become such an enthusiastic and altruistic person, aiming to be a God-centred doctor so he can pay back his gratitude to God to some extent. The following are excerpts of words of gratitude that he offered at the World Shrine at the very significant Mahikari Youth Group event – the Procession of Light 2000 – an event in which I also participated. His complete words of gratitude were published in the *Mahikari Australia-Oceania and Asia Journal* (2001,18:16-21).

When I was ten years old, I was able to receive an Omitama. I expressed my gratitude to God and made a sincere prayer that I would be used by God to help people so that they may live in accordance with divine principles. Throughout my student life, from elementary school to the university, I have been striving to practise the monthly teachings given by Oshienushisama, always thinking about what I can do for God and others.

During my elementary school days, I made special efforts to use polite words. At the same time, with the desire to spread the Light of God, I gave Light to my teachers, my friends and their parents, and spoke to them about Mahikari. From amongst them, I was able to guide five people to attend the Mahikari primary course. Still a fifth grader, and 11 years old, I was allowed to attend the Mahikari intermediate course.

When I entered junior high school, I was bullied by some of the students. They said that my polite language displeased them. They punched me in the face and even kicked me. Despite this, I never lost sight of the fact that they were children of God. When I attended the monthly ceremony at Suza, I made sincere prayers for the salvation of their souls as well as apologised to God for my many spiritual impurities, which I understood from the teachings to be the cause of my undergoing suffering in this way. The next day, all of a sudden, they came to me and said, "Please forgive us for bullying you. We won't do it anymore." I was surprised and deeply grateful. This experience made me awaken to the preciousness of offering sincere prayers at Suza, where Su God is enshrined.

Soon thereafter, with a desire to practise divine teachings along with my teachers and other students, I stood as a candidate for the Student Council and was chosen to be the chairman of the 'year one committee'. One day, seeing that the toilets were badly stained, I decided to clean them. This inspired all the first-year students to also start doing things for the sake of others. Moreover, during the election campaign, even the students who had bullied me helped by joining me in front of the school gate from early in the morning, canvassing students to give their support. Thanks to divine protection, I was elected the vice-chairman of the Student Council.

This role gave me an opportunity to fulfil my desire to practise Oshienushisama's teachings. Oshienushisama gave us a teaching on 'The arrival of the recycling age'. I started promoting the recycling of milk cartons, newspapers and other recyclables with the cooperation of our teachers, students and the local community. This activity helped to foster altruistic love amongst the students. Also, we began a campaign to visit the homes of the aged to talk with them.

At my Mahikari centre, I was a member of the Junior Mahikari Youth Group. It was going to be my last year in this group and I received the unexpected honour of presenting a bouquet of flowers to Oshienushisama at the Grand Purification Ceremony. I will always remember this experience as it allowed me to awaken to the preciousness and magnitude of the missions given to Oshienushisama. It also helped me to deepen my gratitude for having Oshienushisama as the leader of the Sukyo Mahikari Youth Group. I sincerely prayed that I would be able to offer greater service to God.

In the second year of high school, I was elected chairman of the Student Council. At that time Oshienushisama gave us teachings on the importance of greetings and on the need to be pure, cheerful, righteous and accepting of the will of God. Every morning, I would stand at the front gate of our school to greet the teachers and students. In the beginning hardly anybody would reply to my greetings of "Good morning". However, always remembering Oshienushisama's teaching, I persevered with my practice of greetings. Then, without even asking anyone, many of my classmates and students from the lower graders joined me in practising greetings. Six months later, the whole school made a remarkable change to become one filled with cheerful smiles, love and harmony.

During the three years at high school, I had to divide my time between my studies, activities at my Mahikari centre, and the Student Council. Despite this, God allowed me to cope well and I was permitted to gain entrance to the medical department of Tokai University. I attribute all these arrangements to the fact that I always put God and others first and tried to accept everything with gratitude. Presently, I am able to talk about Sukyo Mahikari with my professors and friends at the university.

When I reflect on my life now, if it were not for God's precious arrangements, I would have died at birth or within three years of birth. I now live a healthy life and am enjoying my life on the path of God. What is more, my goal is to practise God-centred medicine. It is thanks to the protection and loving guidance of Oshienushisama that I have been able to make this much progress in life. I am also thankful to my family who have been devoting themselves to serving God in unity and harmony.

§

Mahikari Youth Group members (or youth in general) who wish to become of even greater service and who show suitable aptitude may be recommended to go on to do special training to become what are called *doshis*, spiritual instructors or direct disciples of Oshienushisama. This involves spending a training period at the Doshi Training Institute (*Kunrenbu*), which is located near Takayama, Japan.

Contributions by Mahikari educators

In the Sukyo Mahikari organisation there is a growing number of professional educators who not only give and receive the Light of God and practise universal laws in their lives, but also make significant contributions towards spiritually oriented education in their professions. In some cases the influence has reached education policy bodies, resulting in steps towards designing new curricula for education in that school, state or country. Below are some examples of contributions by professional Mahikari educators with whom I have interacted many times.

Innermost attitudes of educators

Dr Nyuk Nahan was an Associate Professor of Law at the University of Western Australia in Perth, and has guided several academics who have attended the Mahikari course. She gave a report at the 1995 International Educators Conference in Takayama, Japan (Nahan, 1995). Through the practice of the principles learned in Sukyo Mahikari she discovered that the innermost attitudes *(sonen)* precede the spiritual functions of words *(kototama)*. "When the sonen is not right, its impact will be felt by others even if the kototama seems harmless", she said. For instance, she confessed that sometimes when she felt somewhat condescending towards a colleague's view, even though her words were polite and seemingly normal, the results were not so good. She trained herself to maintain the view that "I must harbour no negativity, for that unseen negativity and ego seem to derail my efforts", even though it is sometimes necessary to speak up and act with conviction.

She concluded that every educator is a role model.

What we are, revealed by what we do is the most important . . . In the past 18 months I have had more opportunities to draw from my understanding of divine teachings to motivate, encourage and comfort our students. Frequently I can only listen sympathetically and offer a little kindness. Yet the students seem to become more positive or fortified by these simple contacts. The Dean has observed that the student body seems happier and there is a 'better feeling' about the place. I would like to suggest that divine teachings and universal principles, even when glimpsed, somehow refresh the spirit and strengthen the resolve. This has important ramifications for us because we, as educators, have endless opportunities to 'transmit' them appropriately in acts of kindness to our students and our peers.

Spiritual health: an educational perspective

Ms Betty Szilagyi is a teacher and former health and physical education coordinator of a Catholic girls college in Adelaide, South Australia, and a kamikumite of Adelaide Mahikari Centre. Her efforts have led to changes in the curriculum by her school to incorporate spiritual aspects that had not been included up till then (Szilagyi, 1995). The following are excerpts from her account.

I am a teacher of health, religious and physical education in a girls Catholic college. Over the years since I attended the Mahikari primary course in 1984, I have been able to learn much about the nature of true education. I am very lucky to be working at a Christian school that has a faith education program. Within this program we study many religions and our comparative approach and universal perspective seem to give most students a very good grounding for their lives.

A particular concern of mine has been that state schools are unable or unwilling to provide this type of education. In other words, the spiritual aspect has been ignored and this has occurred for a variety of reasons, for example, fear, teachers needing to clarify their own beliefs, the desire not to impose values on children, secular school policies and so on.

In February 1994, I participated in one of the major health conferences for all schools, and saw that one of the aspects of health being highlighted on an overhead transparency was 'Spiritual Health'. I thought that this could be the avenue through which some type of God-centred education could be implemented.

I went to one of the conference organisers immediately and asked about the spiritual aspect of health. She told me that this was one of her passions in life and that she felt that the time had come for something to be done on this topic.

The session went for nearly two hours. We looked at questions and topics such as:

1. What does spiritual health mean to you?

2. How does spiritual health fit in to the broad picture of health?

3. Different perspectives on spiritual health, for example, belief in a God in a traditional way; belief in a spirit world; the belief that there is something like a universal wisdom that has an influence on how things happen, to mention some perspectives.

Although the twenty teachers were from state schools, their response to this spiritual health discussion was amazing. They came up with fantastic models on spiritual health. One group used the analogy of an orange where the spiritual health aspect was the skin holding all the other aspects of health together, without which the orange couldn't develop or survive. It made me realise that people, in some fundamental way, understand the importance of the spiritual aspect of life, and that there is a desperate need to develop this. Moreover, it must be in a way that unites all people.

We came to the conclusion that spiritual health was all about trying to develop a sense of foundation; a belief system which could help interpret life experience so that individuals could lead a more fulfilling and positive life. I outlined some ideas:

1. Helping students explore their belief systems, values and approach to life.

2. Giving students things to think about to help them develop a healthy value system.

3. Giving students a smorgasbord of religious teachings, thoughts and teachings from great teachers, writers and spiritual people to help them appreciate the deeper aspects of life.

4. Helping students to understand that there are certain universal principles that exist and that are common to all religions, cultures and societies. Furthermore, living by these principles can help to improve the quality of life.

I emphasised that in Health Education and Religious Education the first three aspects would be already dealt with to some degree. I then was able to share my work on 'Universal Principles'. This was a curriculum unit that I'd been presenting to year ten students in my school.

At Ms Szilagyi's college, the course on Universal Principles has been growing since 1994. In 1996 all year 10 classes spent one term on the topic as part of Religious Education. Some of the comments her students gave on the course were:

"It helps us to realise and think about our own morals and ethics."

"I liked the fact that this aspect of religious education was not focussing on a religion, but on humanity."

"This course made me think about myself and how I make decisions and how to improve the person I am."

"It gives you an insight to what better living is like."

Ms Szilagyi said, "I believe the course is one of the most important units we have implemented at the school. It gives students the opportunity to reflect on how to live to achieve happiness . . . there is no other unit of work which gives me so much teacher satisfaction as this one on Universal Principles."

By 1997 the Universal Principles unit became an established part of the Religious Education Curriculum at the college, taught over a period of 10 weeks and comprising 30 lessons (in which students keep a journal and submit four projects). A special student workbook has been produced to assist teachers. In 1997 a similar course was developed for year 12 students, by collaborating with another religious education coordinator, who became impressed by the success of the course for year 10 students.

Betty Szilagyi has presented papers on spiritual health and possible ways of incorporating this in education, at various conferences (Szilagyi, 1996; 1997), including the 1997 Sukyo Mahikari International Educators Conference in Japan.

§

This is an interesting development, because it originated in a Catholic college where traditional Christian teachings about God and related matters are conveyed as a matter of course. In my observations, some children who graduate from religious schools tend to have high-level morals and behaviour whereas others show no significant improvement in their character or behaviour, saying that they are rebelling against the narrow-minded dogma and doctrine they had received. I think it is good to seek ways of enabling people to receive the universal principles of God in a non-threatening, non-imposed way so that they can feel empowered to practise and willingly change themselves in a God-centred way, irrespective of traditional religion, race or anything else.

Spiritually oriented education in New Zealand

Ms Neini Curulala was a Policy Adviser in Education to the Deputy Prime Minister in the government of New Zealand. She has been a kamikumite for a number of years, practising the art of True Light and divine teachings in her home and elsewhere in her daily life. She has been able to introduce a spiritually oriented approach in education that has not only been recognised by the government of New Zealand, but also research data have shown that her approach has led to significant improvement in the academic scores of students. The following are excerpts of her account (Curulala, 1996).

I am an indigenous Fijian born in Fiji. I taught in Fiji before my family moved to New Zealand in 1983. At the completion of my tertiary studies in New Zealand I joined the New Zealand public service as an Education Adviser. Currently I work as the Policy Adviser in Education to the Deputy Prime Minister. Laying the foundation for a God-centred education system in a country plagued with high rates of suicide, teenage pregnancy, school expulsion, suspensions, truancy, bullying and both sexual and physical abuse, is an enormous responsibility.

I awakened to the fact that education in New Zealand can only change for the better when I and others responsible for developing the nation's education policies change and elevate our spiritual contents. I also awakened to the very deep impurities of the 'upstream of society', and that in order to begin the process of change I need to unite strongly with God. Right from the beginning of my endeavour to introduce change I experienced deep joy in being permitted to help fulfil God's vision and plan in the education of New Zealand's future leaders. It is this joy in high-level divine service that has kept me going despite trials and painful training.

As is the practice in my work (as Policy Adviser) I began to plan:
Vision: To lay the foundation for a 'God-centred education system in New Zealand by the year 2000'.
Goals: To promote change in the innermost attitudes of the 'upstream' people in education institutions and government departments, through the practice of universal (divine) principles.
Strategies:
1. Purify key education and government personnel.
2. Purify government institutions.
3. Develop a new education paradigm.
4. Bring in the application of divine principles in education institutions.

1. Purification of key education and government personnel.
As a daily practice I radiate Light directly towards the Prime Minister, other Ministers, chief executives and heads of education institutions in Parliament House and other places of my work. Every day I offer prayers to commence service on behalf of government, community and education institution leaders.

2. Breakthrough permitted after years of purifying government premises.

My work involves attending many meetings and conferences. These take me to other institutions and places nationwide. I value these opportunities to purify government premises.

Since 1992 I had been seeking approval to develop a framework of a new education paradigm. I finally got the approval to develop the God-centred education paradigm, in 1995.

3. Development of a God-centred education paradigm.

The paradigm is called 'True Wisdom'. Its key elements are:
• changing our innermost attitudes;
• working in unity; and
• developing and nourishing the spirit, mind and body.

I am currently aligning our Department's vision, principles and values with the new paradigm.

4. Introducing the application of divine principles in education institutions.

As part of an ethnic minority studying at Victoria University in Wellington in the eighties, I had encountered staff and institutional insensitivity and sometimes racism. At that time I graduated, disliking the institution and what it stood for. In essence I blamed the institution for the failure of many, who like me, are classed by the university as 'disadvantaged groups'.

I realise now that for lecturers at Victoria University to change, I had to change. I was awakened to the fact that lecturers must have a deep sense of failure and insecurity when ethnic minority students fail to qualify year after year. My heart went out to them.

To actualise my innermost attitude change I developed a programme called the 'Professional Development Programme', which the university agreed to trial. The programme was based on the principles of 'innermost attitude change' and 'working in unity'. Its aim was to change ethnic minorities' perception of themselves and at the same time to allow lecturers to change their preconceived notions about ethnic minority students, allowing them to achieve their full potential. To do this we had to unite as equals in an activity that benefited both groups. Students, lecturers, parents, postgraduate students, church leaders, community leaders, the University Council and graduates were involved. They agreed to unite to achieve the common goal, identifying what their roles were and pledged to support each other to fulfil these roles.

To achieve academic credibility, the programme was piloted at Victoria University, Wellington. The activities basically involve students discussing and debating concepts and issues from the lectures and readings, critically *analysing each other's work, sharing shortcuts on how to solve problems and generally being supportive of each other. This support network naturally overflowed to other areas of students' lives. The lecturers and students are supported by a facilitator who is a postgraduate student, well versed in the subject matter, young and a person with whom students can relate easily.*

The pilot programme was an overwhelming success in that more than 80% of the students passed, in comparison with the normal 20% pass rate over the past decade! Students began to value education success through united effort. The programme succeeded in bringing all stakeholders together as equals – a huge change in attitude for some. Negative perceptions and other barriers crumbled. This year, 1996 – one full year after the pilot programme with the Mathematics and Statistics Departments – the Biology, Chemistry, Geography, Botany, Psychology and Zoology Departments have joined and are using unity as the approach to education success.

In 1995 the programme was adapted and piloted at a senior secondary school in Wellington and called the Collaborative Learning Programme. This year, seven schools in New Zealand's largest city, Auckland, are using the united approach. Also this year, the Ministry of Education has included the promotion of the Professional Development Programme and the Collaborative Learning Programme as a priority.

This year I received approval to attend the Sukyo Mahikari International Educators Conference as a New Zealand government official.

In 1997 Ms Curulala presented details and an update of the progress of the Professional Development Programme and the Collaborative Learning Programme at the Sukyo Mahikari International Educators Conference in Japan. Two other universities were considering using the Professional Development Programme. Newspaper reports praised the results of the Collaborative Learning Programme, in which senior high school "students had all passed bursary statistics and calculus, and the mathematics results of the Fifth Form School Certificate students were improving too".

Divine principles in corporate Australia

Amongst the professional educators in the Sukyo Mahikari organisation, there are also people who provide education to both private and public sectors, professional motivators, consultants and coaches, who run workshops and training courses for professional clients. Gary and Lyn Russell of Hobart (now Canberra) in Australia are management and training consultants who have achieved significant breakthroughs with their clients after they introduced spiritually oriented principles in their approach. The following are excerpts of Gary's published account (Russell, 1995).

I have been a kamikumite since 1986. For the past 25 years I have been working with people, from running a youth shelter for homeless young people to assisting needy families and communities. I have a degree in social work and postgraduate qualifications in management.

My wife and I are partners in our consulting and training company. Our mission is 'to reawaken the human spirit' through assisting corporations to become more God-centred.

We focus on the human dimension through teaching, among other programmes, team development and people skills in order to create workplaces of love and harmony based on universal laws and principles.

Through this principled and God-centred approach we teach people to grow, learn and make positive changes through discovering and putting into practice these laws and principles.

Giving True Light to the area where we conduct a seminar always produces a more positive outcome for the participants. We speak openly about the Light when asked 'What are you doing?' Most of our clients are aware and support our approach – primarily because they themselves have experienced 'difficult situations becoming easier' as a result of the Light.

For example, when work relationships are tense and people are in conflict, we notice a greater willingness of people to listen and explore options together after True Light is given.

We try to be positive role models in living our personal and professional lives in accordance with God's laws. In a world of turmoil, confusion and cynicism, business leaders will recognise and accept change when the message and the messenger are congruent. We teach that: 'For things to change, first I must change.'

For example, in a recent course one participant talked about his client who had a large bank debt and also constantly complained and argued with the staff of this particular organisation. The situation changed and this client was able to apologise in writing and willingly begin repayment of his debt when the staff members changed their innermost attitudes from ones of judging, blame and anger, to saying to him, 'How can we work this out together?', and 'We are sorry your situation appears so difficult.'

By offering prayers each day for those business leaders with whom we work, we try to allow God's power to unite with our own.

When people look to us for answers, ego plays a big part in their difficulty: attempts to impress rather than guide; to compete rather than share; and to dictate rather than be humble. Being aware of our personal failings, we encourage people to follow their leaders and managers by filling in the gaps and uniting with one another. Many are at first sceptical about such an approach, believing that a strong competition and a win/lose approach is the very essence of business success. However, our experience is that in encouraging business leaders to begin to act in an accepting, humble way, greater power is given to make positive changes.

Recently a workplace was able to become much happier and enjoyable in spite of constant change and financial cutbacks when staff were shown how to boost their manager who, before the workshop, was heavily criticised as being the cause of much of their hardship.

An Australian colleague recently wrote to our Minister for Education about the educational needs of young Australians, emphasising the need for the school curriculum to reflect spirit, mind and body in the development of our youth. The Minister responded positively and provided opportunities for kamikumite to participate in discussions on developing such a curriculum in our schools.

In our own experience, we have seen many examples of people being able to achieve attitude changes towards their colleagues or manager, after receiving True Light during seminars and reflecting on the significance of God's laws and principles. This occurs even though these people had been to many forms of training, read widely and believed it was a hopeless situation. By following the divine laws and principles of the Creator God, Australian corporations are just beginning to learn new ways of serving our planet.

§

These are some experiences of professional educators I know in the Australia-Oceania Region. Throughout the world there is a growing body of Sukyo Mahikari educators who are making contributions to education. Not only kamikumite professionals but also non-professionals are contributing significantly towards improving education through the Light and universal laws. In Melbourne, for example, kamikumite have purified a number of schools in the metropolitan area, an activity that is done by thousands of kamikumite throughout the world. What particularly attracted my attention, however, was that school principals (who are not kamikumite), in at least three of the schools in Melbourne have written official letters of praise and gratitude for the fact that the purification of their schools has led to significant improvement in the behaviour and well-being of their students, that it has reduced school absenteeism and so on.

Yoko schools

Through purification and proper nurturing of people, it is hoped that a high-quality civilisation, the yoko civilisation, will come to be established. *Yoko* literally means 'yang Light', which really refers to that which is positive, bright and pure. The term 'yoko schools' has been used by some Sukyo Mahikari educators to refer to schools that provide spiritually oriented education in order to help establish the yoko civilisation.

In some sense everyone is a kind of teacher as well as a pupil. As I have indicated, in order to help achieve a high-level education, it is valuable to be a God-centred or spiritually oriented educator at home amongst one's family members; at the Mahikari centre amongst other kamikumite; at one's workplace amongst colleagues; at one's school amongst teachers and students; or indeed, anywhere else. In this sense, every home, Mahikari centre, workplace or school can be a kind of a yoko school.

As spiritually oriented education develops, I envisage that the day will come when yoko schools (other names may be used) will be established as teaching institutions from a structural point of view as well. In other words – even though the true essence of a yoko school is not the structure but the approach to nurturing people in accordance with divine principles – in the future, classrooms and buildings will probably be established, with professional educators, who will impart the Light and universal laws, in addition to the traditional subjects that deal with matters of a more mental and physical nature. Training in spiritually oriented education at this time is laying the foundation for the setting up of such yoko-type schools in the future.

Within the Sukyo Mahikari organisation steps have been taken by some professional educators who are collaborating with staff members at Mahikari centres, in order to provide a yoko school kind of education. When I attended the 1995 Sukyo Mahikari International Educators Conference in Japan, I was moved to hear about the efforts of such education given at the Sukyo Mahikari centre in Mie (Mie Dai Dojo) in Japan, reported by a school teacher, Mrs Hoshijima. More progress has been achieved in the meantime, but I would like to share some of the things I learned from listening to her report in 1995.

Apparently, the number of junior high school students who used to come to the Mahikari centre in Mie was very low (many children attend after-school tutorial schools), which was a cause for regret, as it is important to nurture children so that they can take responsibility for the quality of life in the twenty-first century. The staff and parents thought that it would make it easier for students to come if they held study classes to make up for what was lacking in school education and home education. Therefore, in December 1993, they began to hold what they called 'true education classes' at the centre.

In the beginning, 20 students attended, and by the middle of 1995, 46 were attending. On Saturday nights the centre was normally crowded with parents and children, so the school teachers of the centre, together with some Mahikari Youth Group and staff members, voluntarily offered to provide education from 7 to 9 o'clock every Saturday night. They helped the students with their homework in mathematics, language studies and so on, studies that the students normally had to do in their own schools. Everything was done in a spiritually oriented way.

The weekly procedure was as follows. First of all the students offered their own prayers in front of the divine altar. Then they went to the conference room and prepared the desks by themselves. At 7pm the teaching session started with group prayers and sharing of experiences of gratitude. Then, some minutes were spent studying divine teachings that corresponded with the theme of the teachings that Oshienushisama had given for that month. The educators guided the children on how to pray to God and so on. Then they exchanged True Light on the forehead and gave Light to their books, pencils and other materials. After 40 minutes, they began studying their normal curriculum. Nine o'clock was the official end, completed with prayers of gratitude to God. After closing prayers at 9pm they cleared the room and vacuumed the carpet, full of gratitude to God. Even though 9pm was the official end, many people stayed, cheerfully and gratefully, until 10pm or so.

The two hours passed quickly for everyone. They allowed students who had plenty of questions to remain behind after the regular hours and gave them personal tuition when necessary. Those who had examinations coming also received extra personal help. By mid-1995, approximately 80% of the children in that centre were attending the classes. During the classes, many of the children's parents spent their time at the centre exchanging True Light and offering service in other ways.

The teachers made efforts to unite in love and harmony and to maintain a willing heart in offering service in this way. They praised the children, especially those who found it hard to study, by pointing out their good points, in order to give them confidence. Because the teachers were kind and considerate, the students were encouraged and showed no signs of being tired, even on days when they had attended sports activities earlier. They came to the Mahikari centre smiling cheerfully, greeting the teachers and other people.

Some of the children began the training in a lukewarm way, but they grew to give Light much more earnestly and alertly as time went on. Because the teachers who were conducting the classes praised the children, saying things such as, "You are getting so good at giving Light through attending these classes", the children made efforts more seriously. The teachers wanted to boost the children so they looked for any good points that they could praise. Mrs Hoshijima mentioned that even though they conduct studies like mathematics and English, the main aim is to enable the children to receive the Light of God in abundance, as well as to grasp divine teachings, so that their outlook towards any kind of study and life in general can improve.

Amongst other things, Mrs Hoshijima reported the following about some of her students. There was a 3rd-year junior high school student whose teacher at school had scolded him severely for using a calculator. As a result he hated attending lessons at his school. When his mother asked him to attend the 'true education classes' at the centre, he refused at first, but eventually made a promise that he would come just once. Because the teachers and other people were so kind, he liked the class immediately and began to study enthusiastically again. He became able to follow his English classes at his own school, a subject in which he used to be weak. He even invited one of his friends to attend the classes at dojo. His marks at school went up one grade as a result of attending these classes.

One 5th-grade elementary school pupil who had been bullied at his school and who used to retaliate by scratching, biting and kicking, said that he does not know why, but as a result of his training at the centre, he does not feel like reacting negatively when people criticise him anymore.

Amongst the observations of the teachers were that the children made many friends and grew to enjoy studying. It was common to hear the students say how wonderful it is to study under the Light of God. Even though the educators did not say much about posture, they found that the posture of the students improved naturally as well.

The inspiration and joy grew month after month because not only the staff members, but also the parents noticed wonderful changes in their children. For example, parents remarked on the improvement in the manners and behaviour of their children at home as well as their improved marks at their school. The Mahikari educators found that the children became able to concentrate and listen better at their own schools, and naturally, this helped them in their subjects. Mrs Hoshijima said that there is not a single case of a child whose grades have gone down. Some of the children reported at the centre how they are praised by their teachers at school. There was even a non-Mahikari teacher who came to the centre and reported that whenever her pupil (who attended the studies at the Mahikari centre) came into the room, the atmosphere of the class improved.

Some students brought their report cards to show the centre director the improvement in their school marks. Some of the parents noticed such improvement in their children that they began to come to the centre more frequently as a family, to show their appreciation for the big changes in their children.

The parents and teachers conducting the training also found improvements in their own lives. Two lady teachers had been trying to have children for many years, but were unsuccessful no matter what they tried. As a result of offering this service, they became pregnant and were able to have babies. This training was so infectious that even non-kumite brothers and sisters started coming to the classes as well. Young children were heard to say: "Gee, when I become ten, I want to receive an Omitama too."

A key point for the success of the true education classes was the love, joy and cheerfulness that the teachers and parents displayed. Programs like this cannot work very well if they are conducted reluctantly, as a duty to fulfil. That is why the educators and parents, together with the Mahikari Centre staff members, trained themselves to maintain positivity.

In 1996, 1997 and 2002 I met the director of Mie Dai Dojo again, and she joyfully reported that the number of students participating in the 'true education classes' had multiplied since the report made at the Educators Conference.

World trends in education

In my observations, it is becoming increasingly clear from reports throughout the world that the old approach to education, namely, emphasis on academic achievement and physical skills, is rather limiting.

Dr Gilbert Childs (1991) has given a penetrating presentation of the principles and practice of Waldorf School education – based on the spiritual insights of Rudolf Steiner – something of particular interest to educators who are looking for a deeper understanding of the human being and the educational process. For many years, various kinds of schools such as Rudolf Steiner Schools, Montessori Schools, Brockwood Park School and West Kidlington School in England have been making contributions towards improving the quality of life through education, instead of being content just to impart knowledge.

In his book *Education on Trial*, widely respected lecturer Nathan Rutstein (1992) criticised modern educational practices, and outlined a more enlightened approach, including the incorporation of virtues and moral education.

Leading innovative educators Gang, Lynn & Maver (1992) have outlined some principles of a spiritual education for the twenty-first century, which can prepare human beings for new kinds of relationships. It contains the Education 2000 declaration and shows how education can be transformed by a new set of values.

In their book *Education for the Twenty-First Century*, education researchers Professor Hedley Beare and Professor Richard Slaughter have given a detailed analysis of the necessary changes to education, which should come about partly through the pace of change itself and partly through reassessment of underlying assumptions. The authors showed how schools unwittingly transmit a distorted view of the world and will need to be reoriented towards the future and a one-world outlook (Beare & Slaughter, 1993).

In *The Limits of Competence*, Professor Ronald Barnett (1994) of the Institute of Education, University of London, suggested that universities should provide education for life. This is also a book that goes beyond the limited concepts of academic and operational competence.

Kamikumite Amon-Tanoh (1995), a former Minister of Education of the Ivory Coast, reviewed the major crisis facing modern education and put forward solutions. "If we admit that the crisis in society is essentially of a moral, spiritual nature, we must attempt to overturn the received ideas and achieve sound education through a system of education that, put succinctly, is based on the foundation of universal morality – on the laws of the spiritual world – by which one can live day by day in a practical way." Amongst his proposed solutions are the importance of being a good example, greeting people cheerfully, working for the restoration of nature, cleaning educational institutions, and families meeting regularly to reflect on the education of their children.

Dr Lawrence Le Shan (1996), psychologist and educator, pointed out the need for an ethical system that can help society to survive into the future, in a world with unprecedented technological power but underdeveloped ethical sensitivity. He proposed a system of education based on psychological knowledge and aimed at the clarification of knowledge and the development of self-esteem. He stressed that responsibility and care are only developed by practice, and warned against the "fatal fallacy" that we can change children without changing ourselves.

In 1997, the Centre for Alleviating Social Problems through Values Education (Aberdeen, Scotland) launched the *Journal of Values Education*, a learning forum for a wide range of educators, managers, counsellors and probation officers committed to assisting others to behave more responsibly.

Writer and broadcaster Frances Farrer (2000) described the remarkable story of the values program at West Kidlington School in Oxfordshire. Positive values such as peace, hope, courage, love, appreciation and other aspects form an integral part of the school curricula and activities, with emphasis on the quality of the teachers being the most significant aspect of teaching. Comments from parents, teachers and locals indicate that the program is effective and the atmosphere of the school is special.

Professor James Arthur (2002), Head of the Centre for Educational Research at Christchurch University, shows why the development of character is a central component not only of education but of stable and creative democracies. He considers that teenage problems associated with moral disorder, alcohol and drug abuse, crime, self-centredness and ethical illiteracy should be dealt with by instilling certain virtues so that they become internal principles guiding the pupils' behaviour and decision-making.

§

These are some studies I have come across that indicate that people throughout the world are becoming more and more concerned about the limits of the old approach to education. There are no doubt more researchers calling for change. To me it seems that concerned people are seeking a new approach in education – a whole person approach involving spirit, mind and body.

Spiritually oriented business – the new direction for sound economics

Chapter 9

Spiritually oriented business – the new direction for sound economics

Normally, economics is a field that is viewed only from a material standpoint. Most people probably would not conceive of the idea that economics can have anything to do with the spiritual. However, since universal laws (Sukyo) apply to all fields, they also apply to economics. I was pleasantly surprised when I first learned Sukuinushisama's guidance on a God-centred approach to economics – called spiritually oriented or spiritual economics. It made so much sense, even though my field was far removed from economics. Since then, through personal experience and that of many others, I have come to realise that people in general would benefit greatly if economics was practised in a spiritually oriented way. I have also come to learn that in recent years, increasing numbers of professionals have been promoting more spiritual approaches in economics. In this chapter I deal with some limitations and problems of the old approach and convey my understanding of spiritual economics.

Materialistic economics

I have noticed that the economy is a subject which often dominates the media and people's conversations, no doubt because it has a great bearing on everyday life. Despite the enthusiastic and dedicated efforts of many people in governments, business circles and elsewhere to improve the economy and material well-being, it is ironic and quite a puzzle to understand why in more and more families, both husband and wife have to work just to make ends meet. There is a growing disillusionment with predictions about a better economy. Unpredictable falls in the value of currency are a frequent cause for anxiety. Even when the economy seems to improve on paper, the buying power of money continues to decrease. There seems to be little confidence in the economic theories promoted by experts, be they government officials, economics professors, financial consultants or business leaders. It is interesting, for instance, that there are few if any cases of anyone with a doctorate in economics establishing a company that became a multi-million dollar corporation. Conversely, there are many cases of people who did not know much about economic theories, but who became successful in business after going through much hardship. It seems to me that present economic theory has no clear core or guiding principles to ensure success.

I met Dr Clive Hamilton in Canberra at meetings of academics who were concerned with improving the world. In his book *The Mystic Economist*, Hamilton (1994) concluded that:

> . . . *the economist in fact has almost no idea at all what will happen to the economy and is basing this string of assertions on some theories about economic relationships none of which has been proved or even established beyond a reasonable doubt . . . Some sceptical people have kept records of economists' predictions and tested them against actual outcomes. These studies have shown repeatedly that the economists' forecasts are consistently wrong.*

Paul Hawken is an active campaigner for green policies and was co-founder of a famous United States retail company known for its environmental initiatives. In his book, *The Ecology of Commerce*, Hawken (1994) pointed out:

> *Despite our management schools, despite the thousands of books written about business, despite the legions of economists who tinker with the trimtabs of the $21 trillion world economy, despite and maybe because of the victory of free-market capitalism over socialism worldwide, our understanding of business – what makes for healthy commerce, what the role of such commerce should be within society as a whole – is stuck at a primitive level.*

In addition to the confusion about economic theories, modern economics often involves practices that are of alarming concern. For instance, it is perverted by an addiction to military spending, according to well-known biologist and activist, Dr David Suzuki (1990).

> *Each year, over a trillion [U.S.] dollars are spent worldwide for defence, including the manufacture, sales and use of machines of death. (That's about $20 million every second!) The weapons trade consumes scarce resources but generates enormous profits for major industries and nations. However, it is the diversion of scientific creativity by the military away from socially and environmentally useful areas that is the greatest perversion.*

> *Military research and development now consumes more than 71% of all U.S. R & D while only 9% is spent on health research.*

In the mid-1990s, the U.S. Government spent $30 billion annually on military intelligence while the United Nations Population Agency had a budget of only $240 million. The Indian Government spent 17% of its budget on defence and only 5% on education and health. Most countries in the world show this abnormal, excessive lean towards military and defence spending in their budgets.

In 1990 the Worldwatch Institute, based on various sources, gave comparisons of the valuable improvements that could be achieved if money were not spent on defence programs. For example, they estimated that two weeks of global military expenditure is the same as the annual cost of the proposed United Nations Water and Sanitation Decade. Three days of global military spending would fund the Tropical Forest Action Plan over five years. Two days of global military spending is the same as the annual cost of the proposed 20-year United Nations Action Plan to halt the spread of deserts in Third World countries. The expenses of the Stealth Bomber Program could have been used to cover two thirds of the estimated cost to meet U.S. clean water goals by the year 2000. And so it goes on. I imagine that the budgets for military spending are increasing further as the different countries become involved in war or perceive the threat of war.

In addition to the excessive funding of military projects, there are enormous economic problems that result from the imbalance of salaries and income in society in general. For example, the $20 million paid in 1992 to basketball star Michael Jordan for promoting Nike shoes was more than the entire annual payroll of the Indonesian factories that made the shoes, where thousands of girls and young women workers were paid as little as 15 cents an hour. According to statistics, the top 20% of the world's people enjoy incomes 150 times as high as the lowest 20%. Within the United States alone the income received by the top 1% is greater than the total income of the bottom 40%. According to the *1996 Human Development Report*, which is prepared by the United Nations Development Programme, the world's 358 billionaires, including the Sultan of Brunei and Bill Gates, the founder of Microsoft, have more assets than the combined incomes of countries representing nearly half – 45 per cent – of the planet's population.

There are also numerous cases where big business is jeopardising the safety of humankind and nature. Dr Vandana Shiva (1998), who founded the Research Foundation for Science, Technology and Ecology in Dehra Dun, India, and who has served as an adviser to governments in India and abroad as well as to prominent non-government organisations, has convincingly and powerfully exposed a number of dangers that threaten humankind and nature if large companies continue their 'biopiracy' unchecked. For instance, in the name of 'development of Third World countries', governments of countries are collaborating with a handful of giant food companies, enabling them to genetically engineer 'terminator seeds' that cannot produce progeny, forcing farmers to buy more seeds from the controlling companies. A whole host of unethical and dangerous approaches has arisen – the view that life can be patented, the conversion of common heritage into a commodity and ultimately into an intellectual property right, the dangers of destroying genetic diversity and promoting monocultures, the possible destruction of nature, not to mention the harmful effects on the health of humans and other creatures.

Lack of ethics in business practice, corruption and the like are other causes of various major economic problems. Highly paid directors and senior company officers are often protected from personal liability for their unethical actions. Illegal corporate acts that would bring stiff prison sentences (or perhaps even death sentences in some countries) for individuals, at most lead to fines on the company, which are insignificant in relation to its assets. These are the kinds of things that Dr David C. Korten (1995), one-time Visiting Associate Professor of the Harvard University Graduate School of Business, now president of the People-Centered Development Forum, called, "organised irresponsibility that characterises the corporate sector".

It is estimated that about 95 per cent of the daily monetary transactions in the world are devoted to making money out of money, and only 5 per cent to facilitating the exchange of goods and services.

Even when business is conducted ethically, one person's profit is often another person's loss. Big companies often cause small companies to suffer without trying to do so. A win-win economic situation has been difficult to achieve if one considers society as a whole.

On top of everything else, the manufacturing industry is permeated by an attitude of intentional wastefulness. Goods are purposely manufactured not to last, but to break down so that more goods or parts of them can be sold. Limited product life for the sake of short-term profit is considered more important than the quality of goods, effective use of resources and long-term benefit for people and the environment. This is generally also true for food and other items that have a high turnover. According to Suzuki (1997), in the U.S., people "can choose from 25,000 supermarket items, 200 kinds of cereal and more than 11,000 magazines".

Clearly, the long-term economic situation is not improving for most people, using material-centred, selfish approaches. If such approaches really worked, there would already be a prosperous world, as there are ample resources and very hard-working people dedicated to improving the economy. I believe there is a need for a fundamental shift in approach if long-term improvement in the economy is to be achieved. This shift involves some understanding of the invisible realm as well as attitudinal changes towards appreciation and management of resources from a global point of view.

Spiritual economics

Sukuinushisama gave guidelines on how to achieve economic prosperity, that is, a condition of no financial anxiety, a subject he called 'spiritual economics' or 'spiritually oriented economics'. This is not a quick-fix, self-centred way of becoming rich, but a sensible, mature, altruistic approach that steadily leads to true economic improvement for all society. Though rather simple to explain, I have found his guidelines to be the most far-reaching and effective advice on economics that I have come across. They are not taught at universities, business colleges or schools. They can be practised by anyone, whether directly involved in business or not, as they apply to all economic situations.

I think what makes Sukuinushisama's guidance particularly credible is that he himself had been a very accomplished businessman, a force to reckon with in the business world of Japan. Despite once reaching the position of a multi-millionaire, his wealth disappeared almost overnight. He crashed from 'prince to pauper' at the end of the Second World War. It was through this financial disaster that he awakened to the futility of amassing wealth in a material-centred way based on old approaches that are normally used in business practice.

Just before the end of the war in 1945, all his companies – his entire fortune – were completely destroyed in an air raid by United States war planes. His aircraft factory of 66,000 square metres and surrounding company houses received direct hits and were wiped out. He was left with practically nothing but the clothes he was standing in and huge debts (as a result of loans to run his companies). In other words, he not only lost everything but he had enormous debts to pay. In a humble way, he began working for other people. Eventually, by January 1959, he paid off all his financial debts.

A point that made me think is that Sukuinushisama had been an accomplished businessman according to the traditional understanding of good business principles. He had business acumen, he was a hard-working man, he knew the right people in the right places and he had enormous capital to invest. Despite this, he lost everything due to unforeseen circumstances and unpredictable phenomena. He ended up wondering why he had spent decades of his life building up so-called financial success when at the end of that time it became zero. Can it be called financial success if wealth disappears sooner or later?

There are many examples throughout the world of economic collapse after initial success. Economic well-being cannot be assessed from a short-term, here-and-now viewpoint. There is something operating that Sukuinushisama later referred to as 'theory beyond theories'. Life does not proceed according to conventional human-made theories.

I believe that sound economics can be achieved if there is a spiritually oriented approach, which means to bring understanding of the real existence of the unseen realm, the spiritual realm, into secular activities, and to conduct life so as to produce a positive spiritual influence. My understanding of the guidelines on spiritual economics can be summarised as follows.

• Purify and elevate your spiritual condition (which includes resolving spirit disturbance).

• Recognise the law of cause and effect, namely, that one's present situation is the net result of all the activities of the past, including the activities of oneself and one's ancestors in previous lives, and therefore make an action plan for one's life accordingly.

• Understand that cleansing and waves in life are essential and these may manifest as financial hardships (see chapter 6). Therefore, since one has to receive compensation or cleansing anyway, it is best to do it willingly and with altruistic attitudes.

• Recognise that all natural resources are something created by God and really belong to God, so strive to use them wisely, with gratitude and in order to fulfil the plan of God.

I would like to explain these points separately in more detail, even though they are all connected and cannot really be totally separated.

Spiritual condition and spirit disturbance

Through my experience I believe that no matter how well-meaning and respectable a person is in practising business principles now, if there is a resentful spirit or spirits attached to him or to his family members, sooner or later severe interference or even collapse may occur in the business unless these spirits are saved. As I have pointed out, saying this does not imply blaming the spirits. We need to take responsibility for our lives and recognise that spirit disturbance occurs because we or our ancestors hurt those spirits or their ancestors in past lives. Spirits who are resentful due to financial loss or other material suffering caused by the person or family in the past generally make particularly great efforts to cause financial suffering to the family. Resentful spirits try to prevent the person from succeeding in business by keeping customers away, making equipment break down at crucial times, causing staff members to quarrel instead of cooperate, or whatever they can do. Spirits generally know what will happen in the spiritual realm before the person does, and they are invisible to people, so they can carry on their disturbing activities unnoticed by people in general, which gives them a certain advantage over those they wish to manipulate. The only solution is to save such spirits so that they lose their resentment.

Even though business is a field that is normally associated with physical things such as money, materials and technology, it is just as crucial to take care of the unseen spiritual realm correctly here as it is in any other field, such as health, education or family harmony. The subject of spirit disturbance and how to go about resolving it has been dealt with in chapters 4 and 6. Basically, to resolve spirit disturbance, it is important for the people concerned to give and receive the Light of God as much as possible, as a way of life, with innermost attitudes of gratitude, altruistic love and apology for the suffering caused in the past. At the same time, these attitudes are to be demonstrated by offering genuine service to God.

The purification and elevation of people's spiritual condition is closely connected with the improvement of any spirits attached to them. As a result of steady purification and elevation of the spiritual condition of a person's family, together with the steady improvement of the spirits who are suffering, advantageous arrangements can occur in the spiritual realm and in turn appear in the physical world, arrangements that lead to steady improvement in business – for instance, increasing profits, obtaining contracts or meeting appropriate business contacts.

Another valuable practice that spiritually oriented Mahikari business people can do is to purify their workplace – the office, equipment and materials – with the Light of God every day. Many kamikumite business people have told me how such purification of their workplace, over time, has improved harmony amongst their workers, made the workplace brighter and more pleasant, increased the efficiency, boosted the sales, and resulted in protection from theft and accidents.

Basically, the practices and approach to life are the same in business as they are in family matters or in any other situation: put

God first, then the ancestors and then the matters of the physical world. Even if one worships God correctly and tries to do one's best in a God-centred way by practising spiritually oriented business principles, if the ancestors are suffering, they may even prevent the business from improving until they are taken care of. Taking care of ancestors properly (see chapter 4) is one of the things done to put matters of the spiritual realm in order, and can have a good influence on one's economic situation as it can on all aspects of one's life.

If emphasis is placed on the physical and mental aspects, as has largely been the case in business up till now, it may help people to cope for a while, but I do not think there can be reliable long-term improvement in the economic situation in this present age of baptism by fire (see *Main aspects of the divine plan* in chapter 2). This stands to reason if one recognises that the greatest cause of failure in business is disturbing spirits. How can there be steady improvement or stability if such spirits are suffering and full of hate? Is it really a business success if someone is promoted to become the managing director of the company, say, then due to spirit disturbance, dies in a car crash on the way to a holiday? Whether it is business, health, education or any other aspect of life, the basic approach is the same – to elevate oneself spiritually, which involves purification with the Light of God and helping the spirits attached to oneself and one's family, while striving to improve one's character and compensating with meritorious deeds for the sake of God's plan, society and others.

In short, spiritually oriented business people do not put the main emphasis on the visible realm of money and other materials, but take care of the invisible realm, the spiritual aspects, as they understand that whatever the condition is spiritually, it will materialise physically sooner or later.

Law of cause and effect

Closely related to resolving spirit disturbance and elevating the spiritual condition is to recognise that one's present situation is the net result of what one has done throughout one's whole existence, something that may have begun thousands of years ago, throughout transmigrations and reincarnations over many lifetimes. Similarly, the activities of one's ancestors over many lifetimes also influence one's present condition.

Basically, God has arranged things so that human beings have eternal life and can achieve eternal flourishment (health, harmony and prosperity) as children of God. However, this is something that is achieved progressively over many lifetimes. As human beings we have a certain amount of freedom to choose how we direct our destiny. The present situation is the net result of what one has done up to now. This is the law of cause and effect. As Sukuinushisama taught:

Humans to whom everlasting life has been given go through the training of polishing their soul as they go back and forth between this world and the astral world.

Therefore, your present condition exists as the sum total of the results of your deeds in your previous lives and of your training in the astral world.

In all things a result appears because of a cause. God made arrangements so that one will reap what one has sown.

Spiritual economics means to have this understanding as a foundation and to progressively and actively compensate willingly. It means willingly to sow good seeds which bear good fruit, not bad seeds.

If one is a millionaire now, this is the net result of all one's activities in previous lives, those in the physical world as well as the astral world, including the efforts of one's ancestors. Even though hard work, skill, teamwork and other factors play a role, it is a misconception to think that becoming rich is just something to do with being skilled in business, working hard or becoming lucky at the present time. As is written in the Bible, "As you sow, so shall you reap".

Naturally, if a person's situation is not pleasant financially, that is, if one is living in poverty or material hardships, it is valuable to have a heart of apology and to go about life with new attitudes, taking responsibility for one's situation, instead of blaming the government, society or other people.

Compensation is inevitable
People have made mistakes, produced impurities, knowingly and unknowingly, both directly and through their ancestors, in previous lives as well as the present one, so it is inevitable that compensation or cleansing phenomena will appear from time to time. I have learnt that if there are financial impurities from the past, it is necessary to compensate through materials. This can take place through financial hardships, damaged merchandise, broken promises concerning business agreements, bankruptcy, losing a job and the like. Financial compensation can also occur in such a way that income is lost even though the business may be progressing well, such as a family member suffering from a chronic illness that requires medical expenses which go on year after year, thus keeping the family financially anxious. Whatever the reason for financial compensation, the most valuable approach is to offer willing compensation, with gratitude, that is, to sow good seeds instead of bad seeds. In other words, it is best to use one's money and materials to achieve God's plan, to help society, to

benefit others in some way, as much as possible. This not only results in paying for bad seeds sown in the past, but also becomes the basis of sowing good seeds for the future, in accordance with the law of cause and effect.

I think it is also good to know that it takes time to erase impurities, even with the best of intentions. It is unreasonable to expect that one will have a smooth life financially because one acquires noble motives and now spends time practising spiritually oriented principles at work. It is natural to have ups and downs in life because that is how God created the universe in order for things to progress. People are often good at being grateful when things go well from their point of view, but the key is to have gratitude and use one's means to compensate even when one is in a trough, that is, when going through unpleasant phenomena. If those who are doing well now continue to compensate on their own initiative, they will keep on doing well or do even better.

I believe that voluntary compensation with gratitude is the key to a happy life. Since compensation is inevitable, one might as well do it willingly. The most efficient and pleasant way of compensating is to incorporate the practice of purifying with True Light in one's daily life and to use one's voice, body and materials to serve God. Serving God also means helping others and society. As I have pointed out, all this only has significance if it is done on one's own initiative. In the Sukyo Mahikari organisation there is no coercion to make material offerings or to offer any other kind of service unless one wants to. Indeed, it is really only service when one wants to do it.

Even if a person is reasonably happy now, this may be no indication of what will happen later. Society is full of examples of wealthy people whose fortunes collapsed overnight, including the case of Sukuinushisama himself. Conversely, there are also many people who were born into poverty-stricken situations but went about using their means to help society, and eventually, after going through hardships, came to achieve a more and more prosperous situation.

I do not want to imply that there is something negative about having wealth. It is how we gain and deal with wealth that is important. There have been many wealthy people who have had altruistic attitudes and used their wealth to help their country or society, such as Nelson Rockefeller, Bill Gates, Anthony Robbins and Dick Smith, to name a few. The founder of CNN (Cable Network News), Ted Turner of Atlanta, made a particularly great impact when in 1997 he offered a billion dollars to the United Nations. From

1999 onwards, Bill Gates and his wife have donated more than $23 billion for worthy causes. On the other hand, there are cases of people, even ones in high positions, who have been involved in fraud, embezzlement or other corruption, and even though they appeared to do well for a while, the day came when they crashed.

Many people have wondered why in the past, the rich grew richer, the powerful more powerful, whereas the poor or unfortunate continued to be reduced to lives of suffering, as is apparent in history over the centuries. I feel that this can be understood if one sees things in perspective, unfolding according to the progress of the plan of God (see chapter 2). In order to develop a material civilisation, for many thousands of years God did, in fact, put up with unscrupulous people succeeding materially to different degrees, as a necessary expedient in order for material development to reach the required standards. However, things have changed since 1962, as a result of entering the great turning-point in the divine plan (from material-centredness to spirit-centredness), and now it is more and more difficult for the rich to grow richer unless they fit with God-centred principles. It is harder to exploit people or materials and get away with it. I believe that if one is to be truly successful, there is no solution but to live according to the will of God.

The divine teachings explain that it is now 'a time of exposure' as well as rapid compensation in order to establish a high-quality, holy civilisation. Although in ancient times, when the will of God used to be one of promoting materialism and it was temporarily overlooked to be successful materially even though corruption was practised, today it is becoming less and less likely to happen. There is no way to achieve a quick fix kind of happiness. In my opinion, lasting happiness can only be achieved through steadily practising certain universal laws so as to fit with the will of God.

Natural resources

Another aspect of spiritual economics is to recognise that all natural resources were created by God and really belong to God. This is not some vague religious notion that one reflects on fleetingly and then goes back to considering one's land and house, say, as one's possessions; it is to really strive to have gratitude for what God has been doing, and to be concerned about how to use materials for God's plan.

Natural resources were created over billions of years with great, painstaking efforts by the Creator God through the activities of various deities. It is good to use materials preciously and with gratitude. This means using things sparingly, in other words, not being wasteful, recognising that materials are precious and have a life span. It is also important to take responsibility for the misuse, wastage, destruction, exploitation of and lack of gratitude for material resources, and to change one's way of life so that such mistakes are not repeated.

In the 1950s and 1960s when Japan was undergoing considerable economic growth, Sukuinushisama went so far as to suggest to government agencies that they introduce environmental legislation to make tree planting compulsory when a new building is erected, as lack of oxygen would be a future problem due to the ongoing disappearance of vegetation. He also suggested that they encourage development of clean energy, techniques to convert sea water to fresh water, sensible management of resources, and put an end to a largely consumeristic type of society by developing a society that encourages recycling and a wise use of natural resources, with gratitude to God.

In 1998 Oshienushisama pointed out the importance of spiritual economics for the twenty-first century:

There is an urgent need for the rapid establishment of 'spiritually oriented economics' for the economic development of the future. From the founding of this organisation, Sukuinushisama proclaimed the need to develop spiritually oriented economics. The foundation for spiritually oriented economics should be the establishment of a new system which enables humankind and nature to coexist in harmony. We need to awaken to the fact that the unchecked exploitation of the natural resources God created has reached its limit and a 'new environmentally oriented economics' must be established. We need to develop recyclable products and establish a spiritually oriented world in which all people can lead a peaceful and comfortable lifestyle.

In order to establish spiritual economics, it will also be necessary to discover and develop new forms of energy to replace nuclear energy and fossil fuels. Methane hydrate, hydrogen, the sun and the wind, as well as the vacuum – the so-called new energy of the coming century – will need to be subjects of research and development. To achieve this, we will need to combine human, material and financial resources and thus establish a heavenly society that is a reflection of God's world on earth. Traditional methods of economic development which threaten the well-being of humankind will no longer be permitted by God. Time has run out for humankind to continue making the same mistakes. A new economic system, one that is wholesome and humane, must be developed to the level of being able to protect and promote the welfare of human beings.

In 2000 Oshienushisama once again gave guidance about the new way of going about business:

People in politics and business need to become aware that consideration for the environment is the key to the development of business. When we carry out land development and construction work, it is important that we strive to maintain harmony with nature and consider the impact such work will have on the environment. If business enterprises adopt clean energy and make concerted efforts to recycle as much as possible, the natural environment can be restored to its original state of beauty.

There are all kinds of ways we can use materials more effectively if we want to take some innovative steps. One approach in the workplace, for instance, is to design and operate one's office so that paper is used sparingly and then recycled. It has been estimated that the average office worker throws away about 180 pounds of high-grade recyclable paper every year, and that the average office can save at least 17 trees and keep 60 pounds of air pollution out of the sky for each ton of paper it recycles (MacEachern, 1990). A small drip from a leaky tap can waste over 100 litres of water a day. Electricity, water – indeed, all things that we often take for granted – can be used more efficiently, effectively and with gratitude, if we have a mind to do so.

Sukuinushisama's example
Sukuinushisama's own words (published in the August 1998 issue of *Mahikari Australia–Oceania and Asia Journal*) of his experiences in business when he had fallen into the depths of poverty after the Second World War illustrate a number of aspects of spiritual economics.

If everyone began to consider how things could be done for the sake of society and others, society would improve. However, in today's world, people's basic intentions, innermost attitudes, run contrary to this.

I was able to repay my debts due to God. The amount was so enormous that normally one couldn't have paid it back. When I lost everything after the war, it was the middle of winter. I had only two summer shirts, which were worn out, and a pair of khaki trousers which were supplied by the army. Not only were my possessions reduced to a pair of trousers and two summer shirts, but I also had to repay my debts, so I thought about supplying rubber boots to farmers. I went to Yokoyamacho to buy them. I would buy a pair for ¥365 or something like that, the wholesale price, and I would sell them for ¥700 a pair, according to the recommended retail price. When I took out expenses such as the train fare, I gained a profit of approximately ¥250, so at first I bought only one pair to sell.

I thought that a life as a door-to-door travelling salesman was something dreadful. When you open the front door, people shout at you, 'What do you want?!' It was no use thinking that I used to be president of an aeroplane-

manufacturing company. What I needed was sales. So I would leave saying, 'I'm sorry I troubled you.' As I did this I would arrange their shoes properly at the front door, and if there was waste paper, I would pick it up. I was like a rubbish collector. However, on my next visit they would consider me to be different from a pushy door-to-door salesman. When I visited them again, they would say things like, 'Ah, was that you who organised our shoes the last time?' 'Yes, it was me. I thought your entrance needed a bit of tidying up because if the entrance is messy, perhaps a robber would come in more easily, thinking that the family in the house is slack. I thought I would line up the shoes properly, and also, I thought it would be easier for you to find them when you leave home.' 'You're a strange person, aren't you?' 'Yes, I'm probably a little different.' 'Well then, I might buy something from you', and so it went on.

What did I do? It was the lack of a self-centred ego such as, 'I want to make a profit'. At that time the farmers needed rubber boots and they were expensive on the black market. However, I sold the rubber boots at the recommended retail price, which made the farmers very happy. Eventually, more and more orders came in. I used to say that I could not supply them three pairs at a time, because I did not have enough money to buy them from the wholesaler. And the farmers would say, 'I didn't know you were so poor. Why didn't you tell me? I can pay you in advance.' That is how farmers began to pay me in advance and that allowed me to pay cash to the wholesaler for three, five pairs at a time.

In this way, if you conduct your business with the focus on 'for the sake of society; for the sake of others', you will gain profit naturally. You don't really need to advertise or anything like that. You can do business. I think this is the key to business. Things do not work out well if people's focus is on wanting to make money out of others. I was able to pay back my debts without having to have a single pamphlet to advertise my business. The same applied when I worked for a construction company. I didn't consider my own happiness, but worked hard with the intention of making a profit for the company.

When I indicated that I would resign from the company, they were concerned. The directors came to me one after another, asking me whether my salary was enough, trying to encourage me to stay. So my monthly salary went up without any negotiating for a raise. However, when the due date for repayment of my debts drew near, I was in trouble and was thinking about going to another company. After finding this out, the company asked me to stay as it would pay more for me. They knew that other construction companies were trying to recruit me, knowing that I would not ask for a raise but would bring them a lot of profit. My company's executives thought that if I resigned, other companies would take me on. However, even though the situation was like this, my debt payment was due and I really needed to do something. So I applied to resign from the company. The company president came to visit me, three days in a row, asking me what it was I didn't like about his company. In the end I had to explain to him: 'Finally the due date for repaying a certain amount of debt is drawing near, and if I don't repay it, I'll be in big trouble. A certain company has offered me three times the monthly salary that I receive now and they say they will pay for me, so I was thinking about moving to that company. I'm sorry about doing this. Please forgive me for doing this, but I think I have contributed quite a lot for the growth of this company up until now.' The president said, 'Why didn't you tell me before that you had such a debt? I will pay for it', and so he paid the entire balance of the remaining debt for me. In this way, when people concentrate on working for the benefit of society and others, abandoning their self-centredness, they will prosper, because that is how things are arranged.

I think that changing your innermost attitude is the key. In your business you might want to clean and beautify your shop. Your innermost attitude is crucial when doing this. For example, if you sell apples and polish some poor quality ones, thinking that you will sell them at a higher price by polishing them to look like they are more expensive – such thinking will lead to a decrease in customers. Rather, it is good to make things look nice in your shop by thinking, 'A housewife may come to my shop after quarrelling with her husband. At such a time we will offer her good service in a nice, clean shop. In this way she will feel better and will be able to be happy and harmonious with her husband when she goes home.' Why not have this kind of attitude as you polish your apples? Mysteriously, they will begin to sell. Also mysteriously, customers will gather at your shop. The reason for this is that the spiritual realm of your shop will be different, that is, when someone comes into your shop, the spirit of that person will perceive something very different. Your shop will feel bright. However, if a shop owner has an attitude such as, 'I'm going to take every advantage of customers to make money', the atmosphere that they pick up will be very different from the one they would experience at a shop where the owner conducts business with a genuinely caring attitude.

On top of this, if you respect God and take care of your ancestors, you will receive their help as well. There will not be any ancestors lined up in front of your shop making customers feel negative as they come in, but rather, they will encourage customers to enter. That is why, mysteriously, people will come to your shop.

Even though God has His plan on a grand scale, God also has compassion and love that go down to minute detail. This is why it is important to become a person who is given divine power, not just human power. Furthermore, if people rectify their bad points as well as do what they must do, God will arrange for things to improve naturally as their impurities are erased. That is the bond between God and people.

In going towards God, people must reach a stage where God and humans are closely associated, in other words, living daily life with the thinking that they are working with God. I hope you become like this. This is the key to a path that leads to happiness.

Spiritual economics in practice

Many kamikumite who are in business have told me that they tried to achieve success in business, but that it did not happen until they awakened and started practising the appropriate spiritually oriented principles. One example is Kerry Lam of Sydney. The following are excerpts from his account (Lam, 1995).

Ever since I began my career in business, my main reason for working, like most people I suppose, was to become rich and ensure security and happiness for my family. In 1991, I attended the Mahikari primary course with the aim of solving all my problems. I thought this was possible through receiving an Omitama and serving God. However, after the course, things went from bad to worse; our Gourmet Lunch Bar began to lose business. Due to the recession, I lost many customers. We were affected so badly that in 1992 we made a loss, not a profit. We had to sell the house my wife and I had worked so hard for, in order to pay our debts. We continued to work hard hoping things would improve. They didn't!

During the next two years, I went to the Mahikari centre regularly but was unable to awaken to the spiritual reasons for our problems, despite True Light and guidance from the staff. I attended several studies organised by our centre's business group on Sukuinushisama's teachings about spiritual economics, but I was still unable to awaken to the fact that all our financial difficulties were compensation phenomena arranged by God. God was kindly trying to erase our family's sins and impurities to allow us to achieve real happiness. I didn't realise at the time that service to God and making material offerings were ways of erasing such impurities, not for gaining self-benefit which, I am sorry to say, was my main reason for serving and offering donations at that time.

All through 1992, 1993 and 1994 the staff members were trying to help me awaken to the fact that my financial difficulties were due to spirit disturbance caused by ancestors spirits on both sides of my father's and my mother's family lines (my mother's maiden name is Wong), who were financially ruined by me in a previous life. According to spirit investigations, in some cases in my past life I had even used robbery to take their assets. Therefore, they had deep resentment towards me and vowed to ruin me.

I eventually awakened to the fact that it was God's arrangement to give me various trials and training, and to purify our family through financial difficulties. I then really tried to give up my attachment to selling the Lunch Bar and to abandon my concern over our financial situation. With the help of God and my wife Sylvia, who has never been attached to money and materials like I have, and who has always encouraged me to think in a spiritually oriented way, I started to organise things so that I could work fewer hours and allow myself more time to give Light and help others. Miraculously, God permitted this! He even permitted us to sell the business just before Christmas, which is very unusual for this type of business. We lost over $100,000 when we finally sold the Gourmet Lunch Bar. Amazingly, I was able to accept it as major cleansing and a blessing for our family.

I could then make sense of what had happened to us nine years ago, events that I can now see were due to the suffering we had caused to the Wong family in our previous lives.

The company of my uncle (Mr Wong, my mother's brother) where I was employed as company secretary faced financial difficulties in 1982 and incurred so much debt that they went into liquidation. After investigation by the Corporate Affairs Commission, it was found that the companies had illegally borrowed money from merchant banks and finance companies. Those loans had been initiated by my uncle and I was sure some of those merchant banks had helped set up such illegal procedures so they could lend money to my uncle's companies. Naturally, they denied such knowledge when being investigated. Because some of these loans bore my signature at that time, my uncle and I were both charged by the police for the offences.

However, my uncle happened to be overseas when the police laid charges against us. He has never come back to Australia to face those charges, even up to this day. I was left facing those charges alone, even though I had done nothing illegal! Subsequently, I faced a trial and spent a small fortune in legal fees. I was found guilty of those offences and convicted.

The presiding judge stated at the time of sentencing that even though I had not received any financial benefit at all from those loans and my actions had been probably through blind loyalty to my uncle, because of the magnitude of the amount of money involved, I couldn't be let off with a good behaviour bond. I had to go to jail. I spent 17 months in jail. When I got out, I was barred from practising my profession as an accountant. My whole business career collapsed.

My wife Sylvia and I became very bitter at that time and for even a long time afterwards. She found it very difficult to forgive the Wong family for what had happened to us. Looking back, I now realise that this was all due to resentment from the ancestor spirits of the Wong family and other families. It had taken me nearly four years to realise that what I had heard at study classes given at the Mahikari Centre on spiritual economics was true – that to succeed in business one must erase impurities of a financial nature by material means, either passively by losing money as I had done, or by making offerings for the plan of God, for example, to build the Shrine for the Creator God, to build the Regional Headquarters, to support the Mahikari Centre or other worthy causes. Of course, we must resolve our spirit disturbance as well by saving others. Since then I have been able to offer much more service to God willingly and with gratitude.

This year I awakened to the significance of reattending the primary course. Ever since I first attended the primary course in 1991, and because I always used to put business first, I never reattended the course fully.

On the evening of the first day of the course, on Friday March 24, I went to work at 6 pm. On Saturday, again I went to work after the course, only to find that business had been so brisk during the day that the shop had run out of bread rolls by the time I arrived there. Fancy trying to sell hot dogs without rolls! No rolls meant that we could not trade at all! Miraculously, I was able to borrow about 15 dozen rolls from other shops at that time of the night in order to continue trading until 10pm, the normal closing time for my shop. Usually I'd be lucky to borrow five dozen rolls. However, that night another shop owner had the 'flu' and had to close early. He had 10 dozen rolls he couldn't use, which he lent to me. What a wonderful arrangement from God!

Also, my wife Sylvia had profound awakening from reattending the first day of the primary course. She said to me that during the day she had awakened deeply to God's teachings that we or our ancestors must have caused similar problems in the past to the Wong (my uncle's) family for what we had suffered, and that we should offer sincere apology to God for what we had done to them. Of course, through spirit investigations we had already heard before that we had caused such problems, but until reattending the course we'd never really made a conscious effort to apologise. I readily agreed to offer apology.

On Sunday, the last day of the course, we offered Otamagushi donations for both the Lam and the Wong families and offered our deepest apology to God for our impurities as well as our gratitude for being permitted to change our innermost attitude and have forgiveness in our hearts.

The very next day, Monday, at the close of business, my uncle, who had not contacted me for nearly seven years, phoned me from Taiwan saying he had been in touch with his lawyers, and that there was a chance he might be able to apply for a No Bill through the Attorney-General's office for the charges against him to be dropped so that he could come back to Australia to spend his last years with his family (he is 78 years old).

He asked me if I could help him by providing information to his solicitors. My immediate reaction was that our prayers had been answered! God had given us an opportunity to erase some of our impurities by helping him. Our gratitude to God was overwhelming.

§

A Hobart businessman found that his economic situation kept improving in leaps and bounds after he became a Mahikari member and willingly practised material compensation by making monetary offerings. The following excerpts are from his report (Smith, 1997).

Prior to finding Mahikari, my life was fully absorbed in the pursuit of money and materials, and I lived purely materialistically. From an early age, I was told frequently that wealth could only be measured by the amount of your possessions.

In 1975 I began construction of a huge house with my fiancée and went into business with a long-time friend in the electrical contracting industry. We were both driven by the same sole objective of accumulating as much money as possible. However, his concept of wealth was the amount of money that one could hold in one's hands while mine was related to a big business and many employees. This difference of opinion eventually resulted in our parting, and it marked the beginning of some major financial cleansing in my life.

Firstly, it seemed that whatever I did in business, failed. I had devised some electrical innovations and had approached various suppliers with my ideas. However, they responded by rejecting my ideas. Later I found these same ideas were being marketed as innovative new products. An economic recession developed and work dried up, leaving us with huge business loans that we could not repay, finally resulting in bankruptcy in 1980.

Due to this bankruptcy, the bank took our house, which we had spent years building, and my wife and I were left with nothing. At that time I was offered a job in the north of Tasmania as an estimator/supervisor. I was anxious to forget the misery of the past couple of years, so I gladly took the position.

We returned to Hobart in 1981 and struggled on for another few years, relying on the support of friends and family until work finally started to improve. My wife had a job as a childcare assistant, one that she enjoyed, and I held a contract for the electrical maintenance of the state's biggest shopping centre. We had lived with friends for twelve months, and were finally able to rent a house for ourselves once again. Again we set out to get rich.

Things went well for a few more years and we were able to purchase a house and new cars. The aquaculture industry was just beginning and I was able to find a niche manufacturing the specialised equipment that they required. I felt sure that we were headed for early retirement. However, we soon discovered that although we were turning over huge amounts of money, our costs were so high that we were hardly breaking even; and the future looked grim once more.

At about that time a friend mentioned Mahikari, and my wife began visiting the Hobart Mahikari centre regularly to receive Light. She seemed to be totally involved in this newly discovered practice, and although I didn't really know what it was all about, I didn't raise any objections. It seemed to make her happy, which was something I felt I was never able to do. In the meantime, the business stumbled from one crisis to another, accumulating large debts to the banks, letting clients down, more ideas stolen and so forth.

I began to receive Light myself and to understand the concept of cause and effect. I was able to attend the Mahikari primary course in 1990. For this turning-point in my life I would like to express my gratitude to Su God, Sukuinushisama and Oshienushisama, for the wonderful arrangements which can permit all people to come into contact with the Light and teachings of God.

After this, my business seemed to stabilise for a while, but another economic recession loomed, and work disappeared once more. This time at least we understood why we faced such difficulties, but I still had great resentment, feeling that we had suffered enough. We were forced to sell our home during a slump in the real estate market, but God permitted us great protection in allowing us a quick sale at a good price, thus allowing us to settle with the bank. We took up rental accommodation, moving from house to house over the following few years, each year bringing more difficulties, until finally it seemed that bankruptcy was inevitable again. Although I had been offering service at the Mahikari centre, making Otamagushi offerings with prayers of apology, communicating my circumstances to the centre staff in Hobart, and praying to God for guidance, I was still very focused on thinking physically about my financial problems.

I felt inspired to ring a friend who was the factory manager of a lightning protection company. Surprisingly, he did actually need someone at that time, and he asked whether I could begin work immediately.

In 1993, our Region began fundraising for the new Sukyo Mahikari Regional Headquarters, and after much struggle and thought, I decided to offer a portion of my first meagre pay towards the new Headquarters Building Fund, 10% in fact, or about forty dollars. Almost immediately upon returning to work I was forgiven a debt of twelve hundred dollars. Soon after that, it was arranged for me to do some of my work at home using my own machinery, increasing my income for this work five times.

I then decided to make a regular commitment to God; that is, to offer 10% of my business takings, which was about 25% of my take-home pay, towards the new Regional Headquarters. Of course, I realise that offerings only have significance if they are made willingly, that there are no rules or pressure to do so. However, my wife and I really wanted to make these offerings.

So many blessings have continued to be bestowed by God. The work continued to flow in, and soon I had five people working up to twelve hours a day in a futile attempt to catch up. From each cheque that I received I offered 10% towards the new Headquarters, and every day this happened, I returned home to find that yet another order for more work had arrived. In the end, four families were deriving their living from my company, during a time of recession when these people could conceivably have been in great financial difficulties. Due to these arrangements of God, I was permitted to consistently offer several hundred dollars a month towards our new Headquarters.

One day I received a call from the bank to whom we still owed a great deal of money. Although I was gradually paying off this debt of the past, it was still very large, and I feared the worst. However, after some discussion, the bank came to an arrangement where they wrote off nearly $28,000 of my debt! My accountant, who was as speechless as I, finally blurted out, 'Make them put it in writing.'

From that time, things became even better, although it was hard to believe. When we began looking for a new house, we assessed each possibility with a view to setting up the sacred scroll, Goshintai, in the future, and we were permitted a very suitable house. When we purchased a new vehicle, we did so with the thinking of how we could use it for service. We then found a new vehicle without any difficulty, and at a low cost.

Whenever I offered donations to God for whatever reason, I found that God always returned blessings in some way. For example, I had been paying a debt from my bankruptcy over the years, and decided to send $500 to hopefully clear the debt. To my surprise, the cheque was returned to me with a note asking what it was for. I half-jokingly said to my wife, 'If the bank doesn't want it, I will offer it to our Centre Moving Fund'. Our enquiries to the bank revealed that the account had disappeared out of the system, so we offered the money towards our new centre as promised.

Two years ago, I undertook some work for a company that subsequently fell on hard times and it was unable to pay me for my work. I decided not to pursue the debt, as I remembered how I had been supported by many people in the past. I wanted to take this opportunity to help someone else. Two days after I offered the $500 towards the Centre Moving Fund, I received *a cheque from this same troubled company, for exactly $500. This was eighteen months after I had given up thoughts of ever being paid by them.*

It has taken a great deal of time for me to deal with my materialistic upbringing, and I still find it easy to take things for granted at times. On occasion I wonder why I have been permitted so much; but then again, it is easy to see that God has a long-term plan. Through my business I have been able to make material offerings for God. I have also been able to introduce someone to the Mahikari primary course, and this person's work gives him the opportunity to give Light in the highest levels of government and the military, both in Australia and other countries. In addition, the equipment that we manufacture is shipped all over the world, and I find that I am in a position where I can influence many people in a positive direction.

§

Mr Y. Hori of Brazil is another example of a kamikumite businessman who experienced dramatic changes in his business after he started practising spiritually oriented principles at work. His company manufactures and sells panels that give protection against radioactivity and electromagnetic radiation. His greatest awakening occurred as a result of training in yoko agriculture (see chapter 10). The following excerpts are from his words of gratitude offered at the 37th Anniversary Ceremony of Sukyo Mahikari (Hori, 1997).

The innermost attitude change I underwent at the yoko farm enabled me to make major changes in the way I managed my company. As a result of this divine protection, my company made rapid progress.

I am truly ashamed to say that I used to arrive at the office between nine and ten o'clock each day and seldom greeted my employees. I gave pay rises to people who did well, fined those who did not work well, deducted money from the salary of those who arrived late and demanded special discounts from our suppliers. If a supplier did not deliver merchandise on time, I would claim compensation from him. I was always ready to stop doing business with such suppliers. These are the types of attitudes with which I used to run my business.

Through the practice of yoko farming, I was able to realise the importance of being grateful for all things and of being humble at heart, as well as to understand that our thoughts and conduct are reflected in others and return to us. Thanks to these realisations, I became able to offer heartfelt gratitude to my employees, and of course, to my customers, as well as to the machinery (and the company as a whole), even to rival companies.

I began to arrive earlier at the office and to sincerely greet all the employees. At first the employees looked at me with suspicion, but now they respond to my greetings with much joy. Gradually, the misconceptions they had of me disappeared and they became thankful to me. Mysteriously, there is now hardly anyone who arrives at work late or who is absent from work. As the company's president, not only do I feel gratitude to all the people who work for me, but I also feel a great responsibility for their families.

I became able to forgive our suppliers when they made mistakes. As a result, they began to supply us with materials of finer quality than we had ever received.

We communicate politely with our customers. When we sell our products to customers, we make it a rule to check if they are satisfied with the product. We have developed a good reputation, as our customers have become pleased with our sincerity, and our sales have risen without our spending any money on advertising.

In the one year following the yoko farm training session in Japan, my company made remarkable progress. Our products began to be highly acclaimed by great and famous enterprises both in Brazil and in other countries, and we now receive large orders.

Progressive improvement in economic approaches

Throughout history, wise people have warned about the dangers of becoming too preoccupied with materialism and have proclaimed the importance of spiritual values. Einstein himself, though remembered mainly for his contributions to mathematics and physics, gave wise words about materialism: *I am absolutely convinced that no wealth in the world can help humanity forward, even in the hands of the most devoted worker in this cause. The example of great and pure personages is the only thing that can lead us to fine ideas and noble deeds. Money only appeals to selfishness and always irresistibly tempts its owner to abuse it.*

Human beings can attain a worthy and harmonious life only if they are able to rid themselves, within the limits of human nature, of the striving for the wish fulfilments of material kinds. The goal is to raise the spiritual values of society (Calaprice, 1996).

I find it encouraging that nowadays, growing numbers of professional people throughout the world, from fields that have traditionally emphasised materialism, are questioning old, material-centred values, and are proposing new directives of a spiritual nature.

Dr David Suzuki (1990) argues that we must reinvent a future that is free of obsession with unrestrained consumerism and profit, restructuring our worldwide view to change our attitude towards the natural world and the spiritual value we place on other organisms. He says that we need to get back into balance with the natural world that supports us, as we are biological beings and our very existence depends on the integrity and quality of the web of life (Suzuki, 1997).

Professional motivators, consultants, trainers and business people have been promoting new approaches in order to succeed in the business world or life in general (Renesch, 1992; Block, 1993; Liebig, 1994; Gozdz, 1995; Whitmore, 1997; Gates, 1998). For example, Dr Stephen Covey has helped to improve thousands of mid-sized and small companies, educational institutions and all levels of government. He has had a major impact in opening people's eyes to the importance of being altruistic in dealing with people in order to succeed (being proactive, practising empathic listening, using a win-win approach, synergising and so on). In his popular book *The Seven Habits of Highly Effective People*, Covey (1990) wrote: *I believe that correct principles are natural laws, and that God, the Creator and Father of us all, is the source of them, and also the source of our conscience. I believe that to the degree people live by this inspired conscience, they will grow to fulfill their natures; to the degree that they do not, they will not rise above the animal plane.*

Anthony Robbins is another spiritually oriented motivator who has had a big impact on people's lives, particularly in empowering people to realise that they determine the outcome of their own lives. He said that he wrote his book *Awaken the Giant Within* (Robbins, 1991) so that people can "tap their God-given power". Robbins has given valuable insight into a broad spectrum of issues, including the understanding that true success is related to enduring values and service to others.

According to business research consultants Maynard & Mehrtens (1993), *Many in the Western world are responding to the lack of a sense of balance, purpose, and personal power by bringing spirituality into their lives and work . . . This re-spiritualization of society is manifested in . . . spreading efforts to incorporate spiritual values in the workplace.*

James E. Liebig (1994), another very experienced business researcher, wrote: "What is the world coming to when business leaders begin to talk in terms of *responsibility to the whole, mother nature, soul, consciousness, spirit, love and God?* Maybe something quite worthwhile!"

In his book *Seeds of Greatness*, Dr Denis Waitley (1994), who has helped countless people to become better people, said, "Did not the same Creator make us? Are we not the most marvellous creation of all, with power to think, experience, change our environment and love?"

One of the central arguments by Dr Clive Hamilton (1994) in his book *The Mystic Economist,* is that *we are social beings as well as private economic agents, citizens as well as consumers, and that by denying us our social and ethical natures modern economics constructs a dangerous and self-destructive world . . . Deep within each of us lies a divine self. The purpose of life is to find this Self and to live our lives from it. But the world of modern economics acts unceasingly to obscure our divine Selves from our conscious awareness.*

He indicated that it is not a question of whether we as human beings use natural resources but *how* we use them: *The question is not whether humans stand at the centre of the Earth, but what sort of humans stand at the centre of the Earth. Native peoples such as Australian Aborigines and Native Americans saw it as being in the natural order of things that they should kill some animals to survive. But it was of profound importance to the well-being of the Earth that they adopted the right attitude in killing them. It was not inconsistent to honour an animal and to kill it. This is in acute contrast to our own attitudes when taking from the natural world.*

Paul Hawken (1994) is a successful businessman and a very enthusiastic environmentalist. He asserted that:

The ultimate purpose of business is not, or should not be, simply to make money. Nor is it merely a system of making and selling things. The promise of business is to increase the general well-being of humankind through service, a creative invention and ethical philosophy. Making money is, on its own terms, totally meaningless, an insufficient pursuit for the complex and decaying world we live in.

Hawken predicted that business is on the verge of a great transformation, *a change so thorough and sweeping that in the decades to come, business will be unrecognizable when compared to the commercial institutions of today. We have the capacity and ability to create a remarkably different economy, one that can restore ecosystems and protect the environment while bringing forth innovation, prosperity, meaningful work, and true security.*

Dr David Korten (1995) explained that we need a new economic paradigm – including a new direction of economic progress, new economic theories and policies, and new business values and goals – and that this new economic paradigm must focus on enabling and empowering people to take control over their own lives. He defined the need to transform today's global business system as part of the challenge to "rediscover neglected political dimensions of our societies and spiritual dimensions of our being".

Von Weizsäcker, Lovins & Lovins (1997), leading lights in the worldwide movement for sustainable development, have provided descriptions of dozens of practical and profitable ways of quadrupling resource productivity, and discussed the larger context of efforts towards establishing a brighter civilisation, including the topics of 'green economics' and 'non-material wealth'.

In her innovative book *Rewiring the Corporate Brain*, Dr Danah Zohar (1997) pointed out that human beings are emotional and spiritual beings, not just rational thinkers, and organisations need to generate insightful, creative, 'quantum' thinking in order for businesses to become truly 'leading edge' organisations.

The altruistic approach promoted by Dr Jeff Gates (1998) in which *giving* is emphasised as a key factor in order to achieve financial success, is attracting the attention of people concerned about the world's future. He is advocating that economic decisions be made with sensitivity to a community's values and that private enterprise should involve broad-based personal ownership. A pioneer in the field of employee ownership, Dr Gates is proposing an approach to give capitalism a human face and encourage all participants in the economy to share the responsibilities and reap the rewards of success.

James Robertson (1998) has given radical and carefully considered proposals for a transformation from a dependency-creating 'big brother' structure to an ecologically sustainable people-centred economy with specific proposals on taxes and reform of the financial system.

Dr Hazel Henderson is one of the best-known futurists and is a consultant to corporations, non-government organisations and governments in over 30 countries. She described a global transition to what she calls the Solar Age, and beyond that, the Age of Light. According to Henderson (1991), . . . *the real new world order is based on renewable resources and energy, sustainable forms of productivity and per capita consumption, ecologically based science and technologies and equitable sharing of resources within and between countries as the only path to peace-keeping.* There is much statistical information in her book, including data indicating that some of people's most cherished aims – those concerning safe water, child healthcare, elimination of starvation, reversal of ecological damage – could be achieved for less than a quarter of current military expenditure. Henderson pointed out that our most renewable resource is unconditional love, which she encouraged people to expand into altruistic, cooperative behaviour.

More recently, the expression 'natural capitalism' has been coined (Hawken, Lovins & Lovins, 1999) promoting an approach to making money by cleaning the environment and using alternative sources of energy and energy conservation. The main focus is on new technologies such as resource-efficient, non-polluting hypercars; waste reduction; energy-efficient manufacturing; whole-system design and engineering; resource-efficient, re-usable materials; green buildings; textiles; timber; food and agriculture; water; and so on. They also promote a tax shift from taxes on incomes, employment and financial savings to taxes on resources and pollution of all kinds.

§

There are many other concerned authors who have put forward constructive viewpoints to look at economics in a more spiritual way than in the past. I am not implying that all these views fit with the guidelines of the spiritual economics outlined in this chapter. However, any steps to develop economic systems that respect God, humans and nature, that are altruistic and sustainable, are surely steps in the right direction. I find it interesting in itself that economics, a field that has been largely viewed only in a materialistic way, is viewed more and more spiritually throughout the world.

Yoko agriculture – a collaboration between God, humans and nature

Chapter 10

Yoko agriculture –
a collaboration between God,
humans and nature

Limited understanding of nature

In my childhood and youth I was raised on a mixed farm in the south-east of South Australia. For many years I had opportunities to interact directly with nature – animals, the land, trees and crops. When I began primary school at the age of five, I had to ride to school (about seven kilometres) on a pony with my twin sister. This little school in the country had one teacher who had to take care of seven grades at once, consisting of less than twenty children for the whole school, all farmers' children. Later, together with my two brothers and sister, we went to school in a horse and cart. When I was a little older, I had to milk a cow in the morning before going to school. I helped my father take care of about 300 hens. At different times we had up to 20 different kinds of pets. My father helped the property owner to take care of sheep – dipping, shearing them and so on – so we children often joined in as well. He also grew several hectares of potatoes commercially. I learned to drive trucks, motorbikes, tractors and all kinds of old cars. I ploughed the land. Throughout our childhood and adolescence, we children were involved in all kinds of enjoyable nature activities such as climbing trees, building aboriginal-type houses, walking through swamps, playing with frogs and walking for miles to observe the rabbits.

As we were living a long way from any town, we generated electricity from our own power supply. There was no running hot water; we had to boil water in a big copper kettle and carry it in buckets in order to have a warm bath. We grew our own vegetables. Most of the time, if we needed anything, we ended up building it ourselves. Even after I moved to Adelaide for college and university studies, during vacations I earned money by working on farms or in the forest, doing jobs such as digging potatoes, carting hay and transporting logs.

Having had such a background, for years I thought I knew a lot about nature compared with the city people I spent most of my time with later in my life. Of course, country people do, in fact, acquire many valuable skills from rural experience. However, it is only through training in yoko agriculture that I have come to realise how little I really knew about nature.

We viewed nature with preconceived ideas, something that all the farmers of the day seemed to do. Vegetables in the garden or crops in the field were viewed as something that we human beings could use at will, control to different degrees and even exploit. We had demands and expectations from the plants, even about how big they should grow and the size of the yield. To make things grow better it was considered normal to use agricultural chemicals. For example, every year I helped my father spread the recommended fertiliser, superphosphate, on the potato fields. We used to judge vegetation as good plants or weeds, with the positive and negative attitudes that go with such categorising. Similarly, animals were categorised as good animals or pests. Insects were by and large considered a nuisance and sometimes dangerous, although we recognised that there were some friendly ones as well. Snakes were always viewed as dangerous and had to be killed without a second thought. There really was no feeling of unity between God, humans and nature. In fact, many farmers and people in general openly made it known that they did not believe in God. Even people who respected nature and admired its wondrousness often did not attribute the wonders of nature to divine power. Nature was viewed without much thought that it can be a teacher or that there are greater depths to it if one quietly observes things with an open mind. Similarly with the products of nature – the delicious vegetables and fruits that we ate – not really much time was spent on being grateful to God or nature for them. On top of everything else, one of the most limiting things about having had experience with conventional agriculture, be it farming, commercial horticulture or gardening, I feel, is that one can become arrogant and think that one knows more about nature and growing produce than people who have not been exposed to such things.

Now, years later, having had some experience with yoko agriculture, I feel somewhat humbled and ashamed at how little I really knew about agriculture or nature in the past. I am still a beginner in yoko agriculture, but I feel that at least I have had enough experience to realise that this spiritually oriented form of agriculture, which involves the practice of universal laws (sukyo), is of a high order, as it relates to all aspects of life, not only gardening and farming.

Some readers will probably find various parts of this chapter unbelievable or "too good to be true", possibly too emotional or lacking commonsense. All I can say is that the truth of many of these things can be verified by personal experience, as has happened for me.

What is yoko agriculture?

Ever since the beginning of the Mahikari organisation, Sukuinushisama and later Oshienushisama have been giving guidance about the preciousness of nature, the importance of achieving unity between God, humans and nature, the dangers of pollution and other misuse of nature and how to overcome various crises facing humankind and nature. Since 1984 Oshienushisama has clarified what has come to be called "yoko agriculture" (yoko farming and home yoko gardening). As a goal given to the Mahikari Youth Group, Oshienushisama announced the plan to construct a yoko farm in Takayama, Hidama, a farm to be managed and developed by the Mahikari Youth Group as the main working body, under the guidance and direction of Mahikari staff members. Since then, beginning with Japan, yoko farms and gardens have been steadily increasing throughout the world. *Yoko* literally means *yang (positive, bright, sun) light* and is the same as the *yoko* of *yokoshi* or Mahikari practitioners (see chapter 2).

Significance, aims and basic guidelines of yoko agriculture

I have learnt that yoko agriculture is a movement in which people are nurtured to become genuine God-centred human beings, and the soil is nurtured in order to restore it to its original or natural, pure and fertile condition. It is a type of organic growing that helps achieve unity between God, humans and nature.

Normally, the term 'agriculture' refers to something to do with soil, crops, garden tools and the like, something very physical. However, if there is an attitude of separation from God and people, it is not yoko agriculture.

The attitude of trying to 'conquer nature' is best replaced with the attitude of harmonising with nature. A basic point of understanding is that all living things are to coexist and co-prosper. It is important for human beings to elevate their attitudes towards God and divine matters, their attitudes towards human beings and also their attitudes towards nature. For too long, many people have looked upon nature as a commodity to be used for the pleasure and profit of human beings, something that one can exploit at one's convenience rather than something that is a precious creation of God and intimately connected with all existence. Therefore, treating nature preciously, learning from it, and living so that unity can be achieved between God, humans and nature is important.

Thus, yoko agriculture is not a technique. It is not a task-oriented practice in which one tries to achieve a desired condition of the soil or yield of certain crops, but a spiritual training in which one strives to change in order to fit with the will of God in all aspects of life. As a result of spiritual elevation, which involves one's relationship with God, nature and people, by and large, God bestows nutritious, spiritually-enriched produce in abundance.

In addition to the personal training to elevate one's spiritual quality, the aims of yoko agriculture are:

1. To revive the earth to its original pure and clean condition as in ultra-ancient times, by protecting and developing it with true-hearted gratitude, recognising that it is precious and lent to us by God.

2. To eliminate the poisonous energy from the earth by purifying it with True Light, thus helping to revive it to a pure and clean condition that will result in produce full of the spiritual energy of the soil.

3. To nurture people who are wholesome and healthy in spirit, mind and body, and who make efforts to eat pure and clean produce without poisoning the body any further.

4. To establish a system of self-sufficiency, and develop emergency food supplies in order to overcome food crises.

Let me explain the thinking behind these four aims, as there is more to them than meets the eye. A major concern for the future of humankind is to nurture people who can develop a high-level civilisation in the twenty-first century. This nurturing, as well as providing the appropriate environment and food, can be gradually achieved to a significant degree through practising yoko agriculture, I believe. By being in touch with nature and perceiving its truth, goodness and beauty, people's innermost attitudes can be elevated more readily. In this way, people can become more spiritually oriented and can perceive God's protection and arrangements, and so offer gratitude to God more deeply.

As regards self-sufficiency in providing food, many economists, biologists, demographers, politicians and concerned professionals have predicted global food crises, particularly in certain countries and communities. In the mid-1990s in particular there were numerous reports from government organisations, scientists and the media concerning the new food crisis in the world. In 1996, for example, it was reported that at one time the world had only 30 days' supply of grain in store, the lowest level in history. In general, the main conclusion was that the population has been growing too rapidly while at the same time natural resources are becoming depleted. These factors certainly play a role, but I feel that there are other more important issues that have not been considered seriously by professionals.

Firstly, food, natural resources, other materials and nature in general have not been taken preciously by most of humankind but have been treated wastefully, particularly for the sake of profit. There are many cases throughout the world where farmers, governments and other official bodies have haggled over the prices of crops or produce, and because they could not obtain their desired profit, left the crops to rot or even dumped them in the sea. That is, profit is often given greater importance than the preciousness of food to feed people. How can one expect God to permit high-yield harvests later?

Another major reason for food crises is that the environment is being destroyed by deforestation, extinction of plant and animal species, acid rain, the spread of deserts and the use of agricultural chemicals – all problems caused by human beings. Land is exploited rather than revived. In general, if land becomes unproductive for crops, it is discarded and new land is opened for farming, without much thought about the precious earth. Through yoko farming it is possible to use the same land regularly, indefinitely, planting crops every season, providing the soil is being revived in the proper way, as is practised in various kinds of organic growing.

Abnormal changes in climate, which are also a major threat to food production, are due not only to increasing areas of barren land, global warming and so on, but also to humankind's degenerating innermost attitudes. As Oshienushisama said in March 1984, if humankind does not have the innermost attitude of carefully and respectfully using all creatures and things, including mountains, rivers, grass, trees, animals, insects and fish, which were created by God over billions of years for the sake of humankind, "then the oceans will become angry, the mountains will become angry, the forests will become angry, and will begin a counter-attack in silence, and finally humankind will be judged by nature".

This point is probably not easy to grasp by people in general, I think. Up till now the issue of possible food shortage has been viewed largely from a physical point of view. However, my understanding from divine teachings and experience is that in order to overcome crises such as food shortages resulting from drastic changes in the world's climate, natural disasters and worsening international conflicts, it is not only the sustainability of the soil, the area of land used for planting or other physical aspects that are important, but the innermost attitudes – the purity and elevation of human beings – as these influence how people deal with the land and what kind of arrangements God permits. Through the practice of yoko agriculture, the earth becomes purified and human beings improve, resulting in more favourable arrangements from God in which spiritually-enriched food can be obtained in abundance.

In other words, even though for most people yoko agriculture is primarily a training in order to elevate their spiritual quality, it is nevertheless also necessary to have a source of food so that people can be self-sufficient. No matter how much progress is made in science, medicine, education and other fields, we need food to survive. We need oxygen to breathe, and water is also essential. How we deal with nature and the produce it provides is a very important matter for all humankind. Providing food for people on a large scale applies mainly to professional farmers, so it is particularly important that farmers practise yoko agriculture where possible.

As part of nurturing people to become God-centred, it is also advisable that people eat food that is spiritually enriched and pure. That is why yoko farms are valuable. It is not just a matter of eating food that has not been grown with artificial chemicals. The point is that much of the produce grown today is spiritually very poor. The practice of yoko agriculture enables the soil to be revived to its original fertility, richness and power. The crops are grown with positive, encouraging, cheerful innermost attitudes and words, as well as the purifying effects of the Light of God. Experience shows that plants, microorganisms and so on, all respond better if they are given encouraging and grateful vibrations and words. We believe all this improves the spiritual quality of food.

The practice of yoko agriculture
From a practical point of view we consider four main aspects:
1. Positive, elevated innermost attitudes.
2. Cheerful, positive, kind 'spiritual functions of words'.
3. True Light.
4. Compost.

Even though they normally apply to growing crops, fruit or vegetables, the core practices within these aspects are equally effective in daily life in one's home, school, workplace or anywhere else.

In order to help make the training in yoko agriculture as practical as possible, the Yoko Agriculture Committee of Sukyo Mahikari International Headquarters has given six guidelines to practise in the field. These are:

1. Be grateful and cheerful in offering service to God and doing all things.
2. Greet the field or garden before beginning and offer gratitude to it afterwards.
3. Treat the tools and other materials preciously, greeting them with gratitude before beginning and thanking them afterwards.
4. Be careful not to step on the garden beds.
5. Avoid criticism, slandering, anger or other negativity.
6. Have cheerful, bright, positive words, smiles and behaviour.

I have come to realise that one's innermost attitudes, that is, the mindset or convictions, influence everything – people, surrounding materials, nature. Many people have found that their convictions influence the outcome of their farming. For instance, I heard that when children were given rather old seeds and told that they were wonderful seeds that would grow into healthy plants, they tended to believe it and, in fact, the majority of the seeds did just that. When seeds from the same stock were given to professional farmers who were told the age of the seeds, there were cases where hardly any germinated because the farmers believed they were too old to germinate. If a person tries to grow tomatoes but does not really like tomatoes, then the chances of producing a large, healthy crop are not as great. Relying on God, having trust in nature, recognising that it is doing its best: such attitudes in themselves influence everything to function better.

Similarly, the spiritual significance or functions of words (*kototama*) affect everything, as these are a materialisation of innermost attitudes. I have pointed out in earlier chapters, that according to divine teachings and personal experience, the innermost attitudes and words of people have a considerable influence on the whole environment, including the destiny of people – both themselves and others around them. For instance, even if the soil is neither fertile, rich, nor full of valuable microorganisms, but a person lovingly grows tomatoes in this poor soil, with lots of encouragement, gratitude, cheerful attitudes, thoughts and words, the tomatoes will tend to grow enthusiastically and there may be a huge yield.

At the same time as one tries to have positive innermost attitudes, thoughts and words, it is also important to avoid any negativity such as being irritated, upset or angry. Negative thoughts cannot be hidden from nature, it seems. They influence it as they do people. Through training with yoko agriculture, it is often possible to discover that it is very real. This is why Oshienushisama has pointed out that yoko agriculture is something to practise in a sensible way so that it does not become a pressure, a task-oriented burden, but something that can be enjoyed.

Those who do not have ready access even to a small garden can practise yoko agriculture by growing a plant in a single pot. Even a single plant in a pot can be an effective teacher and produce a surprising yield if it is nurtured well.

As regards greeting the tools and communing with other materials, in the Mahikari primary course one learns that all matter consists of very small particles, and that inherent in each particle is the will, wisdom and love of God. As the elements build up to form creatures, whether it is a chicken or a human, there are different degrees of this wisdom, will and love of God. Even though the human is God's highest creation, animals also are living beings with which one can have communication. So are plants. So are spades, rakes and hoes, although to a lesser degree. Dealing with materials gratefully – treating them well, showing appreciation and care – is always rewarded by more effective functioning and a decrease in accidents or other problems. In April 1987, Oshienushisama said:

> . . . those who are involved in the yoko farm, if you are grateful for the precious soil, show this gratitude by saying, 'Thank you very much', as you use the tools such as the plough and the hoe to plough the fields. If you show gratitude to the tools and crops saying, 'Thank you very much', you will be able to smell the fragrance of the vegetables even more. Many reports have been received from those who are involved in service at the farm such as, 'With gratitude, phenomena such as increased growth and fragrance of the vegetables actually occurred'.

A useful approach in practising yoko agriculture is to imagine oneself as being the plant or object one is dealing with, trying to imagine what it would feel like. For example, if you were a potato plant and people walked past without greeting you, how would you feel? You would certainly feel more encouraged and willing to make efforts for humans if they looked at you with joy and gratitude and encouraged you with positive words. Similarly, even if a person was not necessarily ill-mannered or unkind, but grew you only for the sake of profit and exploited the soil only for personal gain, how would you feel? You would certainly be much more encouraged if the person treated you well and looked upon you as a wondrous creation of God, quite apart from the monetary gain he or she would receive.

Being loving and kind does not mean showing nothing but gentle positivity, however. Just as children sometimes need to be reared with a strict aspect of discipline, plants will also achieve their roles more effectively when they receive training, such as some water deprivation at appropriate times, for instance. Staff members at the yoko farms in Japan have observed that plants that went through hardships, especially while young, often yielded a greater harvest than those that did not receive such training.

The effects of various influences can be verified through experience by closely observing nature with the humble attitude of wanting to learn. If one is willing to be taught by nature, one can be inspired with awe. In yoko agriculture one practises observing nature closely, communing with it so that one can perceive its truth, goodness and beauty. As Oshienushisama said, . . . *as you work on yoko farms, perceive the intricate arrangements of nature and the very profound protection from the Parent God that lies behind these arrangements.*

Observing nature is a practice that can be done at deeper and deeper levels. Observing the beauty, the intricacy of the arrangements and processes, feeling the wonder of nature and so on can be joyful and elevating. One can come to appreciate more deeply and be inspired by imagining the sophisticated arrangements of God in achieving the creation of all the different aspects of nature – from the minute to the large – including the biological processes involved, the functioning of the microorganisms, the social structure of the insects and the like. With experience, careful observation can lead one to perceive things spiritually more and more, to see things without preconceived notions, grasping the condition as it actually is, before deciding which words to utter or what action to take. There is no judging of things as good or bad. It is like going beyond the physical and mental eyes and opening the spiritual eyes in order to see things from God's perspective, not people's perspective. What humans see as a desirable outcome may be seen otherwise by God, according to the divine principles. It is good to be flexible in learning to explore new perceptions, new ways of managing the land and crops. Nature is a wonderful teacher if one tries to observe and learn from it with a humble attitude.

Most of the world's people live in cities and do not have much contact with nature, let alone realise its profundity. It is often easier to awaken to the arrangements of God when in contact with nature.

§

These six guidelines are not a set of rules, but a means to help us learn a new way to live with nature. Being grateful, for example, has a powerful effect on improving all things, whether it be the growth of plants, human relationships or the functioning of equipment. It is a quality that is valuable to cultivate anywhere, quite apart from in the garden or on the farm. However, by practising it in gardens and farms, often startling responses from plants can be seen, encouraging people to make the practice of gratitude a habit elsewhere in daily life.

The practice of offering apology is related to gratitude. It becomes natural to offer apology to God and to nature if one reflects on people's desecration of nature, misuse of materials, poisoning and pollution of the earth, destruction of the homes of all kinds of animals (including insects and microorganisms) and the eradication of many species. On top of that, there are the impurities of the people dealing with the land, impurities from previous lives such as having killed people or made them suffer in other ways. Without apology for the mistakes or impurities from the past (including those of one's ancestors), I do not think one can completely understand the physical phenomena that may occur in nature. For example, two growers may have similar plots of land side by side, but one grower's impurities may be deeper than the other's and therefore, even if both practise agriculture in a similar way, the one with more impurities may have to spend some years with smaller crop yields or other misfortune in agricultural practice, in order to compensate before being permitted to receive a greater harvest.

§

Another guidepost is to not use artificial chemicals but to purify everything with the True Light of God. It has become clear that the precious earth has been ruined to different degrees throughout the world in all kinds of ways, particularly by the use of artificial chemicals, both applied purposely in the form of agricultural chemicals (fertilisers, herbicides, insecticides and fungicides) and also through pollution in the environment (waste industrial chemicals, exhaust fumes from motorcars, acid rain, to name a few). It is valuable to give True Light to the soil, plants and other aspects of nature with an innermost attitude of gratitude and apology. The Light is not to be considered as a kind of fertiliser to make things grow better in a forceful way. It is to purify everything – the divine, astral and physical aspects. Of course, since it is the basis of all life, the Light is also valuable for plants to grow and function, just as it is valuable for all of God's creatures, including humans. It is also true that the Light of God purifies the soil and vegetation, gradually removing the impurities that have accumulated through the use of agricultural chemicals and other pollution in the environment. However, things go deeper than that. When people purify their land with the Light of God, it also helps in removing the impurities of their wrongdoings in previous lives, including wrongdoings involving the land itself.

§

I think that the greatest problem that results from using artificial chemicals is that the microorganisms in the soil are gradually killed. Also, the soil becomes both toxic and hard. This is why another guidepost of yoko agriculture is to use compost. There are many approaches in making organic mulches and compost, but the essence is to provide organic matter which is broken down, providing the soil with valuable nutrients, organic structure and microorganisms. Compost is not just some kind of organic fertiliser that makes plants grow better; it is nutrition for the microorganisms in the soil. If plants are force-fed with artificial chemical fertiliser, they may grow quickly at first, but the soil will not become healthier. In yoko agriculture, compost is spiritually enriched as it is made with love, positivity and True Light.

My early experiences with yoko agriculture

In August 1995 I participated in the International Yoko Agriculture Training held for one week at the Nyukawa Yoko Farm, the main training yoko farm of the Sukyo Mahikari organisation, located about 30 minutes' drive from Takayama. I was told that the previous owners had used the land for a melon farm, but after years of saturating it with artificial chemicals, the land became unable to sustain plant life to any significant degree and was abandoned. Apparently, when Sukyo Mahikari members first began to revive the soil in 1985, it was so hard and devoid of microorganisms that straw buried years ago had not even decomposed. When I first visited Nyukawa Yoko Farm in 1992, it was already flourishing, a nature paradise full of bountiful vegetation, earthworms, frogs and dragon flies – an impressive model of what can be achieved by practising yoko agriculture.

In the past, I had given lectures about yoko agriculture, but from the training at Nyukawa I realised that I had not really grasped the depths. I had been transmitting the words, but could not feel the reality of much of Oshienushisama's guidance. I suppose it is something like giving a cooking lesson after studying a recipe book when one does not really cook much anyway. A teacher who enjoys cooking and does it often does not have to say much. People in the class can almost pick up the vibrations of joy, enthusiasm, skills, key points and so on, from the person's very being.

Much was permitted to change for me by training at Nyukawa Yoko Farm. At first I was concerned whether nature would accept me because of my past arrogance and insensitivity. In the end, somehow it did, I feel, and for this I am grateful.

As a scientist with more than ten years of brain research experience, in the past I could not readily believe the stories I had heard that cucumber tendrils twirl around one's fingers when we communicate with them appropriately. However, I personally had this delightful experience several times at Nyukawa, but not when I first tried it, full of doubt. On one occasion I went to the cucumber hothouse alone, towards the evening so that nobody could see me. There were no demands from other people for me to perform well. There was no pretending. I selected a cucumber plant in which the tendril was actually curving in the opposite direction from me, and put my index finger near it saying, "Dear little cucumber plant, I am only a beginner in these matters but I would like to be a friend of nature and learn to genuinely communicate, from my heart. If you care about me, please show this." Within seconds the cucumber tendril started curling towards me, wrapping itself around my finger! I became very moved and excited. Words of genuine gratitude and encouragement to the cucumber started pouring out from my mouth. The tendril wrapped itself even more tightly around my finger! It was difficult to remove my finger when I wanted to leave a few minutes later. I felt that the plants were accepting me. Scientists have a lot to learn about nature, I thought.

I suppose that sceptics could say that such experiences do not mean much, because climbing plants cling on to whatever they can anyway. Basically true – but my experiences with the cucumber plants at the yoko farm revealed that the tendrils did not curl around my finger at first when I had arrogant or suspicious feelings, but responded within seconds when I had warm and positive feelings.

One of the activities at the yoko farm was to make compost. I was particularly jubilant in helping to make that compost. I felt like a little boy, singing and laughing with the other participants, dancing around in bare feet on the straw, the manure squishing between my toes. There was no pretending. I loved the smell of the bran and straw, the feel of the manure, the energy of nature, the happy sounds of the people that poured out spontaneously. It reminded me of my childhood and youth on my parents' farm. I had no self-centred motive at Nyukawa – only to learn as much as I could, tuning in to nature with joy and gratitude.

When the activity was over, I felt extremely elated, very energised, much more than if I'd had a very refreshing sleep or received exciting news. This surprised me, as the day was rather warm (about 35 degrees Celsius) and there had been other activities which had made many of the participants somewhat tired. Later I had a wonderful and strong cleansing from the bowels, something I had not had for a long time. I knew I must have received much Light during the compost making, as I have previously experienced such intense cleansing through the bowels after receiving much Light at Mahikari ceremonies and courses. I remember thinking how exhilarating it is to receive so much of the Light of God when one abandons oneself, and like a child, becomes totally absorbed in altruistic activities just for the joy of doing them.

What amazed me later was that the big varicose veins on my left leg were reduced by about 60%. It was only in the evening that I noticed this, as I normally do not pay much attention to my legs in daily activities. For me this was a miracle from God, because I know that no matter what I had done over the past 20 years, the varicose veins on my legs did not become smaller. I have been able to give Light to people every day, help resolve the spirit disturbance of many people, receive Light every day and offer other kinds of service over many years. However, the varicose veins on my legs just continued to grow bigger. I love jogging in the morning, my diet is good most of the time, but nothing seemed to decrease my varicose veins, especially those on my left leg. My wife, who knows this very well, was quite surprised to see a clear decrease in my varicose veins after I had joined in to make compost that day.

When I reflected on this later, I realised that if I had made the compost with an ulterior motive of seeking personal benefit, such as wanting my legs to improve, God might not have granted me this improvement. I can honestly say that I did not even think of any personal gain at the time. My sole aim was to master the principles of yoko agriculture, to be bright, grateful and accepting like a child, just as we were guided. I cannot help marvelling at God's great love, even in such detailed personal matters that are of little consequence to others. This experience has inspired me to show even more gratitude to God.

One of my great joys at Nyukawa Yoko Farm was to experience plants moving when I greeted them. Talking to the plants at Nyukawa came to feel normal, just as it is when interacting with people. In fact, we sometimes made requests to the plants. Whenever we needed to harvest something, we asked the plants, "Who wants to be harvested?" Very often we noticed reactions such as the plants moving or a fragrance being emitted, sometimes even a fruit falling into the hand as one's hand came near.

I will never forget the first time I experienced plants responding to my words. I was with one of the instructors and was asked to harvest the Japanese white radish (daikon) which was to be offered on the divine altar the next day, at the ceremony to be held in the Shrine for the Creator God. Hoping to offer vegetables of high quality, I was wondering how I would be able to assess the shape, size and quality of the daikon when most of it is beneath the soil. I asked my instructor and he casually replied, "Just ask the plants, who wants to be harvested?" At first I thought he was joking but I observed that he seemed quite normal when he went to the edge of the field and called out, "Daikon-san, who wants to be harvested for the ceremony?" I noticed that the leaves of some daikons rustled but those of many others did not. Once again, being a kind of experimenter, I insisted on trying it myself. It was the most exhilarating feeling. I called out in English, "Who wants to be harvested for the ceremony?" There were definitely leaves of daikon plants that rustled even though there was no breeze, and leaves of other daikon plants did not move. When I pulled out a daikon whose leaves had moved, it was a truly splendid daikon, long, fat, succulent-looking and healthy, an excellent choice. I repeated this in English and in Japanese three times, and on each occasion I was able to pull out a very high-quality daikon.

This impressed me, probably because it was my first time to ask plants whether they wished to be harvested. Now it has become a way of life whenever I harvest anything, including fruit and vegetables in my home garden in Canberra. Naturally, not all plants respond in the same way, nor can one always reliably observe whether they respond at all. Some plants may rustle their leaves. I have noticed that when tomato plants are greeted, they sometimes emit a stronger fragrance. There may well be many kinds of communication that can be studied, but plants communicating with people is a phenomenon that can certainly be experienced. Of course, if one does this in a mocking way, with disbelief or derision, there may not be a response. Learning to communicate with nature is just as much an art as is any other kind of communication, I think. We were frequently told that it is not only the words but the innermost attitudes or vibrations that communicate powerfully, so if a person is feeling negative but pretends and uses positive words, it is the negativity that communicates.

The influence of the innermost attitude can manifest in subtle ways that may not be immediately obvious. We were told, for example, that if one is only interested in the harvest of say cucumbers, for personal consumption or gain, the next day there may not be as many cucumbers to harvest. However, if one harvests cucumbers with the attitude of providing food for many people, in other words, with an attitude of altruistic love, more cucumbers will be ready for harvesting the next day. The experienced instructors often commented that they can often see, just by looking at the plants, whether people working in the fields have been doing so with dissatisfaction or positivity.

Not all my experiences were positive. I learned from mistakes as well. At the time of an Autumn Grand Ceremony, I was able to do a day's training at Nyukawa Yoko Farm with only the people who lived there. One of the tasks was to grind up tatami matting in a rather temperamental machine, so the matting could be used for making compost in the future. I started off joyfully and the machine kept on accepting all the straw I put in without stopping. After a while, I felt that this task was getting a little boring and wished that the people would show me some other task. The instant I had a feeling of dissatisfaction, the machine stopped! I started off cheerfully again and the machine kept working. Some minutes later I again started to wonder how long the task would go on. The instant that complaint and dissatisfaction appeared, the straw became jammed and the machine stopped. As a scientist, I couldn't help repeating this process several times, just to check whether it was really true or not. Sure enough, whenever I projected words of encouragement and gratitude to the machine, it just kept on working, even when I was somewhat careless with the straw. The moment I started feeling a little dissatisfied, even though I tried to work carefully, the machine stopped. I do not think that one's innermost attitude can influence so obviously machines that normally work well, but to me this experience was an eye-opener to realise more deeply that everything, even inanimate objects like machines, can respond to the vibrations that people give out.

Another matter I learned concerning coexistence and co-prosperity is that insects that are traditionally considered dangerous or harmful need not be so if one projects kindness and appreciation rather than fear, dislike or other negativity. Bees, for example, often make people fearful and end up being killed. Yet, bees do wonderful work, such as pollinating flowers, eating many insects and producing honey. It seems that if a bee is feared or hated, it picks up this vibration and often stings the person. If it is appreciated and treated kindly, it is unlikely to sting.

One morning at Nyukawa I noticed that one of the other participants was talking to a big bumble bee on the breakfast table. The bee was huge, much bigger than the ones I had seen in Australia. In the past, whenever I came near bees, I had an uneasy feeling that I could get stung, and even though I never really fled in fear, I did not take any chances with bees. I always used to avoid them. This time, however, I communicated with the bumble bee with genuine gratitude and pleasure, without any fear. To my surprise, the big bumble bee landed on my right hand and moved around looking for something sweet with its proboscis. At first I felt somewhat apprehensive, but decided I would go through with this even if the bee stung me. However, the bee quietly walked all over my hand for several minutes without leaving it. In the end, I went to a tree and asked the bee to leave, feeling deep gratitude. It was a moving, warm experience to realise that there need be no fear if one can work towards achieving harmony between God, humans and nature.

Since the yoko agriculture training at Nyukawa in 1995, I have awakened still further through practising yoko agriculture in Australia at the yoko farm near Canberra, the yoko garden at the Regional Headquarters and in my home garden. Many experiences continue to amaze me. For example, in my back yard I planted a small persimmon tree that I had bought from the local nursery. They told me it should bear fruit in three years. Persimmons are slow to begin bearing fruit. I love persimmons and I often made this known to the tree. I could not help talking to it or noticing it with warmth whenever I came near it. I enjoyed watering it lovingly. Sometimes I would just look at it approvingly in silence, with a smile on my face. Within only a few months, not years, nine persimmons appeared! These ripened to become delicious fruit, less than one year after the little tree was put into the ground. The tree was still a 'baby', less than a metre tall. I can only ascribe this to the power of love. Since then, the little tree is covered with dozens of persimmons every season.

Healthy persimmons about nine months after planting

Another experience (a confession really) concerns zucchinis. Shortly after I married in 1980, years before I knew anything about yoko agriculture, zucchinis grew prolifically in many gardens in Canberra. It seemed that everybody's garden was full of zucchinis, including our own. Zucchinis were even growing out of the compost heap. My wife loves zucchinis and we often had zucchinis to eat. At one stage I grew tired of zucchinis and emphatically said something like, "I'm sick of zucchinis! All we eat is zucchinis!" Years passed, and even after my training in Nyukawa Yoko Farm in 1995, I have to confess that even though most plants have been growing rather well in our garden, I had no success with the zucchinis, despite trying to project good innermost attitudes, positive words of appreciation and taking care of the soil, just as I did with the other plants. At first I thought it was due to having old seeds, so I obtained seeds from my friend's garden. None germinated. I bought seeds. None germinated. I even obtained seeds from a friend who knew they were from last year's season. From this batch I managed to get only one seed to germinate. The one seedling that sprouted I covered with a plastic bottle just in case the snails would find it too tempting. Then, one day while I was away, a strong wind suddenly came up and blew the bottle over. By the time I got home two or three hours later, the seedling had already been nipped at the stalk by a snail and was dying. It was only after that incident that I recalled my negativity towards zucchinis some years ago. That recollection was truly like an inspiration!

I told my wife and children about this, and in front of our sacred altar (Goshintai), offered a prayer of sincere apology to God for having felt and spoken so negatively about zucchinis in the past. Next morning I went into the garden and walked around apologising out aloud for my negative attitudes towards zucchinis in the past, telling them I now wanted to love and take care of them. After that I planted five zucchini seeds. Three came up and flourished to a degree that I could not believe. Even though snails appeared, they did not eat the zucchinis. The zucchini plants produced big yields. This was a very important lesson for me, a lesson about the power of innermost attitudes and words, in this case, expressing apology. Since then I have been continually able to grow zucchinis that have produced healthy and high-yielding harvests.

Learning from people

Although learning from personal experience cannot be substituted, learning from people who are experienced in yoko agriculture can also be invaluable.

The director of the yoko farms of Sukyo Mahikari, Mr Masayuki Nakagawa, who is a professional farmer of many years' experience, opened my eyes considerably by relating experiences that he has had with growing produce – experiences that cannot be explained in terms of traditional agriculture. For example, one year in Japan there was much less rain than normal and farmers had to use underground (bore) water for their rice paddies. In his district there was the problem of too much salt in the bore water. The rice plants in the fields of neighbouring farmers died, but none died in his field, even though he was using the same bore water. He had been practising yoko agriculture, whereas the other farmers were using the traditional chemical approach.

He also related that rice farmers normally have problems with weeds, particularly in summer, when it is hot and wet in Japan. In addition, the so-called 'jumbo mud snails' are feared by Japanese farmers, because they eat the tasty rice seedlings but do not eat the weeds. In Mr Nakagawa's case, however, he found that the jumbo mud snails ate the weeds in his rice paddy but left the rice plants. This happened particularly when he was offering service by guiding people about yoko agriculture in the summertime (when weeding of the rice paddies is normally very important). Such things do not happen by practising a technique. I feel that they are arrangements that result from making efforts to achieve unity between God, humans and nature.

Sukyo Mahikari International Headquarters in Japan has published a number of accounts about Mahikari farmers and the unique arrangements they have received from practising yoko agriculture with love and sincerity. For example, in 1993, the conditions for growing rice in Japan were devastating, mainly because of abnormal weather. The summer temperatures were the lowest ever recorded in Japan and the amount of sunshine for summer was the lowest in the past 30 years. In that year, kamikumite dedicated a rice paddy to God in Mie Prefecture. After the planting ceremony on 9th May, the weather was particularly bad for rice, very rare in Japan's history. Therefore, many kamikumite came to give Light to the rice paddy every day. God must have admired such united efforts of service and made special arrangements for this paddy. Although all the other farmers in the area experienced huge losses in their rice crops that year, this particular rice paddy was exceptional, yielding a greater harvest than ever before.

*Left – rice paddy dedicated to God (vertical plants);
right – neighbour's rice paddy*

Furthermore, the area was pounded by three consecutive typhoons, including typhoon number 13, the most devastating typhoon since World War II. At that time the rice plants of all the surrounding areas were flattened into the water. However, the rice plants in this paddy did not fall down. On the contrary, they supported each other and endured the violent storm. The differences were obvious to the naked eye.

The neighbours made comments in amazement such as, "We used the same species of rice plants, but why is there such a difference? This must really be a rice paddy for God". Everyone involved was moved to see the big difference between receiving and not receiving divine power.

In that year, the harvests were close to zero in the northern islands and the north-east region of Japan in particular, as a result of the devastating effects of the cold summer. There are kamikumite rice farmers in these areas. When they sensed that the year was going to be a very poor one because of the cold summer, some of them felt that because it was their livelihood and they needed to harvest as much grain as possible, they had to use chemical fertilisers. It turned out that in these farms, the chemicals caused a certain disease to develop in the rice crops, which devastated the entire crop. There were some other kamikumite farmers who sprayed their rice crops with agricultural chemicals. In the end, they found that not only did the chemicals fail to prevent the occurrence of disease, but they were left with the loan that they had taken out in order to purchase the agricultural chemicals.

It takes a lot of perseverance for farming people to be successful in producing abundant crops, overcoming the initial trials and losses, yet still continuing to practise yoko agriculture principles, rather than a profit-centred approach to agriculture. There were Mahikari farmers who received rich and abundant harvests of rice, despite the extremely abnormal climatic changes in their region. These harvests could not be compared with those of the surrounding farmers.

When these people were asked what their secret was, they simply replied, "It's just a matter of practising love and truth as indicated by Oshienushisama." They said that whether it rained, whether the wind blew or whether the storms came or not, they walked through the rice fields every day, giving Light and projecting words of love, saying things such as, "Please do your best, rice plants, even though it is very cold." Also, because they were in touch with the rice plants every day, they could sense their condition and were able to adjust the water in the paddy according to the changes in the weather.

There are kamikumite who think that as long as they do not use agricultural chemicals but use organic compost and give Light from time to time, they are practising yoko agriculture. This is a limited view, I feel, although it is a step in the right direction. The basic aspect of yoko agriculture is the practice of divine teachings in all aspects of one's life. As people practise persistently, with sincere attitudes towards God, divine power will be granted and improvements are likely to be permitted. The everyday practices of gratitude, humility and love and harmony in daily life are all part of yoko agriculture.

'Weeds' and 'pests'

Normally, when gardening or farming, people talk about 'good plants' and 'weeds'; 'useful creatures' and 'pests' or 'predators'. In other words, there is an attitude of conflict or confrontation. The truth of the matter is that all plants, all creatures, all life forms, have a purpose. Whether it is a blade of grass or an insect – everything has its role or mission. Rather than having a negative viewpoint, it is important to ask, "What is the purpose of this plant (creature)? Why has it appeared? What does it mean?" In yoko agriculture it is understood that all creatures, all life forms, are to exist together and flourish.

I was able to learn about this in more depth at the Nyukawa Yoko Farm, particularly from Mr Nakagawa, who spent years practising conventional (chemical) forms of agriculture as a farmer before he learned to see things from nature's point of view. His own father had been a well-known agriculturist who successfully used chemical fertilisers, pesticides and other agrichemicals. However, when Mr Nakagawa took over from his father, he found that he could not continue to grow crops well by using agricultural chemicals anymore. This forced him to study nature very closely, even to the point of sleeping out in the fields and observing phenomena such as the dew in the morning and how plants withered at night. He dug up parts of the soil and found that the rootlets were heading towards areas where there was no chemical fertiliser. This made him think that plants may actually choose to avoid artificial chemicals. He started using organic materials such as compost and mulch. Some years later he encountered Sukyo Mahikari and is now an active kamikumite as well as a farmer. His farm is flourishing. Moreover, he revealed that nowadays on his own farm he does not even bother much about making compost anymore, but just has an attitude of love. His farm continues to flourish and the crop, fruit and vegetable yields are enormous.

He taught that when the soil becomes poor or imbalanced, plants willingly sacrifice themselves to help revive the soil in order to enable future generations of plants to grow well. What are called 'weeds', are in fact grasses or other plants that have a strong vitality. We believe that one of their functions is to absorb the toxicity from the soil and sacrifice themselves after converting the toxicity into a non-toxic form, which then goes back into the soil as organic matter and helps to revive the soil. In other words, since the soil is the basis of any growth, if there is any degeneration or imbalance of the soil, nature brings various mechanisms into play in order to help restore its fertility. This is one reason why so-called 'weeds' grow. If one just blindly and mechanically tries to kill off weeds without any concern about their possible function, this may lead to the degeneration of the soil to the point when it will not be able to sustain plant life anymore. Where artificial chemicals are used in agriculture, the soil gradually degenerates because the microorganisms are killed, toxicity builds up and the soil hardens. It is only extremely hardy grasses and plants ('weeds') that can survive, and they are used by God in attempts to restore life to the soil.

Weeds no doubt play other roles as well, depending on the plant and the condition of the soil. Weeds help to anchor the soil, preventing the harsh sun and the pounding rain from hardening or washing it away. Various kinds of weeds also help the soil to retain moisture. There are also weeds that drive their roots deep into the ground, making the soil more friable and enabling the air and water to penetrate, thus helping other plants to grow better. Weeds are homes for various kinds of insects that play important roles. Certain weeds can be eaten, not only by animals but by humans. There may well be other purposes of weeds that we have not yet come to understand, but in short, an important approach is to recognise that all plants have a purpose. It is valuable to approach nature with a humble attitude, as a student learning from a teacher, rather than trying to impose one's will, project negativity or have unreasonable expectations that exploit nature.

I do not wish to imply that it is necessarily wrong to weed the garden. Indeed, without some weeding, in many cases the strong, rapidly-growing grasses would choke young vegetable seedlings or block out the sunlight. It is more a case of looking at weeds without negativity, trying to study why they are appearing, with gratitude and respect, and dealing with them in an appropriate way depending on the circumstances. In my own garden, when grasses appear close to young vegetable seedlings, I pull them out with respect and lay them on the soil with the words, "Thank you very much. Please become valuable mulch..." or something like that. When the vegetables grow large enough, I do not touch the weeds. They serve as a valuable water-retaining mat. Besides, if the weeds are in the shade (such as under pumpkin leaves) they do not grow so much anyway.

As regards so-called pests and predators, creatures such as termites, ticks, snails and so on, similar reasoning applies. If 'nature knows best', the question to ask is, "Why do pests appear?" At the yoko farm we were taught that it may be because the plant is not able to sustain life in the weakened soil, and therefore calls a certain pest, such as a snail, for example, to eat some of its leaves so that the rest of the plant can continue to grow in the impoverished soil. Or, the plant may call certain insects to 'destroy' it so the plant can return to the soil in order to help nourish and restore it to fertility. Nature has the fundamental will to enable descendants to come into being, so if the soil is not good enough to sustain a plant, the plant may bring on its own death by attracting pests as a step towards making the soil better for the future, before it is denuded beyond repair.

In other words, insects offer themselves for the good of the soil, the prosperity of future generations of plants and ultimately for the prosperity of humans. Blindly killing off so-called pests may provide a short-term solution, but it invites long-term disaster. If the soil is made fertile, there will be less need for the plants to call pests. Trying to kill off pests is like having a leaky roof in a house and putting buckets underneath to catch the water, rather than repairing the leak. Destroying insects with negativity and pesticides leads to destroying the balance of nature and gradually destroying human beings in the process. If the soil is revived so that it is of high quality and teeming with microorganisms, experience shows that so-called pests do not appear so much or do not cause the damage that they used to even if they do appear.

There may be other reasons why nature sometimes arranges pests to appear. The unnecessary removal of vegetation no doubt results in the destruction of the natural homes of various creatures, such as aphids, bugs and snails. If every blade of grass in the vegetable patch is removed, what else can these little creatures eat but the vegetables? Besides, is it really so bad to let them feed on some parts of the vegetable plants? Experience suggests that if crops, vegetables and fruit are dealt with according to yoko agriculture principles without negativity towards pests, the pests eventually eat only some of the desired produce, leaving most of it behind. Again, however, I am not implying that some short-term compromise against pests cannot be used (such as, say, a mechanical snail-fence) until the soil is sufficiently revived, even though, strictly speaking, this does not fit with yoko agriculture principles.

I have personal experience with different approaches towards pests, from my own garden in Canberra. Canberra gardens are notorious for snails, particularly when it rains. For years I had seen our little cucumber and cabbage seedlings disappear (partly or wholly) within hours or days after germinating, due to snails. People who do not understand spiritually oriented agriculture often view snails negatively and use poisoned bait to kill them off. After learning about yoko agriculture but not understanding it deeply, I had the misconception that it would be all right to keep ducks in the garden to eat up the snails during winter, so that I would be able to grow vegetables in spring. This, of course, does not fit with yoko agriculture principles, but with my limited understanding before I had done the training at Nyukawa, I felt it was better than using artificial chemicals. In short, I tried to introduce predators for the snails. However, I did not achieve much this way. The two ducks that I put into our backyard were chased away by my pet dog within minutes. One flew over the house never to return and the other kept flying into the neighbour's yard, no matter how many times I brought it back under cover of darkness. I gave up my intention to keep ducks in our backyard.

After I did the yoko agriculture training at Nyukawa Yoko Farm, I returned to Canberra without any attitude of conflict towards snails or any other creatures. I just continued to give Light with a heart of love, gratitude and apology and went about communicating positively (in my attitudes, thoughts and words) with the soil, the plants and creatures. I grew to feel very close to the garden, and amazingly, I noticed that even though many snails appeared, as many as before, mysteriously, they no longer ate the vegetables to the same degree. Previously, on average I would lose up to about 90% of the seedlings if I did not take any steps to prevent the snails from reaching the plants. Nowadays, however, it is more like losing only about 5% or less, depending on the plant. It is quite remarkable to see many plants flourish in our garden now, plants that just did not grow in previous years.

Moreover, earthworms, ladybirds, dragonflies, frogs and bees are appearing more and more. I remember Mr Nakagawa's story about a married kamikumite couple who live on the top floor of a 10-storey apartment block in Tokyo. They decided to make a garden with a little pond on the roof and practise yoko agriculture. Some weeks later frogs appeared in the garden. Where did they come from? In our experience, elevating one's innermost attitudes, purifying the soil and reviving it to its original fertile condition, with the approach of achieving coexistence and co-prosperity with nature, results in the spontaneous appearance of such creatures, traditionally considered as 'good'.

§

When I participated in the 1995 yoko farm training at Nyukawa, kamikumite from the yoko farm in Brazil and a professional kamikumite farmer from Bolivia raised the matter of the sauva ants (leaf-cutting ants) in Brazil. Apparently, these leaf-cutting ants have been considered to be pests – even a plague – for more than two hundred years, because they destroy farm crops. Farmers have been trying to destroy them by using insecticides, setting up explosions inside ant hills, setting bait (which is taken by the ants to the depths of their nests and produces noxious gas when it comes into contact with water, thus destroying the food source of the ants) as well as by other means. The kamikumite were very frustrated about how to solve the problem without using such drastic tactics, because apparently, in the yoko farm in Brazil, within one night half a bed of vegetables was damaged by the ants, and on another occasion, a whole bed was damaged. They became upset, discouraged and even very angry towards the ants. Even the cherry trees were not spared. They really wanted to learn how to solve this problem amicably.

The answer that they received at Nyukawa is that humans have been ruining nature while farming, and it is necessary to ask forgiveness for this. They were also told that there is no such thing as coincidence and that the insects have been sent by God for some reason. There was something the kumite of Brazil had to awaken to. They were also told that all changes are for the better. The instructors pointed out that even what is usually called a plague has a mission. Also, when there is an imbalance in nature or in the land, the vegetation itself appeals to insects, inviting them to infest the vegetation. The plants then become 'sick', dry up and return to the earth in order to help the earth to become rejuvenated.

The kamikumite from Latin America were at first a little confused by the guidance but decided to put it into practice. One year later, some of them participated in the 1996 yoko agriculture training at Nyukawa and reported startling awakenings, practice and results. The following excerpts are from their report. (A more detailed report in English is given in the Mahikari journal of the North American Region, *Sukyo Mahikari*, 1997 no. 45, vol. 9(1), pp. 30-35).

The first realization we had was that the leaf-cutting ants had lived on the land before we did. Therefore, they were not the invaders; we were.

Then we tried talking to the ants, asking them for forgiveness. We offered them a part of the land and part of the plants, requesting permission to cultivate the remainder, but nothing very meaningful happened. Then, with great humility, we offered them all of the plants. However, even after doing this, the big change we expected did not occur.

Even though we understood theoretically that the ants had a purpose for existing and that there is a special mission for each creature, it was very difficult to sincerely accept them and to erase the image that they were a plague that was devastating the plants. With difficulty, we changed our innermost attitude and continued to observe nature.

With careful observation over time the kumite came to realise that ants are true farmers. They cultivate fungus from raw materials by cutting leaves and sticks, then they eat the fungus. Different ants fulfil the four roles of cutters, carriers, farmers and the breeder. Then they noticed something very startling on the yoko farm in Brazil:

. . . A certain weak tree became strong with time and bore beautiful leaves and flowers even though everything else around it was stripped. This fact attracted our attention and made us curious. There was a very leafy tree right in the middle of a big ant hill. We were concerned for its welfare. However, we realized that none of the leaves of this tree were being cut by the ants.

From this the kumite began to observe things more closely and realised that only the leaves of weak trees were cut by the ants; the soil where the ants damaged the trees was depleted soil; the leaves of weak trees have a weak smell, whereas the leaves of strong trees have a strong smell; and leaves of weak trees seem to be better for the cultivation of fungus. By digging to the depths of the soil, the ants leave the soil smooth and allow water and air to enter the soil; the soil becomes rich due to the organic material brought in by the ants for the production of fungus; the work of the ants is similar to the work done by earthworms, which fertilise the soil; and, on researching other places, it was found that the soil became rich in every place where the ants built their nests.

From such observations as well as discussions with experienced organic farmers they were able to happily accept that the leaf-cutting ants really do have a mission to preserve the balance in the soil. In the area where the soil is not well formed, it seems that the plants offer their bodies to become organic fertiliser. For that purpose, they apparently invite the leaf-cutting ants to come and fulfil their mission. In places where the soil is rich, there is no need for the ants. The more one uses agricultural pesticides, the more the soil becomes unbalanced, and the more the need for the ants increases. It seems that God Himself is protecting the ants, preventing them from becoming extinct, even causing them to multiply more when necessary. When the leaf-cutting ants finish their service, they leave the area where the trees and plants have become healthy and go on to another area to offer their service.

§

The whole subject of weeds, pests, crop disease and related aspects is something that requires study through experience, maintaining the understanding that there may be various reasons for the apparent 'problems' observed in nature, just as there are with human beings. For instance, the staff member in charge of yoko agriculture told me that there was a Mahikari husband and wife whose crops were threatened by a certain bug, and even though they went to the edge of the field, offered apology and gratitude, and gave Light every day, the plants continued to deteriorate. It was only when they awakened more deeply, went to their Mahikari Centre to offer apology in front of the sacred altar (Goshintai), and demonstrated their apology by offering a day of service to God at the Mahikari primary course, that they found their crops began to improve.

Even very experienced practitioners of yoko agriculture may not yet have all the answers as regards so-called weeds and pests. As the years pass, we may understand their role more deeply. It is already obvious that there are different reasons for 'problems' occurring with crops. As mentioned earlier, a farmer with deep impurity from the past may have to go through all kinds of hardships by way of compensation, before he is permitted satisfactory yields of produce, even if he diligently practises God-centred organic agriculture at this time.

The practices with the Light of God, elevating the innermost attitudes and positive words, that is, the invisible aspect concerned with the soul and mind, make up at least 80% of yoko agriculture, and the basic guidelines about these do not change. However, there is room for experimentation as far as the soil is concerned, for example, the use of different kinds of compost or other organic materials to stimulate the production of microorganisms. Of course, even though the soil and compost represent the more physical aspect (about 20%) of yoko agriculture, its quality is also greatly determined by the Light, innermost attitudes and words, so it can never be regarded as merely physical.

Effects of practising yoko agriculture principles

Many people have remarked that the crops, vegetables and fruit from a yoko farm were the most delicious they have ever eaten. Many have also remarked on the increased power and energy they receive when eating yoko agriculture produce.

The practice of yoko agriculture principles has helped numerous people in other aspects of life as well. In my own case, what I was able to learn at Nyukawa Yoko Farm has helped me to interact with people more amicably and respectfully, and to nurture kamikumite as well as my own children more effectively. In my early years with Mahikari, I had often preached the divine teachings to people without looking sufficiently sensitively at their individual differences or levels of understanding. When we observe nature carefully without preconceived notions we can learn to become better stewards of nature. By observing carefully how plants grow, how the soil, plants, animals and insects interact, or whether the plants are having 'problems' in some way, we can more effectively tune in and take the next step to help improve things. It is a gentle, altruistic, non-judging interactive process. It is the same with people. It feels good to do this with nature, and it feels so good to do this with people as well.

As a father, in the past I often imposed my will on my children, demanding what I thought was good for them from God's point of view as well as a parent's point of view. However, they could not always follow, which led to frustration, irritation or other negativity. We cannot force vegetables to grow in the way we want, so why do we do it with children? We can only observe their situation, and by communing altruistically, help them to achieve what they need to do. Rough words can make plants wither, just like spraying them with herbicide. Parents arguing must have devastating effects on their children, I feel. Cheerful, encouraging words make all things live better. I am trying to practise this much more with people, having observed the influence on plants.

In chapter 8 I related how many school teachers have learnt to be careful with their innermost attitudes and words in the classroom, as a result of experiencing what this does to plants and animals. In chapter 9 I gave a case of how a company president was able to change towards his employees and clients as well as achieve great success in his business as a result of practising the principles he learned while training in yoko agriculture. Below are some more experiences of kamikumite who have been able to improve in daily life and in their professions, as a result of training in yoko agriculture. The following three excerpts are from cases that have been published in the *Mahikari Australia and Asia Journal* (1995), vol. 13 (10).

Learning from plants

Liane Hinds (mother, Canberra, Australia)

Recently, my 4-year-old daughter Eliza, two-and-a-half-year-old son Tom, and 2-year-old friend Matthew Quixley, lovingly planted some tomato seeds in Eliza's 'mini glasshouse', which is about the size of a shoe box. Remarkably, the seeds sprouted within only two days and quickly proceeded to grow energetically. Each morning Eliza and Tom greet the plants and I give the seedlings True Light before we take them outside for the day.

One morning Eliza wanted to have a look at the seedlings before we took them out. Tom tried to have a look at them too, but Eliza wouldn't share the seedlings. A tussle for the glasshouse broke out. Remembering the fundamental yoko agriculture principle of positive words, I resisted the urge to speak sharply to the children in front of the plants. Then Tom, who had become quite frustrated, started shouting loudly. Eliza then left the room, leaving Tom and me holding the glasshouse between us. As Tom screamed, I saw all the seedlings droop at once until they were completely bowed over!

I had an overwhelming feeling of sadness and showed Tom that the seedlings were hanging their heads. I explained that they probably were sad because they love him and Eliza and it hurt them to hear the two of them arguing and shouting. Tom's face fell and he was silent. Before he could start to cry, I quietly asked him to say 'sorry' to the seedlings. Tom held the glasshouse, apologised to the seedlings and bent over and gave them a kiss. As soon as he lifted his head, we both saw the seedlings bounce straight back to their original upright position as though something that had previously been holding them down had been removed! Tom was happy and danced around in the kitchen.

Without human logic and scientific theory, Tom at two-and-a-half-years of age accepted that his attitude had affected his environment and sought to help the plants. How much could be achieved if I as an adult were able to remove the limitations I place upon myself, nature and others, with human logic?

Students and teachers improve by communicating with a plant

Deenishnee Naidoo (high school relief teacher, Durban, South Africa)
Two months ago I began teaching at a high school. Initially I was confronted by a class of pupils who were rough and unruly. They gave me the impression that they were not interested in studying. They flung both books and verbal abuse across the room. On one occasion five boys drank a whole bottle of alcohol during my absence (of a few minutes) and were too intoxicated to stand. Many other pupils were sent to the principal for disciplining during this time.

Unaware of what I was going to do, I said to them, 'Please meet the new member of our family,' and held up a pot-plant, Greeny. I then related some moving experiences which the director of the Durban Mahikari Centre had related to us about the eggplants, the pumpkins and the cucumber plants communicating with him at Nyukawa Yoko Farm in Japan. I thereafter guided the students to be bright and smiling in class, to leave all their problems on the doorstep before entering the class.

In the first week, three of Greeny's leaves vibrated when spoken to. This awakened many pupils to the unseen dimension of the life within the plant. I know this left us all dazzled.

A few days later I took a class out to attend a talk on epilepsy. Another teacher and her pupils occupied my class. Unaware of Greeny, she spoke loudly, with anger, trying to get the students settled. I walked in, only to find that there was a lot of disharmony, something unfavourable to Greeny. In the next period, the pupils and I sadly discovered that the same three leaves which had first vibrated, now drooped lifelessly. Later they became brown. I mentioned this to the teacher. She surprised me when she took five minutes of her lesson to come in and apologise to Greeny. Thereafter she came in every day for one week to apologise to the brown leaves. Miraculously, the tip of one leaf became green again even though it had turned completely brown and shrivelled. A pupil asked Greeny if it needed anything and the leaf that was half green and brown vibrated as if crying out for nourishment.

By the third week one of the classes became disruptive again. Some students slipped up a few times and said things they shouldn't have said. They became irritated with each other. Within myself I cried out for them not to fall back into the old behaviour. I was forced to remove Greeny for five minutes to another class and then spoke to the students about not having any respect for themselves, least of all for a humble plant. When I brought

Greeny back to the class, all the tall stems had dropped almost ninety degrees. This had all occurred within a period of five minutes. I became emotional because I felt that Greeny was unhappy about the disharmony.

The following class, shocked by this, began to apologise to Greeny, truly from the bottom of their hearts, and gave it water and kind words. At the end of that period they brought to my attention that amazingly, the stems of Greeny were standing upright again. This change occurred within thirty-five minutes.

Some of the behavioural changes that have moved me most have been when pupils come to class late, they naturally walk over to Greeny to apologise for the disturbance. They use words like, 'Please be silent' and 'Please be quiet'. Teaching a multi-cultural class, students talk in English, Arabic and Zulu to Greeny, as they feel more comfortable with this. Lullaby tunes and melodies are slowly becoming a practice.

When I asked the students why they wanted to keep Greeny, they replied that having Greeny has brought harmony and peace into their class. They felt it taught them not only to respect plants, but each other as well. Some said they have been out of trouble since Greeny has been around. Others felt that their personal relationships with people within and outside school had improved miraculously. Fifteen pupils of a class of thirty three proudly said that they have stopped defacing desks, awakening to the fact that everything has life.

Learning through my home vegetable patch

Dawood Ebrahim (high school teacher, Johannesburg, South Africa)

In January 1992, we moved into the home in which we currently live. At that time, we set aside a piece of ground approximately 36 square metres in size for yoko gardening. I resolved to begin in earnest with the prayer that we as a family could purify the soil with True Light and share any produce that was permitted amongst our neighbours as an expansion activity. In this way we could help distribute the Light of the Creator God.

With the understanding that one should not have any expectations, we planted beetroot, lettuce, tomato, eggplant and pepper seedlings. I tried to purify the soil as regularly as possible and soon realised that this vegetable patch was indeed going to be a classroom for the training of my soul. Greater effort than I had originally expected was going to be required. My re-education began almost immediately after the seedlings were in the ground.

In the very first week, birds had pecked off some of the young leaves of the eggplant seedlings. Some of the seedlings (5 cm tall at the time of planting) were not even visible.

My son pointed out one to me that was like a matchstick stuck into the ground. We gave it True Light and fed it some liquid that had collected *at the bottom of one of the grass-filled refuse bags that I had been saving for compost. By the next morning, four tiny leaves had grown on that 'matchstick'. Nature had presented me with the first lesson: 'If you don't judge or despair, but make an effort with the heart of nurturing, miraculous change can be permitted'.*

The tomato seedlings flourished without any setbacks, but I noticed that the weeds seemed to be making things difficult for them. I realised that there must have been a lot of impurities in the soil and the weeds should be allowed to do their work of removing these impurities. By cutting down the size of the weeds, the roots would still remain and grow strong.

I apologised to the weeds and cut them down to about 5 cm in height. The stems thickened and new branches sprouted from them. But now there was an influx of insects. I suspected that they too were an arrangement for the purification of the soil and did not worry about them. Accepting the arrangements of nature with the understanding that there is a reason for everything, allowed me to witness another miracle. Not a single tomato leaf was eaten by the insects; only the weeds were touched. I was so amazed that I could not help thanking all the plants and insects for the work they were doing.

The tomato plants grew very strong and bore fruit profusely. We were able to distribute these to many people.

The eggplant also flourished and bore many fruit that were 20 cm in length on average. I found out later from people in the area that some of them had tried to grow eggplants but nobody seemed to have succeeded.

One neighbour, who also does a little vegetable growing and whose eggplants had died during a spell of heavy rain and wind, was quite amazed when he saw ours. Like most other people in our street, he maintained an immaculate lawn, and when he was given some of those vegetables, he commented, 'And we are growing grass'.

I must add that another person had also experienced failure; this was with cucumbers. Apparently, in our region, cucumber plants reach maturity, bear flowers and the cucumber fruit begins to form. But soon afterwards they wither and die. None of this happened in our vegetable patch. We were permitted many healthy specimens. The real difference in our methods was purification with True Light and no use of chemicals.

Further evidence of the power of True Light was with the lettuce plants. They were just about ready for harvesting when we had a few days of extremely hot weather. Normally this would have caused withering if no heat protection was installed such as shade nets. Because I was working on a very limited budget, I had not erected shade netting, and by the end of the second day the lettuce heads were showing signs of going limp. I spoke to them, giving them encouragement, watered them and gave them True Light.

They survived with flying colours. Once again we were permitted a fine crop. They were beautifully green, crisp and well-formed.

I love potatoes and can eat them daily without ever tiring of them. However, I was always prejudiced against eggplants and only ate them reluctantly. The eggplants grew and produced way above what I expected, but the potatoes failed miserably. I have now realised that I did a lot of enquiring and investigating about growing potatoes (wanting them solely for my own use) but I did not become an obstacle to nature when it came to the eggplants. This, to me, was the most valuable of all the lessons. I had started off with an attitude of God-centredness but wavered when it came to potatoes. I wasn't going to fool God.

§

In summary, yoko agriculture is a movement consisting of two main aspects – reforming humans and revitalising the soil. It is an agriculture of love. By being grateful and kind, showing apology for the impurity and mistakes of the past, and having a humble attitude of learning from nature without preconceived notions, remarkable things can be steadily achieved. At the same time, the soil is revived in a spiritually oriented way, with the understanding that it is alive. Yoko agriculture provides a collaborative way of living between God, humans and nature in order to help make a better world.

I do not think these are matters that can be learned in a course on horticulture or through advice from traditional farmers. They cannot be proved with formulae, mathematics or intellectual arguments. They need to be experienced. If one does not believe in such things, the disbelief already hinders the discovery of the phenomena. One of the things that inspires me about yoko agriculture is that it is something like learning about God – there is no end to the depths of understanding that can be achieved if one makes efforts.

Establishing the yoko civilisation

Chapter 11

Establishing the yoko civilisation

In this book I have tried to convey my understanding of the basics of Sukyo Mahikari – how and why it began, how it is developing, and some of the main concepts. I have outlined how the Light and the universal laws are relevant to religion, medicine, science, education, economics and agriculture. They are equally relevant to the humanities, architecture, music, art, sport or any other field. This chapter deals with where all this is leading – the future yoko civilisation – which, of course, is being established by not only Sukyo Mahikari practitioners but by all people, with essential contributions from academic, technological, professional and other people of expertise.

Cooperating to make a better world

Sukuinushisama taught a lot about creation, the purpose of the human being and the development of the divine plan. In my understanding, God created human beings, and although they have different skin colours, their origin is one and the same. That is, humankind consists of brothers and sisters who have the same origin.

Similarly, even though the Creator God of heaven and earth has been referred to by different names throughout the world at different times and in different cultures, the Creator God is one and the same for everybody. According to the teachings, in extremely ancient times, comparable to ages now referred to as those of mythology, people followed God directly and God directly gave guidance on how to live. Communication was said to have been through a high priest or leader, a kind of spiritual mediator, who was both a representative of God to the people and a representative of the people to God.

Originally the earth was created by God for all humankind, that is, there is only one earth for all races. The land where people were first created was called the 'land of the origin of spirit'. In extremely ancient times there were no separate nations with borders. People just lived in different places. Similarly, all resources were shared. Just as air is provided for all humankind, it was understood that all materials were for the common good of people. There was no notion that something belonged to only a certain group of people. In those times, people recognised these things and lived peacefully.

The earth looked very different from the earth of today. According to divine teachings, in a certain period in history, tens of thousands of years ago, the land of origin or 'motherland' was a huge continent in the Pacific Ocean, referred to as the Mu Continent by various authors (although not the mainstream view of most historians). From there, people spread to different parts of the world, resulting in different civilisations. Most of the Mu Continent is said to have submerged in the ocean about 12,000 years ago, leaving the mountainous areas, which today include the islands of Japan, Hawaii, Tonga, Fiji and so on.

Over eons of time, people gradually became distanced from each other in all kinds of ways, to the point where there were not only borders between nations, but barriers between races and barriers between cultures, resulting in all kinds of conflict, even wars. God's will is that such barriers be eventually overcome and human beings learn to live together in harmony like brothers and sisters, as they did originally, without conflict about race, religion or anything else. One of the major aims of the Sukyo Mahikari organisation is for people to live in harmony with God, each other and nature, assisting God in establishing a high-quality, peaceful world.

This is called the 'yoko civilisation' ('yang light' or 'sun light' civilisation), a term Sukuinushisama used to describe a civilisation in which people live in peace and harmony, according to the universal laws of God, practising high-level science, medicine, education, agriculture and other pursuits, and sharing resources in ways that are both people-friendly and environment-friendly – irrespective of race, creed, birth or other differences. Yoko – yang light – like sun light, illuminates everything and enables everything to grow and prosper. Establishing the yoko civilisation is promoting the development of a flourishing civilisation of truth, goodness and beauty, as it was in ultra-ancient times, except that the civilisation of the future is also to incorporate the beneficial aspects of modern technology and material culture.

According to Sukuinushisama, we are now in the dawn of such a civilisation. He taught that the twenty-first century would be called a "holy century" because it will be a period of great change from emphasis on material-centredness to emphasis on spirit-centredness or a spiritually oriented approach. It may take a while for this ideal, peaceful situation to be achieved. Nevertheless, since it is God's will to achieve it, God has given people the opportunity to radiate the Light of God and has provided divine teachings in order to help restore the world to a high-quality, harmonious condition.

Even though people are given the Light and valuable teachings through Sukyo Mahikari, this does not mean that this organisation can achieve such a peaceful world on its own. Everyone can contribute to making a better world.

In addition to the value of practising the art of True Light and the teachings of God in daily life by people in general, it is also important for people of academic, technological, professional and other kinds of expertise to cooperate, in order to help establish the yoko civilisation.

The role of scholars

Since the dawn of history, humankind has been seeking happiness and truth, and has found certain answers in religion, philosophy, the arts, science, technology and other fields, resulting in various kinds of civilisations and cultures. At this time of the turning of the century, we can be particularly impressed with the rapid development and contributions that science and technology have made to humankind in terms of living in comfort in material abundance.

On the other hand, however, modern civilisation has brought with it numerous crucial problems of global concern, such as environmental destruction, widespread contamination of people and nature, climatic abnormalities, increasing conflict, gradual economic collapse, the population explosion and spiritual and moral desolation. In general, society promotes unrestrained consumerism and the pursuit of excessive leisure and pleasure. In other words, it is clear that modern civilisation is far from the ideal civilisation that humankind has been really seeking.

Many independent thinkers over the years have tried to analyse the causes for the chaos and crises that are occurring more and more on a global scale, but by and large there is not much integration. Some have pointed out that it is due to the greed of human nature, others talk about political mistakes, still others propose new economic theories. What our materialistic culture seems to lack is an essential value system that is acceptable to all people.

Sukuinushisama indicated that the nature of modern civilisation involves fractionation, separation and analysis, which has resulted in a flat (two-dimensional) civilisation – emphasis on the physical and mental – and this limited framework leads to confrontation, resulting in disunity. Therefore, we must develop a new civilisation – aiming to establish a three-dimensional and stable civilisation where things of opposite or different nature are harmoniously integrated. The three dimensions refer to divine, astral, physical or spirit, mind, body.

As Oshienushisama said in her opening address at the First Yoko Institute International Conference for Europe, in Luxembourg in 1993, *As material civilisation has developed, ideologies have produced further ideologies and all aspects of human life have become segmented, developed separately in disunity and have gone out of control . . . This is due to the principle of placing priority on material development. It has brought humanity to the point where the irreplaceable earth has been contaminated and there is even a threat to the survival of humanity.*

It is therefore necessary to embrace new ideals in order to overcome the problems, and these should be acceptable to people of all backgrounds because they are proven to be sound and viable, not because of some imposed faith or ideology. The approach of imposing beliefs on others has already been tried, often resulting in rejection due to indifference at best and serious conflict at worst. However, if people of the world from different backgrounds and beliefs, through open-minded discussion, study and research, can discover the reality of common, universal laws or principles and willingly agree to implement such integrated principles for humankind to live by, it will be a different matter. That is why it is important to do appropriate research and collate relevant information in order to help create a new civilisation.

From my studies, it seems that Sukuinushisama's vision was to provide a forum so that true dialogue can occur between scientists, people of religion, educators, medical doctors, agriculturists, economists and learned, concerned people of other fields, to try to find new, yet universal, ways by which humankind can live correctly. In this vision, the first priority is the restoring of spiritual values. The path towards a prosperous future for humankind does not lie in more technological and scientific development, but in a fundamental change in attitudes and perspectives. In fact, a total revision of lifestyle, a U-turn of 180 degrees, is to be made in many aspects where material values have come first, to ones where spiritual values are of primary importance. This new approach is a kind of crossing or integrating of seemingly different and even opposing aspects into a united whole, the "forum for crossing". ('Forum' means a meeting place for public discussion and it existed as an institution in both ancient Greek and Roman culture. In a forum, all viewpoints, all disciplines and all people are to be represented.) At the core of Sukuinushisama's vision was the perception that "the origin of the world is one, the origin of humankind is one and the origin of all religions is one".

Sukuinushisama considered it important to provide such a "forum for crossing" where scientists, doctors, educators and other scholars, irrespective of whether they are Mahikari members or not, could conduct activities to build up research data and collate appropriate information that will become credible evidence to help validate the practice of the principles of God or universal laws. Specifically, the aims of the forum are to cooperatively validate, practise and promote these principles in a scientific manner so that all humankind unites with the will and great love of the Creator God; the aspects of spirit (divine), mind (astral) and physical (material) are integrated; and all kinds of spiritual, mental and physical sciences are integrated.

In order to promote such studies, it is necessary to develop networks of learned, capable people throughout the world, people who have the desire to integrate viewpoints through inter-disciplinary study and are willing to explore new methodologies. Any research results should be such that they can be accepted by scholars and others throughout the world on the basis of their scientific credibility and acceptability, not just through blind belief.

I suppose that for some people who are strongly immersed in their own discipline, such a meeting place of seemingly irreconcilable approaches may sound unreasonable. For instance, in my observation there are still scientists who cannot accept that anything of a religious nature can be compatible with science. There are also people of religion who are hesitant to become involved with anything too scientific for fear that it will undermine their faith. However, such views can melt away, I feel, if there is frank, open-minded discussion based on research which shows that science and religion are really one and the same, with both disciplines involving the study of universal laws, but from opposite positions.

The 'crossing' or combination of principles or disciplines has the potential for creating new and deeper meaning and it seems that from one point of view such meaning is what is largely lacking in global culture. Science has provided tremendous know-how, but not much on *why*. Much of humankind is at a loss as to what to do with all the know-how. Even the ability to live a decent, respectable and sensible life has been lost by many. Throughout the world there seems to be much emphasis on how to satisfy desires, but not much about the significance of the human, human values or the meaning of life.

Through cooperative, multi-disciplinary study, humanity should be able to restore the lost meaning of life and see how the different aspects all emerge from a common source that is at the centre of all existence. In religious terms this source is called God and in more scientific or philosophical terms it is called Cosmic Intelligence, Cosmic Consciousness, the Creative Source, the Great Designer and the like. Through this great core there is intention in the universe, but

345

this is not always recognised by scholars in the different disciplines or by people in general.

If intimate relationships exist behind the different specialised and fragmented disciplines, as members of humankind we must try to find them and establish anew their interconnection and interrelation in order to produce new meaning, meaning that is essential in order to advance. It is an important task for learned people to research how to integrate the different fields so that their valuable aspects can be utilised, in order to establish a stable, high-quality civilisation free of conflict. In this way, such new principles are to be formulated to help achieve lasting peace.

In 1959, Sukuinushisama predicted that the age of the supremacy of self-centred materialism would soon come to an end, and he founded the Yoko Civilization Research Association in which he outlined his vision of establishing a civilisation in which various principles are to be integrated. To actualise Sukuinushisama's vision, in 1985 Oshienushisama established the Yoko Civilization Research Institute with herself as president and Sukyo Mahikari as its sponsor.

In my opinion, the three Yoko Civilization International Conferences held by the institute so far have been of some significance. I attended all three conferences and I have observed steady progress in the process of integrating various contemporary issues and perspectives from the sciences, social sciences, medicine, the humanities, education, philosophy and spirituality, an observation shared by others. As an example, the following excerpts are observations made by Dr Ellen Tabak of Washington, D.C., a kamikumite research analyst in a science-based government agency, who attended the Third Yoko Civilization Conference in Takayama, Japan, in order to seek ways to integrate science and spirituality in her work, and to help people that she meets through her profession to do the same. Her article is published in full in the North American magazine, *Sukyo Mahikari* (2000) no. 82, vol. 12 (4), pp. 48–53).

The conference began with a welcoming speech by Oshienushisama. Oshienushisama set the tone by pointing out that life exists on more than just the physical level. She said that the body is material, but life is spiritual, and that the universe consists of unseen energy that allows human life to exist. Oshienushisama said that from now on we must overcome all borders of nationality, religion, and so on, gathering all the spiritual wisdom of the world in order to learn how as human beings we can live in harmony with nature.

The keynote address was given by a professor at the solid state materials laboratory at Pennsylvania State University. He opened the conference discussions by saying the achievements of contemporary science's analytic mode of exploring the world must be balanced with the understanding being revealed by modern physics that there is no objective reality 'out there' and that many different views of reality must be considered.

The next two days of the conference were devoted to three parallel tracks of thematic sessions. The themes were 'Universe and Life', focusing mainly on scientific and spiritual data and world views, 'Life and Healing', focusing mainly on health issues, such as genetics and healing, and 'Our Livelihood and Environment', focusing on such issues as sustainable agriculture methods, food technology, and more equitable economic systems.

The first session I went to was about 'cosmic purpose', given by a professor at Georgetown University. He described the work of Alfred North Whitehead, who suggested that the universe is evolving toward continuously more complex expressions of beauty, beauty being defined as the harmony of contrasts and ordering of novelty. He said that our universe has been moving from simple toward ever more complex expressions of beauty. In this view, humans are not separate from nature – we do not create beauty; we are part of beauty. I was excited by this wonderful, evocative, and integrative beginning to the conference, a view of the universe that is more expansive than the view of any one individual, any one discipline, even any one culture.

In subsequent thematic sessions and panels, I listened to a physicist who specialises in the physics of elementary particles at the University of

Texas, discuss the importance of including consciousness in the study of the natural world. A theologian talked about issues related to genetic engineering and bio-diversity, and afterward, participants from Europe, Asia, Africa, Australia, and the Americas discussed the human genome project and ethical issues relating to modern fertility treatments. A geneticist remarked that it is clear to her that life is more than DNA, that there is something in our cells that gives the order to activate the DNA. For some scientists, that 'something' is chemicals, she said, for others it is God. Participants pondered the ultimate questions, including how as scientists we can best help people without interfering with the natural order.

I listened to sessions in which a psychologist provided data on the effects of intercessory prayer on distant patients and a biologist described research measuring the effects of people's thoughts on the pH level of water, the development time of insect larvae, and the activity of enzymes. Another biologist talked about extremely low frequency electrical energy emitted from the human body, stating that because this energy is measurable, it opens up new frontiers for studying phenomena, such as consciousness, that we have not thought could be measured and that as a result have seemed mysterious or part of a separate realm from science.

In a plenary panel on the fourth day, a quantum physicist from France described the brain as being like a light bulb that can emit light but only when consciousness energizes it. His belief is the universe is filled with consciousness, and that consciousness affects the physical world, which could help begin to explain phenomena such as absent healing, telepathy, and the Jungian collective unconscious. He believes these are matters that can be tested by science and that quantum physics is already beginning to find some clues.

A particle physicist from Sweden agreed, saying the views of science that have been strongest until now hold that reality is composed of separate, independently acting parts. But, he said, our lives are much more than just a collection of separate atoms. As human beings, we are capable of compassion and love, yet these aspects seem to have no place in current science. In his understanding, the 'theory of everything' that scientists are trying to develop cannot be 'everything' if love, truth, and other values are left out. These are irreducible elements of life, and without them, life has no meaning. He presented his view that all life has consciousness to some degree, and that consciousness affects the observed world, a scientific perspective that has existed since the ancient Greeks but has not been the dominant approach. In the discussion, some participants cautioned against anthropic thinking, citing scientific findings, while others countered that even natural phenomena that seem nonsensical or contradictory might have more profound reasons for being allowed to occur if viewed from a wider perspective than our own.

A theologian suggested letting science do what it does and leaving it to metaphysics to study values, purpose, and meaning. But the physicists felt that the study of these things should not be assigned only to one field, because science has something to offer to the examination of these issues, at the risk of having to change itself. For better or worse, science is our current knowledge system, one physicist said, and what it does not study is considered wishful thinking or romantic thought. We cannot say, 'Today I am in my science room, and tomorrow I will go into my spiritual room'. He said there is only one big room, and the other panelists seemed to agree that we must explore reality from many points of view and synthesise all findings.

Attending the conference helped me see in new ways how it is possible for science and spirituality to be integrated and that many people are already thinking along those lines. I had been creating my own roadblocks to progress by believing that science and spirituality are separate and could never understand each other. I was moved by the depth of God's love for humankind and the world in having brought together so diverse a group of high-level scientists and theologians from many countries, cutting across fields of endeavor in order to find solutions to problems that affect everyone in the global community. The truth we learn in the primary course became clearer to me, that God did not create the world and then retire to watch at a distance, but rather is actively working to take the world to a higher, more integrated level. I believe deeply that people in the scientific world can help by working on the problems of the world with God's perspective in our minds, guiding the questions we ask in our research, and informing our actions. The conference inspired me to make greater efforts to tell other people about this new way of looking at things and to share with them the power of God's Light.

Some of the publications issued by the Institute include:

Creating the Future of Mankind (1987). Proceedings of the First Yoko Civilization International Conference. Yoko Civilization Research Institute: Tokyo.

What Does it Mean to be Human? (1991). Proceedings of the Second Yoko Civilization International Conference. Yoko Civilization Research Institute: Tokyo.

Human Responsibilities – Approaching the Twenty-first Century (1995). Proceedings of the Yoko Institute International Conference (May 1993, Ansembourg). L.H. Yoko Shuppan Europe S.A.: Luxembourg.

Spiritual Values: The Hope For Mankind (1995). L.H. Yoko Shuppan Europe S.A.: Luxembourg.

Life and The Universe: Scientific and Religious Viewpoints. Life and The Environment (2001). Proceedings, vol.1, of the Third Yoko Civilization International Conference. Yoko Civilization Research Institute: Tokyo.

Life and Healing: Healing of Nature, Healing Our Civilization and Healing Humankind. Life and The Environment (2002). Proceedings, vol. 2, of the Third Yoko Civilization International Conference. Yoko Civilisation Research Institute: Tokyo.

Our Livelihood and The Environment: Technology and Our Safety in Society. Life and The Environment (2002). Proceedings, vol. 3, of the Third Yoko Civilization International Conference. Yoko Civilization Research Institute: Tokyo.

Panel Discussion and Plenary Session. Life and The Environment (2003). Proceedings, vol. 4, of the Third Yoko Civilization International Conference. Yoko Civilization Research Institute: Tokyo.

Merging of science and religion

From the late 1950s onwards Sukuinushisama taught that religion and science are essentially one and the same, as they deal with the laws of the universe, but from opposite points of view. He predicted that science and religion will gradually merge to the point that one will be indistinguishable from the other. Science and religion will eventually become one, as the spiritually oriented civilisation is established.

From my observations and studies, many scientists and other scholars have expressed the view that science and religion are compatible; that science is heading in a spiritual direction; and that materialism and spirituality can be combined (Richardson & Wildman, 1996; Tart, 1997; Barbour, 1998; Templeton & Giniger, 1998). David Lorimer (1998) has edited a book that reviews the thinking of many well-known 'mystics and scientists' over the past two decades or so, that supports Einstein's famous words: "Science without religion is blind, religion without science is lame".

Several Secretaries-General of the United Nations – Dag Hammarskjöld, U Thant, Javier Perez de Cuellar – advocated the integration of spirituality and science. The 1993 Parliament of the World's Religions was also anxious to "develop the Science and Spirituality of the Parliamentary Programme".

In 1995 the John Templeton Foundation and the Center for Theology and Natural Sciences announced eleven winners of the Templeton Prize for outstanding books in the field of theology and natural science, which included *The Mind of God* by physicist Professor Paul Davies. In this book Davies said, "If we wish to progress beyond, we have to embrace a different concept of 'understanding' from that of rational explanation. Possibly the mystical path is a way to such understanding." All the books give different perspectives on how religion and science are not only compatible but are really a study of universal principles from different angles. I think it is interesting that the Templeton Prize for Progress in Religion in 1996 was won by Professor Davies, who is a respected, down-to-earth scientist, not a religious professional.

Some of the finest thinkers in physics have been mystics in a sense. They include Wolfgang Pauli, Werner Heisenberg, Arthur Eddington and Albert Einstein. Einstein is probably one of the better known of the brilliant scientists who not only acknowledged the existence of God, but indicated that his equations could not be explained unless there was a controlling Mind or Power behind the universe. On one occasion Einstein wrote, "Everyone who is seriously involved in the pursuit of science becomes convinced that a spirit is manifest in the laws of the Universe – a spirit vastly superior to that of man, and one in the face of which we with our modest powers must feel humble."

Professor Charles P. Steinmetz, the famous inventor and electrical engineer, was once asked: "What line of research will see the greatest development during the next fifty years?"

I think the greatest discovery will be made along spiritual lines, Steinmetz replied. *Here is a force which history clearly teaches has been the greatest power in the development of man. Yet we have been merely playing with it and have never seriously studied it as we have the physical forces. Some day people will learn that material things do not bring happiness and are of little use in ·making men and women creative and powerful. Then the scientists of the world will turn their laboratories over to the study of God and prayer and the spiritual forces which as yet have hardly been scratched. When this day comes, the world will see more advancement in one generation than it has in the past four* (Wagoner, 1965).

Nobel laureate, physicist Dr Charles H. Townes spoke of the convergence of science and religion as follows:

Science and religion should at some time clearly converge . . . Perhaps by the time this convergence occurs, science will have been through a number of evolutions as striking as those which have occurred in the last century, and taken on a character not readily recognisable by scientists of today. Perhaps our religious understanding will also have seen progress and change. But converge they must, and through this should come new strength for both (Townes, 1966).

Renowned for his great contributions to physics, Max Planck said: "We must assume behind this force [in the atom] the existence of a conscious and intelligent mind. This mind is the matrix of all matter."

The great historian, Toynbee, said: . . . *though the successes of science and technology have been sensational, I am still more impressed by the limitations of what they can do for mankind. Our greatest need is for a spiritual improvement in ourselves and in our relations with our fellow human beings, but this is a need that science and technology in themselves cannot meet* (Toynbee, 1971).

In his book *The Mind of God*, Professor Davies (1992) wrote, *Through my scientific work I have come to believe more and more strongly that the physical universe is put together with an ingenuity so astonishing that I cannot accept it merely as a brute fact. There must, it seems to me, be a deeper level of explanation.* His conviction is that the laws of physics are simply "too special" to be products of chance. He indicated, "These rules look as if they are the product of intelligent design. I do not see how that can be denied".

Dr Robert Barry (1993) went a step further and referred to the 'mystical universe', calling for a complementary relationship between scientific and mystical understanding. He explained, *Science is simply a rational approach in establishing relationships between various observations. As such, it can offer only relative truths. In order to progress from this position, it must always borrow at least one absolute truth from outside its own system.* He examined the major religious traditions and found the same fundamental message, namely, the need for humanity to recognise and serve an underlying unity, and a need for self-denial on the path of spiritual progress. None of this is in conflict with science, Barry concluded.

Nicholas Hagger (1993) is another scholar who has brought understanding about the view that science and religion are ultimately one. He considers that the materialistic reductionism of much of science and the linguistic reductionism of modern philosophy are out of date. His grand, unified 'Theory of Everything' postulates that the primal source of being is Light or Fire. This ultimate energy brings back matter and consciousness into existence, rather perhaps as an impulse of energy can bring both a particle and an anti-particle into existence.

In recent years, in particular, scholars have presented very convincing views on the compatibility of religion and science (Haught, 1995; Polkinghorne, 1996 a, b; 1998; Wilkinson, 1996; Richardson & Wildman, 1997; Parkinson, 2002). The Reverend Canon John Polkinghorne, KBE, FRS, is both a mathematician and a theologian, and therefore well qualified to make such a conclusion. Similarly, the Reverend Dr David Wilkinson FRAS, an astrophysicist with a degree in theology, argued that a scientific explanation for the origin of the universe does not refute belief in God. Dr Frank Parkinson (2002), whose career spans engineering, philosophy, teaching, business management, literature and religion, has proposed ground-breaking views for a new vision for science and religion.

Interestingly, in recent years a new biology is emerging in which scientists are not only discovering crucial areas of conflict with prevailing material-centred paradigms, but their discoveries are leading into new realms of explanation involving terms such as "non-linear dynamics", "complexity theory", and "chaos", to name a few. In short, there is a growing number of scientists who acknowledge and theorise from their data that there is purpose in the universe; that there are creative forces, that the fields traditionally known as 'science' and 'religion' are merging.

Expanding frontiers of medicine

Medicine, particularly whole person medicine (see chapter 6) is another field in which the boundaries are expanding. As a member of the Scientific and Medical Network (founded in London) I am frequently exposed to contributions made by open-minded, innovative, courageous and sincere researchers who are building bridges or 'crossing opposites', so to speak, elucidating universal principles that will no doubt help to achieve the yoko civilisation.

For example, Dr Larry Dossey (who participated in a Yoko Civilization International Conference) is a cardiac specialist who thoroughly reviewed the medical and scientific literature and found an enormous body of evidence, over 100 experiments, exhibiting the criteria of "good science" (many conducted under stringent laboratory conditions), over half of which showed that prayer brings about significant changes in a variety of living beings. His books (1993, 1996, 1999, 2001) are a landmark in the field. Even though a number of sceptics have tried to dispel the results of research on prayer as being nothing but the power of suggestion or belief (which no doubt can play a role as well), there is excellent evidence that the power of prayer often works when the people prayed for do not even know that they are being prayed for.

One example is a 1988 study by cardiologist Dr Randolph Byrd of San Francisco General Hospital. Byrd took 393 patients in the coronary-care unit and randomly assigned half to be prayed for. To eliminate the placebo effect, the patients were not told of the experiment. Remarkably, Byrd found that the control group was five times as likely to need antibiotics and three times as likely to develop complications than those who were prayed for.

From his review of the literature, Dossey found that the effects of prayer did not depend on whether the praying person was in the presence of the people being prayed for or far away; healing could take place on site or at a distance. Nothing seemed capable of stopping or blocking prayer, even shielding from all forms of known electromagnetic energy; the effect still got through. In short, Dossey brings together the lessons of religious teachings, medical research, psychology, parapsychology and modern physics to show how prayer can be a potent force to deal with illness in oneself and others. His view is that in the evolution of medical treatment we have gone through the era of focusing on mechanical approaches; then the era of mind-body medicine; and have now entered the era of non-local or transpersonal medicine, which involves time-displacement healing. Dossey (1999) concludes that we cannot make sense of our lives unless we acknowledge that our mind operates non-locally.

At Duke University School of Medicine, cardiologist Dr Mitchell Krucoff and nurse-researcher Suzanne Crater organised distant prayer for patients undergoing invasive cardiac procedures such as angioplasty. In their double-blind study, patients receiving prayer had a 50 to 100 percent reduction in side-effects compared with controls (Krucoff, 1999).

In another high-profile study, physician Dr Elisabeth Targ and colleagues at the University of California School of Medicine, San Francisco and the California Pacific Medical Center, studied the impact of distant healing in two double-blind studies of patients with advanced AIDS. In the pilot study, 40 percent of the AIDS patients died, while no deaths occurred in the distant healing group. In the larger follow-up study, AIDS patients receiving distant healing experienced fewer AIDS-related illnesses, had fewer and shorter hospitalisations, and experienced a higher level of psychological well-being. Interestingly, their clinical outcome was not correlated with whether they believed they were receiving distant healing or not (Sicher, Targ, Moore & Smith, 1998).

Dr Deepak Chopra (1990), a physician, has also contributed greatly to the understanding and achieving of health by involving the spirit of the person. Similarly, Dr Andrew Weil (1995), another physician, has diverged from conventional medicine in his emphasis on the body's natural healing ability. Chopra has become something of a spiritual guide for countless people, whereas Weil and Dossey are more research-oriented in their approach.

Harvard University's Dr Herbert Benson has moved beyond the purely pragmatic use of meditation into the realm of spirituality in his book *Timeless Healing* (1996). He considers that humans are actually engineered for religious faith. In a five-year study of patients using meditation to battle chronic illnesses, Benson found that those who claimed to feel the intimate presence of a higher power had better health and more rapid recoveries. He wrote, "Our genetic blueprint has made believing in an Infinite Absolute part of our nature . . . humans are also wired for God." In Benson's view, prayer operates along the same biochemical pathways as the relaxation response. In other words, praying affects epinephrine and other corticosteroid messengers or 'stress hormones', leading to lower blood pressure, more relaxed heart rate and respiration and other benefits. Recent research demonstrates that these stress hormones also have a direct impact on the body's immunological defences against disease.

As Dr Eric Ram (1995), Director of World Vision, Switzerland, said, "Health is more than medical care or even an absence of disease. Health is a harmonious and balanced relationship of the spiritual, physical, mental, social and economic well-being of a person in harmony with God, others and the natural environment."

In the mid-1990s, only three (of the 125) medical schools in the U.S.A. taught courses on religious and spiritual issues. By 1997 there were 30 (Levin, Larson & Puchalski, 1997). By the end of the decade this number doubled and dozens of other medical schools formally expressed their desire to introduce such courses. In chapter 6 I already mentioned Koenig's (2001) report that the number of research articles on spirituality and health increased sixfold over a decade, and Levin's (2001) data showing that religions and spiritual practice can improve people's health.

Dr Craig Brown (1998) emphasised that healing involves finding wholeness and harmony, including "developing spiritual awareness and values".

In my opinion, HRH The Prince of Wales (1998) has demonstrated great vision, open-mindedness and enthusiasm in his promotion of "integrated healthcare":

Health should be much more than the mere absence of disease or infirmity; and we should strive to ensure that everybody can fulfil the full potential and expression of their lives . . . The goal we must work towards is an integrated healthcare system in which all the knowledge, experience and wisdom accumulated in different ways, at different times and in different cultures is effectively deployed to prevent or alleviate human suffering . . . We must respond to what the public are clearly showing they want by placing more emphasis on prevention, healthy lifestyles and patient-centred care. Integrated healthcare is an achievable goal.

From David Lorimer's (2003) informative book *Radical Prince*, it is clear that the Prince of Wales has a consistent and profound world-view that the sacred or spiritual aspect of life is central for all kinds of fields, not only medicine.

Dr C. Norman Shealy (1999), founder of the American Holistic Medical Association, defines sacred healing as the life-giving power of a higher energy source and documents examples of cures of seemingly incurable diseases when the options of conventional medicine have been exhausted. His book, a powerful statement of a future more spiritualised medical theory and practice, covers a wide range of themes around energy and spirituality, giving historical contexts when appropriate.

Professor Rustum Roy (2001) of the Pennsylvania State University considers that integrative or whole person medicine – medicine that involves the spirit, mind and body – is "the greatest advance in the history of medicine".

Interestingly, this approach in medicine was known long ago by Hippocrates, who said, "It is better to know the person who has the disease than the disease the person has."

The future

Beginning in the late 1950s, Sukuinushisama predicted that soon humankind will enter an unprecedented period of sweeping changes. Looking at the trends throughout the world, to me it is clear that there have been considerable changes in recent years, much more so than have been observed over previous centuries. Moreover, the ability to create change as well as the attitude that change is desirable is now sweeping the world. Throughout history, stable continuity rather than change has been promoted, up till recent times. There is also considerable global instability – in the climate, politically, medically, economically – and in many other ways, which is continuing to increase.

This book is not aimed at reviewing all the valuable contributions made by others. I merely refer to some of the more significant studies that I have come across in various fields, which help to illustrate an important point I am making: a high-quality civilisation, or yoko civilisation, will come to be achieved as people validate and practise universal laws or principles, principles that operate through the divine, the astral and the physical realms – or spirit, mind and body. This involves both people in general and academic researchers, whose data will lead to the formulation of appropriate theories that can be accepted by the world, irrespective of race, creed or birth. The previous chapters in this book – on the integration of religions, whole person medicine, frontier science, whole person education, a spiritual approach in economics, the new direction in agriculture – deal with some of the progress in this direction.

There are various other areas of great change. Energy flow and energy use is a topic that has been revived in recent years, and discoveries are suggesting that we may be only at the beginning of understanding and utilising various energies of a potential that we used to dream about (Gerber, 1996; Coghill, 1997; O'Leary & Kaplan, 1999).

Research reports on bioelectromagnetics, psychoneuroimmunology, epigenetics, consciousness and other frontier science fields are yielding claims that challenge a number of dominant world views in biology (Rubik, 2001).

The information explosion is mind-boggling. Even technocratic experts find it difficult to adjust psychologically to the rapid pace of development, where information, ideas and images are zapped across the globe in nanoseconds. At the turn of the century there was already a microchip with one billion transistors on it – the equivalent of sixteen super computers – that cost less than one hundred dollars. Many people are saying that the danger now is too much information, decreasing our ability to understand underlying meanings. Some people are saying that nanotechnology and robotics is accelerating the dehumanising process, leading to a monoculture.

However, there are clear signs that as communication technology is crossing all the artificial boundaries that had been erected, a spiritual and psychological reorientation is also taking place, as mentioned earlier.

In my opinion, the divine plan has reached a stage where it is important to recognise that there cannot be narrow-minded beliefs, such as the old-fashioned approach of living with separate concepts amongst scientists, politicians, doctors and people of religion. We have to embrace the notion of unity between different kinds of people, as well as a partnership between the divine and humankind. We also have to unite with nature. As regards this planet earth, we humans did not create anything, so we should respect and treat preciously what has been created. We should play the role of stewards or guardians of the earth, on behalf of God, rather than simply be consumers or exploiters of its resources. We must become free of the obsession with limitless consumption and profit, restructuring our world view to have caring attitudes towards the natural world and elevating the spiritual value we place on other organisms.

As regards conflict, a preferred approach for us as human beings is if we want to have peace, we do not prepare for war. War will not be prevented by outward, material-centred approaches alone. It has to start from within, the purification of the spiritual aspect, the upstream of the river, so that people will naturally respect other lives and strive to live in harmony. The manifestation of world peace begins with peace within one's innermost attitudes and in one's immediate environment such as the family, the workplace or the school. This involves working on understanding and practising the universal laws concerned with the actually existing spiritual realm.

There is a growing body of researchers who have studied various aspects of the global situation and are sincere in proposing workable approaches to make a better world (Feuerstein & Feuerstein, 1993; Slaughter, 1996; Ehrlich & Ehrlich, 1996; Laszlo, 1997; von Weizsäcker, Lovins & Lovins, 1997; Brown, Flavin & French, 1998; 2000a, b; Starke, 1999; Hawken, Lovins & Lovins, 1999; Pearce & Barbier, 2000; Moss, 2000; Porritt, 2000).

Scholar Nicholas Hagger (1993) has gone a long way in promoting what he calls 'universalism', a new unifying perspective "based on a metaphysical premise of unity, an intrinsic connectedness rather than intrinsic separation". He considers universalism as something that defines the human "in relation to the mystical experience of a universal energy experienced as Fire or Light in the divine part of ourselves". Universalists believe that a metaphysical unity lies behind creation; that this undivided One permeates man and nature and is experienced by mystics; that the essential core of mysticism is the experience of the Fire or Light; that this experience – often interpreted as the vision of an immanent God – provides the existential foundation of the world's religions; that this encounter with the Fire or Light is the driving force in history behind the rise and fall of religions, civilisations and cultures; that the positivist and reductionist assumptions of modern science are limited by a solely materialistic outlook; that philosophy should offer a coherent explanation of the universe and human experience – rather than focus on language and logic; and that universalism can provide the basis for a universal civilisation – a new, benevolent, metaphysically-informed world and a global ethic.

To me, much of this is a more academic way of stating some of the views of the Sukyo Mahikari organisation, and helps to show that truth is universal and can be discovered in different ways. It is important to establish unity of purpose, the sharing of elevated human values, and to integrate the various fields of endeavour, in order to establish a high-quality civilisation, the yoko civilisation. As Oshienushisama said in 1995:

The new civilisation that is being established will be one of harmonisation. It will mark the advent of a cross civilisation in which the opposite elements of fire and water are united in a cross.

Although the origin of the earth is one and the origin of humankind is one, the new civilisation that the Creator, Su God, wants to establish is not a civilisation like a single-coloured crude piece of fabric. It is a spiritually oriented, three-dimensional civilisation like a multi-coloured brocade, maximally utilising the cultures and traditions from each region.

In order to establish a heavenly civilisation, we must transcend the barriers of religions and denominations, of races and of national borders. We must respect, love and nurture each other, thus creating a world of love and harmony. It will not be possible to actualise a heavenly civilisation as long as there are conflicts between religions and their denominations, between races and nations.

The new spiritually oriented civilisation will be the actualisation of a world made brilliant by the vibration of living entities who emit the Light of God.

References

ADDLESTONE, C. (1997) *Many Paths, One Truth: The Common Thread.* Humanics Ltd: Atlanta.

ALMEDER, R. (1992) *Death And Personal Survival.* Rowman and Littlefield: Lanham, MD.

ALVAREZ, M.J. (1995) The preciousness of Divine Light. *Mahikari Australia and Asia Journal,* 13 (11):19-21.

AMON-TANOH, L. (1995) The crisis of national education – an outline solution. In: *Human Responsibilities Approaching the 21st Century,* Proceedings of the Yoko Institute International Conference, 1993, Ansembourg, pp.175-180. L.H. Yoko Shuppan Europe S.A.: Luxembourg.

ARTHUR, J. (2002) *Education with Character. The Moral Economy of Schooling.* Routledge/Falmer: London.

AUSTRALIAN VACCINATION NETWORK (1998) *Vaccination Roulette: Experiences, risks and alternatives.* Australian Vaccination Network: Bangalow, N.S.W.

BAILEY, L.W. & YATES, J. (1996) (editors) *The Near Death Experience: a Reader.* Routledge: London.

BALDWIN, W.J. (1995) *Spiritual Releasement Therapy: A Technique Manual.* Headline Books: Terra Alta, W.V.

BALDWIN, W.J. (2003) *Healing Lost Souls: Releasing Unwanted Spirits From Your Energy Body.* Hampton Roads Publishing Company: Charlottesville, VA.

BARBOUR, I.G. (1998) *Religion and Science.* SCM Press: London.

BARNETT, R. (1994) *The Limits of Competence.* Open University Press: London.

BARROW, J.D. & TIPLER, F.J. (1986) *The Anthropic Cosmological Principle.* Oxford University Press: Oxford.

BARRY, R. (1993) *A Theory of Almost Everything.* One World Publications: London.

BEARE, H. & SLAUGHTER, R. (1993) *Education for the Twenty-First Century.* Routledge: London.

BECKER, C.B. (1993) *Paranormal Experience and Survival of Death.* S.U.N.Y. Press: Albany.

BENNETT, C. & BENNETT, K. (1994) Recovery from acute multi-organ failure considered medically impossible. *Mahikari Australia and Asia Journal,* 12(1):25-29.

BENSON, D. (1996) *Timeless Healing. The Power and Biology of Belief.* Scribner: New York.

BERGSON, H. (1960) *Creative Evolution.* Macmillan: London.

BERNARD-MIRTIL, L. (1998) *Sukyo Mahikari: Une Nouvelle Religion du Japan.* Bell Vision: Bretagne.

BHUGRA, D. (1996) (editor) *Psychiatry and Religion: Context, Consensus and Controversies.* Routledge: London

BLOCK, P. (1993) *Stewardship. Choosing Service Over Self-interest.* Berrett-Koehler Publishers: San Francisco.

BOHM, J. (1980) *Wholeness and the Implicate Order.* Routledge: London.

BOUMA, G.D., SMITH, W. & VASI, S. (2000) Japanese religion in Australia: Mahikari and Zen in a multicultural society. Chapter 3, in *Japanese New Religions in Global Perspective*, pp.74-112. Edited by P.B. Clarke. Curzon Press: Richmond, Surrey.

BRAYBROOKE, M. (1996) *A Wider Vision*. One World: London.

BROWN, C. (1998) *Optimum Healing: A Life-changing New Approach to Achieving Good Health*. Rider: London.

BROWN, L.R. (2001) *Eco-Economy*. Earthscan Publications: London.

BROWN, L.R., FLAVIN, C. & FRENCH, H. (1998) *State of the World 1998*. Earthscan Publications: London.

BROWN, L.R., FLAVIN, C. & FRENCH, H. (2000a) *State of the World 1999*. Earthscan Publications: London.

BROWN, L.R., FLAVIN, C. & FRENCH, H. (2000b) *State of the World 2000*. Earthscan Publications: London.

CALAPRICE, A. (1996) *The Quotable Einstein*. Princeton University Press: New Jersey.

CARBONELL, J.E.V. (1987) More experiences of a Catholic priest. *Mahikari Australia Journal*, 5 (7):16-18.

CARSON, R. (1962) *Silent Spring*. Houghton Mifflin: Boston.

CHANG, S.E. (1994) Aiming at actualising the dream of a Yoko civilisation. *Mahikari Australia and Asia Journal*, 12(1): 10-14.

CHELVARAJ, S. (1994) Practising Mahikari in dentistry. *Mahikari Australia and Asia Journal*, 12(1): 20-24.

CHILDS, G. (1991) *Steiner Education in Theory and Practice*. Floris Books: Edinburgh.

CHOPRA, D. (1990) *Quantum Healing*. Bantam: London.

CHRISTIE, I. & WARBURTON, D. (2001) *From Here to Sustainability: Politics in the Real World*. Earthscan Publications: London.

CLARK, R.W. (1971) *Einstein: the Life and Times*. Avon Books: New York.

CLARKE, P.B. (2000) 'Success' and 'failure': Japanese new religions abroad. Chapter 10, in *Japanese New Religions in Global Perspective*, pp. 272-311. Edited by P.B. Clarke. Curzon Press: Richmond, Surrey.

COGHILL, R. (1997) *Something in the Air*. Coghill Research Labs: Gwent, U.K.

CORNELL, T. (2002) *Investigating the Paranormal*. Helix Press: New York.

CORNETT, C. (1998) *The Soul of Psychotherapy*. The Free Press: New York.

CORNILLE, C. (1991) The phoenix flies West: The dynamics of the inculturation of Mahikari in Western Europe. *Japanese Journal of Religious Studies*, 19(2-3):265-285.

CORNILLE, C. (1994) Jesus in Japan: Christian syncretism in Mahikari. In: *Japanese New Religions in the West*. Edited by P.B. Clarke & J. Somers, pp.88-102. Japan Library/Curzon Press: Kent.

CORNILLE, C. (2000) New Japanese religions in the West. Between nationalism and universalism. Chapter 1 in *Japanese New Religions in Global Perspective*, pp. 10 – 34. Edited by P.B. Clarke. Curzon Press: Richmond, Surrey.

CORNWELL, J. (1996) *The Power to Harm: Mind, Medicine and Murder on Trial*. Viking Penguin: New York.

COVEY, S. R. (1990) *The Seven Habits of Highly Effective People*. The Business Library: Melbourne.

CURULALA, N.D. (1996) Laying the foundation for a God-centred education system. *Mahikari Australia-Oceania and Asia Journal*, 14(8):16-20.

DALAI LAMA (2000) *Transforming the Mind.* Thorsons: Blue Ridge Summit, PA.

DAVIDSON, J.H. (1992) *Natural Creation or Natural Selection?* Element Books: London.

DAVIES, P.C.W. (1992) *The Mind of God.* Penguin: London.

DAVIES, P.C.W. (1994) *The Last Three Minutes.* Weidenfeld and Nicolson: London.

DAVIES, P. C.W. & GRIBBEN, J. (1992) *The Matter Myth.* Penguin: London.

DAVIS, W. (1980) *Magic and Exorcism in Modern Japan.* Stanford University Press: Stanford.

DOI, H. (1991) Trinitism in human beings. In: *What Does it Mean to be Human?* Proceedings of the Second Yoko Civilization International Conference, Oct.28-Nov.1, 1989, Takayama, Japan, pp.287-289. Yoko Civilization Research Institute: Tokyo.

DOSSEY, L. (1993) *Healing Words. The Power of Prayer and the Practice of Medicine.* Harper Collins: San Francisco.

DOSSEY, L. (1996) *Prayer is Good Medicine.* Harper Collins: San Francisco.

DOSSEY, L. (1999) *Reinventing Medicine.* Harper Collins: San Francisco.

DOSSEY, L. (2001) *Healing Beyond the Body: Medicine and the Infinite Reach of the Mind.* Shambhala: Boston.

DUPRÉ, J. (2001) *Human Nature and the Limits of Science.* Clarendon Press: Oxford.

DYSON, F.J. (1979) *Disturbing the Universe.* Harper & Row: New York.

ECCLES, J.C. (1987) The effect of silent thinking on the cerebral cortex. In: *The Brain-Mind Problem. Philosophical and Neurophysiological Approaches.* Edited by B. Gulyas, pp.29-60, Leuven: Leuven University Press.

ECCLES, J.C. (1994) *How The Self Controls Its Brain.* Springer Verlag: Berlin.

EHRLICH, P.R. (1986) *The Machinery of Nature.* Simon & Schuster: New York.

EHRLICH, P.R. & EHRLICH, A. (1996) *Betrayal of Science and Reason.* Island Press: Washington DC.

FARRER, F. (2000) *A Quiet Revolution.* Rider: London.

FENWICK, P. & FENWICK, E. (1995) *The Truth in The Light.* Headline: London.

FENWICK, P. & FENWICK, E. (1999) *Past Lives.* Headline: London.

FEUERSTEIN, G. & FEUERSTEIN, T.L. (1993) *Voices on the Threshold of Tomorrow: 145 Views of the New Millennium.* Quest Books: London.

FIORE, E. (1987) *The Unquiet Dead: A Psychologist Treats Spirit Possession.* Doubleday: New York.

FISHER, J.A. (1994) *The Plague Makers.* Simon & Schuster: New York.

GANG, P., LYNN, N. & MAVER, D. (1992) *Conscious Education.* Dagaz Press: Oakland, CA.

GATES, J. (1998) *The Ownership Solution. Toward a Shared Capitalism for the Twenty-first Century.* Addison-Wesley: New York.

GERBER, R. (1996) *Vibrational Medicine: New Choices for Healing Ourselves.* Bear & Co: Santa Fe, NM.

GILBERT, A.G. & COTTERELL, M. (1995) *The Mayan Prophecies. Unlocking the Secrets of a Lost Civilization.* Element Books: Brisbane.

GLANZ, J. (1996) Collisions hint that quarks might not be indivisible. *Science*, 271: 758.

GLEICK, J. (1987) *Chaos.* Cardinal: London.

GLENN, J.C. & GORDON, T.J. (2000) *State of the Future at the Millennium.* American Council for the United Nations University: Washington.

GOODWIN, B. (1994) *How The Leopard Changed Its Spots: The Evolution of Complexity.* Weidenfeld & Nicolson: London.

GOTTLIEB, G. (1992) *Genesis of Novel Behaviour: Individual Development and Evolution.* Oxford University Press: New York.

GOZDZ, K. (1995) (editor) *Community Building in Business. Renewing Spirit & Learning.* New Leaders Press (Sterling and Stone): San Francisco.

GREENWOOD, G.A. (1995) *All The Emperor's Men.* Strictly Literary: Queensland, Australia.

GREYSON, B. (1993) Varieties of near-death experiences. *Psychiatry,* 56: 390-399.

GREYSON, B. (2000) Dissociation in people who have near-death experiences: out of their bodies or out of their minds? *The Lancet,* 355: 460-463.

GUIRDHAM, A. (1982) *The Psychic Dimensions of Mental Health.* Sterling: New York.

HAGGER, N. (1993) *The Universe and the Light.* Element Books: London.

HAMILTON, C. (1994) *The Mystic Economist,* Willow Park Press: Fyshwick, A.C.T.

HARMAN, W. & SAHTOURIS, E. (1998) *Biology Revisioned.* North Atlantic Books: Berkeley, California.

HAUGHT, J.F. (1995) *Science and Religion – from Conflict to Conversation.* Paulist Press: Mahwah, New Jersey.

HAWKEN, P. (1994) *The Ecology of Commerce.* Weidenfeld & Nicolson: London.

HAWKEN, P., LOVINS, A.B. & LOVINS, L.H. (1999) *Natural Capitalism: The Next Industrial Revolution.* Earthscan Publications: London.

HEAD, J. & CRANSTON, S.L. (1967) *Reincarnation in World Thought.* Julian Press: New York.

HENDERSON, H. (1991) *Paradigms in Progress: Life Beyond Economics.* Knowledge Systems Inc.: Indianapolis.

HO, M-W. (1998) *Genetic Engineering: Dream or Nightmare? The Brave New World of Bad Science and Big Business.* Gateway Books: Bath, U.K.

HORI, Y. (1997) Perceiving the existence of God. *Mahikari Australia-Oceania and Asia Journal,* 15(2):16-20.

HOSAKA, K. (1993) Omitama and salvation in the astral world. *Mahikari Australia and Asia Journal.* 11(7):27.

HURBON, L. (1991) Mahikari in the Caribbean. *Japanese Journal of Religious Studies,* 18(2-3):243-264.

ILLICH, I. (1976) *Limits to Medicine.* Marion Boyars: London.

IRWIN, H.J. (1994) *An Introduction to Parapsychology.* (2nd Edition) McFarland: Jefferson, NC.

KAKU, M. (1994) *Hyperspace.* Oxford University Press: London.

KAUR, B. (1995) Miraculous recovery from a coma. *Mahikari Australia-Oceania and Asia Journal,* 13(7):26-28.

KNECHT, P. (1995) The crux of the cross. Mahikari's core symbol. *Japanese Journal of Religious Studies,* 22(3-4):321-341.

KNOBEL, M. (1995) The big chill. *Mahikari Australia and Asia Journal,* 13(7):23-25.

KOENIG, H.G. (2001) Religion, spirituality and medicine: how are they related and what does it mean. *Mayo Clinical Proceedings*, 76: 1189-1191.

KOEPPING, K-P. (1967) Sekai Mahikari Bunmei Kyodan. A preliminary discussion on a recent religious movement in Japan. *Contemporary Religions in Japan*, 8 (2):101-134.

KORTEN, D.C. (1995) *When Corporations Rule The World*. Kumarian Press: West Hartford, CT.

KRUCOFF, M.W. (1999) The MANTRA study project. Interview by Bonnie Horrigan. *Alternative Therapies in Health and Medicine*, 5(3):74-82.

KÜNG, H. (1996) *Yes to a Global Ethic*. SCM: London.

LAM, K. (1995) Awakening to my sins and impurities and the importance of fully reattending kenshu. *Mahikari Australia and Asia Journal*, 13(7):15-20.

LASZLO, E. (1993) *The Creative Cosmos. A Unified Science of Matter, Life and Mind*. Floris Books: Edinburgh.

LASZLO, E. (1996) *The Whispering Pond*. Element Books: London.

LASZLO, E. (1997) *3rd Millennium: the Challenge and the Vision*. Gaia: London.

LASZLO, E. (2003) *The Connectivity Hypothesis*. S.U.N.Y. Press: Albany.

LAZAROU, J., POMERANZ, B.H. & COREY, P.N. (1998) Incidence of adverse drug reactions in hospitalized patients. A meta-analysis of prospective studies. *Journal of the American Medical Association*, 279(15):1200-1205.

LE SHAN, L. (1996) *An Ethic For The Age of Space*. Samuel Weiser: York Beach, ME.

LEVIN, J. (2001). *God, Faith and Health: Exploring the Spirituality-Healing Connection*. Wiley: New York.

LEVIN, J.S., LARSON, D.B. & PUCHALSKI, C.M. (1997) Religion and spirituality in medicine: research and education. *Journal of the American Medical Association*, 278(9):792-793.

LIEBIG, J.E. (1994) *Merchants of Vision. People Bringing New Purpose and Values to Business*. Berrett-Koehler Publishers: San Francisco.

LIM, D. (1996) Eating 'nightmare' solved so simply. *Mahikari Australia-Oceania and Asia Journal*, 14(4):26-27.

LIM, J. (1996) My efforts in trying to become a good role model for the youth of the world. *Mahikari Australia-Oceania and Asia Journal*, 14(9):19-22.

LORIMER, D. (1990) *Whole in One*. Arkana: London.

LORIMER, D. (1998) (editor) *The Spirit of Science. From Experiment to Experience*. Floris Books: Edinburgh.

LORIMER, D. (2003) *Radical Prince. The Practical Vision of the Prince of Wales*. Floris Books: Edinburgh.

MacEACHERN, D. (1990) *Save Our Planet*. Dell Publishing: New York.

McVEIGH, B.J. (1992a) The vitalistic conception of salvation as expressed in Sukyo Mahikari. *Japanese Journal of Religious Studies*, 19(1):41-68.

McVEIGH, B.J. (1992b) The master metaphor of purity: the symbolism of authority and power in Sukyo Mahikari. *Japanese Religions*, 17(2):98-125.

McVEIGH, B.J. (1992c) The authorization of ritual and the ritualization of authority: the practice of values in a Japanese new religion. *Journal of Ritual Studies*, 6(2):39-58.

McVEIGH, B.J. (1993) Building belief through the body: the physical embodiment of morality and doctrine in Sukyo Mahikari. *Japanese Religions*, 18(2):140-161.

McVEIGH, B.J. (1995) Learning morality through sentiment and the senses: the role of emotional experience in Sukyo Mahikari. *Japanese Religions,* 20(1):56-76.

McVEIGH, B.J. (1997) *Spirits, Selves, and Subjectivity in a Japanese New Religion. The Cultural Psychology of Belief in Sukyo Mahikari.* Mellen Press: New York.

MAHARAJ, B. (1996) As a medical doctor, I am amazed by the Light of God. *Mahikari Australia-Oceania and Asia Journal,* 14(9):12-15.

MATSUNAGA, L. (2000) Spirit first, mind follows, body belongs. Notions of health, illness and disease in Sukyo Mahikari UK. Chapter 7 in *Japanese New Religions in Global Perspective,* pp.198-239. Edited by P.B. Clarke. Curzon Press: Richmond, Surrey.

MAYNARD Jr., H.B. & MEHRTENS, S.E. (1993) *The Fourth Wave. Business in the 21st Century.* Berrett-Koehler Publishers: San Francisco.

MELTON, J.G. & JONES, C.A. (1994) New Japanese religions in the United States. In: *Japanese New Religions in the West.* Edited by P. Clarke, pp.33-55. Japan Library/Curzon Press: Kent.

MENDELSOHN, R.S. (1979) *Confessions of a Medical Heretic.* Contemporary Books: Chicago.

MILTON, R. (1994) *Forbidden Science.* Fourth Estate: London.

MOODY, R.A. (1975) *Life after Life.* Mockingbird/Bantam Books: New York.

MORAN, G. (1998) *Silencing Scientists and Scholars in Other Fields.* Ablex Publishing: Greenwich, Connecticut.

MORLION, A.F. (1987) The calling of Mahikari for the coming spiritual civilization. In: *Creating the Future of Mankind. (Proceedings of the First Yoko Civilization International Conference),* pp.25-30. Yoko Civilization Research Institute: Tokyo.

MOROWITZ, H. (1968) *Energy Flow in Biology: Biological Organization as a Problem in Thermal Physics.* Academic Press: New York.

MORSE, M. (1994) *Parting Visions. Uses and Meanings of Pre-Death, Psychic and Spiritual Experiences.* Villard Books: New York.

MOSS, N. (2000) *Managing the Planet: The Politics of the New Millennium.* Earthscan Publications: London.

NAHAN, N.Y. (1995) Expansion amongst educators. *Mahikari Australia-Oceania and Asia Journal,* 13(9):28-31.

NANAUMI, H. (1993) My son's grades. *Mahikari Australia-Oceania and Asia Journal,* 11(8):26-27.

NASR, S.H. (1968) *The Spiritual Crisis of Modern Man.* George Allen & Unwin: London.

NASR, S.H. (1993) *The Need for a Sacred Science.* State University of New York: New York.

NASR, S.H. (1996) *Religion and the Order of Nature.* Oxford University Press: Oxford.

OCHI, T. (2002) Progress of rheumatoid arthritis and its medical treatment Religious attitude can alter the course of the disease. In: *Life and The Environment,* Proceedings, vol. 2, pp. 9-27, of the *Third Yoko Civilization International Conference,* August 1999, Yoko Civilization Research Institute: Tokyo.

O'LEARY, B. & KAPLAN, S. (1999) Miracle in the void: The new energy revolution. *Network (The Scientific and Medical Network Review)*, No.70, pp.3-10.

ONODERA, T. (1995) Medical treatment and the practice of 'love and truth'. *Mahikari Australia and Asia Journal*, 13(1):22-26.

OWENS, J.E., COOK, E.W. & STEVENSON, I. (1990) Features of "Near-Death Experience" in relation to whether or not patients were near death. *The Lancet*, 336: 1175-1177.

PARKINSON, F. (2002). *Jehovah and Hyperspace. Exploring the Future of Science, Religion and Society.* New European Publications Ltd: London.

PARNIA, S. WALLER, D.G., YEATES, R. & FENWICK, P. (2001) A qualitative and quantitative study of the incidence, features and aetiology of near death experiences in cardiac arrest survivors. *Resuscitation*, 48:149-156.

POLKINGHORNE, J. (1996a) *Serious Talk*. SCM Press: London.

POLKINGHORNE, J. (1996b) *Scientists as Theologians*. SPCK: London.

POLKINGHORNE, J. (1998) *Science and Theology*. SPCK: London.

POPPER, K. & ECCLES, J.C. (1985) *The Self And Its Brain*. Springer Verlag: New York.

PORRITT, J. (2000) *Playing Safe: Science and the Environment.* Thames & Hudson: London.

PRINCE OF WALES, THE HRH (1998) Integrated healthcare: A way forward? *Network (The Scientific and Medical Network Review)*, No.66, pp.14-15.

RABY, P. (2001) *Alfred Russel Wallace – a life*. Chatto & Windus: London.

RADIN, D.I. (1996) Frequently asked questions about parapsychology. *Network (The Scientific and Medical Network Review)*, No. 61, pp.5-11.

RADIN, D.I. (1997) *The Conscious Universe: The Scientific Truth of Psychic Phenomena*. Harper Collins: New York.

RAM, E.R. (1993) Healing the whole person. In: *Human Responsibilities – Approaching the 21st Century*, pp.11-19. L.H. Yoko Shuppan Europe S.A: Luxembourg.

RAPHAEL, S.P. (1994) *Jewish Views of the Afterlife*. Jason Aronson Inc.: New Jersey.

RAWLINGS, M. (1979) *Beyond Death's Door...* Sheldon: London.

RENESCH, J. (1992) (editor) *New Traditions in Business. Spirit and Leadership in the 21st Century.* Berrett-Koehler Publishers: San Francisco.

RICHARDSON, W.M. & WILDMAN, W.J. (1997) (editors) *Religion and Science – History, Method, Dialogue*. Routledge: London.

RIFKIN, J. (1991) *Biosphere Politics*. Crown Publishers: New York.

RING, K. (1980) *Life at Death. A scientific investigation of the near-death experience*. Coward, McCann & Geoghenan: New York.

RING, K. & COOPER, S. (1999) *Mindsight. Near-Death and Out-of-Body Experiences in the Blind*. William James Center for Consciousness Studies: Palo Alto, CA.

ROBBINS, A. (1991) *Awaken the Giant Within*. Simon & Schuster: New York.

ROBERTSON, J. (1998) *Transforming Economic Life: a Millennial Challenge*, Green Books: Totnes, Devon UK.

ROSENTHAL, R. (1976) *Experimenter Effects in Behavioral Research*. John Wiley: New York.

ROSENTHAL, R. (1991) Teacher expectancy effects: a brief update 25 years after the Pygmalion experiment. *Journal of Research in Education*, 1:3-12.

ROY, A. (1996) *The Archives of the Mind*. SNU Publications: Stansted, Essex UK.

ROY, R. (2001) Whole person healing. In: *Life and The Environment, Proceedings*, vol. 1, pp.15-34, of the *Third Yoko Civilization International Conference*, August 1999. Yoko Civilization Research Institute: Tokyo.

RUBIK, B. (2001) The emerging worldview in biology. In: *Life and The Environment, Proceedings*, vol. 1, pp.197-210, of the *Third Yoko Civilization International Conference*, August 1999. Yoko Civilization Research Institute: Tokyo.

RUSSELL, G. (1995) Divine principles in corporate Australia. *Mahikari Australia-Oceania and Asia Journal*, 13(9):32-34.

RUSSELL, R. (2000) *The Vast Enquiring Soul*. Hampton Roads: Charlottesville, VA.

RUTSTEIN, N. (1992) *Education on Trial*. Oneworld: Boston.

SABOM, M. (1982) *Recollections of Death: A Medical Investigation*. Harper & Row: New York.

SAND, L. (2000) *Medicine for the Coming Age*. Capall Bann Publishing: Chieveley, Berkshire, UK.

SCHEIBNER, V. (1993) *Vaccination*. Scheibner: Blackheath, New South Wales.

SCHRODER, G.L. (1990) *Genesis and the Big Bang. Discovery of Harmony Between Modern Science and the Bible*. Bantam Books: New York.

SHEALY, C.N. (1999) *Sacred Healing*. Element Books: London.

SHELDRAKE, R. (1994) *Seven Experiments That Could Change The World*. Fourth Estate: London.

SHELDRAKE, R. (1998) Experimenter effects in scientific research. *Journal of Scientific Exploration*, 12:73-78.

SHIBATA, K. (1993) *Daiseishu. (Great and Holy Master)*. L.H. Yoko Shuppan: Tokyo.

SHIMADA, Y. (1996) *Niju-isseiki no Shukyo. (Religion of the Twenty-first Century)*. *Seiho to Gyakuho no Tenkan Ten ni Tatte*. Shukyo Jiji Kenkyusho: Kawasaki. [In Japanese]

SHIVA, V. (1998) *Biopiracy. The Plunder of Nature and Knowledge*. Green Books: Totnes, Devon UK.

SICHER, F., TARG, E., MOORE, D. & SMITH, H. (1998) A randomized double-blind study of the effect of distant healing in a population with advanced AIDS: report of a small-scale study. *Western Journal of Medicine*, 169:356-363.

SLAUGHTER, R.A. (1996) *New Thinking for a New Millennium*. Routledge: London.

SMITH, G. (1997) God's calculator. *Mahikari Australia-Oceania and Asia Journal*, 15(3):11-15.

SNELLMAN, H. (1995). Scientific knowledge and human responsibility. In: *Human Responsibilities Approaching the 21st Century*, Proceedings of the Yoko Institute International Conference, 1993, Ansembourg, pp.124-131. L.H. Yoko Shuppan, Europe S.A.: Luxembourg.

SOMERS, J. (1994) Japanese new religious movements in Britain. In: *Japanese New Religions in the West*. Edited by P. B. Clarke & J. Somers, pp.54-77. Japan Library/Curzon Press: Kent.

STARKE, L. (1999) (editor) *Vital Signs: the Environmental Trends that are Shaping our Future*. Earthscan Publications: London.

STEMMAN, R. (1997) *Reincarnation – True Stories of Past Lives*. Piatkus Books: London.

STEVENSON, I. (1977) The explanatory value of the idea of reincarnation. *The Journal of Nervous and Mental Disease*, 164:305-326.

STEVENSON, I. (1997a) *Reincarnation and Biology: a Contribution to the Biology of Birthmarks and Birth Defects*. Praeger: Westport, CT.

STEVENSON, I. (1997b) *Where Reincarnation and Biology Intersect*. Praeger: Westport, CT.

STOVE, D. (1995) *Darwinian Fairy Tales*. Avebury Books: Aldershot & Brookfield, U.S.A.

SUZUKI, D. (1990) *Inventing The Future*. Allen & Unwin: Sydney.

SUZUKI, D. (1997) *The Sacred Balance: Rediscovering our Place in Nature*. Allen & Unwin: Sydney.

SZILAGYI, B. (1995) Spiritual health: an educational perspective. *Mahikari Australia-Oceania and Asia Journal*, 13(9):35-37.

SZILAGYI, B. (1996) Spiritual health. In: *Proceedings of the 20th Biennial National International ACHPER Conference*, 14-19 January 1996, Melbourne.

SZILAGYI, B. (1997) Spiritual health – facilitating the development of healthy values in our students. In: *Proceedings of the Health and PE-Twilight Workshop*, 10-20 February 1997, Adelaide.

TANIKADO, K. (1996) Disappearance of Methicillin-resistant staphylococcus. *Mahikari Australia-Oceania and Asia Journal*, 14(5):17-19.

TART, C. (1997) (editor) *Body, Mind, Spirit*. Hampton Roads: Charlottesville, VA.

TAYLOR, R. (1979) *Medicine Out of Control*. Macmillan (Sunbooks): Melbourne.

TEBECIS, A.K. (1982) *Mahikari. Thank God For The Answers At Last*. L.H. Yoko Shuppan: Tokyo.

TEMPLETON, J. M. & GINIGER, K. (1998) (editors) *Spiritual Evolution*. Templeton Foundation Press: Radnor, PA.

THIRUVIKKAL, J.L. (1995) My medical experiences with True Light. *Mahikari Australia-Oceania and Asia Journal*, 13(1):19-21.

TOMBERG, V. (1992) *Covenant of the Heart: Meditations of a Christian Hermeticist on the Mysteries of Tradition*. Element Books: Shaftesbury, Dorset UK.

TOWNES, C.H. (1966) The convergence of science and religion. *Think*, 32:2-7.

TOYNBEE, A.J. (1971) *Surviving the Future*. Oxford University Press: London.

UUS, U. (1994) *Blindness of Modern Science*. Tartu: Seattle, WA.

VAN LOMMEL, P., VAN WEES, R., MEYERS, V. & ELFFERICH, I. (2001) Near-death experience in survivors of cardiac arrest: a prospective study in the Netherlands. *The Lancet*, 358:2039-2045.

VON WEIZSÄCKER, E., LOVINS, A.B. & LOVINS, L.H. (1997) *Factor Four: Doubling Wealth, Halving Resource Use*. Earthscan: London.

WADE, J. (1996) *Changes of Mind*. S.U.N.Y. Press: Albany.

WAGONER, C.P. (1965) *Steinmetz revisited*. Spectrum, April, pp.82-87.

WAITLEY, D. (1994) *Seeds of Greatness*. Brolga Publishing: Ringwood (Victoria).

WALKER, M. (1993). *Dirty Medicine*. Slingshot Publications: London.

WEIL, A. (1995) *Spontaneous Healing*. Alfred A. Knopf: New York.

WEITZ, M. (1980) *Health Shock.* Reed: Sydney.

WHITMORE, J. (1997) *Need, Greed or Freedom: Business Changes and Personal Freedom.* Element Books: London.

WILKINSON, D. (1996) *God, The Big Bang and Stephen Hawking.* Monarch Publications: London.

YOUNG, R.F. (1993) Magic and morality in modern Japanese exorcistic technologies. A study of Mahikari. In: *Religion and Society in Modern Japan. Selected Readings.* Edited by M. R. Mullins, S. Susumu & P. L. Swanson, pp. 239-256. Asian Humanities Press: Berkeley.

ZOHAR, D. (1997) *Rewiring the Corporate Brain.* Berrett-Koehler Publishers: San Francisco.

Glossary

Amatsu Norigoto
Amatsu Norigoto prayer ("Heavenly prayer"), the most important and frequently chanted prayer of purification, usually recited before giving Light, at ceremonies and at other important activities.

Dojo
A Mahikari centre of a certain spiritual level; literally, 'training place'. In the case of the Mahikari organisation, it is a training place for the soul.

Goshintai
Sacred object or scroll, the most holy part of the divine altar through which Su God is enshrined. In the Sukyo Mahikari organisation, True Light, the Light of the Creator God, emanates from Goshintai.

Kamikumite
Members or practitioners of Sukyo Mahikari; literally, 'those who join hands with God'.

Kotodama (or kototama)
Spiritual functions (significance, power or essence) of words (or syllables).

Kumite
Members or practitioners of Sukyo Mahikari (abbreviation of **kamikumite**).

Mahikari
True Light, the Light of the Creator God, sometimes used as the abbreviated name of the organisation Sukyo Mahikari.

Mahikari no waza
Art of True Light; practice of True Light.

Mioya Motosu Mahikari Omikamisama
The full name of Su God, the Creator God.

Omitama
Sacred locket, which is connected with Su God by a spiritual cord and is worn around the neck on a chain, enabling the person to radiate True Light.

Oshienushisama
Literally, 'Great Teacher' or 'Master of Teachings', the spiritual leader of Sukyo Mahikari.

Su, Su God, Sushin, Su no Mikami, Su no Omikamisama
The Parent God, the Creator God, Almighty God.

Sukuinushisama
Literally, 'Great Saviour' or 'Master of Salvation' – Kotama Okada, the founder of the Mahikari organisation.

Sukyo
Universal laws or principles, universal teachings for humankind that transcend the barriers between religions.

Yoko civilisation
'Yang light' or 'sun light' civilisation, a bright civilisation of peace and harmony, a flourishing civilisation of truth, goodness and beauty.

Yokoshi
Members or practitioners of Sukyo Mahikari; literally, 'sun (positive, yang) light children'.